Children, Chu... Christian Learning

Edited by

Leslie J. Francis
and
Jeff Astley

SPCK

First published in Great Britain in 2002 by
Society for Promoting Christian Knowledge
Holy Trinity Church
Marylebone Road
London NW1 4DU

The authors and editors gratefully acknowledge permission to rework material originally published in the following journals: *Journal of Education and Christian Belief*, *International Journal of Education and Religion*, *British Journal of Religious Education* and *Tufton Review*.

British Library Cataloguing-in-Publication Data
A catalogue record for this book is available from the British Library

ISBN 0-281-05532-7

10   9   8   7   6   5   4   3   2   1

Typeset by FiSH Books, London WC1
Printed in Great Britain by Creative Print and Design (Wales), Ebbw Vale

Contents

Contents

Preface

Ministry among children must be seen as a central component of the Churches' strategy for ministry and mission in the twenty-first century. It is a strategy which properly involves the three-way partnership between home, congregation and school.

Currently a new sense of commitment is pervading the Christian community to found new church schools, to foster a vocation to teaching among committed Christian people, to resource churches for all-age learning and worship, to provide new accredited training programmes for specialist ministries among young people, to stimulate imaginative approaches to religious education and school worship, and to equip Christian parents for nurturing their children into faith. *Children, Churches and Christian Learning* has been designed as a contribution to these crucial developments.

We wish to express our gratitude to all who have helped shape this volume: to Robin Keeley who originally proposed the idea and to Elizabeth Marsh who has remained patient and supportive throughout the writing process; to Anne Rees, Evelyn Jackson and Susan Thomas who have shaped various stages of the manuscript; to Carol Roberts, Michael Fearn and Mandy Robbins who compiled the indexes; and to Diane Drayson who has copy-edited and harmonized our texts.

Leslie J. Francis
Jeff Astley
Easter 2002

Contributors

The Revd Professor Jeff Astley is Director of the North of England Institute for Christian Education and Honorary Professorial Fellow in Practical Theology and Christian Education, University of Durham. He wrote Chapters 6, 8, 9, 10, 11, 15, 18, 20, 23, 25, 26, 27, 31 and 32.

Dr Geraint Davies is Senior Lecturer in Education, Trinity College, Carmarthen. He wrote Chapter 21.

The Revd Anne Faulkner is Parish Development Adviser, Diocese of Oxford. She wrote Chapters 40, 41, 42, 43 and 44.

The Revd Professor Leslie J. Francis is Director of the Welsh National Centre for Religious Education and Professor of Practical Theology, University of Wales, Bangor. He wrote Chapters 5, 7, 12, 13, 14, 16, 17, 19, 28, 20, 30 and 34.

The Revd Dr William K. Kay is Director of the Centre for Pentecostal and Charismatic Studies, University of Wales, Bangor, and Senior Lecturer in Religious and Theology Education, King's College, London. He wrote Chapters 35, 36, 37, 38 and 39.

Dr David W. Lankshear is Deputy Secretary and Schools Officer of the National Society and Schools Officer of the General Synod Board of Education, London. He wrote Chapters 22, 24 and 33.

The Revd Dr William Strange is Director of the Centre for Ministry Studies, University of Wales, Bangor. He wrote Chapters 1, 2, 3 and 4.

PART ONE
BIBLE AND CHURCH

Children in the Old Testament and in Early Judaism

Introduction

The Old Testament has a great deal to say about children, from God's command to Adam and Eve to 'be fruitful and multiply' (Genesis 1.28), through its stories about children (such as the boy Samuel in 1 Samuel 2.18—3.18), and on to Zechariah's vision of a rebuilt Jerusalem which 'shall be full of boys and girls playing in its streets' (Zechariah 8.5). Judaism likewise is a faith in which family and children play a central part. The purpose of this chapter is to understand what the Old Testament has to say about children, and what part they played in the family life of Old Testament Israel and of the Jewish nation in the time of Jesus.

Jewish family life: biblical times and today

> ### The Jewish family as a religious community
>
> Since the home is regarded as the focus of religious activity in Judaism, the family plays a role, not only as the basic unit of social life, but also as the primary milieu of ritual expression. All the festivals are permeated by home-based rituals, and the *Shabbat* is structured around the family meals.
>
> Alan Unterman, 1981, p. 200

Modern Judaism places a high priority on family life. As the previous quotation indicates, the family has a religious as well as a social significance. This is something which has been a constant of Jewish life over many centuries, and stretches right back into biblical times, when several festivals were home-based and often involved the participation of children. Passover is a very clear example:

> And when your children ask you, 'What do you mean by this observance?', you shall say, 'It is the passover sacrifice to the Lord, for he passed over the houses of the Israelites in Egypt, when he struck down the Egyptians but spared our houses.' (Exodus 12.26–27)

However, there have been major changes in Jewish life and worship over the centuries. Modern Judaism is not exactly the same as Judaism in the time of the New Testament, nor was New Testament Judaism the same as the religion of Israel in, say, the time of David and Solomon. We can distinguish three important phases in the development of Israelite and Jewish life during biblical times:

1   Early Israel before about 1000BC. This is the period before the formation of the kingdom under David and before the building of the Temple under Solomon. The Israelites were peasant farmers in the hills of Palestine without either a central place of worship or a centralized form of government. The Bible speaks of a nomadic period which came even before the period of settlement in the land.

2   The period of the kingdoms. From about 1000BC until 586BC the Israelites were ruled by kings. In this period they had a centralized form of government, and probably began to develop social institutions such as schools to provide literate staff for the royal court and the temple.

3   The exile and Second Temple Judaism. In 586BC Jerusalem fell to the Babylonians and many Judeans were taken into exile. After 539BC some were allowed back, and a start was made on rebuilding the Temple. As the new structure replaced King Solomon's first temple, this period is sometimes called 'Second Temple Judaism'. Only the tribe of Judah survived these terrible events in recognizable form, so the people from this point can be called 'Judahites' or 'Jews' (rather than 'Israelites'), and their religion can be called 'Judaism'. This period came to an end in AD70 with the destruction of the Temple by the Romans.

The place and role of children may well have changed considerably between the simple peasant existence of the early period and the more sophisticated society of the late Second Temple period, during which Jesus was born and lived. We have to beware, then, of putting everything in the Old Testament or in later Jewish writings together as if there only ever has been one Jewish view of children.

The Israelite household

The fundamental social unit in early Israel – and this seems to have persisted through the period of the monarchy also – was the household, which the Old Testament calls *bayit* or *bêt 'ab* ('house' and 'house of the father'). It was not a nuclear family such as has become common in modern Western society, but an extended or composite family, which included several generations. It was likely to include also people not related by blood but dependent on the main family, such as war captives, debt slaves or resident aliens (sojourners). The composition of the 'house of the father' was too familiar to the writers of our Old Testament texts to need description, but its typical composition is hinted at in several passages, such as the Sabbath commandment, which draws a brief picture of the members of a typical Israelite household:

> Six days shall you labour and do all your work. But the seventh day is a sabbath to the Lord your God: you shall not do any work – you, or your son or your daughter, or your male or female slave, or your ox or your donkey, or any of your livestock, or the resident alien in your towns. (Deuteronomy 5.13–14)

The laws on incest in Leviticus 18 and 20 give an equally useful insight (though this is not its intention) into the kinds of relations who might all be found living in a single 'father's house' and therefore presumably sexually available.

Archaeology seems to confirm the importance of the 'father's house' in early Israelite society. Recent investigations of early Israelite dwellings in the pre-monarchical period show a consistent picture of rectangular pillared houses.

Archaeological evidence for the 'father's house'

The houses [of early Israelite settlements] appear in clusters of two or three, with one or more walls in common, apparently sharing common courtyard space and, presumably, the activities carried out in that space ... These dwelling clusters constitute evidence for a family unit in early Israel larger than that of the nuclear family (or conjugal couple with unmarried offspring). Each pillared house in a cluster may represent the living space of a nuclear family or parts thereof, but the shared courtyard space and common house walls of the linked buildings indicate a larger family grouping. Early Israelite dwelling units were thus complex arrangements of several buildings and housed what we might call extended families.

Carol Meyers, 1997, p. 16

The value of children

At the most basic level, children had an economic value in ancient Israel. They consumed resources, and were in that respect a drain on households which were often living near the edge of viability, but they had an economic usefulness which quickly began to counterbalance the need to provide food and clothing for them. They could perform small tasks for the household, either in the home or out in the fields. When they were old enough, but still too young to undertake adult tasks such as warfare, they could look after animals in the field, or run errands for their elders, as we find David doing for Jesse (1 Samuel 17.15).

However, children also represented the guarantee of the future. Through them, and especially through male children, a man's 'name' was perpetuated: his line carried on, and his household continued. This is the thinking behind the custom of 'Levirate marriage', under which a man was meant to take his deceased brother's wife in marriage, so that together they might produce an heir who would perpetuate the 'name' of the dead man (Deuteronomy 25.5–10).

It was also prudent to have a large family: by having a good number of children a couple could ensure that there would be someone around to care for them in old age. Jesus' command to leave one's children in order to be his follower (Mark 10.28–30) may not, therefore, be an injunction to abnegate responsibility for dependants, but a challenge to renounce the security for the future which children represented.

All peasant societies place this kind of value on children, but the Israelite and later Jewish understanding of children went far beyond simple material calculation. The procreation of children was seen as a commandment from God (Genesis 1.28). Children were protected from harm by several laws of early Israel, and in later Judaism were shielded by a positive attitude toward the value of young children's lives which made the Jews unusual, if not unique in the ancient world.

The protection of children

The treatment of children in ancient Israel seems to have fallen into the category of issues dealt with by the father of the family. Little is said about it, therefore, in the legal texts of the Old Testament, which codified the community and priestly law of Israel, but left a wide area of life still under the authority of the head of the 'father's house'.

Occasional narratives or prophetic texts give us some idea of how children were dealt with, and in general we may say that while fathers at an early stage seem to have power of life and death over their immediate family (Genesis 38.24–26), later law and custom curtailed or entirely removed this power (e.g. Deuteronomy 21.18–21).

We must assume, though, that Jews took what we would regard as a humane attitude toward children. We can say this if we may judge from the one area on which specific Jewish writing to do with the treatment of children has survived: infanticide. Several law codes in the Ancient Near East contain laws protecting unborn children from harm caused by violence, similar to the law found in Exodus 21.22–25. None, though, had laws which explicitly banned infanticide and abortion, but that is precisely how later Judaism interpreted this important law. The Jews of the New Testament period found themselves in contact with – and often living among – people who did not share this view of the sacredness of infant life. It was a common custom in Greek and Roman society either to reduce family size by procuring abortions, or to expose unwanted children to die. Jews of this period were distinctive in their refusal to countenance such acts, and Jews who tried to explain their ancestral ways to gentile readers often drew attention to this issue.

A first-century Jew explains his people's protection of children

The law, moreover, enjoins us to bring up all our offspring, and forbids women to cause abortion of what is begotten, or to destroy it afterward; and if any woman appears to have so done, she will be a murderer of her child, by destroying a living creature, and diminishing human kind; if any one, therefore, proceeds to such fornication or murder, he cannot be clean.

Josephus, *Against Apion*, 2.202

Birth and circumcision

Women in labour were customarily attended by midwives. Perhaps because this was the most vital life-and-death task exercised by women in ancient Israel, the midwife was a figure associated with a wisdom which could outwit kings and save a nation from destruction (Exodus 1.15–22).

Children in early Israel received a name, it would seem, at birth. This contrasts with some ancient societies (such as the Romans) who withheld naming a child until the child had shown its viability by surviving for its first perilous days. In several Old Testament stories, the mother gave the child its name (Genesis 19.37–38; 29.32–35; 30.6–13, 1 Samuel 1.20; 4.21). The father may have exercised a veto over unsuitable names (Genesis 35.18). In some circumstances, the community of neighbours had a say in the naming of a child (Ruth 4.17). Luke 1.59–63 tells of the naming of John the Baptist, and is interesting in several respects. In this instance the naming is a debate between mother, neighbours and father, in which the father has the final word. Here, too, the naming is postponed until the circumcision on the eighth day – perhaps Jews by this later period were beginning to be influenced by gentile customs.

After naming, circumcision was the next major event of a boy's life. Circumcision may well have begun as a pre-nuptial rite performed in early adulthood, and traces of this earlier function may be reflected in stories such as Genesis 17.25; 34.13–17 and Exodus 4.24–26.

Circumcision was not unique to Israel. In fact it was common to most of early

Israel's neighbours. It was not practised by the Babylonians among whom the Jews were exiled in the sixth century BC, so it is likely that it was during that exilic period that circumcision came to be seen as the distinctive mark of the Jewish male. What does seem to have been unique to Israel was the practice of infant circumcision. The Jewish Scriptures traced this practice back to God's command to Abraham (Genesis 17.12) – in other words, it was seen as foundational to the whole relationship between God and his people. By the time of Second Temple Judaism, infant circumcision was regarded as the defining sign of the covenant. During the persecutions of Antiochus Epiphanes in the second century BC, Jewish mothers suffered martyrdom rather than allow their sons to be left uncircumcised (1 Maccabees 1.60–61).

Boys and girls

Male and female roles were quite distinct in Israelite and Jewish society. So it is not surprising that boys and girls were treated rather differently as they were growing up.

There was no equivalent to circumcision for girls, no rite which marked their entry into the community. This was because of the way in which girls were being prepared for what was essentially a private, inner-household life, while boys were being prepared for responsibility outside the household, in the fields, among the markets, at the shrine or (later) in the synagogue. Our knowledge of the upbringing of girls in ancient Israel, and their expectations of adult life, is very restricted indeed.

The sphere of women's work was, generally speaking, in and around the house. Although they could work in the fields when necessity drove them (Ruth 2.2–3, 8), this kind of unprotected public work exposed women to dangers (Ruth 2.9, 22) and families which could seclude their womenfolk from such public roles probably did so. The writer Jesus ben Sirach (c. 200BC) advised that a 'headstrong daughter' should not be allowed out in public to 'parade her beauty before any man'. Not only should men not be able to see her, she should not even be allowed to have a lattice window through which she might catch sight of men (Sirach 42.11–12). To counterbalance this picture of strict control over girls and women (perhaps more characteristic of the later Second Temple period than of earlier Israel), Proverbs 31.10–31 praises the industry and good sense of the mistress of a wealthy household. It portrays a woman with many contacts and concerns which stretch beyond the confines of the house. But while her manifold activities brought her into contact with merchants and others outside her family, even this powerful figure is mainly a household manager.

A girl's upbringing, therefore, must have consisted largely of learning from her mother or other significant females of the 'father's household' how to fulfil the various domestic tasks which contributed to the efficient running of the household unit – even if some of these tasks became virtually a cottage industry (Proverbs 31.24).

Education

In the previous section we noted that we know very little about the upbringing of girls in ancient Israel. In fact we know little more about that of boys.

Their introduction to their communal and religious role began with circumcision. Today in the Jewish community it is brought to fruition in the ceremony of *bar mitzvah*, or 'son of the covenant', in which a boy at around 12 or 13 publicly takes on the responsibility to fulfil Torah for himself. We have no evidence for such a ceremony in Israel or in early Judaism, though the boy Jesus accompanying Mary and Joseph to Jerusalem at about the age of 12 and displaying remarkable understanding (Luke

2.41–51) may suggest that this age was already a significant one for a Jewish boy of the late Second Temple period.

A boy's education was fundamentally the responsibility of his father, much as the girl's was of the mother. He was expected to teach his son such practical skills as swimming, and to induct him into a trade. Indeed, this latter was so important that a rabbi of the first century AD, Hillel, maintained that negotiating one's son's apprenticeship was on a level with reading Torah: it could even be done on the Sabbath.

Formal schooling could only be provided in a relatively organized society. In Israel this probably meant that the first schools began under the monarchy, and that their aim was to provide literate, well-mannered and sage men to serve the royal court. Quite likely these schools were similar to the schools of the great cultures around Israel, especially those of Egypt. They would have turned out young men able to read, write and reckon numbers, men able to speak more than one language and so engage in foreign relations for the king (see 2 Kings 18.26), men also steeped in the wisdom teaching of Israel, as it is summarized for us in the book of Proverbs.

This schooling would have been based on rote learning and on conforming the young man to a tradition established by his elders and which he would be expected to pass on to another generation. It would strike us as dull and unstimulating. We might think that the Israelite boy at school did little more than learn a series of moral and social platitudes. But as the following extract points out, such a reaction fails to understand what the schooling of ancient Israel was trying to provide.

Teaching and learning in ancient Israel

These sayings about how to behave and what to do were addressed to people's reason and good sense, which in a civilized society is a *common* sense; they were intended to win assent without further explanation or argument; they were designed to be memorable and repeated (platitudinously) over and over again. By reciting or copying out these proverbs, the schoolboys of Israel were being initiated into the moral consensus of their community – and that was a major part of their education in wisdom.

Eric Heaton, 1994, pp. 91–2

References and further reading

Heaton, E. W. (1994), *The School Tradition of the Old Testament: The Bampton Lectures for 1994*, Oxford, Oxford University Press.

Kraemer, D. (ed.) (1989), *The Jewish Family*, New York, Oxford University Press.

Meyers, C. (1997), 'The family in early Israel', in L.G. Perdue *et al.* (eds.), *Families in Ancient Israel*, Louisville, Kentucky, Westminster John Knox Press, pp. 1–47.

Perdue, L. G. *et al.* (eds.) (1997), *Families in Ancient Israel*, Louisville, Kentucky, Westminster John Knox Press.

Safrai, S. and Stern, M. (eds.) (1976), *The Jewish People in the First Century*, Assen/Amsterdam, von Gorcum.

Unterman, A. (1981), *Jews, their Religious Beliefs and Practices*, London, Routledge.

┌─────┐
│ 2 │
└─────┘

Children in the New Testament

Introduction

Christian readers will not be disappointed if they turn to the New Testament looking for something about children. There are a number of stories and sayings in the Gospels in which children feature, as well as passages in the letters of Paul and others which deal with the topic of children.

Readers may be disappointed, though, if they expect a clear set of instructions which can simply be read off from our texts and put into practice today. This is partly because there are cultural differences between the New Testament world and our own, and partly because different parts of the New Testament speak about children from different points of view. Only when we have noted these differences can we bring together the ideas we have encountered and begin to form an overall picture.

We should beware, also, of imposing our values on the text, rather than listening to what it has to say. Many modern-day readers, for example, are pleased by what they hear Jesus saying about the value of children, but displeased by what they read in, say, 1 Timothy about keeping children 'submissive and respectful' (1 Timothy 3.4). This outlook seems paternalistic at best, downright patriarchal and outmoded at worst – something to be repudiated rather than embraced.

It would be wise to suspend judgement on any of the voices we hear from the New Testament until we have listened to a cross-section of them, and attempted to integrate them as part of a whole. We need also to recognize that these voices come to us from cultures significantly different from our own.

The place of the child in New Testament society

It is a very modern concept in the Western world that the child – the future – is important and in a position of privilege. In the past the child was seen as belonging to the father, the family, the group, the community – not to the future. The father, the head of the household, the spokesman for the family and the group ruled.

Megan McKenna, 1994, p. 67

Children in the ministry of Jesus: the objects of care

Caring for children was a major part of Jesus' ministry, according to the Gospel narratives. On at least three occasions, Jesus was asked to intervene to heal or exorcize

9

a child (Mark 5.21–24; 35–43; 7.24–30; 9.14–29; each with parallels in at least one other Gospel). Children were brought by the crowds when they came to hear him teach (Matthew 14.21), and were put in front of him for him to 'touch' (Mark 10.11) – presumably because it was thought that his touch conveyed a blessing. The Gospels give the clear impression that people perceived him as concerned with children.

Caring for children was part of his ministry which he explicitly passed on to his followers. This care shaded over into general concern for the weak and vulnerable in the community. His words on 'welcoming one such child in my name' (Mark 9.37) stand alongside his saying on not despising 'one of these little ones' (Matthew 18.10), and not putting a stumbling block in front of 'one of these little ones who believe' (or 'who believe in me') (Mark 9.42). Some commentators apply these sayings to despised (adult) members of the community of Christ's followers. However, it seems that Mark 9.37 certainly, and the other sayings possibly, should be taken to refer to care for actual children, even if they could also refer to adults whose vulnerability made them like children.

In Mark 9.37, Jesus' saying is prompted by a quarrel among the disciples about who was the greatest. He took a child, put his arms around him (see also Mark 10.16), and declared: 'Whoever welcomes one such child in my name welcomes me, and whoever welcomes me welcomes not me but the one who sent me.' In Jewish society, a man could be represented by an authorized agent (*shaliach*), and the way such an agent was received and treated was taken as treatment given to the man himself. Here, then, Jesus is saying that the treatment given to a child is given to him. It may be that this saying also refers to those whose frailty and lack of status place them in a similar position to children and who are also Jesus' representatives, but we should not take away from the impact of this saying, nor from the great importance it places on the care of children.

Children in the teaching of Jesus: examples to disciples

The disciples of Jesus were prone to argue about status and their own place in the hierarchy which (they assumed) Jesus was setting up in his 'kingdom' (Matthew 18.1). Jesus' answer to such argument was to take a child, put him among them, and say 'truly I tell you, unless you change and become like children, you will never enter the kingdom of heaven. Whoever becomes humble like this child is the greatest in the kingdom of heaven' (Matthew 18.3–4). Similarly, as a rebuke to the disciples when they tried to stop people bringing children to Jesus, he said to them: 'Let the little children come to me, and do not stop them, for it is to such as these that the kingdom of heaven belongs' (Matthew 19.14; Mark and Luke add: 'Truly I tell you, whoever does not receive the kingdom of God as a little child will never enter it', Mark 10.15/Luke 18.17).

'Becoming like a child' and its meaning

Jesus was speaking specifically about how a person enters the kingdom of God, and in looking at children it was not their subjective characteristics, but their objective position in society which made them models for discipleship. He meant that just as children occupied a socially inferior position, dependent on others, and at the beck and call of others, so also his followers must live as servants in the kingdom. To enter the kingdom of God means to renounce self and self-seeking and to take a status of no consequence.

William Strange, 1996, p. 51

The kingdom of God is a realm of paradox, where the first are last and the last first, and where the greatest has to take the status of the least. One aspect of that paradox is that, whereas children are 'normally' expected to transform into adults (1 Corinthians 13.11), in the kingdom of God adults have to learn to become like children.

Hard sayings on family and children

Considerable attention has been given in recent study of the Gospels to the prominence of the theme of renunciation of family ties in the teaching of the early Church and in the teaching of Jesus himself. While there are very positive things said about children in the Gospels and affirming things done for and to them, there are hard sayings on family and children there too.

Luke's Gospel begins with the rejoicing of the childless couple Elizabeth and Zechariah over the conception of their child, who is to become John the Baptist (Luke 1.24–25, 57–58). Luke also says more about the conception, birth and youth of Jesus than any other Gospel (Luke 1.26–56, 2.1–52). So it is something of a surprise after this affirmation of family life and the significance of children, to find this saying in Luke's Gospel: 'Whoever comes to me and does not hate father and mother, wife *and children*, brothers and sisters, yes, and even life itself, cannot be my disciple' (Luke 14.26). The parallel in Matthew is slightly less stark: 'Whoever loves father or mother more than me is not worthy of me; and whoever loves son or daughter more than me is not worthy of me' (Matthew 10.37). These are part of a cluster of sayings critical of the family and of the strong ties with which it bound people in first-century Palestine (Matthew 8.21–22/Luke 9.57–62; Matthew 10.34–36/Luke 12.51–53; Matthew 19.10–12; Matthew 19.23–30/Mark 10.23–31/Luke 18.24–30).

How are we to understand these hard sayings on family and children? Some interpreters argue that these were not sayings directed at all Jesus' followers, but only to those who literally left everything to follow him as wandering charismatic preachers (e.g. Theissen and Merz, 1998, pp. 378–9). The sayings themselves, though, do not contain any clue that their scope is restricted in this way (note 'whoever' in Luke 14.26). More likely, the thrust of these sayings is to make the call of family upon the follower of Christ a *relative* rather than an *absolute* one in the light of the total demands of life in the kingdom of God. We must remember that to have a child in the society of Jesus' day was not simply to generate a person who would be a dependant (though children clearly did depend on their parents: Matthew 7.9–11/Luke 11.11–13) and would then become independent. Your child would eventually be your provider, and you would be dependent on them in old age or illness (Mark 7.11–12). So these hard sayings on family and children are probably to be taken as calls to 'strive first for the kingdom of God and his righteousness' (Matthew 6.33), rather than put one's trust in human provision.

Taking children seriously: Colossians and Ephesians

Ephesians and Colossians instruct children

Children, obey your parents [in the Lord], for this is right. 'Honour your father and mother' – this is the first commandment with a promise: 'so that it may be well with you and you may live long on the earth'. And, fathers, do not provoke your children to anger, but bring them up in the discipline and instruction of the Lord.

Ephesians 6.1–4

> . Children, obey your parents in everything, for this is your acceptable duty in
> the Lord. Fathers, do not provoke your children, or they may lose heart.
>
> Colossians 3.20–21

These instructions to children and to fathers are part of sections in both letters which deal with reciprocal relationships in the family or household: husbands–wives (Ephesians 5.22–33, Colossians 3.18–19), parents–children (Ephesians 6.1–4, Colossians 3.20–21), and masters–slaves (Ephesians 6.5–9, Colossians 3.22—4.1). These belong to a form of ethical instruction which scholars have called 'household codes'. These household codes give instructions on moral living to different groups within the family, and they are to be found elsewhere in the New Testament as well as in other ethical writings from the ancient world, both Christian and non-Christian.

Explaining the parent's role in Ephesians

Most significantly, it is here for the first time in Christian literature that instructions are given about the Christian socialisation of children: fathers are to raise their children 'in the discipline and instruction of the Lord' (*en paideia kai nouthesia kyriou*, 6.4). The precise nature of the two nouns here – *paideia* and *nouthesia* – is difficult to determine. *Paideia* can mean formation in the educational sense ('training') or merely 'discipline'; the two were closely associated in Antiquity by the assumption that lessons were best beaten into children! *Nouthesia* can mean merely 'warning', but it seems to have the sense here of 'instruction' in more than merely a negative sense. In any case, the combination of these two nouns with the genitive *kuri/iou* [of the Lord] signals a perception that there is a specifically Christian way of raising children, and perhaps a specifically Christian body of instruction to be imparted to them.

John M. G. Barclay, in Moxnes, 1997, pp. 76–7

Modern readers will notice that these instructions accept the hierarchical structure of the family without question, and that in fact they reinforce the need for the 'subordinate' household members (wives, children, slaves) to show reverence, respect and obedience to the 'superior' figure (husband, father, master). Some interpreters are disappointed to find these features in the New Testament, and argue that they represent an importing of pagan values into the Christian community and so are a decline from the insights and example of Jesus (Osiek and Balch, 1997, pp. 118–21).

If we focus particularly on the parts dealing with children, though, we should notice something else: the letters to the Colossians and to the Ephesians are unique in early Christian literature because they contain injunctions addressed *to* children. Even if the content of the instruction seems conventional, the fact that children were spoken to and not merely talked about is very significant.

These two letters envisage children as disciples. We know from little snippets of information elsewhere in the New Testament that children were present when the Christian assembly gathered in someone's house or elsewhere for worship (Acts 20.7–12; 21.5). Ephesians and Colossians show that at least sometimes something positive was made of their presence: alongside adults, they were instructed in how to live as Christians. No doubt the teachers who helped 'equip the saints for the work of ministry' (Ephesians 4.11–12) would have taken up this theme from the letters and continued to teach children in the congregation. These simple instructions to children, therefore, amount to evidence that children were taken seriously. To that extent we would have to say that Ephesians and Colossians are not importing pagan values, but expressing the same outlook as that of Jesus himself, who also paid attention to children in their own right.

Children as the church's invisible members: the Pastoral Epistles

In Ephesians and in Colossians, responsibility is given to fathers to bring children up 'in the discipline and instruction of the Lord' (Ephesians 6.4). In these letters the church community itself had some role in nurturing children in faith. But eventually the responsibility for teaching children in the faith was handed entirely to parents, and children's discipleship came to be seen as part of their parents' discipleship. They were not instructed directly, but their parents were instructed on how to teach them. They became the church's invisible members.

We can see this tendency in, for example, 1 Peter. This letter, like Ephesians and Colossians, has ethical instruction in the form of a 'household code', but in this instance the only relationships dealt with are slaves and masters, and husbands and wives. Children have slipped out of the picture (1 Peter 2.18—3.7). Similarly in the case of Titus 2.1–9, we find the targeted instruction is for older men, older women, younger men, younger women and slaves – but not children.

It was important that children should receive the good news and grow in faith. However, in the letters known as the 'Pastoral Epistles' (1 and 2 Timothy; Titus) the teaching given to the churches emphasizes that men should control their households, including specifically the task of keeping children 'submissive and respectful in every way' (1 Timothy 3.4–5, 12; Titus 1.6). The positive nurturing of children seems to be the role of the mother: 1 Timothy 5.10, 14.

We appear to find, then, that the first Christians took children seriously. They also regarded the home as the principal arena of Christian nurture and instruction – so much so that the home eventually became the *only* place of specific Christian teaching for children. The meeting of the church itself became a more purely adult affair at which children, if present, were given little attention or none at all. The following quotation expresses the post-New Testament Church's understanding of where responsibility lay for the Christian education of children.

An early Christian reminds his readers of the mother's responsibility to nurture children in the faith

Let us first of all teach ourselves to walk in the commandment of the Lord; next teach our wives to remain in the faith given to them, and in love and purity, tenderly loving their husbands in all truth, and loving all others equally in all chastity, and to educate their children in the fear of God.

Polycarp, *Philippians*, 4.1–2 (about AD120)

Conclusion

The example of Jesus pointed Christians to a positive understanding of children. Their Jewish background, of course, already disposed them to regard children as important. The extra element which Jesus seems to have added was to make his disciples regard them as important, not just for the *potential* of what they would become, but for what they already *are*. 'It is to such as these that the kingdom of heaven belongs' is a saying which has puzzled Christians down the centuries – not surprisingly, when we remember that it was first spoken as a rebuke to Jesus' first followers. As long as this saying and others like it were there to be read in the Gospels, along with the stories of Jesus touching and even embracing children, then Jesus' followers could not wholly ignore children.

The hard sayings on children and family which we have noticed helped to fuel an anti-family, anti-children outlook in some parts of the early Church, in which the bearing and raising of children came to be regarded as a spiritually and morally doubtful thing to do. But the Church did not forget children. Even in the rather patriarchal 'household codes' which we have read here, and in the churches in which instruction of the young was delegated to the family, the importance of children was at least affirmed. And it was not just the children of the Christian community: in AD374, when the Roman Empire was becoming Christian, one of the first enactments of the Christian Emperors was to outlaw infanticide. This one simple law expressed eloquently the difference made to the world by Christianity's Jewish heritage and by the Church's continued attention to the teaching of Jesus.

References and further reading

Barton, S. C. (1994), *Discipleship and Family Ties in Mark and Matthew*, Cambridge, Cambridge University Press.

Barton, S. C. (ed.) (1996), *The Family in Theological Perspective*, Edinburgh, T. & T. Clark.

Barton, S. C. (1998), 'Living as families in the light of the New Testament', *Interpretation*, 52, 130–44.

McKenna, M. (1994), *Not Counting Women and Children*, Tunbridge Wells, Burns & Oates.

Moxnes, H. (ed.) (1997), *Constructing Early Christian Families: Family as Social Reality and Metaphor*, London, Routledge.

Osiek, C. (1995), 'The New Testament and the family', *Concilium*, 52, pp. 1–9.

Osiek, C. (1996), 'The family in early Christianity', *Catholic Biblical Quarterly*, 58, pp. 1–24.

Osiek, C. and Balch, D. L. (1997), *Families in the New Testament World: Households and House Churches*, Louisville, Kentucky, Westminster John Knox Press.

Strange, W. A. (1996), *Children in the Early Church*, Carlisle, Paternoster Press.

Theissen, G. and Merz, A. (1988), *The Historical Jesus: A Comprehensive Guide*, London, SCM Press.

Verner, D. C. (1983), *The Household of God: The Social World of the Pastoral Epistles*, Chico, California, Scholars Press.

3

Theology of Childhood

Introduction

Christian theology has not generally made children a central focus of concern. When Christians have thought about children theologically, it has usually happened in passing, when dealing with such topics as baptism, abortion, education or family life.

Christians today are beginning to challenge this neglect of children as a focus of concern, and more attention is being given to developing a theology of childhood. We will here draw together some of the theological ideas which Christians past and present have held about childhood, by looking at three of the sayings of Jesus to do with children, and by using them as an introduction to considering the nature, the value and the place of children in Christian theology.

Jesus, children and the kingdom of God

Let the little children come to me; do not stop them; for it is to such as these that the kingdom of God belongs.

Mark 10.14

Original sin

The influence of this saying of Jesus has been immense, especially in the area of baptism. As early as AD200 Christians were already appealing to it to justify infant baptism (interpreted as 'bringing children to Christ'). The saying that the kingdom of God belongs 'to such as these' has made many Christians take a positive view of the nature of children in the sight of God. However, many other Christians have also regarded children as tainted by 'original sin'. The Christian theological understanding of children and childhood has, in consequence, had both a positive and a negative aspect.

The earliest Christians seem to have believed that children were 'innocent', in the sense that they were born, so to speak, with a clean sheet. Christians in the first three centuries seem also to have thought that humans have a propensity to sin, but that children are not *guilty* of sin until they reach the age of discretion and become responsible for their own actions, or until they have reached an age to experience sexual temptation.

Augustine (AD354–430) was the first theologian to take any substantial notice of children and to reflect about them, about their nature and about their standing before God. He more than anyone else was responsible for changing the earlier Christian view of childhood as a state of innocence. In Augustine's understanding, Scripture taught clearly that human beings are born already with a taint of sin and guilt upon them. He drew this from such texts as Psalm 51.5 ('I was born guilty, a sinner when my mother conceived me'), and Romans 5.12. Augustine thought that Paul was saying in Romans that every member of humanity throughout time actually sinned when Adam fell, because we were all contained potentially in our first forefather. Augustine also believed that this scriptural truth was borne out by empirical evidence, if we observe what children do.

Are children innocent?

It can hardly be right for a child, even at that age [babyhood], to cry for everything, including things which would harm him; to work himself into a tantrum against people older than himself and not required to obey him; and to try his best to strike and hurt others who know better than he does, including his own parents, when they do not give in to him and refuse to pander to whims which would only do him harm. This shows that, if babies are innocent, it is not for lack of will to do harm, but for lack of strength.

Augustine, *Confessions*, 1.8

Augustine's view of original sin (or birth sin) obviously tied in well with belief in the necessity of infant baptism. Baptism was the only means by which this taint could be washed away, and by which a child could be assured of an eternal destiny in heaven. Indeed the early rites of baptism – including the baptism of infants – included exorcism before the baptism itself, and this fact alone is a significant testimony to the general view of children's pre-baptismal spiritual state.

Limbo

Christians, though, were seldom willing to pursue the logic of Augustine's theology of childhood, and to believe that children who died unbaptized were damned. In the Middle Ages Thomas Aquinas (1225–74) struggled with the legacy of Augustine. On the one hand, he could not contradict what the greatest thinker of the Western Church had said on the subject. But on the other, Thomas was convinced that children were not guilty of actual sin, and that any punishment had to fit the sin being punished. The punishment for the guilt of original sin must, in all justice, be less than that for actual sin.

Thomas' answer to this dilemma was to propose that two classes of people – the 'fathers' of the old covenant who died before Christ, and unbaptized children – went neither to heaven nor hell, but to a third place which he called *limbus* – 'limbo'. Limbo was not a place of punishment, merely of deprivation of the joy of heaven. In the case of the fathers, this was only a temporary resting place in which they remained until Christ freed them after the resurrection. In the case of unbaptized children, limbo was their eternal resting place, but it would be bearable for them, because they would recognize and accept (since they would have become fully rational souls) that in their unbaptized state they could never have attained heaven.

Limbo: what and why

[Commenting on the phrase 'the pains of death' in Acts 2.24] But there are no pains in the limbo* of the fathers, nor indeed in the limbo* of children, who are not being punished with a punishment which can be felt, but only with the punishment of being condemned for original sin.

Thomas Aquinas, *Summa Theologica*, 3.52.2.2

(*In this passage he uses the word *infernum*, 'hell', but he means the state which he elsewhere calls 'limbo'.)

It should be added that the Eastern Church did not share Augustine's view, and did not develop a theology of limbo. The Eastern Orthodox Church sees baptism as absolutely necessary for salvation, but has been content to leave the fate of the unbaptized child to God's mercy.

A new look at the nature of childhood

It was only when Western Christians began to question Augustine's view of the effect of original sin, from the eighteenth century onwards, that the saying of Jesus 'it is to such as these that the kingdom of God belongs' could again begin seriously to influence Christian thinking about the nature of children. Once Christians started to doubt whether original sin was transmitted from Adam as Augustine argued, they could look at children and childhood in a different way. In Anglo-American society, at least, there was a shift in attitude in the late eighteenth to early nineteenth centuries, from a general assumption that children were wicked, to a growing assumption that they were potentially good.

In the nineteenth century, theologians began – apparently for the first time – to ask what it was about children to which Jesus was drawing attention when he said: 'it is to such as these that the kingdom of God belongs. Truly I tell you, whoever does not receive the kingdom of God as a little child will never enter it.' Some thought that it was their innocence. F. D. E. Schleiermacher (1768–1834) argued that what lay behind Jesus' words was the child's ability to live in the moment.

The child lives in the moment

The peculiar essence of the child is that he is altogether in the moment... The past disappears for him, and of the future he knows nothing – each moment exists only for itself, and this accounts for the blessedness of a soul content in innocence.

Friedrich Schleiermacher, in Bunge, 2001, p. 339

Developing a theology of childhood

Some nineteenth-century theologians have been criticized – and were criticized by their contemporaries – for basing their understanding on an idealized view of childhood. Something similar might also be said of the pre-Augustinian view of childhood as a time of innocence. If receiving the kingdom of God as a child means returning to a state of innocence, then it seems to set an unattainable and inappropriate goal for discipleship: the life of a person who has experienced estrangement from God and has been redeemed must in some sense reflect that experience and cannot be a simple return to a supposed innocence, as though nothing had taken place.

So this saying of Jesus may be drawing attention to some aspect of childhood other than innocence, an aspect which is appropriate as a model or goal for the adult disciple. The Roman Catholic theologian Karl Rahner (1904–84) suggested that the crucial element was the child's dependence, that they are 'those who *know* that they have nothing of themselves on which to base any claim to his help, and yet who trust that his kindness and protection will be extended to them and so will bestow what they need upon them'. In this sense the child is an appropriate model for the adult who will receive the kingdom of God.

More than this, Rahner argued, childhood is not merely to be seen as a temporary and imperfect state from which we progress to something better. Those who live as children of God remain open to 'expect the unexpected' and so preserve their original childhood. In fact, they more than preserve it – they grow into it. They do not stop being a child in order to be an adult: they develop a mature childhood.

The theological meaning of childhood

Now this also implies, however paradoxical it may appear, that we do not really know what childhood means at the beginning of our lives until we know what that childhood means which comes at the end of them; that childhood, namely, in which, by God-given repentance and conversion, we receive the kingdom of God and so become children. It is in this sense that we only recognize the child at the beginning of life from the child of the future.

Karl Rahner, 1971, p. 43

Schleiermacher had already formulated something similar to Rahner's view in a short aphorism: 'Being a child should not prevent becoming an adult: being an adult should not prevent becoming a child' (in Bunge, 2001, p. 349).

The value of children

Jesus on the value of the child

Whoever welcomes one such child in my name welcomes me.

Mark 9.37

This saying of Jesus identifies the child as effectively his own representative. Through Christian history the potentially revolutionary impact of this saying and its negative counterpart (Mark 9.42) has largely been overlooked.

The ancient world in which Christianity was born had no concept of a general care for the welfare of children. Parents would normally try to look after their own offspring – though even they might be grossly neglectful without attracting strong censure – but nobody considered that they had any responsibility for other people's children.

Jesus' teaching on the value of the child began to change this, but it was slow to have its effect. The first Christians were aware of the need to care for widows and orphans – a concern which came down to them from their Jewish background (see James 1.27). However, it is only in the Middle Ages that we begin to see the words of Jesus making a difference to the treatment of children. The medieval Church began the practice of taking in and caring for orphans and foundlings, children abandoned because they were born out of wedlock or because they were born to parents whose poverty made abandonment the only option. Pope Innocent III (Pope 1198–1216) is the first prominent Christian known to us to have taken action on behalf of children out of a sense of Christian responsibility, when he set up the Hospital of Santo Spirito, an orphanage for abandoned babies in Rome.

Pope Innocent III puts Jesus' words into action

Innocent's social awareness in regard to children would have developed from his support for the *vita apostolica*, the movement which had arisen out of the spiritual ferment of the twelfth century. With such spiritual inspiration, Innocent would constantly have had in mind the gospels and the sayings of Jesus. There, in Matthew and Mark, he would have found the advice to 'suffer little children... because of such are the kingdom of heaven.' This demanded an approach to children by others than those in the parental relationship, which was perhaps not at all common at the time ... It is not clear when Christ's injunction – not to offend against his little ones – became a guiding principle for the church, but by the turn of the twelfth century some attempts were obviously being made.

Brenda M. Bolton, in Wood, 1994, p. 166

The challenge of these sayings of Jesus has continued to inspire a succession of Christian initiatives, from the orphanages and schools of A. H. Francke in seventeenth-century Germany, through the Foundling Hospital of Captain Thomas Coram in eighteenth-century London (now Coram Family), to Dr Barnardo's Homes in the nineteenth century, and on to the work of numerous societies such as National Children's Homes (now NCH Action for Children) or the Children's Society in the contemporary world.

It could still be asked, though, whether the value of children implied in the sayings of Jesus poses an even deeper challenge to Christians. Some people criticize modern capitalism for turning children into commodities, or consumers, whose value lies only in their economic contribution. It is doubtful whether capitalism is alone in this – previous economic systems also lent themselves to the ruthless exploitation of children. However, if the world economic system in which we live does in fact leave millions of children in poverty, and if it does in practice deliver millions more to a narrow materialism, then present-day Christians have some very practical questions to address in their world, when they accept Jesus' valuing of the child as his own representative.

The place of children

Jesus on honouring parents

You know the commandments: . . . 'Honour your father and your mother.'

Mark 10.19

It is impossible to investigate a Christian theology of childhood without recognizing that a major emphasis through Christian history has been on the *subordination* of the child to his or her parents. Most Christians of the past believed that bringing children into subjection to their elders was a necessary part of their socialization (at the least), and many Christians regarded 'breaking the child's will' as utterly necessary for their eternal salvation. Through most of Christian history, physical beating was assumed to be an appropriate means of achieving this subordination.

It is for this reason, and in view of the theological estimate of children as tainted by original sin, that some modern writers have accused the Christian Church (and especially European and American Protestant Churches) of creating a 'poisonous pedagogy'. On this view, the theological views which Christians held about children legitimated violence against them, and so permitted and sanctioned the physical abuse of children (Miller, 1983; Greven, 1991). The Christian view of childhood, it has been claimed, lies at the root of modern child abuse.

The truth or otherwise of this charge against Christians' view of childhood can be investigated in two ways:

1 We could ask whether Christians (even those who held the Augustinian view of 'original sin') have been necessarily violent or cruel to children in their care. The evidence on this seems to be mixed. Some Christians who held what might appear to be very severe views about original sin were not thereby driven to harsh treatment of children (Bunge, 2001). And those Christians who have treated children badly need not have been doing so *because* of their theological views. It is quite difficult to prove a link between a particular theological view of childhood and actual patterns of behaviour.

2 We could ask whether the injunction to honour your father and your mother, and the insistence on the subordination of children, is an entirely one-way process in Christian thinking. Some of the New Testament evidence, which apparently affirms the subordination of children, actually goes a long way toward calling hierarchical models of family life into question. The letters to the Ephesians and Colossians, for instance (Ephesians 6.1–4; Colossians 3.20–21), address children directly and give parents a responsibility toward children as well as giving children duties toward their parents.

'Honour your father and your mother' in a Christian context

Colossians and Ephesians make the responsibilities of parents and children mutual. If children owe their parents the duty of respect, no less do parents owe their children the duty of consideration. This was quite a radical idea in the culture of the time, where a far more one-way relationship would be the norm. The commandment quoted in Ephesians 6.2, 'Honour your father and your mother', enjoined the normal social respect for parents. Ephesians does nothing

---

to undermine this respect; it builds it into a wider vision of a family which can be a living expression of life in Christ. So here the relationship of parents and children is part of the mutual concern characteristic of all Christian living, which is profoundly and simply set out in Ephesians by the maxim at the head of its ethical list: 'Be subject to one another out of reverence for Christ' (Ephesians 5.21).

William Strange, 1996, p. 74

The fact that these letters directed teaching toward children suggests that children in the Christian community are not merely subsumed under their parents. The evidence of Ephesians and Colossians recognizes, in a potentially fruitful way, that children have a discipleship of their own.

References and further reading

Barton, S. C. (ed.) (1986), *The Family in Theological Perspective*, Edinburgh, T. & T. Clark.

Bunge, M. J. (ed.) (2001), *The Child in Christian Thought*, Grand Rapids, Michigan, Eerdmans.

Greven, P. (1991), *Spare the Child: The Religious Roots of Punishment and the Psychological Impact of Physical Abuse*, New York, Alfred A. Knopf.

Miller, A. (1983), *For Your Own Good: Hidden Cruelty in Child-Rearing and the Roots of Violence*, New York, Noonday.

Rahner, K. (1971), 'Ideas for a theology of childhood', in K. Rahner, *Theological Investigations VIII*, London, Darton, Longman & Todd, pp. 33-50.

Strange, W. A. (1996), *Children in the Early Church*, Carlisle, Paternoster Press.

Whitmore, T. D., with Winright, T. (1997), 'Children: an undeveloped theme in Catholic teaching', in M. A. Ryan and T. D. Whitmore (eds.), *The Challenge of Global Stewardship: Roman Catholic Responses*, Notre Dame, University of Notre Dame Press, pp. 161–85.

Wood, D. (ed.) (1994), *The Church and Childhood: Studies in Church History 31*, Oxford, Blackwell.

4

Baptism and Confirmation

Introduction

Christians cannot agree about baptizing children. Some Churches will and do baptize children while others will not and do not. To complicate the picture further, some ministers and clergy in Churches which allow the baptism of infants are willing to baptize any baby or child brought to them, while others operate policies that permit only believing parents to bring their children to baptism. Churches which baptize children usually have some further ceremony (confirmation) to mark the young person's entry into the Church as an adult.

Clearly there are issues of principle at stake here. We will have to look at what baptism is and how children fit into the Church if we are to understand the deep differences between Christians over baptism.

How have we come to be the way we are?

What do we mean by baptism?

Very often, the first words I hear when I answer my study phone are, 'I want the baby baptised, Vicar.' My usual response is, 'Why?' After a short pause, back comes the reply, 'Well, it's the right thing to do, isn't it?' Another reply I often hear is, 'Gran says I must in case something should happen to the baby.'

Clifford Owen, 1991, p. 267

People in society at large are often unclear about what baptism is. As the conversations reported in the quotation above show us, parents requesting baptism are not always asking for the same thing as the Church thinks it is offering. Parents requesting baptism of their child would get a variety of responses depending on the view held by the minister with whom they were speaking: some Christians think children cannot be suitable candidates for baptism ('believers' baptism'); some think any child may be baptized, while others still think that some may be, but not all should be.

Christians are divided over the issue of baptizing infants or children because the New Testament itself says nothing clear about it. The evidence of the New Testament and the early Christians can be seen in two quite different ways, as with a puzzle picture. People with different ways of looking at the evidence see two quite different pictures.

Believers' baptism

Those who support the idea of believers' baptism will take into accout the following issues:

- *What a Christian really is.* A Christian is someone who has consciously accepted Christ as Saviour and Lord.
- *What baptism really is.* Baptism is a public profession of faith in Christ in which the believing person states in front of a congregation that they have accepted Christ. Since children cannot make this step, they should not be baptized.
- *What the New Testament says.* Nowhere in the New Testament do we find any evidence of children being baptized. All those who were baptized were adults who had become Christians. So there is no New Testament warrant for baptizing infants.
- *How a false view of baptism came about.* In the early Church, probably around AD200, parents started to worry about their children dying unbaptized, so began to ask that they should be given baptism. Eventually baptism came to be seen as a rite which would guarantee that a child went to heaven if he or she died (see the grandmother's view in the quotation above).
- *How the true view of baptism was recovered.* At the Reformation in the sixteenth century the major reformers failed to tackle this issue. But a group known as the Anabaptists ('Re-baptisers') recovered the original New Testament teaching about baptism. Following them, the Baptist Churches have upheld the authentic New Testament link between profession of faith and baptism.

Biblical support for believers' baptism

In contrast to the many lines of approach used by the advocates of paedobaptism [infant baptism], the baptist's approach is disarmingly simple. For him it is sufficient that, in his judgement, every doctrinal statement about baptism in the New Testament presupposes that baptism will be administered to those who consciously believe in Christ, and that it will be the token of their faith in him. For him it is decisive that every instance of baptism recorded in the New Testament is of men or women who have consciously believed in Christ and who thus wish to express their faith.

Donald Bridge and David Phypers, 1977, p. 55

Infant baptism picture

Some of those who agree with the baptism of infants think that the believers' baptism case is correct to suppose that children were not baptized in the time of the New Testament. Others do not concede this, and think the evidence is strong that children were baptized from the very first. This outline takes the second version of the 'picture':

- *The precedent of circumcision.* Infant Jewish boys were (and are) admitted to the covenant community by the rite of circumcision. Although the New Testament says nothing specific about this, we should expect the first Christians to admit their children to the covenant community by the corresponding rite of baptism.
- *Jesus welcomed children.* The words of Jesus, 'Let the children come to me, do not hinder them, for to such belongs the kingdom of God', were being used to justify

infant baptism as early as Tertullian (c. AD200). Some argue that this text has no reference to baptism, but others urge that indirectly it demonstrates that children should be initiated by baptism into the kingdom community of the Church.

- *Household baptisms in the New Testament.* In apostolic times, when the head of a household was converted the entire household was baptized, and it is fair to assume that children would have been included (Acts 16.33; 1 Corinthians 1.16).
- *Children were treated as baptized.* New Testament letters assume that all the hearers were baptized (Romans 6.3–4; 1 Corinthians 10.1–4; Ephesians 4.4). Yet children are addressed in some letters (Ephesians 6.1–4; Colossians 3.20–21). The conclusion must be that they had been baptized.
- *What happened in the early Church.* Admittedly, there is no direct evidence of infant baptism before AD200, but when it is first reported, nobody claimed it was an innovation, and some people (such as Origen) already held that it was a practice of the apostles. So it is most likely that infants were baptized from the time of the apostles onwards.

Biblical support for the baptism of infants

Careful investigation of scripture points to an origin of infant baptism in the very origins of the church, with roots in the Old Testament. Anglicans today are in a position to say that, even if a superficial reading of the Reformation period might suggest that the tradition was sustained without sufficient critical scrutiny, it is no mere accident of history, but scriptural conviction, which makes us ready in principle to baptize infants today.

Colin Buchanan, 1998, p. 243

Why do we stay the way we are?

There seems no immediate prospect of ecumenical agreement on infant baptism, because of deep differences over the nature and operation of sacraments (or as the Protestant tradition would say, 'ordinances') such as baptism. These differences are accompanied by disagreements about the nature of the Church: the believers' baptism position tends to fit well with the 'gathered Church' concept, a Church which draws the boundaries of its membership quite clearly, while infant baptism accords with a more open form of Church, and in this form of Church the concept of membership is less clear.

There are pastoral and practical reasons for the wide spectrum of approaches taken by Churches today to the baptism of infants. The following paragraphs indicate some of these reasons.

Believers' baptism as the guarantee of discipleship

Those in Baptist Churches, Pentecostal Churches and others which practise believers' baptism, maintain that by not baptizing infants or small children they are following a policy which is not only scriptural but also pastorally sound. They maintain that by baptizing infants, other Churches are giving the impression that faith is not necessary, and that one can become a Christian without professing a conscious faith in Christ.

Children are to be valued and brought up so that they will have an opportunity and encouragement to come to baptism as believers, but parents and others should not be deluded into thinking that the sprinkling of an unconscious infant will have any effect upon him or her. The only effect of infant baptism is like that of innoculation – by receiving a harmless dose of 'religion' at the font generations of people have been given the impression that this is all that is required, and so have been prevented from seeking real faith.

The Baptist critique of infant baptism

New Testament baptismal theology only fits New Testament baptismal practice where the candidate is at the point of conversion on profession of faith. To apply it to an infant is to claim too much for the infant and to give baptism an almost magical quality... We cannot escape the conviction that too sacramentarian an understanding of baptism undermines, if not denies, the necessity of personal faith and tends to produce a Christianity that is impersonal, magical, and lacking in evangelical thrust.

Baptist Union of Scotland, in Thurian, 1987, p. 234

Baptism for the children of believing parents

A portion of those who belong to Churches which baptize infants believe that only the children of believing parents should be baptized. They have come to this conclusion on scriptural grounds, because they believe that the only children baptized in the New Testament were those belonging to parents who had requested baptism for themselves, and who then belonged to the first Christian communities. They maintain that at the Reformation, Churches such as the Church of England stipulated that every baby should be baptized because they assumed that everyone was a Christian. In today's more secular society, not everyone is a believing Christian. So to be true to the New Testament and to the intention of the Reformers, the Churches should restrict infant baptism to the children of parents who can profess faith. Such believing parents will be able to bring their child up as a Christian, a truly baptized person.

The difficulty with this view is that it contradicts the expectations of many parents who do not perceive the link between on the one hand having their baby christened, as generations before them have, and on the other hand committing themselves to beliefs they have not previously held and practices they do not understand. 'Parents may well be moved by little more than social convention', wrote a Church of England report on initiation, 'or they may have profound but inarticulate feelings of their child's need for God's favour; they are likely to have very little sense of what may be expected or asked of them' (Church of England, 1995, p. 85). The question is whether a positive construction should be put on these inarticulate feelings, or whether baptism should be reserved for children of parents who have identified clearly with the Christian community.

Reforming baptismal practice

The Church may be distracted by inexplicable requests – and sometimes truculent demands – from parents who, though they are far outside the life of the Christian community, somehow still want baptism for their offspring. But we have a clear duty before God to practise infant baptism as a stewardship held from him, and to minister the sacrament in accordance with the biblical revelation. In particular we must so minister infant baptism that its unity with adult baptism, and its standing as true baptism, can be discerned. Because we are in a period of transition from Christendom to pagandom the task is not always easy... It is far better to come to terms with the realities than it is to live in a world of pretence.

Colin Buchanan, 1993, p. 175

Open baptism

Within Churches that practise infant baptism, some would want to put a more optimistic interpretation on the motives of those who bring children to baptism, inarticulate though these may be, and would wish to interpret Scripture and Christian tradition in a different way.

Jesus welcomed children openly, and the Church should do the same. It is the faith of the Church, represented by godparents, and not of the parents specifically, which is exercised in baptism. The sacrament looks forward to the child's growth in faith, and he or she is therefore a fit subject for baptism, whether or not his or her parents conform to any notion of either believing or belonging. In the case of the Church of England in particular, the baptism of any child is not only allowed but positively enjoined by the Church, and nothing which has happened in society in recent decades has substantially changed the appropriateness of this 'open' policy.

A Church following such an 'open' policy will necessarily be unsure about its boundaries, and contain many half-committed people. But this is how it has always been and accords better with the expectations of those who bring their children for baptism.

Today's parents and baptism

It is not sentimental to suggest that [the desire for baptism] has also been linked – and still is – with 'a stirring of religious awareness aroused by the mystery of birth and a new life; a desire to give thanks, and to do their best for the helpless infant now entrusted to them' [B. S. Moss]. The Church has told them that that 'best' was baptism. They have brought their children as they were told to, and the language of the service has made it plain that they acted rightly. Their descendants today are rarely aware of the latest theological currents. They bring their children now in the same spirit. They are bewildered if it is suggested to them that they are wrong to do precisely what they have been told to do. They are resentful too if they are told that they are not qualified to have their children baptized. It is their children for whom they are seeking baptism, and they have never been told before that the child's right to baptism depends on their own spiritual state.

Mark Dalby, 1989, p. 92

Baptism: the sacrament of rebirth

The Roman Catholic Church maintains that baptism is a sacrament which is absolutely foundational for all Christian life. Infants are rightly seen as subjects for this sacrament because their Christian life begins with it, and all other Christian formation flows from it. Baptism is a declaration of God's grace before it is a statement of human faith.

In 1980 the Catholic Church issued an *Instruction on Infant Baptism* which reiterated the Church's commitment to the baptism of infants, and instructed against the delay of baptism until the stage when the individual can make a personal commitment (the believers' baptism model). However, the Catholic Church demonstrated in the 1980 *Instruction* its recognition of the place of faith in baptism and of the importance (in normal circumstances) of parental faith and commitment.

Grace and faith in infant baptism

[Two principles should govern the practice of infant baptism]

(a) Baptism, which is necessary for salvation, is the sign and means of God's prevenient love, which frees us from original sin and communicates to us a share in divine life. Considered in itself, the gift of these blessings to infants must not be delayed.

(b) Assurances must be given that the gift thus granted can grow by an authentic education in the faith and Christian life, in order to fulfil the true meaning of the sacrament. As a rule, these assurances are to be given by the parents or close relatives, although various substitutions are possible within the Christian community. But if these assurances are not really serious there can be grounds for delaying the sacrament; and if they are certainly non-existent the sacrament should even be refused.

Sacred Congregation for the Doctrine of the Faith, 1980, pp. 14–15

Confirmation

Most Churches which baptize infants have a later rite which admits young people into adult membership. In many Churches this is known as 'confirmation', and in those Churches which have bishops it is usually performed by the bishop. Nobody knows for certain how confirmation began, but it is likely to have been something like this:

- Early Christian baptism came to include additional rites alongside washing with water. These were performed by the bishop and were intended to express God's blessing of the candidate and the coming of the Holy Spirit. Among the rites was the laying-on of hands.
- As the Church grew, water baptism was performed by priests, who were more numerous and available to the people, while the right to lay on hands remained with the bishops, who were fewer and not in regular contact with all congregations.
- The rite of initiation became split in two in the Western Church, with baptism by the priest at birth being followed by the laying-on of hands by the bishop at a later stage. This split seems to have happened by AD400 (though in the Eastern Church, priests also lay hands on the baptized infant, so that water-baptism and the laying-on of hands are performed together).

In the medieval Church, confirmation by the laying-on of the bishop's hands came to be seen as a separate sacrament, which conveyed the Holy Spirit and was a necessary gateway to communion. At the Reformation the Church of England rejected the view that confirmation is a sacrament, but retained it as a rite which was a necessary preparation for communion.

The Lutheran Church also retained confirmation, but in a different form, administered by the pastor. The Methodist Church, too, kept a rite of confirmation, and made the minister of the circuit responsible for administering it.

The Roman Catholic Church retained confirmation as a sacrament but not as the necessary preliminary to communion. Children are commonly admitted to communion before confirmation, having received adequate instruction and preparation beforehand.

References and further reading

Bridge, D. and Phypers, D. (1977), *The Water That Divides*, Leicester, IVP.

Buchanan, C. (1993), *Infant Baptism and the Gospel: The Church of England's Dilemma*, London, Darton, Longman & Todd.

Buchanan, C. (1998), *Is the Church of England Biblical?* London, Darton, Longman & Todd.

Church of England (1995), *On the Way: Towards an Integrated Approach to Christian Initiation*, London, Church House Publishing.

Dalby, M. (1989), *Open Baptism*, London, SPCK.

Owen, C. (1991), *Baptise Every Baby?* Eastbourne, Marc.

Sacred Congregation for the Doctrine of the Faith (1980), *Instruction on Infant Baptism*, Vatican City, Sacred Congregation.

Thurian, M. (ed.) (1987), *Churches Respond to BEM: Official Responses to the 'Baptism, Eucharist and Ministry' Text*, 2, Geneva, WCC (Faith and Order Paper 135).

Yates, A. S. (1993), *Why Baptize Infants? A Study of the Biblical, Traditional and Theological Evidence*, Norwich, Canterbury Press.

5

Children and Communion

Introduction

Within some Churches (notably Roman Catholic and Orthodox) there is a long-established practice for children to receive communion. Within most Protestant Churches, however, communion has been restricted to adults or adolescents who have been able to demonstrate the level of understanding appropriate for some form of mature Christian commitment, as expressed through confirmation, reception into membership, or believers' baptism. If children have been present at communion services they have not shared the bread and wine, while in many churches children have been withdrawn from the services to attend their own classes.

Many Churches are now reconsidering their position on children and communion. The report *Children and Holy Communion* by the British Council of Churches Consultative Group on Ministry among Children (1989) suggested that a number of factors have been influential in stimulating this debate, including:
* the more central place of communion in the local church
* the move toward fuller participation by children in worship
* fresh discussion on the pattern of Christian initiation
* new understandings of how faith develops
* growing emphasis on the Church as community
* fresh insights as to how children learn by participation
* demands both from children and parents for fuller participation
* recognition of changing practices ecumenically and internationally

A matter of doctrine

Whether or not a Church admits children to communion must be consistent with its broader theological understanding of issues like sin, grace, faith, salvation, the nature of the Church and the sacraments of initiation. From a doctrinal point of view the following questions need to be addressed:
* Is baptism a full qualification for receiving communion, or is something else needed?
* Is communion the sign of conversion and commitment having taken place, or is it a means of grace and a prompt toward conversion?
* If communion is a means of grace, should this means of grace be denied to children?
* If communion presupposes understanding, can even adults be said to understand?

A matter of worship

Changing patterns of worship reflect changing theological understanding of the nature of the Church. The view that communion is central to the worship of the people of God is now held by many Christians of all traditions. For such Christians, this has led to the following features in worship:
- an integration of word and sacrament
- the weekly celebration of communion as the main service
- an emphasis on the corporate nature of the liturgy
- an understanding of the congregation as a community

A matter of nurture

Important distinctions have been made in recent years between the concepts of education, instruction, training, indoctrination and Christian nurture, and nurture has been emphasized as the proper educative task of the Christian community. In nurture the emphasis is less on being taught the facts of the Christian tradition and more on being integrated into the Christian community. According to this view, it is argued that:
- The child has a rightful place in the worshipping community.
- The communion service becomes a key influence in the process of growth.
- Parents and congregation have key parts to play in the process of Christian nurture.
- Faith is caught rather than taught.

A matter of commitment

Commitment is generally seen as an important element in the process of Christian growth. So is faith. Different traditions have placed different emphases on the relationships between commitment, faith and communion. The following points promote reflection:
- Children can have faith, as their prayers reveal.
- Children can show commitment, appropriate to their stage of development.
- It is necessary to distinguish forms of faith and forms of commitment as appropriate to different stages in life.

A matter of childhood

A number of features of twentieth-century life have sharpened the distinction between childhood and adulthood. The danger is that childhood is seen as something to outgrow and to leave behind. Such a view may see children in the Church as having to wait until they approach adulthood before being ready to become proper members of the Church. Such a Church is dominated by an adult model of the faith. The following points promote reflection:
- All persons are complete and yet always becoming.
- Three-year-old persons, for example, are not deficient because they are only three.
- Three-year-old persons, for example, can be 'in Christ' and can have faith.

Orthodox view

The Orthodox Churches maintain the close link between baptism and communion. For the Orthodox, infant baptism (followed by chrismation) and communion are part of the one act of initiation. Here communion is administered in one kind only, the wine, since the young infant is unready to receive solid food. From this point onwards the child is welcome to receive the sacrament.

For the Orthodox Churches the communion of infants and children has been practised since the days of the ancient Church. It is understood, therefore, as an apostolic tradition which was never at any time interrupted and never had its legitimacy questioned.

An Orthodox parish priest reflects

At the eucharistic liturgy we have the mothers with their babies and the father and mother with their small children and older children. They are there very naturally. First of all, they bring the babies to holy communion. If the baby does not want holy communion and cries, we do not insist... Other children are never afraid at all and immediately smile and open their mouths. There is something very mysterious there.

Children and Holy Communion, 1989, p. 20

Baptist view

The Baptist Churches also maintain the close link between baptism and communion. For the Baptist, baptism is delayed until the individual believer is able to make a mature declaration of faith, reflecting understanding and commitment.

Quaker view

The Quakers (or the Religious Society of Friends) do not use bread and wine or a eucharistic liturgy in their worship at all. Their view is that every meal is in memory of Christ's last supper. For Quakers, therefore, there is no real question about children and communion.

Roman Catholic view

The characteristic stance of the Roman Catholic Church has been to separate communion from baptism. Baptism is administered in infancy. Then a period of preparation is given prior to first communion. Here the prerequisite for first communion is the act of penance demonstrated in the sacrament of confession. As a general rule, children are admitted to first communion around the age of seven. In some countries, however, children are admitted to communion much younger than this, while in other countries there is serious questioning as to whether the age of seven is too young.

An adult Catholic looks back

It was like Christmas Eve for about six months. We received hours of instruction from teachers and priests and spent many afternoons rehearsing our first confession and communion. The teachers warned us not to smile or

---

wave at our friends or families, not to push or shove on the way to or from the altar rails, not to talk and, above all, not to let the host [the bread] fall on the floor.

Children and Holy Communion, 1989, p. 19

During the early 1970s the Roman Catholic Church took an important initiative in developing eucharistic liturgy designed to recognize the distinctive needs of children. The *Directory of Masses with Children*, published 1 November 1973, required that the presidential prayers which had been composed for adults should be so adapted in masses with children that children will consider them to be expressions of their own religious life. Three eucharistic prayers for masses with children were subsequently approved by the Pope for an experimental period. In 1980 the Congregation for Divine Worship extended the use of these prayers 'indefinitely until further notice'.

Eucharistic Prayer for Children 1

God our Father
you have brought us here together
so that we can give you thanks and praise
for all the wonderful things you have done.

Eucharistic Prayers for Masses with Children and Masses of Reconciliation, 1975,
p. 14

Helpful suggestions on how to make best use of these new eucharistic prayers were provided in two books by Father Edward Matthews, *Celebrating Mass with Children* (1975) and *Children Give Thanks* (1976). Father Matthews had been a member of the working party set up by the Congregation for Divine Worship to produce the *Directory for Masses with Children*.

It is also seen as appropriate, at least sometimes, to take children out of the Mass for the Liturgy of the Word, so as to receive different educational experiences.

Presbyterian view

The debate in the Church of Scotland was stimulated by the publication *Children at the Table* edited by David G. Hamilton and Finlay A. J. Macdonald (1982). The following recommendation was presented by the Board of Education to the 1982 General Assembly:

Our consideration has been comprehensive and it has led us to the conclusion that participation of baptized children in the Lord's Supper would be entirely consistent with the doctrinal standards of the Church of Scotland.

The response from the Presbyteries, however, meant that the recommendation was not implemented at that time.

Methodist view

In 1987 the Methodist Conference in England approved the report *Children at Holy Communion: Guidelines*. The report finds no inconsistency between admitting children to communion and Wesley's own practice and teaching. According to this report Wesley gave communion to children at his own services and regularly communicated children in America.

An adult Methodist explains

Children sometimes ask why they cannot receive the bread and wine and some express dissatisfaction at receiving only a blessing... It is our conviction that the correct approach is to tell the Gospel to such young enquirers in ways appropriate to them and then to invite them to share in the Lord's Supper if they desire it.

Children and Holy Communion, 1989, p. 18

Anglican view

Historically Anglican doctrine and practice have been rooted in the 1662 *Book of Common Prayer*. Here the rubric says:

And there shall none be admitted to the holy Communion, until such time as he be confirmed, or ready and desirous to be confirmed.

The age of admission to communion, then, has been linked to the age of confirmation. The *Book of Common Prayer* links confirmation to 'those that are baptized and come to years of discretion'. According to the *Book of Common Prayer* those who have come to years of discretion:

can say the Creed, the Lord's Prayer, and the Ten Commandments; and can also answer to such other Questions, as in the short Catechism are contained.

In practice, however, the age of confirmation has varied widely between one Province and another, between dioceses according to the view of the bishop, between Anglo-Catholics and Evangelicals, and even between neighbouring parishes.

The theological link between confirmation and admission to communion was irrevocably undermined in the Church of England by the Ely Report, *Christian Initiation* (1971), which concluded that baptism was a complete sacrament of initiation and was 'sufficient' basis for admitting children to communion prior to confirmation. Subsequently the Knaresborough Report, *Communion Before Confirmation?* (1985), concluded that it was desirable to permit the admission of baptized persons to holy communion prior to confirmation and proposed a set of draft regulations.

The Fourth International Anglican Liturgical Consultation, held in Toronto during August 1991, argued that:

Baptism is complete sacramental initiation and leads to participation in the eucharist. Confirmation and other rites of affirmation have a continuing pastoral role in the renewal of faith among the baptized but are in no way to be seen as a completion of baptism or as necessary for admission to communion.

Many Provinces in the Anglican Communion have taken the initiative to admit children to communion and to give serious attention to the need for educating children, parents and congregations for this new practice. A good example of such materials is provided by the programme *Life in the Eucharist* produced by the Anglican Church of Canada (1986). Other Anglicans have seen the admission of children to communion as a betrayal of biblical roots and of Anglican tradition. This view is well argued by Alan Langdon (1987) writing from the Anglican diocese of Sydney, Australia.

An Anglican parent reflects

Children have always been present, but taking part fully in the eucharist confirms and symbolises that we are a family of people who belong to God, not a collection of qualified and part-qualified disciples.

An Anglican child reflects

We're all one together. It's not mummy and daddy and then us and then more grown ups. We're the same as you when we all kneel together. And that's special!

Jenny Hyson and Anne Faulkner, 1997, pp. 22–3

Practical implications

If children are to be welcomed to communion, the liturgy and the way in which the service is conducted must reflect their presence. The following points need careful consideration:

1 Some Churches have deliberately prepared a *different* form of the liturgy for use when children are present. In particular such liturgies will include specially crafted eucharistic prayers. The strength of such developments is that the adult eucharistic prayers may be especially difficult for children to understand. The weakness of such developments is not only that eucharistic prayers for children have proved difficult to craft with integrity, but that children then outgrow such prayers. Other Churches have preferred to ensure that children are introduced to the adult liturgy.

2 There are now many attempts to develop communion books for children. Examples include *The Lord is Here!* by Paul Jenkins and Leslie J. Francis in the Church of England, and *Peter and Paula at a Communion Service* by Michael Prowting and Wilfred Tooley in the Methodist Church. Some of these texts include the whole text for children to follow, while others concentrate on *describing* what is taking place. As Churches provide more and more alternatives within the eucharistic liturgy, so it becomes more difficult to provide a children's communion book. What is important is that those conducting the service take note of what it is like to follow the service in the children's book.

3 Attention has to be given to the length of the service, and in particular to the ministry of the word. The danger is that communion services try to fulfil two very

different functions: an act of celebration and an opportunity for teaching. Children learn in quite different ways from adults.

4   Opportunities need to be given both for adults and children to explore the significance of the components of the communion service, in ways appropriate to their own stages of faith and of development. Examples of programmes designed to meet these aims are provided in an Anglican context by *Bread for All God's Family* by Leslie J. Francis and Diane Drayson, and by *Children and Holy Communion* by Steve Pearce and Diana Murrie.

5   Children feel most at home in the communion service when they are practically involved in the service. Opportunities exist for children to contribute to the offertory, to lead prayers, to assist with the music and to prepare the church for the service beforehand. It is also important to make good use of the hymns and musical traditions enjoyed in local schools.

6   There are additional problems which need to be faced by those denominations, like the Anglican Church, which now embrace a variety of different practices regarding the admission of children to communion. On the worldwide scale there is the problem, say, of the 8-year-old child who has been admitted to communion in Canada, visiting or relocating to a Province where it is less general for children to receive communion. On the more local level, there is the problem of the 8-year-old child who has grown up in a parish where it is the practice for children to be admitted to communion then moves to a new parish where very different rules seem to apply. Are such children in danger of experiencing excommunication?

References and further reading

Anglican Church of Canada (1986), *Life in the Eucharist*, Toronto, Anglican Book Centre.

British Council of Churches (1989), *Children and Holy Communion*, London, BCC.

Church of England (1971), *Christian Initiation: Birth and Growth in the Christian Society*, London, Central Board of Finance of the Church of England (The Ely Report).

Church of England (1985), *Communion Before Confirmation?* London, CIO Publishing (The Knaresborough Report).

Francis, L. J. and Drayson, D. (1997), *Bread for All God's Family*, Leominster, Gracewing.

Hamilton, D. G. and Macdonald, F. A. J. (eds.) (1982), *Children at the Table*, Edinburgh, Church of Scotland Department of Education.

Hyson, J. and Faulkner, A. (1997), *We Welcome You...: Preparing a Parish for the Admission of Children to Holy Communion*, Oxford, Diocesan Church House.

Jenkins, P. and Francis, L. J. (1978), *The Lord is Here!* London, Collins Liturgical Publications.

Langdon, A. A. (1987), *Communion for Children? The Current Debate*, Sydney South, Christian Education Publications.

Matthews, E. (1975), *Celebrating Mass with Children*, London, Collins Liturgical Publications.

Matthews, E. (1976), *Children Give Thanks: A Guide to the New Eucharistic Prayers for Children*, London, Collins Liturgical Publications.

Methodist Church (1987), *Children at Holy Communion: Guidelines*, London, Methodist Church Division of Education and Youth.

Pearce, S. and Murrie, D. (1997), *Children and Holy Communion*, London, National Society and Church House Publishing.

Prowting, M. and Tooley, W. (1985), *Peter and Paula at a Communion Service*, London, Chester House Publications.

Roman Catholic Church (1975), *Eucharistic Prayers for Masses with Children and Masses of Reconciliation*, Great Wakering, Mayhew-McCrimmon.

6

Sunday School Movement

Introduction

When asked to think about 'children, Churches and Christian learning', most people over the age of 50 are likely to make some reference to 'Sunday schools'. In this chapter we describe the rise, fall and metamorphosis of the Sunday school movement.

Beginnings

Although Sunday schools had existed prior to the eighteenth century (some were founded by the Archbishop of Milan in the sixteenth century), the Sunday school movement really took off in Britain in Gloucester in 1780 with the work of Robert Raikes. Raikes (1735–1811), an Anglican layman, was a prison reformer and newspaper publisher.

The Sunday school began as a school for the poor, at a time when most children had no formal education and their families needed the little money their offspring could bring in from paid employment. Raikes believed that education was not to be restricted to the privileged. It was his idea to provide schools to teach 'reading and religion' on a Sunday, when the children were not employed, leaving them free to work during the week. The focus was primarily on teaching reading, writing and 'the reformation of manners'; but catechetical instruction, reading the Bible and attendance at church were regarded as central from the outset.

The curriculum of Sunday schools

VIII THAT nothing whatever be taught in the schools but what is suited immediately to the design of the sabbath day, and preserving young people from idleness, immorality, or ignorance.

The Rules of the Birmingham Sunday Schools, 1784

This 'harmless and innocent' experiment, as Raikes described it, was welcomed by many parents and at first commended by the Churches. Magistrates and others noted that Sunday schools, aimed originally at the children of the very poor, seemed to have a beneficial role in controlling crime, in 'the orderly and decent comportment of the Youth' and in encouraging their pupils 'cheerfully to submit to their stations'.

The effects of the Sunday school

Some of the clergy in different parts of the country bent upon attempting a reform among the children of the lower class, are establishing Sunday schools, for the rendering of the Lord's day subservient to the ends of instruction, which has hitherto been prostituted to bad purposes... In those parishes where this plan has been adopted, we are assured that the behaviour of the children is greatly civilized. The barbarous ignorance, in which they had before lived, being in some degree dispelled, they begin to give proofs that those persons are mistaken, who consider the lower orders of mankind as incapable of improvement, and therefore think an attempt to reclaim them impracticable, or at least not worth the trouble.

Robert Raikes, article in the *Gloucester Journal*, 1783

Later, however, opposition to the schools began to stir. This came from the farm owners who believed that education would ruin agriculture, but also from those who argued that those schools that taught writing as well as reading were breaking the Sabbath rules on work and from those who feared that a more learned working class would eventually turn against the established order (being taught, as one bishop put it, 'to despise... the laws and all subordination'). But Raikes himself was no political radical. Although his Sunday schools aimed at 'the reformation of society', he was primarily concerned with the plight of individuals – especially children – within society and with the crime to which this led. 'Ignorance', he wrote, 'is generally the principal cause of these enormities.' Despite his great concern with prisons and poverty, unlike later reformers he was not concerned with faults built into the structure of society.

The early Sunday school

If good seed be sown in the mind at an early period of human life, though it shows itself not again for many years, it may please God, at some future period to cause it to spring up and to bring forth a plentiful harvest.

The great principle I inculcate is, to be kind and good natured to each other; not to provoke one another; to be dutiful to parents; not to offend God by cursing and swearing, and such little plain precepts as all may comprehend.

Robert Raikes

The improvement of these children in learning has been wonderful, and when they sing to the praise and glory of their maker, they appear a tribe of embryo-angels training for the skies. Every Christian heart glows with triumph; and heaven seems for a moment transplanted upon earth.

Manchester pamphlet, 1785

By 1787 over 200 Sunday schools had been established, educating 10,000 pupils. Ten years later there were over 1,000 such schools and nearly 70,000 pupils. By 1831 there were nearly 12,000 schools and the number of scholars had risen to over 1,000,000. The nineteenth century was a great time of growth for the Sunday school movement, the number involved soon outstripping church membership and peaking at 5,000,000 pupils, some 19 per cent of the population.

With the founding of weekday day schools, particularly from 1830, the Sunday schools came to concentrate more on Bible reading, the formation of children in Christian belief and their 'habituation' to regular worship. This shift to a more exclusively religious emphasis – a focus on *Sunday* rather than *school* – was accompanied by a move from professional (or, at least, paid) teachers to voluntary helpers. The Sunday schools also became less ecumenical and more denominational, and were increasingly seen as providing an induction into the particular tradition (Nonconformist or Anglican) of the Churches that ran them, despite the early slogan 'Doctrine divides, service unites'. (Interestingly, Roman Catholic Sunday schools were always a relatively insignificant part of that Church's Christian education endeavour.)

Change and decline

The good times did not, however, last in Britain. From the second decade of the twentieth century both Sunday school and church membership were in decline, the former decline well outstripping the latter. Sunday schools were down to 3,000,000 scholars in total by 1951. A decrease in membership by 40 per cent was reported by the Methodist Church between 1950 and 1966, and a 61 per cent fall in the number of Church of England Sunday school scholars was recorded between 1953 and 1980 (membership now stands at less than 10 per cent of its 1900 value). The explanation most commonly presented for this steep decline was the rise of car ownership and weekend leisure pursuits. Sunday afternoons – the preferred time for most Sunday schools – became unsustainable and the schools began to meet on Sunday morning, at the same time as 'adult' church services.

This led, however, to another, more theological, problem for those children who still attended the Sunday school. Increasingly their numbers were restricted to children whose parents went to church, whereas in the 'great days' of Sunday schools the majority of pupils had been 'sent' by parents who themselves did not attend, or only occasionally attended, church worship. (Until very recently this 'religion by deputy' practice was still generally considered to be strong evidence for the parents' religious commitment: Williams, 1999, p. 164.) One difficulty with Sunday school for children of churchgoing parents was that they experienced Christian nurture, worship and prayer in separation from the main act of communal worship and away from their parents.

A different approach of integrating children with the congregation developed through the 'Family Church' Movement. This was commended by Herbert Alfred Hamilton (1897–1977), the Congregational Principal of Westhill College in the 1940s and 1950s, and was soon embraced by many nonconformist Churches. It took on eucharistic form in the Church of England's increasingly popular Parish Communion Movement, with its 'family communion' or 'parish eucharist' which children were encouraged to attend.

Hamilton writes

This training of persons to worship and to act to others as persons, demands the kind of relationship in which they can both learn in experience what it is

---

to be significant and to be secure in Christian fellowship, and also what it means to 'see' – to see life and men so as to see God at work and to have a worshipful attitude to life. This has increasingly come to me to be the main task of Christian education. It is more and more clear that *the possibility of this is governed decisively by the quality of life in a Christian community whether in the home or in the Church.*

Herbert Alfred Hamilton, quoted in Cliff, 1986, p. 240

The arguments for the *separation* of children from adults include the following:
- The intellectual, social, moral and spiritual development of children is often such that they cannot understand or appreciate adult worship, and sermons in particular.
- Many adults are disturbed in their worship by the presence of young children, whose training in and propensity for 'sitting still and keeping quiet' seem to them sadly lacking.
- Worship, teaching and preaching that is suitable for an 'all-age' congregation (see Chapter 28) is more difficult to prepare and conduct effectively than for adult learners and worshippers.
- Children themselves often feel alienated from, and unwelcomed in, the 'big church' setting and congregation.
- Children at school are now used to 'active learning' and are encouraged to participate and ask questions, whereas adult services encourage a more passive and structured response.

The point of the Sunday school?

It may well be argued that most children would not want to stay in church and would, in fact, prefer to go out to Sunday school; that the Sunday school offers a welcome relief for both children and adults alike. If this is so then it could be that the Sunday school, far from preparing children for church is in fact providing them not only with a welcome alternative, but with a likely way out. To the question 'Why do you think we have Sunday schools', one child replied: 'So that the adults can have peace and quiet in church.'

Rosemary Nixon, 1985, p. 11

On the other hand, the arguments for *integration* are strong:
- Excluding children from the main Sunday service (or even a part of it) splits the Church and puts a question mark against the Christian identity of children as a full part of the body of Christ.
- Churches that practise infant baptism may appear to deny the significance of this sacrament if they make children into 'second-class Christians'.
- Children do not just learn from teachers: they learn best what it is to be an adult worshipper by seeing and hearing other adults worship.
- Adults also have a lot to learn from children. Jesus placed a child in the centre of the group of disciples to illustrate the nature of true (adult) discipleship (Mark 9.33–37; Luke 9.46–48) – especially that discipleship is not about status, power or prestige.

- Separating Sunday school may wrongly suggest that Christian education is *only* for children, and not for adults as well. (Interestingly, some of the great Lancashire schools of the 1920s were 'all age'.)
- Although Christianity is certainly an 'adult religion', this should not be taken to mean that it is a matter of intellectual and social achievement and competence, rather than about the sort of spiritual insight, love and fellowship that can be shown by children in their own way.

Sunday school failures?

Virtually all who attended at all found Sunday school a pleasant experience as a small child, at the stage of drawing pictures and listening to stories. From about the age of eight, however, they began to get bored. They complained of being talked at, told the same things over and over again, having a sense of forever going over the same ground.

Bernice Martin and Martin Pluck, 1977, p. 16

It has taken almost . . . two hundred years to come to recognize that religion cannot be learned from a book, even if that book is the Bible. Many noble souls have given years of devoted service to the Movement, and in the course of time a large number of lives must have been enriched in a number of ways, but it has not produced church members directly. But, in the end, Sunday school teachers cannot do for parents what they must do themselves. The class-room is no substitute for the family, and that family of families, the Church.

Philip Cliff, 1986, p. 322

What should we make of the history of the Sunday school? Rosemary Nixon writes that 'the decline of the Sunday school is probably a blessing in disguise! Instead of bemoaning its demise we must have the courage of its founders and consider what God is saying to the Church' (Nixon, 1985, p. 67). Perhaps she is right. The Sunday school movement was a valid and appropriate response to the needs of the age. As our age is so very different, Christian education may need a very different response.

The future?

The future of Christian education in liberal mainline denominational Churches will be in the creation of new-old intergenerational Sunday schools where persons will gather to witness through word-and-deed to the Christian story and way of life as their story and way of life.

John Westerhoff, in Ferguson, 1981, pp. 195–6

Sunday school teachers

At the beginning of the twentieth century educational reform impacted on the Sunday schools with 'grading' of pupils of different ages into different 'departments'. Such reforms were much more marked in the United States. The American Sunday school in mainstream Protestant denominations eventually developed into a pedagogically reflective 'church school': 'a lavish educational institution, that is one modelled after the best of public [state] schools, a *real school*, consistent with modern psychology and pedagogy' (Westerhoff, in Ferguson, 1981, p. 185). Some American Sunday schools have adult departments also, reflecting the much greater emphasis that the American Churches place on Christian education in the parish.

Sunday school teachers in Britain often trained as day school teachers when teacher training began in earnest in the early nineteenth century, and the Sunday School Union soon drew up courses for its own teachers. Nevertheless, changes in educational philosophy and child learning were often slow to have an impact on the British Sunday school. Even grading into age groups took time to become adopted. The Canadian George Hamilton Archibald visited Britain in 1902 and stressed the importance of 'knowledge of children', taking up the themes expounded by Froebel and other educationalists. Under his influence, the Westhill Easter Conference at Swanwick trained hundreds of Sunday school teachers in pedagogical method. The Cadbury family founded Westhill College in Birmingham in 1907 to train teachers for both day and Sunday schools; St Christopher's, Blackheath, was founded in 1908 with a similar aim.

The situation is markedly different today, for where there are still Sunday schools they are frequently dependent on untrained – and often young – teachers. Those that use trained and experienced teachers, or at least parents, and are willing to devote time and energy to preparation work, provide a greatly superior experience of Christian education for their pupils. This is true, of course, of all the work that the Churches do with their children.

References and further reading

Booth, F. (1980), *Robert Raikes of Gloucester*, Redhill, National Christian Education Council.

Cliff, P. B. (1986), *The Rise and Development of the Sunday School Movement in England, 1780-1980*, Redhill, National Christian Education Council.

Ferguson, J. (ed.) (1981), *Christianity, Society and Education: Robert Raikes, Past, Present and Future*, London, SPCK.

Hutchins, C. (1974), *Christian Education on Sunday Mornings*, Nottingham, Grove.

Knoff, G. E. (1979), *The World Sunday School Movement: The Story of a Broadening Mission*, New York, Seabury.

Lynn, R. W. and Wright, E. (1980), *The Big Little School: Two Hundred Years of the Sunday School*, Birmingham, Alabama, Religious Education Press.

Martin, B. and Pluck, M. (1977), *Young People's Beliefs*, London, Board of Education of General Synod.

Nixon, R. (1985), *Who's the Greatest? A Study of the Sunday School in Contemporary Society*, London, National Society.

Phillips, T. M. (1988), *All God's Children: The Sunday School in Scotland*, Milngarie, The Scottish Sunday School Union for Christian Education.

Reid, I. (1980), *Sunday Schools: A Suitable Case for Treatment*, London, Chester House.

Williams, S. C. (1999), *Religious Belief and Popular Culture in Southwark, c. 1880–1939*, Oxford, Oxford University Press.

7

The Child in the Church

Introduction

Current thinking about the place of children in the Church owes a great deal to the report published in 1976 by the Consultative Group on Ministry among Children of the British Council of Churches, under the title *The Child in the Church*. The working party responsible for this report was chaired by Bishop John Gibbs and drew significantly on the insights of Professor John Hull. The present chapter explores the argument advanced by the report and traces its influence.

The Child in the Church is rooted in a clear analysis of the changes taking place in both the Church and wider society in Britain. It also takes informed account of contemporary changes in the understanding of childhood (including issues concerned with social development, emotional development and intellectual development) and in the understanding of Christian faith (including issues concerned with doctrine, the Bible, the Church, ethics and inter-faith dialogue).

Introducing Christian nurture

The key concept advanced by *The Child in the Church* was the notion of Christian nurture. Christian nurture is clearly distinguished from related concepts like education, instruction and indoctrination.

Christian nurture

We understand Christian nurture first of all when we see that it springs out of the nature of the Christian life itself as a process of continuous growth. The growth does not take place in isolation, but in company with others who are also working in the same way. Our understanding of nurture is thus bound up with our understanding of the Church, the community of the way.

The Child in the Church, 1976, p. 19

The report recognizes that Christian nurture must become more self-conscious and more specific in a society in which different religious traditions exist side by side in mutual respect and in which secular values may predominate. Parents committed to the Christian faith cannot leave the responsibility of nurture into that faith in the hands of society as a whole or the schools operated by that society. In a plural society parents need to choose, implicitly or explicitly, the influences which will shape their children.

Applying Christian nurture

This emphasis on Christian nurture carried major implications for the ways in which Churches relate to children. Children are to be respected in their own right and their contribution to the Church is to be properly recognized. The child's proper place is part of the worshipping congregations, and congregations must be prepared to adapt and grow accordingly.

> ### *Understanding children*
>
> Our understanding of children now is such that we have no excuse for seeing them merely as the recipients of tradition or only as adults in the making. Nurture must mean taking seriously each stage of children's growth. It must be 'child-related' in the sense that techniques of nurture, in order to be effective, must take into account our ever increasing knowledge of child development. The child must always be taken seriously *now*.
>
> *The Child in the Church*, 1976, p. 33

The report argues that the presence of children is essential at the centre of Christian worship, with the whole worshipping community. Participation in such worship is not the *goal* of Christian nurture but the very *means* of nurture. Accordingly, to separate children from the community in worship and to make special provision for them (say in Sunday school) is to bring them up in something less than the fullness of Christian experience, and will impoverish their nurture.

Recommendations

The Child in the Church offered the Church five main areas of recommendation.

1   The first area of recommendation concerned *adult education*. A Church which is able to take seriously the Christian nurture of children needs to begin by equipping adults for this task. Four points were made under this heading:
   - Churches should give greater priority to training resource persons to offer effective leadership in nurture.
   - Clergy education (initial or in-service) should include the study of Christian nurture.
   - Churches should give greater attention to parent education, including the psychology of children and the practice of Christian education in the home.
   - Such work should be undertaken ecumenically.

> ### *The integrity of childhood*
>
> The human being has a perfection proper to his stage of development whatever that stage may be, and in this sense, even a child, unlike a half-formed product of the conveyor belt, is truly finished. A child of three years old, or even three days old, is not defective because he cannot do what an adult can do.
>
> *The Child in the Church*, 1976, p. 15

2   The second area of recommendation concerned *theology*. Christian nurture needs to be theologically informed. Two points were made under this heading:
  •   Renewal of the Church's ministry in nurture requires a theology which sees critical openness springing from Christian commitment.
  •   A study outline on childhood and the Christian faith should be prepared for local churches.
3   The third area of recommendation concerned the *development* of knowledge and resources. Christian nurture needs to be properly resourced. Two points were made under this heading:
  •   A research project should be established to promote Christian nurture.
  •   A chain of ecumenical Christian Learning Resource Centres should be established.
4   The fourth area of recommendation concerned the child and the *adult congregation*. Christian nurture needs to be fully embraced by the local congregation. Three points were made under this heading:
  •   The process of Christian initiation should reflect the view that children are not merely in preparation for adult membership of the Church.
  •   Times, places and patterns of worship should promote the appropriate integration of children and adults.
  •   Services should provide greater opportunity for the participation of children.

Involving children in the Church

If we ask what makes anyone feel that he 'belongs' to any community we should probably say: a sense of fellowship; a sense of enjoyment, which includes happiness and laughter; a sense of significance, the recognition that one belongs and that one matters; a sense of responsibility, of being given tasks to do, tasks where it really matters if one does not do them properly; and a request for service, being asked to give time and energy in the service of others.

The Child in the Church, 1976, p. 41

---

5   The fifth area of recommendation concerned *schools*. Christian nurture needs to operate within a proper appreciation of the role of schools. Three points were made under this heading:
  •   Schools not founded by religious bodies cannot be expected to accept responsibility for religious nurture.
  •   Schools not founded by religious bodies should concentrate on an open descriptive approach to religious education.
  •   Church schools should distinguish between religious education and Christian nurture.

Understanding Christian nurture

The Consultative Group on Ministry among Children produced a sequel to *The Child in the Church* five years later, under the title *Understanding Christian Nurture*. This sequel had a more limited and more specific aim than the original report. It was produced as a direct response to the recommendation in *The Child in the Church* for proper theological clarification of the nature of Christian nurture and of the relationship between Christian nurture and critical openness. Once again the working party drew significantly on the insights of Professor John Hull.

Critical openness

Christian nurture is like the closed and dogmatic instruction of the Christian sects in that its content is the Christian faith and its object the deepening of faith but it differs in that it possesses the spirit of critical openness. It is similar to secular education in placing a high value on critical openness but differs in that it deliberately seeks to deepen Christian faith.

Understanding Christian Nurture, 1981, p. 6

Influencing the denominations

While by no means all the recommendations set out in *The Child in the Church* have generated the response hoped for by the working party, the widespread influence of the document is well attested by the way in which its key emphases have been reflected in a number of denominational reports. Illustrations are provided from the Baptist Church and from the Church of England.

In the report *Children in the Church: A Baptist View*, David F. Tennant develops the implications of the position advanced in *The Child in the Church* for the Baptist tradition. At a practical level this is quite straightforward. Tennant emphasizes the following three considerations:

- The child is part of the worshipping congregation.
- The child is to be nurtured in the faith.
- The child belongs to the fellowship.

At a theological level, however, the position advanced in *The Child in the Church* presented a greater challenge to the Baptist tradition. In that tradition the emphasis on believers' baptism clearly offers an *adult* model of what it means to be a Christian, while *The Child in the Church* argues equally clearly that it is inappropriate to impose adult models of Christian identity on children. Bringing these two perspectives together, Tennant concludes that 'we must not allow our views of adulthood to determine the views of childhood as that which is to be passed through and left behind'.

A Baptist view

The Child in the Church concludes that 'because Christ was a child, a child can be a Christian'. Few Baptists would accept that. Yet it raises the question of what is a Christian? If answers given to that question are along the lines, 'one who accepts Jesus Christ as personal saviour' or 'a follower of Jesus Christ' or 'one who repents of sin and turns to Jesus the Saviour in faith', then it may be that children are capable of those responses. If the response is the one sought for baptism as a believer, then on that argument children are eligible for baptism.

David F. Tennant, 1978, pp. 30–1

The Church of England report, *Children in the Way*, published in 1988, takes as its starting point the following quotation from *The Child in the Church*:

> The Church that does not accept children unconditionally into its fellowship is depriving those children of what is rightfully theirs, but the deprivation such as the Church itself will suffer is far more grave.

From this starting-point, *Children in the Way* develops two models which have become increasingly central to an Anglican understanding of ministry among children and young people. The first model is that of the *pilgrim Church*. According to this model adults and children are travelling the same faith journey on which both may learn from each other. The pilgrim Church displays the following characteristics:

- Teaching comes from all members of the community.
- Learning comes just as much from informal as formal situations.
- Sometimes children lead the way and are not always the followers-on.

The pilgrim model

Imagine a group of people of all ages going for a long walk together. At times the children and adults will walk along together, talking as they go, sharing stories with first one person and then another, each observing different things and sharing their discoveries. At times the children will lag behind . . . At other times, though, the children will dash ahead making new discoveries and may, perhaps, pull the adults along to see what they have found.

Children in the Way, 1988, p. 32

The second model is that of *all-age learning and worship*. According to this model, churches are challenged to provide opportunities for all members of the pilgrim Church to learn and to worship together. All-age learning and worship may include the following opportunities:

- Saturday workshops
- holiday project days
- evening meetings
- Sunday festivals

Often different learning groups may work on a common theme and come together to share the fruits of their learning experience in a common act of worship.

All-age learning

The nurture of children is parallel to and also continuous with the education and growth of teenagers and adults. As adults and children work together questions may well be raised which adults need to develop and pursue at a different level in adult groups. It appears – both in theory and practice – that much of our learning and growing could be done in all-age groups.

Children in the Way, 1988, p. 44

Influencing the local church

The Child in the Church did so much more than simply influence the direction of further Church reports. The real influence of *The Child in the Church* is to be seen in the work of local churches and congregations.

Ten years after the publication of *The Child in the Church*, Leslie J. Francis published a review of the ways in which local churches had responded to the challenge of the report. In this book, *Making Contact: Christian Nurture, Family Worship and Church Growth*, a series of authors tell their stories about good practice in their own church.

Andrew Bowden, for example, describes how children and adults from a small Cotswold community prepared to celebrate the feast of All Saints in the village church. The very village environment itself provided the key resource for the celebration of All Saints' tide. The theme proved as real for the adults as for the children.

All Saints at Sapperton

The headteacher at Sapperton is a wonderful teacher of local history; she is also an inspired producer of children's drama. No sooner had I begun to explore with her the theme of the All Saints' celebration than she had begun to evolve a pageant in homage of our village ancestors. The development of this pageant embraced many aspects of the school curriculum and at the same time caught the imagination and interest of the wider local community.

Leslie J. Francis, 1986, p. 48

In her book *Leaves on the Tree*, Dorothy Jamal published a series of letters in which churchgoers describe their experiences of all-age learning and worship. These letters draw particular attention to ways in which adults have been enriched by welcoming children into these churches.

An elderly churchgoer reflects

The best part for me was during the time for intercession when we were all given a cut-out figure which represented ourselves and we were invited to offer our own prayers either by writing or drawing them on the figure. Then ... we brought our prayers ... and placed them in the sanctuary. For the first time in my life I had been asked to share something of myself in worship and it was a moving experience to see my figure lying next to many others, belonging to both adults and children.

Dorothy Jamal, 1990, p. 47

Another set of inspiring stories about how local churches have responded to the ideas promoted by *The Child in the Church* is provided by Leslie J. Francis and Anne Faulkner's book, *All God's People*. These accounts show how the many resources of the local community can be focused on worship. For example, Betty Pedley describes how young children learn about God the Holy Spirit at Pentecost.

Celebrating Pentecost

We made and decorated kites. We blew up balloons and drew pictures on them. We took them outside to play. We tied the strings of the balloons to the children's wrists so the children could watch the balloons blow in the wind but would not be distressed by losing them. We released a few balloons when the wind was at its height and watched them tossed over the trees. We watched our kites with delight as some of them soared high into the sky.

Leslie J. Francis and Anne Faulkner, 1997, p. 47

Identifying issues

The Child in the Church clearly stimulated considerable change in the ways in which Churches thought about children and ministered among them. Such change properly provoked the need for further focused enquiry. The range of issues raised is illustrated by three working party reports from the Church of England.

The first issue concerns the admission of children to communion. In 1985 the Knaresborough Report, *Communion Before Confirmation?* examined the implications for church practice of the fact that children were increasingly present during the main mid-morning Sunday communion service in Anglican parishes. The report questions whether the practice of blessing children at the altar rail is an appropriate substitute for admitting them to receive the sacrament (see Chapter 5).

Are children welcome at communion?

Valiant attempts have been made to include children in the action of worship: they have been welcomed to the altar rail. But instead of receiving there the sign of belonging they receive a gesture which, in an adult setting, reinforces the impression of their unacceptability.

Communion Before Confirmation? 1985, p. 36

The second issue concerns the question of faith development and Christian education. In 1991 the report *How Faith Grows* responded to the growing interest in faith development theory and research shown by clergy and lay people responding to new opportunities and challenges posed by ministry to children in the Church. Faith development theory has its roots in the work of James Fowler and his associates, largely based on research conducted in the United States (see Chapter 10).

How can faith development research help?

We should pin our colours to the mast at the outset. It is our view that faith development theory offers an illuminating and practically relevant contribution to the practice of the church, particularly in the areas of Christian education and pastoral care. We are not uncritical of the approach, however.

Jeff Astley *et al.*, 1991, pp. ix–x

The third issue concerns the Church's contact with and responsibility for the large number of children growing up outside the ministry of the Church. Because *The Child in the Church* placed increasing emphasis on ministry to children within the congregation, Churches saw less point in maintaining a separate ministry to children through institutions like Sunday schools. Traditionally, however, Sunday schools had reached out to those children whose parents had little or no contact with the local congregation. In effect the demise of the Sunday school weakened the Church's ability to reach such children. In 1991 the report *All God's Children?* faced the problem concerning the child who was not in the Church.

How can churches reach children?

There can be little doubt that the move away from the classroom to the experience of the Christian community was right theologically... However, the consequences of this richer but narrower approach have to be faced and these consequences are of particular concern for a national church seeking to minister to the entire community and with a concept of the care of souls for all within parish boundaries.

All God's Children, 1997, pp. 8–9

Unfinished business

A decade and a half after *The Child in the Church*, the Consultative Group on Ministry among Children recognized that there still remained much unfinished business concerning children and the Churches. The report of this working group, published in 1995 under the title *Unfinished Business*, is concerned with *all* children, both those who have an involvement in church life and the majority who effectively have no contact with the Church.

The two key questions addressed are these. How can churches become 'child-friendly' within their own premises and within society? How can the Churches work with and for all children? *Unfinished Business* provides both an audit and an incentive for the Churches to:

- explore what it means to be a child in today's world
- promote the place of children in their life and worship
- act on behalf of all children as an advocate for them

These aims are set in the conviction that the child is a gift of God and a sign of the kingdom.

References and further reading

Astley, J. *et al.* (1991), *How Faith Grows: Faith Development and Christian Education*, London, National Society and Church House Publishing.

British Council of Churches (1976), *The Child in the Church*, London, BCC.

British Council of Churches (1981), *Understanding Christian Nurture*, London, BCC.

Church of England (1985), *Communion Before Confirmation?* London, National Society and CIO Publishing (The Knaresborough Report).

Church of England (1988), *Children in the Way*, London, National Society and Church House Publishing.

Church of England (1991), *All God's Children? Children's Evangelism in Crisis*, London, National Society and Church House Publishing.

Council of Churches for Britain and Ireland (1995), *Unfinished Business: Children and the Churches*, London, CCBI.

Francis, L. J. (1986), *Making Contact: Christian Nurture, Family Worship and Church Growth*, London, Collins Liturgical Publications.

Francis, L. J. and Faulkner, A. (1997), *All God's People*, Leominster, Gracewing.

Jamal, D. (1990), *Leaves on the Tree: All Age Learning and Worship*, London, National Society and Church House Publishing.

Tennant, D. F. (1978), *Children in the Church: A Baptist View*, London, Baptist Publications.

PART TWO
CHILDREN AND FAITH

$\boxed{8}$

Approaching Christian Education

Introduction

In this chapter we shall explore different meanings of the phrase 'Christian education', before surveying a number of different approaches that have been developed for the task of Christian education in general and the Christian education of children in particular.

Defining 'Christian education'

'Christian education' is a phrase that sounds innocent enough, but its employment can lead to considerable confusion and misunderstanding, partly because different people use it to mean such different things. There are three main uses of the term.

Education about Christianity

In this sense, Christian education takes place in all types of schools, wherever children are taught about the Christian religion, its practices, experiences and beliefs, as a part of the school's religious education curriculum. Most teachers of RE will be very careful to distinguish this ('non-confessional') education about the Christian faith from an attempt to induct children into, or help them grow up in, the Christian faith.

A Christian approach to education

Some people are willing to describe the teaching of any subject, and more particularly the general ethos of a school, as examples of Christian education, in the sense that these activities and relationships are motivated by and express Christian values and principles such as a love of truth, caring for others and treating them as ends in themselves.

Education into Christianity

On this third definition, Christian education covers those educational processes through which children (and adults) *learn to be Christian and to become more Christian*. It includes both Christian nurture or formation, in which Christian beliefs, attitudes and dispositions are learned, and the development of 'Christian criticism' through the learner's own thoughtful evaluation of Christianity.

In the rest of this chapter, we shall focus on this *third understanding* of Christian education, as a process of helping children embrace and grow into the Christian faith.

Education, learning and Christianity

Although philosophers of education have often argued that the term 'education' must be restricted to valuable learning that involves understanding and critical reflection, the word is in fact used more widely to cover all those processes through which learning takes place, where learning is defined equally generally as a long-term change brought about by experience. Such learning may include changes in attitudes, values and skills, as well as in knowledge and critical understanding. On most accounts, education involves a teacher or educator who intends that the learner learns, although we sometimes speak of life experience as itself serving as 'an education'.

A broad definition of the term 'Christian education', therefore, would label those processes (usually involving teaching) through which Christian beliefs, attitudes, values, dispositions to act and to experience, and other dimensions of being a Christian are learned.

Approaches to Christian education

We may think of children, young people and adults being educated into Christianity in a wide range of ways. The five different approaches outlined below each show somewhat different aims and objectives, and understandings of the role of the teacher and the learner, as well as different contexts and styles of Christian teaching and learning.

The faith community approach

On this approach, Christian education is something that best takes place in the context of the local church's community of worship and fellowship; in fact the Church may be said to be the main agent of such Christian education. Sometimes its life and worship may be deliberately structured so that people are helped to learn to be Christian, but often the Church exercises this role without knowing it. The process that is taking place when a child learns Christian ways by being part of a community is sometimes called *socialization* or *enculturation*. Here learning is a sort of osmosis: the child is encompassed by the Christian community, immersed in its prayer and practice, and so 'picks up' and 'absorbs' the Christian ways of thinking, feeling and acting. The faith community approach acknowledges and welcomes the potent influence of the 'hidden curriculum' of the Church. This phrase describes a set of learning experiences which do not advertise themselves as 'educational', but through which people learn anyway. In the Church this covers such things as experiences of worship, fellowship and friendships, finance meetings, social action, even Church art and architecture.

On the faith community approach, Christian education is understood very much as a matter of 'nurture' or 'formation' (see Chapter 9), through which we learn the 'languages of faith'. Important though this is, many argue that it needs to be supplemented by a cooler critical reflection that may best be done outside the Church's fellowship and worship, for it is hard to distance yourself from and critically to reflect on the Christian faith at the same time as you are embracing and celebrating it.

The Church's worship is a potent medium for Christian education, through which children see and hear Christian beliefs, feelings and values expressed, and find themselves sharing in that expression. It makes sense, then, to welcome children into a worship experience from an early age. The attitudes, symbols and rituals of worship will communicate a great deal well before the child can intellectually comprehend and analyse the beliefs that go with them.

What is Christian education?

Catechesis is more a process of nurture and conversion than of education, though it is concerned for deliberate, systematic, and sustained efforts. Catechesis is a process that is, without apology, value-laden, a process which aims to introduce persons into a community of Christian faith with its distinctive values, understandings and ways, a process which aims to aid persons to internalise and adopt the community's faith as their own and to apply that faith to life in the world.

John Westerhoff, 1978, p. 287

Critical Christian education

The faith community approach treats Christian education as part and parcel of the Church's life and work. The critical Christian education approach, however, understands it as a much more distinctly organized and separate affair. The difference may be captured by the implied (not often real) distinction between the *images* of the 'junior Church' and the 'Sunday school'. A school is often regarded as a place for explicit education. It is a distinctively educational community, where children learn about and come to reflect critically on the belief-claims of others.

On the critical Christian education approach a great deal of stress is laid on the cognitive (thinking) aspects of Christianity and the child's critical reflection on them. 'Understanding' and 'evaluation' are the key terms here, and 'critical' is not a dirty word.

What is Christian education?

Let me answer the question from the perspective of the Christian community. It is the process of exploring the Church's tradition and self-understanding in such a way that persons can understand, assess, and therefore respond to the truth of the gospel for themselves. It can always be the hope, but never the objective of the teacher that the understanding and the assessment will lead to a response that will transform the person as he or she receives the gift of faith.

Sara Little, in Seymour and Miller, 1982, pp. 41–2

Christian education as development

Children may be said to *develop* in their moral and religious thinking and the way they hold their faith. Such development is driven largely 'from within', but many interpret the task of the Christian educator as assisting this internal change. It is not our job, however, to hurry children through these developmental stages, but to support and encourage them as they change. On this view, the Christian educator acts rather like a counsellor or spiritual friend, although he or she may also provide learning experiences that will help the child to complete any developmental transition on which she has already embarked. James Fowler, taking a term from the psychologist Erik Erikson, views this educational ministry in part as one of *sponsorship*. It is to be seen in the context of a climate within the faith community that expects such development.

Sponsoring faith

By sponsorship in this context I mean the way a person or community provides affirmation, encouragement, guidance and models for a person's ongoing growth and development. The sponsor is one who walks with you; one who knows the path and can provide guidance. The sponsor is one who engenders trust and proves trustworthy in supporting you in difficult passages or turns. The sponsor may, as needed, confront you, insisting that difficult issues be faced and that self-deceptions or sloth be avoided. The sponsor or sponsoring community should be able to provide both models and experiences in education and spiritual direction that deepen and expand one's initial commitments and provide the nurture for strong and continuing growth.

James Fowler, 1981, p. 287

Christian education as liberation

Those who embrace this approach to Christian education often argue against the three earlier approaches. For them, the faith community approach is too conservative – passing on a Church culture and replicating the beliefs and values of its members, while the developmental approach is too 'individualistic' and the critical Christian education approach too intellectual – often treating 'criticism' as no more than rational agonizing over the truth-claims of religion. For liberation educators, *all* education must be critical, but it must embrace criticism in a moral, social and political way, rather than merely as an intellectual, logical exercise. Education, after all, is about opening people's eyes to reality, especially to the social reality that confines, determines and oppresses their lives.

Liberation Christian educators may applaud the fact that children often rebel against and reject the views of their 'elders and betters'. This is a good and healthy sign, for education is not about inheriting, ingesting and absorbing the past, but about changing the present and moving on to a new, revised future.

Where the faith community approach welcomes the influence of the hidden curriculum of the Church's life and worship, the liberation educator is more likely to encourage children to resist the learning that comes this way, as potentially oppressive and manipulative. For this approach, freedom as a dominant idea is 'in' and the assumed authority of the Church's sub-culture and its ways may be at risk of being thrown out.

Christian education as political?

By what we reclaim from our past heritage or propose for our future, by what we ignore from our past and refuse for our future, Christian religious educators are being political. We have no choice about whether or not Christian education will have political implications. It is inevitably political and our choice is about the direction in which we should shape the future of society by our present engagement as Christians within it.

Thomas Groome, 1980, p. 26

Christian education as faith translation

Although one or two of the approaches to Christian education outlined above tend to conflict, as we have seen, most of them are complementary and overlapping. This last approach may properly be said to identify a feature common to all the others. It treats the relationship between the Christian tradition (its culture, beliefs, values, stories, texts, rituals, etc.) and the Christian learner (with her present and past experiences, concerns, actions, beliefs, reasoning, spirituality, etc.) as being similar to what happens whenever we learn a different language. We need to translate what we hear or read so that we can 'get our tongues round' another and alien 'tongue'. All translation is interpretation: putting one set of ideas into a form that a different language-culture can recognize and understand. On the translation/interpretation model, Christian education is rather like a conversation, with the tradition ('the text') speaking and the learner responding out of his or her own experience and situation. In this dialogue of interpretation, the learner's 'horizon' – the limits of her field of vision and understanding – has to touch and fuse with the horizon of the tradition. Only then can the learner learn what the tradition has to teach her. And she can only learn that, in and from her own perspective.

The Christian educator is not to be seen here as a transmitter of an unchanged signal or message, but as a *translator* who stands in between the gospel tradition and the learner, interpreting the one to the other in a dialogue between the 'Christian story' and the learner's own story about their own experience: a dialogue that has the potential to change both stories.

Telling the tale

There are times when the Story comes to us as a source of affirmation, encouragement, healing, and hallowing. But knowing that we – in our personal, interpersonal, and social/political lives – are never completely faithful to our faith commitments, there are also times when the Story confronts us, calls us in question, and calls us forward. God's self-revealing and reaching out into the world should always be recognized as both consolation and confrontation, encouragement and correction, affirmation and invitation. Conversely, as our stories respond to the community Story, there are whole dimensions of the larger Story with which our own lived experience resonates (since it arises from the lived experience of the Christians who went before us). Thus we can readily affirm it. On the other hand, there may be dimensions of the larger Story...in which we recognize limitations.

Thomas Groome, 1980, pp. 217–18

References and further reading

Astley, J. (ed.) (2000), *Learning in the Way*, Leominster, Gracewing, chapters 1 and 2.

Astley, J. and Day, D. (eds.) (1992), *The Contours of Christian Education*, Great Wakering, McCrimmons, Chapters 1, 3 and 10.

Astley, J. and Francis, L. J. (eds.) (1994), *Critical Perspectives on Christian Education: A Reader on the Aims, Principles and Philosophy of Christian Education*, Leominster, Gracewing, Chapters 1, 2 and 3.

Fowler, J. W. (1981), *Stages of Faith: The Psychology of Human Development and the Quest for Meaning*, San Francisco, California, Harper & Row.

Groome, T. H. (1980), *Christian Religious Education: Sharing Our Story and Vision*, San Francisco, California, Harper & Row.

Groome, T. H. (1998), *Education for Life: A Spiritual Vision for Every Teacher and Parent*, Allen, Texas, Thomas More.

Harris, M. (1989), *Fashion Me A People: Curriculum in the Church*, Louisville, Kentucky, Westminster John Knox Press.

Hughes, F. (1992), *What Do You Mean – Christian Education?* Carlisle, Paternoster Press.

Nichols, K. (1997), *Refracting the Light: Learning the Languages of Faith*, Dublin, Veritas.

Seymour, J. and Miller, D. E. (eds.) (1982), *Contemporary Approaches to Christian Education*, Nashville, Tennessee, Abingdon.

Seymour, J. and Miller, D. E. (eds.) (1990), *Theological Approaches to Christian Education*, Nashville, Tennessee, Abingdon.

Warren, M. (ed.) (1983 and 1997), *Sourcebook for Modern Catechetics*, Volumes 1 and 2, Winona, Minnesota, St Mary's Press.

Westerhoff, J. (1978), 'Christian education as a theological discipline', *Saint Luke's Journal of Theology*, 21, pp. 280–8.

9

Christian Nurture

Introduction

The Churches' thinking about education in religion has often centred on the phrase 'Christian nurture', understood in terms of fostering and deepening (and perhaps initiating) religious commitment. The nineteenth-century American theologian Horace Bushnell seems to have first popularized the term. He was reacting against an individualistic, revivalist form of Christian education that laid great stress on first convicting the child of sin and then demanding her conversion to a very different life. For Bushnell, by contrast, children should be brought up 'in conversion', not 'for conversion'. Parents particularly should work as God works, bringing up children in the 'nurture and admonition of the Lord' (Ephesians 6.4) through appropriate caring and nurturing relationships in the discipline of the family. Bushnell's ideal of Christian education was *'that the child is to grow up a Christian, and never know himself as being otherwise'*.

Nurture versus conversion

The aim, effort and expectation should be, not, as is commonly assumed, that the child is to grow up in sin, to be converted after he comes to a mature age; but that he is to open on the world as one that is spiritually renewed, not remembering the time when he went through a technical experience, but seeming rather to have loved what is good from his earliest years.

Horace Bushnell, 1861, p. 10

Bushnell particularly emphasized the non-verbal, implicit Christian nurture that takes place by passing on the Christian character and spirit through living together and parenting, rather than any specific teaching of belief. Since Bushnell's time, however, discussion of religious nurture has widened to include more overt, intentional teaching or *instruction*.

Nurture versus education

One of the fundamental debates over religious education in schools relies on distinguishing *education* from *nurture*. In the 1970s in Britain strenuous and successful attempts were made to justify religious education in school on 'educational grounds', rather than religious ones. This contrasted with the views of earlier writers on education, many of whom viewed the teaching of RE as a matter of evangelism and nurture. Increasingly this view was rejected as religiously 'partisan'. The nurturing of religious commitment was inappropriate to, and could not be justified in, schools; it was a task solely for churches and Christian families. Education, many claimed, involved the open questioning of a variety of options, not the inculcation of one set of beliefs. As one Professor of Education (Paul Hirst) famously put it, a sophisticated approach to education is concerned with objectivity and the development of reason. It therefore forbids 'the presentation of particular commitments as if they were not radically disputable on rational grounds' (Hirst, 1981, p. 87). In other words, when and where *real* education is 'in', religious nurture must be cast 'out'.

So the distinction was made between, on the one hand, religious education that aimed at understanding and evaluating religions, and, on the other, nurture (and evangelism) that encouraged children to adopt and grow in a particular religious faith. This is often described in terms of the distinction between an acceptable 'non-confessional' religious education in schools and an unacceptable 'confessional' one.

Confessional religious education This form of 'teaching religion' or 'education in religion' aims at religious commitment and gives the child an understanding of a religion by helping her to adopt it and participate in it.	*Non-confessional religious education* This is mainly restricted to a 'teaching about religion' which develops the child's understanding of the religions and develops empathy with believers, but is not aimed at her conversion to, or formation in, religious faith. However, it may also include the encouragement of the child's own quest for a 'faith to live by'.

Exceptions to the rule?

As the debate proceeded, however, a number of problem areas were identified.

What about Church schools?

Church schools are a sort of 'half-way house' between the Church and a more secular state with its 'community schools'. Church schools practise professional education, but they have a Church base which gives them a concern for helping children to 'grow into Christ' as well. Is this forbidden? (See Chapter 22.)

What about moral education?

Most parents, teachers and politicians accept that schools should not just teach *about* morality. They also expect that schools will develop in their pupils particular moral values and dispositions. Yet, despite claims about 'generally accepted' or 'common' values, there is perhaps as much disagreement about morality as there is over where the truth lies in questions of religion. If 'moral nurture' is acceptable in school, why not religious nurture?

What about spiritual education?

Spiritual education is a traditional aim of education that has been given enhanced status in recent educational legislation (see Chapter 26). Is there any difference between promoting specific 'spiritual beliefs' and values and experiences, on the one hand, and nurturing children in religion on the other? After all, people also differ over their spiritual values, spirituality is not easily separated from religion, and the spirituality of a religion is an absolutely essential part of it.

Nurture as a part of education?

In any case, *is* nurture an un-educational activity? Education must initiate the child into a way of believing, speaking, valuing and experiencing *as a condition* of that child engaging in any rational 'disputation' or evaluation at all. Some sort of initial culture or world-view must be formed before rational criticism can begin. And *some* beliefs and values are so basic that they seem to demand that they be taught as firm, fixed and indisputable. (Scientific beliefs about laws of nature and moral beliefs about respecting other people may serve as examples.) This 'initiation' phase is particularly significant for young children. Might it not also include religious elements, provided that the child is not so formed in religion that she finds it difficult to recognize the proper criticisms that can be made of religion as she gets older? This question relates to the thorny question of indoctrination, which is discussed later in this chapter.

In fact, Paul Hirst himself has recently modified his views on education in general and religious education in particular (Hirst, 1993). He now stresses the priority in education of induction into certain 'social practices' that constitute 'a flourishing life', rather than (while not neglecting) the learner's critical reflection on those practices. His earlier position was too concerned with rational grounding and theory; he recognizes now that religious education crucially involves 'directly introducing pupils to the kinds of practices' that are involved in religion, as well as getting them to reflect critically on them.

Other metaphors

The word 'nurture' (from the Latin *nutrire*, to nourish or suckle) means 'to bring up, train, foster, rear'. 'Nurture' is really a metaphor. But it is not the only metaphor used for this type of education. Debates about the topic draw on a number of other examples of metaphorical language, as described below.

'Formation'

A useful distinction can be made between *formative education*, in which the learner receives and is formed in a tradition of values, beliefs and dispositions, and *critical education*, in which the learner is taught how to reflect on and evaluate that tradition (and also other traditions). 'Formation' is a metaphor derived from activities where form is given to something that is unformed, like the potter at her wheel or the wood-turner at his lathe. The value of the metaphor is that it concentrates attention on producing an educational end-product of a particular nature; but if it is taken too literally the word could suggest that the learner is entirely passive in education and has nothing worthwhile to contribute of her own.

'Moulding' or 'shaping'

These very similar metaphors generate similar misgivings. If I shape or mould your beliefs or values, am I not doing something *to* you (instead of *with* you or even just *for* you) that robs you of your independence? But we are all inevitably shaped by parents, teachers, friends, television, films, newspapers, music, architecture, geographical location and 'the culture' in general, and we rarely regard these agents as violating our freedom, autonomy or rationality.

'Gardening' or 'suckling'

Gardening metaphors used to be very common in educational thinking. Perhaps the idea of nurture comes closest to the model of the gardener manuring his plants or the mother nursing her baby. There is less of a sense of control or domination in such language compared with some images. We might say that the learner, like the plant or child, is being helped to develop *according to her own nature*, with the assistance of the input ('milk' or 'manure'!) provided by the teacher. Religious people sometimes happily speak of their own work, even their work as teachers or real gardeners, as *co-creating* with God, and of respecting the independence of what they 'create'.

Nurture and critical openness

Nurture itself can have a critical aspect: full Christian nurture may have both 'formative' *and* 'critical' dimensions. John Hull and others have written of such a Christian nurture leading to 'critical openness' through 'Christian criticism'. They claim that this humble, testing, enquiring attitude should be encouraged by those engaged in Christian nurture. It is appropriate, they argue, because the outcome that is being sought here is not a completely uncommitted mind or heart, nor a rigidly closed one, but an interdependent, self-critical and reflective attitude that is open to other evidence, arguments and world-views. A learner who adopts such an attitude is 'critically open', but she remains committed to her Christian viewpoint, affirming the beliefs and values of the Christian tradition. This critical openness is appropriate if, as Hull would claim, our theology sees God not as a dictator but as one who seeks with us a 'fellowship of minds', encouraging our reasoning rather than trying to put a stop to it (cf. Chapter 7 and Hull, 1984, chapter 18).

What about indoctrination?

This 'I-word' is usually introduced at some stage or another in debates about teaching religion. 'You can't do that to the poor kids', someone will say. 'That's indoctrination.' But what exactly is this dreadful activity, and why does it matter? There are several definitions of indoctrination. One is that to indoctrinate someone is to develop in them unshakeable beliefs: that is, beliefs that they cannot later change, even in the face of strong negative evidence.

Such a definition is couched in terms of *outcomes*. Others define indoctrination by specifying:

- 'anti-educational' *methods* that lead to such fixed beliefs
- a suspect *intention* in those teachers who want to control their pupils' minds in this way or
- the teaching of controversial *subjects* that are based on opinion rather than on 'facts' and 'sound evidence' (politics, morality and religion have all been accused of falling into this category)

Although the debate about indoctrination can become quite technical, four points that might provide parents and teachers with some defence against what is often a charge that has not been properly thought through should be appreciated:

1 If we do not intend to close children's minds, or use methods that we know will do so, and if our children do actually develop the capacity to think for themselves and to evaluate and perhaps reject what they have been taught, then we have *not* indoctrinated them, on any definition. This is the usual situation. Indoctrination is rarer than many think, and is rarely very successful when it is attempted in an open society. In any case, most teachers and parents intend quite the opposite results from their teaching.

2 We want our children – and the adults they will grow into – to have flexible, open minds: minds that are able to weigh evidence, and can and will reject unwarranted beliefs. But a window stuck open is worse than a window stuck closed. What we really want is for our children to grow up to have a *critical* (reflective, thoughtful) openness about their beliefs, not to grow up with unthinking minds that they are for ever changing. It is good to stick to your beliefs and your principles, sometimes even in the face of apparently contradictory evidence. That is the method followed by the best scientists – and by the best lovers and parents also.

3 Many beliefs are not 'open to conflicting evidence' in the same way as our beliefs about tables, chairs and leprechauns. (Take, for example, the beliefs that my memory is largely to be trusted and that all of my experience is not just a dream.) Perhaps the indoctrination charge cannot be levelled against such very general beliefs. But isn't the belief that a loving God made and keeps the whole world in existence just such a general belief? Christians acknowledge that much counts against it, but that nothing counts (or could count?) decisively against it. The belief is not immune to falsifying evidence, but it may properly be *resistant* to it.

4 While religion is about beliefs, it is also about right attitudes (such as worship, penitence and forgiveness), right values (particularly evaluations of the importance of power, wealth and relationships) and right behaviour (treating people as ends in themselves, and not only as a means to my ends; acting as stewards of the gifts of the earth, and so on). Indoctrination charges do not stick as well in areas such as these.

Practical implications

All this talk about the value of openness and the dangers of indoctrination can easily unnerve Christian parents and teachers. But there is no need for alarm. Sensible teaching in an atmosphere of respect and affection will do no harm, even when we are teaching our own, firmly held, moral and religious beliefs. Six issues need to be borne in mind:

1 *Honesty is important.* If you have doubts, or you know that *others* have doubts, you should find ways of communicating that fact. Your child will certainly develop her own doubts, and it helps to know that she isn't alone. 'Many believe that...' is one way of not being too dogmatic. 'The Bible (or the creed or the Church) teaches...' signals that this is an important belief, but it also positions it a little further away than does the introduction, '*I* believe that...' The child will come to recognize and appreciate the difference.

2 *But context is important too.* Schools, including Church schools, are patently more 'neutral' and 'public' institutions, and we have a responsibility to recognize in them something of the wide range of views of the diverse society that supports them. The families we create should be allowed a more particular view.

3 *Listening is even more important.* No child, however young, is without her own beliefs, thoughts, ideas, and theological explanations – however naive or silly. Her beliefs matter to her, and they should matter to you. The question, 'What do *you* think?' does not give her a licence to believe any old thing. Parents and teachers should be gently probing of her beliefs, getting her to be self-critical of them, often opening them up to correction and amendment. But we must also take them seriously, or the child will never take the beliefs of Christianity seriously either.

4 *Don't do everything all at once.* Parents and teachers don't need to keep interrupting themselves while they tell the Christmas story to introduce critical remarks about the plausibility of angels or the difficulty of reconciling the different versions in Matthew and Luke. With young children particularly, it is your attitude (reverent, but not dogmatic; open to their doubts and reflections, not closed to them) that will best communicate the fact that this story is open to discussion and debate, activities that will perhaps come much later.

5 Above all, *be clear what YOU believe.* (The word is *clear*, not *certain*. There are few things about our religion, perhaps, of which we can honestly say we are totally certain.) Teaching, and indeed just talking to children, forces us to think through what we think ourselves about the story of Noah and the Ark, or the problem of evil, or the effects of the death of Christ. You don't have to say all that you do believe, nor all that you don't believe, about these things. But you will find it easier to speak to children positively and faithfully about them if these doctrines and stories have become part of your positive, thought-through, reflective adult faith. You will have discovered what lies at the heart of these beliefs, at least in the case of one believer. Your children should be allowed to share that.

6 *Don't make the mistake of eschewing any religious teaching* or moral formation for your child, waiting for her to grow up until she can 'freely choose her own faith and values'. That is not how it works. If you do not play your part in forming her, you will simply leave the task to her peers, other adults and society (and the mass media). She *will* be formed, somehow or another. And she *will* hear about God, Christ and the Church from other sources, which may not be as well informed, nor as sympathetic, nor perhaps as critical as yourself. The silence of the overmeticulous liberal may only communicate that he doesn't take these things very seriously.

References and further reading

Astley, J. (1994), *The Philosophy of Christian Religious Education*, Birmingham, Alabama, Religious Education Press; London, SPCK, Chapters 1, 4 and 5.

Astley, J. and Day, D. (eds.) (1992), *The Contours of Christian Education*, Great Wakering, McCrimmons, chapters 4 and 5.

Astley, J. and Francis, L. J. (1994) (eds.), *Critical Perspectives on Christian Education: A Reader on the Aims, Principles and Philosophy of Christian Education*, Leominster, Gracewing, Sections 4 and 6.

British Council of Churches (1981), *Understanding Christian Nurture*, London, BCC.

Bushnell, H. (1861), *Christian Nurture*, reprinted Grand Rapids, Michigan, Baker Book House, 1979.

Hirst, P. H. (1981), 'Education, catechesis and the Church school', *British Journal of Religious Education*, 3, 3, pp. 85–93 and 101.

Hirst, P. H. (1993), 'Education, knowledge and practices', in R. Barrow and P. White (eds.), *Beyond Liberal Education*, London, Routledge, pp. 184–99.

Hobson, P. R. and Edwards, J. S. (1999), *Religious Education in a Pluralist Society: The Key Philosophical Issues*, London, Woburn Press.

Hull, J. M. (1984), *Studies in Religion and Education*, Lewes, Falmer.

Nelson, C. E. (1976), *Where Faith Begins*, Atlanta, Georgia, John Knox Press.

Thiessen, E. J. (1993), *Teaching for Commitment: Liberal Education, Indoctrination and Christian Nurture*, Leominster, Gracewing.

Westerhoff, J. H., III (1976), *Will Our Children Have Faith?* New York, Seabury Press.

10

Faith Development

Introduction

The word 'faith' is used in a great variety of different ways, by non-religious as well as religious people.

Talking about faith

'I really hope that my children will grow up to have a faith of their own.'
'He still has a very strong faith in justice.'
'I lost my faith when I was about seventeen.'
'I came to faith when I was in hospital after having Sarah.'
'Keep faith with your convictions, son.'
'It is difficult to believe all the tenets of the faith.'

According to the American Methodist theologian and psychologist of religion James Fowler, 'faith' is a very general term indeed. It labels the almost universal human activity of:
- creating or finding meaning in life
- knowing, valuing and relating to that which we take to be meaningful, in commitment and trust

Human and religious faith

This is a very broad understanding of what might be termed 'human faith'. Human faith is not necessarily religious. We all 'believe in' something or someone: especially people, objects, ideas or values. We all have an image of what we take to be of ultimate concern. This constitutes our world-view, which is what Fowler calls our 'ultimate environment'.

For Fowler, religious faith differs from other forms of faith primarily in having specifically religious objects or *faith contents*. These are religious 'centres of value' and 'images of power', such as God, Christ and the Holy Spirit, and religious 'master stories' of the sort that underlie the doctrines of creation, incarnation and redemption. Other religious traditions have different objects for their faith, in so far as they believe in different truths and realities.

Most religious, and indeed most non-religious, people are interested in *what* people believe and what they believe in. They are interested in the content of faith. Thus Christians talk about 'The Faith' and its tenets, principles or doctrines. Fowler, on the other hand, wants to draw our attention to the *form of faith*: the ways in which we have faith, or the 'how' of faith.

> ## *Fowler on faith*
>
> Faith is an active or dynamic phenomenon. A verb, not a noun, faith is a way-of-being-in-relation – a stance, a way of moving into and giving form and coherence to life.
>
> James Fowler and Sam Keen, 1978, p. 24

The focus of Fowler's work is therefore on faith-as-a-process. It is difficult to talk about the form of faith without talking about its content, but perhaps we can see the point of the distinction – and the value of this more general (and not specifically religious) interpretation of faith.

> ## *Faith of mind and heart*
>
> Faith is not merely assent to the truth of propositions but is the surrendering of the heart to a transcendent centre of value and power.
>
> Rodney M. Moseley and Ken Brockenbrough, 1988, pp. 105–6

Faith aspects

What do children *do* that might be described as part and parcel of faith? Faith is a dynamic process, best described in terms of verbs rather than nouns. It is about trusting, committing yourself, relating to others and to God, valuing them, feeling positively about them. It is about making and finding meaning, thinking things through, getting them into perspective, forming a judgement and adopting a system of beliefs.

Fowler argues that the form of faith can be viewed under a number of interrelated aspects, listed below. These aspects are sometimes described as 'windows into faith'. This is a useful metaphor, for different windows give us different, partial views into a building, while much of it may remain forever out of sight of the observers.

According to Fowler, there are seven aspects or elements within our human faith:
- our *reasoning* – the way we think
- our *perspective-taking* – our ability to adopt another person's perspective
- our *moral judging* – the way we make moral judgements
- our *social awareness* – how and where we set the limits to our 'community of faith'
- our *relation to authority* – how and where we find authorities on which to rely
- our *forming a world-view* – our way of 'holding it all together'
- our *relation to symbols* – our understanding of, and response to, symbols

Stages of faith

Children, young people and adults can show a number of different stages or styles of faith. As we develop, our way of being in faith changes.

A family of three children in church with their mother

Sarah is nearly four years old. She fidgets a lot during the readings and the sermon, but likes to stand and pretend to follow the hymns in the hymn book. She particularly enjoys the candles and the little processions, and is fascinated by the statues and the pictures in the windows. She is giggling to herself now, because her Mummy has reported to her that Mrs Jones has died, and has explained that she is 'in paradise, alive but without a body'. Sarah is imagining her with her legs sticking out of her head.

Ben is eight. He is listening intently to the story the vicar is telling. He wants to know from his Mum if it is a made-up story. (He doesn't seem to mind that it is.) But when the vicar has finished the story proper and goes on to discuss its 'moral', Ben's interest wanders back to his book.

Stephen is twelve. He was embarrassed walking to church in case he was seen by his friends. He likes to listen to the arguments in the sermon though, when there are any, although he is now more influenced by his history teacher who is very dismissive of religion. Stephen isn't quite sure when he will be grown-up. He wonders about it, and at the diversity of views grown-ups have about Church. Soon he will be a prickly adolescent, difficult to talk to, having a world-view that he doesn't yet recognize that he has, and being influenced in his faith in ways he can hardly acknowledge.

The children's mother has been through all these stages. She knows at least this about the faith of her children: that it will change, as they change. It does not yet appear what they shall be. The same claim, she muses, can be made about her own faith. She is nearly forty, and although she believes in many of the same things that she did when she 'came to faith' at the age of sixteen, she seems to believe in them now in a very different way.

Fowler argues that the way we hold our faith can pass through up to seven stages (0–6). At each stage we 'faith' differently. As we move from one stage to another we suffer the trauma of losing one familiar way of being in faith before we can take up a new style of faith. As we develop, the faith contents (beliefs) from each earlier stage are carried over and reworked by the different structures of thinking and relating of the new stage of our faith.

At each developmental stage, a person's faith will exemplify a particular form of reasoning, of perspective-taking, of moral decision-making, and so on. The *transition* from one faith stage to another is marked by a change in one or more of these aspects of faith, as this dimension of faith changes to the form that is more characteristic of a later stage. It is only when the other faith aspects have changed in a similar way that the person can be said fully to have moved to the next stage.

According to Fowler, we pass through these stages in sequence, without omitting a stage or regressing (except in illness or old age, perhaps, when it is possible that we may revert to using the structures of an earlier stage). Most of those who embrace faith development theory assume that this pattern of change is the same for everyone, although Fowler himself does not go so far as to claim this. But many of us do not get very far in our faith development. And note that hardly anyone is at Stage 6!

Fowler's theory is contentious, and many researchers prefer to think of different *styles* or *patterns* of faith rather than a developmental sequence of *stages*, an account that better fits the influence of a person's life history and social context on her way of being in faith. Other criticisms include the following (cf. Dykstra and Parks, 1986; Astley and Francis, 1992; Astley and Kay, 1998):

- The developmental psychology on which Fowler relies underestimates the cognitive (thinking) capacities of younger children.
- Data from research interviews is not specific enough to test his wide-ranging hypothesis.
- The form and content of faith cannot be so easily distinguished, and what makes faith religious is more than a difference in content.

Researching faith development

Fowler claims that this scheme of faith development is supported by several hundred in-depth interviews that he and others have done with children, young people and adults. Each semi-structured interview lasts from 2½ to 3 hours and tries to find answers to a range of questions (appropriately worded), such as:
- 'What makes an action right?'
- 'What does death mean to you?'
- 'Are there any beliefs, values or commitments that are important in your life right now?'
- 'If you have a question which you cannot decide, to whom or what would you look for guidance?'

These interviews are recorded and typed up, and the responses coded by trained coders who identify the stage of development they reveal.

Faith stages in childhood and adolescence

Stage 0: Faith as nursed and foundational

Fowler's 'Primal Faith'
Age 0–4 approximately

Obviously, this is not a period that is open to study by interview techniques. The foundations for faith are laid down in our early experiences of being picked up and nursed, when trust is first formed. Fowler writes of the way we are nursed into 'our first *pre-images* of God', which are mediated through 'recognizing eyes and confirming smiles' (Fowler, 1981, p. 121). Dependable parenting is crucial during this period and the next stage.

Stage 1: Faith as chaotic, unordered and impressionistic

Fowler's 'Intuitive–Projective Faith'
Age 3/4–7/8 approximately

Thinking is intuitive rather than logical at this stage, so the child's relatively uninhibited imagination and her own experience result in a chaos of powerful images.

Reality is perceived more like a disorderly bundle of film cuttings from the floor of the editing suite than a completed reel of the movie. Symbols are viewed magically and are treated as being what they represent. Since the powerful symbols of Christian experience, ritual and sacrament can provide the child with deep and lasting images at this stage of her faith, some would argue that we should not exclude these young children from 'adult' forms of worship.

Stage 2: Faith as ordering

Fowler's 'Mythic–Literal Faith'
Age 6/7–11/12 approximately, and some adults

At this stage the child (or adult) can order her experience because of her developing cognitive skills, especially her ability to trace patterns of cause and effect. Story-telling is her primary way of doing this, which explains the importance at this stage of the child telling her own story – and the story of the Christian community to which she belongs. 'Belonging' is itself of considerable significance for self-image at this stage; junior school aged children are particularly keen to belong to some club or group. This communal belonging expresses the child's new skills in simple, concrete perspective-taking, abilities that make her unlike her egocentric younger siblings. She is now beginning properly to enter into the world of the other person.

Stage 3: Faith as conforming

Fowler's 'Synthetic–Conventional Faith':
Age 11/12–17/18 approximately, and many adults

Many view the ability to think abstractly as the most significant development in thinking and religious judgement (see Chapter 14). By Stage 3, this skill has fully developed, along with a new capacity for adopting the perspective of others. The adolescent or adult can now see herself as others see her. Interpersonal relationships and what other people think, particularly others in her peer group, are of considerable significance at this stage. This is a time of going with a particular 'faith-current' or 'faith-crowd', and submitting yourself to what Sharon Parks has called 'the tyranny of the "they"' (1986, p. 76). At this stage, Christian educators can engage their students in more abstract teaching and discussion. However, the learners are not yet 'thinking for themselves', but rather unconsciously adopting the beliefs and values of others. Faith or meaning-making is thus largely 'second-hand', and adolescents are not yet able properly to reflect either on their beliefs and values or on the way in which these are held.

Imagining God at different stages

At Stage 1 children tend to image God in terms of the 'air' or the 'sun'. At Stage 2 they are most likely to adopt 'anthropomorphic' imagery, seeing God in human form, as a Big-Daddy-in-the-Sky. But at Stage 3 this has been exchanged for a more sophisticated notion of the personal qualities of a transcendent deity, as friend, comforter or guide.

Adult faith stages

Beyond childhood and early adolescence lies a continuing journey of faith development. At Stage 4 ('Individuative–Reflective Faith') we come to choose our own faith and fully acknowledge and evaluate our own beliefs and relationships for the first time. At this stage, 'I can now no longer tolerate having my faith at second-hand; I must know who I am for myself, when I am not being defined by other people' (Astley *et al.*, 1991, p. 27).

Where Stage 4 faith is very concerned with definition and conceptual clarity, collapsing tensions and ambiguities to ensure these ends, Stage 5 ('Conjunctive Faith') allows for a new style of faith which is rather less tidy, and is more willing to live with paradox and ambiguity. The stage may emerge particularly through coping with failure and living with the consequences of our earlier decisions. Adults at this stage may be more tolerant of the differing beliefs and value perspectives of children and young people than they were in early adulthood, which is perhaps one reason why some grandparents are more open-minded than parents.

The transition to Stage 4 takes place from about 17/18 years onwards, or from the 30s and 40s; Stage 5 is rare before age 30. However, nearly a quarter of the adults that Fowler interviewed were still at Stage 3, and nearly 1 per cent at Stage 2.

References and further reading

Astley, J. *et al.* (1991), *How Faith Grows: Faith Development and Christian Education*, London, National Society and Church House Publishing.

Astley, J. and Francis, L. J. (eds.) (1992), *Christian Perspectives on Faith Development: A Reader*, Leominster, Gracewing; Grand Rapids, Michigan, Eerdmans.

Astley, J. and Kay, W. K. (1998), 'Piaget and Fowler', in W. K. Kay and L. J. Francis (eds.), *Religion in Education, Volume 2*, Leominster, Gracewing, pp. 137–68.

Blazer, D. (ed.) (1989), *Faith Development in Early Childhood*, Kansas City, Sheed & Ward.

Dykstra, C. and Parks, S. (eds.) (1986), *Faith Development and Fowler*, Birmingham, Alabama, Religious Education Press.

Fowler, J. W. (1981), *Stages of Faith: The Psychology of Human Development and the Quest for Meaning*, San Francisco, California, Harper & Row.

Fowler, J. W. (1987), *Faith Development and Pastoral Care*, Philadelphia, Pennsylvania, Fortress Press.

Fowler, J. and Keen, S. (1978), *Life Maps: Conversations on the Journey of Faith*, Minneapolis, Minnesota, Winston Press; Waco, Texas, Word Books.

Fowler, J., Nipkow, K. E. and Schweitzer, F. (eds.) (1992), *Stages of Faith and Religious Development: Implications for Church, Education and Society*, London, SCM Press.

Moseley, R. M. and Brockenbrough, K. (1988), 'Faith development in the pre-school years', in D. Ratcliff (ed.), *Handbook of Pre-school Religious Education*, Birmingham, Alabama, Religious Education Press, pp. 101–24.

Parks, S. (1986), *The Critical Years: The Young Adult's Search for a Faith to Live By*, San Francisco, California, Harper & Row.

Slee, N. (1996), 'Further on from Fowler', in L. J. Francis, *et al.* (eds.), *Research in Religious Education*, Leominster, Gracewing, pp. 88–91.

11

Moral Development

Introduction

Whether it arises within or outside a religion, much of morality is a matter of *learning* moral attitudes, beliefs, disposition, behaviour and ways of thought (see Chapter 25). But it appears that other changes do not originate from outside, but from 'within' the person following a developmental pattern as she matures.

One aspect of our morality that has been regarded as subject to development proper is our moral understanding and judgement. This *cognitive* developmental approach stresses the importance of advances in the child's powers of thinking as she or he moves from a stage of egocentric, externally influenced ways of thinking to a stage of more self-directed moral responsibility. This focus on moral thinking contrasts sharply with the non-rational, emotive accounts of moral development of Freud and others.

The work of Piaget

The Swiss psychologist Jean Piaget (1896–1980) explored the nature of children's moral judgements by talking with children, not only about the particular judgements they made about right and wrong, but also about more general things such as their attitudes to rules, and their notions of justice and fairness. Very young children played games (Piaget investigated the game of marbles) with no reference to common rules, but later adhered to the rules of the game strictly, treating them as immutable. Only around age 11 were children willing to treat rules as modifiable, useful conventions. Piaget regarded this change as an important clue to the child's understanding of moral rules.

The child's growing ability to co-operate with others emancipates her from a 'heteronomous' obedience to outside authority, so that self-determination ('autonomy') may develop. Piaget found that young children regarded actions as right if adults approved of them. They also judged actions by their consequences rather than the agent's intention: actions were 'naughtier' the more mess they made, regardless of whether these consequences were intended or accidental (see Chapter 37). Around the age of 11, children gradually move from this heteronomous *conventional* stage or type of morality (in which they show 'unilateral respect' and obedience to adult commands and guidance, and uncritical adherence to rules), to a less rigid *rational morality* in which they recognize themselves as formulating their own moral rules by mutual agreement and apply them according to circumstances. This change comes about, Piaget argued, through a process of cognitive restructuring of the ways in which the children were thinking morally.

Such a change is essentially a difference in the 'structure', 'form' or 'logic' of the child's thinking about morality, rather than its 'content'. That is to say, the change is a change in how she comes to make a moral judgement and how conscious she is of what she is doing in making this judgement, rather than a change in what that judgement actually is. Such a view fitted Piaget's (now more contentious) claims about the development of children's thought toward more abstract modes, although the moral stages are not so clear-cut and he argued for an overlapping continuum. (While autonomy usually begins about age seven and is well formed by the age of 12, there are examples of each stage in much older and younger people, and sometimes a mixture of responses.)

Piaget's stress on the importance of reciprocity (mutual respect) in the development of autonomy has been criticized, as has his blanket condemnation of the external morality of heteronomy:

> We see a different process at work. Rules are laid down by, and attitudes observed in, respected adults. They are progressively extended and interiorised through the process of identification. Thus interiorised moral feelings of guilt arise when they are broken; and such sense of guilt develops into the autonomy we call 'conscience' ...Autonomy, we conclude, is born of heteronomy – not of reciprocity. (Bull, 1969, pp. 41–2)

The work of Kohlberg

The American researcher Lawrence Kohlberg (1927–87) built on Piaget through his own extensive empirical work. He argued that the structures of every child's moral thinking and understanding change through the same series of six possible stages of irreversible development, in interaction with their environment. Movement from one stage to the next is driven by the child's inability at a 'lower stage' to cope with the conflict of competing interests in a given moral situation with the resources she can muster for moral thought. Kohlberg defines a 'stage' here as 'a way of thinking, which may be used to support either side of an action choice; that is, it illustrates the distinction between moral form and moral content' (Kohlberg, in Munsey, 1980, p. 31).

- At *Stage 1*, morality is understood in terms of obedience to some powerful authority and avoidance of punishment, i.e. doing what you are told. (For example, 'I shouldn't take the cake because I will be smacked later if I do.')
- At *Stage 2*, morality is seen in terms of self-interest, rewards and satisfaction of one's own needs, and co-operating with others for our mutual interest. ('You scratch my back and I'll scratch yours.') Fairness is important to children at this stage, but mainly where their own interests are concerned. ('I should help at home because I want the money Dad will give me for doing it.')
- At *Stage 3*, the child's judgement is based on conformity to the expectations of other people, so as to maintain his or her relationships with them and gain approval (the 'good boy/nice girl' syndrome). At this stage there is considerable emphasis on trust and loyalty, and intention is now a major consideration. ('I shouldn't cheat because if I do the teacher won't like me anymore.')
- At *Stage 4*, morality is understood as a matter of keeping rules for the sake of society and one's own self-respect. This has been described as a 'law and order' orientation. ('I should visit Grandma in hospital, because it is my duty.' 'I shouldn't steal, because it would be breaking the law, and society would collapse if we don't follow the rules.') Stages 3 and 4 are described as representing the *Conventional Level* of moral reasoning, where morality is viewed in terms of role conformity in family and society, regardless of consequences.

- At *Stages 5 and 6* (the *Postconventional Level* or *Principled Level*), morality most truly comes into its own, as a morality of self-accepted moral principles. Now moral judgements are seen more in terms of a *social contract* of moral obligations to safeguard the rights of others (Stage 5) or as a set of *abstract and universal ethical principles* of justice, equality, respect for human beings as such, and other universal human rights (Stage 6).

Kohlberg claims, rather unconvincingly, that this developmental account follows a necessary logical sequence: that is, that the stages *must* occur in this order. Initially, he treated Stage 6 as representing the best form of moral judgement, indeed the only 'real morality' in which a person adopts self-conscious, universal principles of what is right and just. Unfortunately Stage 6 is very rare. In fact only a minority of people get beyond Stage 4, and they seldom do so before the age of 16. Other stages of moral reasoning represent progressively closer approximations to the ideal state of moral judgement. But many argue that we should not dismiss these less mature forms of moral reasoning; Kohlberg himself later broadened his definition of a 'principled person' to include States 5, 4 and even 3. Kohlberg also insists that the *moral worth* of all persons is the same; a Stage 6 person is not 'of higher worth' than a Stage 3 person. Yet he rejected moral relativism and claimed that the higher stages of moral reasoning are morally better than the earlier ones, and that basic moral values are universal.

Moral educators are sometimes encouraged to present children with moral arguments that are suitable to a stage *beyond* their present one, thus challenging their present thinking so as to help them move on to the next stage. The notion of 'stage mixture' is sometimes proposed to explain why moral development can sometimes progress more quickly where the child faces more challenges, new experiences and intellectual and moral conflicts which provide her with complex stimuli that her present stage of development cannot fully grasp. (Kohlberg thinks of this as involving 'cognitive stimulation', rather than directly teaching the child the content of morality.) Nevertheless, there is little correlation between moral development and IQ or 'mental age', and Kohlberg insists that there is more to moral maturity than cognitive maturity, however that is measured. Yet there is also strong evidence that comprehension of moral concepts does correlate positively with Kohlberg's stage development.

'The Heinz dilemma'

One of the most famous of the dilemmas that Kohlberg used in his research on children's moral thinking is the story of Heinz. Heinz steals a new and expensive drug to save his dying wife, because he could not afford the inflated price and negotiations with the druggist have failed. Typical responses to the 'Heinz dilemma' at the six different moral stages include the following:

- *at Stage 1* 'Heinz shouldn't have stolen it because he might be put in jail.' 'He should have stolen it because he'll be in trouble if his wife dies.'
- *at Stage 2* 'Heinz should have stolen it, because he needed his wife to look after him.' 'If Heinz was sent to prison she would die anyway, so he shouldn't have stolen it.'
- *at Stage 3* 'Good people don't steal – so he did wrong.' 'Good husbands take care of their wives – so he did right.'
- *at Stage 4* 'It was wrong because he was breaking the law. He'll always feel guilty.' 'Anyone who has a sense of honour and duty would have to save her.'

- *at Stage 5* 'It is wrong to steal, but to let his wife die would be worse in the eyes of Heinz and the community.' 'Every violation of the law has long-term bad effects.'
- *at Stage 6* 'Heinz broke the law but the inherent worth of the individual is the central value.' 'Heinz would always condemn himself for not living up to his own standards of honesty and respect for others' property.'

Dilemmas in the classroom

Let us now be more concrete about means of moral education in the school. It is not always necessary that the matters discussed be ones of the immediate and real-life issues of the classroom. I have found that my hypothetical and remote but obviously morally real and challenging conflict situations are of intense interest to almost all adolescents and lead to lengthy debate among them. They are involving, because the adult right answer is not obviously at hand to discourage the child's own moral thought, as so often is the case. The child will listen to what the teacher says about moral matters only if the child first feels a genuine sense of uncertainty about the right answer to the situation in question. The pat little stories in school readers in which virtue always triumphs or in which everyone is really nice are unlikely to have any value in the stimulation of moral development. Only the presentation of genuine and difficult moral conflicts can have this effect.

Lawrence Kohlberg, in Munsey, 1980, p. 75

Criticisms

Critics of these cognitive approaches, particularly Kohlberg's account of the development of 'justice reasoning', include those who argue as follows:
- Young children may have a far richer sense of morality than Kohlberg allows. They do not act solely out of fear of punishment, but also from considerations of fairness and for other reasons.
- Morality is more a matter of appropriate attitude, 'moral vision', character or emotion than of reasoning. (Kohlberg dismissed this view as advocating context-dependent, short-lived 'bags of virtues'.)
- 'Moral judgement' is ineffective unless it issues in moral action; less sophisticated thinkers may sometimes behave better than more mature thinkers (but Kohlberg claimed that 'advance in moral judgement seems to correlate with more mature moral actions'). Some researchers (e.g. Damon, 1990) argue that although moral ideals can have an increasing influence on conduct as children mature, this is not automatic and depends on their 'moral identity' – that is, their use of moral principles to define themselves (when 'people should be honest' becomes '*I* want to be honest'); and that is not a matter of a different developmental level of thinking.
- Kohlberg's account, in concentrating on the form of moral judgement, misses the importance of the *content* of a person's moral thinking, especially basic rules and moral virtues.
- People often think very differently in different moral situations.
- Carol Gilligan notes that Kohlberg's focus on justice and moral autonomy (deciding for yourself) represents an 'ethics of rights' or duty, which is concerned with interests, fairness, contracts and power. She argues, however, that women and girls more commonly show an 'ethics of responsibility' centred on care and

compassion, relationships, service and interdependence. Whereas Kohlberg's early interviews were with boys, and dealt with hypothetical moral dilemmas about other people, Gilligan also interviewed women and girls, some of whom faced an immediate and personal moral dilemma about whether they should undergo an abortion.

Sex and morality

In dealing with hypothetical moral dilemmas differently, males seem more content to abstract the 'essential elements' from a situation and apply abstract principles to it; detachment and disinterestedness are basic to this approach. Females, however, are more concerned with the detail and view each situation as a unique set of interpersonal relationships that needs further explanation. They do not distance themselves from the dilemmas in the ways that males do.

So girls are more likely to want to know about Heinz's *relationship* with his wife, his friends and the man who has the miracle drug. Their responses in interviews often place girls lower than boys in Kohlberg's stage hierarchy, but Gilligan argues that this is because of a different – but no less mature – female understanding of morality.

This arises from a concern for relationships, a 'belief in communication as the mode of conflict resolution', and an unwillingness to seek out right solutions and to be above reproach. Women are more likely to speak of moral dilemmas as a matter of choosing 'the lesser of two evils'. Gilligan writes that moral education for both boys and girls should 'focus on developing the understanding of both justice and responsibility' (Gilligan, in Fowler and Vergote, 1980, p. 248).

It should be pointed out, however, that recent studies have claimed that boys and girls at the same educational level *do not* differ markedly between emphasizing caring and emphasizing rules and justice. In any case, Kohlberg's revised scoring system is said to take care and responsibility into account at each stage level, which may go some way to meeting the criticisms of Gilligan and others.

References and further reading

Bull, N. J. (1969), *Moral Education*, London, Routledge & Kegan Paul.

Clouse, B. (1985), *Moral Development: Perspectives in Psychology and Christian Belief*, Grand Rapids, Michigan, Baker Book House.

Damon, W. (1990), *The Moral Child: Nurturing Children's Natural Moral Growth*, New York, Free Press.

Dykstra, C. R. (1981), *Vision and Character: A Christian Educator's Alternative to Kohlberg*, New York, Paulist Press.

Fowler, J. W. (1984), *Becoming Adult, Becoming Christian*, San Francisco, California, Harper & Row, Chapter II.

Fowler, J. W. and Vergote, A. (eds.) (1980), *Toward Moral and Religious Maturity*, Morristown, New Jersey, Silver Burdett.

Gilligan, C. (1982), *In a Different Voice: Psychological Theory and Women's Development*, Cambridge, Massachusetts, Harvard University Press.

Kay, W. K. (1998), 'Piaget, Kohlberg and Gilligan', in W. K. Kay and L. J. Francis (eds.), *Religion in Education, Volume 2*, Leominster, Gracewing, pp. 169–98.

Kohlberg, L. (1984), *Essays on Moral Development, Vol. 2: The Psychology of Moral Development*, San Francisco, California, Harper & Row.

Munsey, B. (ed.) (1980), *Moral Development, Moral Education, and Kohlberg*, Birmingham, Alabama, Religious Education Press.

Piaget, J. (1932), *The Moral Judgement of the Child*, London, Routledge & Kegan Paul.

Van der Ven, J. A. (1998), *Formation of the Moral Self*, Grand Rapids, Michigan, Eerdmans, Chapter 5.

12

Attitude toward Religion

Introduction

Attitudes are fundamental to the learning process in general and fundamental to development in the Christian faith in particular. The aim of the present chapter is to discuss the nature of attitudes, to examine the place of attitude formation within Christian education, and then to provide an introduction to a body of research begun in the early 1970s into the way in which a positive attitude toward Christianity is shaped during childhood and adolescence.

What are attitudes?

Since the mid 1920s social psychologists have been fascinated by the idea of attitudes and by attempts to assess and to measure them. Attitudes are thought to lie at the heart of so much of human behaviour. By very definition, however, attitudes are not themselves visible. What we are able to observe are the range of behaviours to which attitudes give rise. Attitudes are reflected in what people do and in what people say.

Psychologists are generally agreed that attitudes are deep-seated underlying predispositions to respond in certain ways, the hidden mechanism which helps to shape what we do and what we say. Beyond this level of agreement, however, there is some disagreement among psychologists as to precisely how attitudes should be defined. Some psychologists argue that there are three components to an attitude which they see as cognitive (beliefs), affective (feelings), and behavioural (actions). Other psychologists argue that attitudes are focused on one component, the affective. The present author agrees with that simpler view.

To say that attitudes are concerned with the affective component means that they are concerned with our evaluations, with how we feel about specific things, ideas or people, either positively for these or negatively against these. Thus, someone's attitude toward an object, a concept, or a person comprises the sum total of his or her evaluative responses relevant to that object, concept or person. To become clearer about this idea of attitude, it is helpful to distinguish attitudes from other related ideas, like opinions and beliefs.

Opinions are held without the same unconscious emotional commitment as attitudes. Opinions live near the surface, but attitudes live deep down in our psyche. Opinions are by this definition inherently unstable and may change from day to day. I may have a deep seated positive attitude toward Christianity, but nonetheless hold the opinion that the carol service I attended yesterday was awful.

Beliefs are generally related to claims about the existence of something or to claims about its nature. Beliefs may or may not be held with emotional force. Beliefs are modifiable in the light of evidence or argument in a way in which attitudes are not so easily modified. I may have a firm belief in the existence of God and of God's revelation in Jesus and in Scripture, but nonetheless have a very negative attitude toward Christianity.

Other constructs which are generally distinguished from attitudes include traits, values and motives.

Attitude toward religion

Attitude toward religion has been defined as 'a relatively permanent and enduring evaluative predisposition to a positive or negative response of an affective nature which is based upon and reflects to some extent evaluative concepts or beliefs learned about the characteristics of a referent or group of referents which come within a definition of the religious'.

William K. Kay and Leslie J. Francis, 1996, pp. 186–7

Attitude toward religion and educational aims

During the late 1960s a main concern in religious education was focused on conceptual development, following the influential research of Ronald Goldman (see Chapter 14). In his book *Religious Thinking from Childhood to Adolescence*, Goldman (1964) had indicated that children were unable to deal with religious concepts in the same way as adults dealt with them until they reached the level of formal operational thinking around the age of 13 or 14. In his subsequent book, *Readiness for Religion*, Goldman (1965) cautioned against introducing children to religious concepts prematurely.

Building on and criticizing Goldman's work in the 1970s, Leslie J. Francis tried to divert attention from concern with conceptual development to concern with affective development. He argued that the Churches' primary job in Christian education among pre-school children and children in the primary school age range was to concentrate on affective development rather than on conceptual development. In other words, the primary concern of the Christian educator working with children among this age range was to be focused on shaping their attitudes (how they feel about religion) rather than on their concepts (what they understand about religion). He argued that, if the 'right attitudes' were developed during this period of life, the children would still feel positive about religion and about the Church and be motivated to develop the 'right thinking' slightly later in life.

This philosophy about locating the education of attitudes at the heart of Christian education among children was expressed through a eucharistically based catechetical programme published by Leslie J. Francis in 1981 under the title *His Spirit is With Us* alongside a companion eucharist book, *The Lord is Here* (Jenkins and Francis, 1978).

Promoting a positive attitude toward religion

Between the ages of seven and eleven children are beginning to develop the attitudes which will shape their later lives. At this stage attitudes are beginning to determine the areas in which the child will concentrate attention and about which he will learn to think maturely at a later stage. Unless positive attitudes are being developed toward the Church at this age, little real learning is likely to take place for some years subsequently.

Leslie J. Francis, 1981, p. 10

Leslie J. Francis' concern with putting the education of attitudes at the heart of Christian education continued with catechetical programmes based on the lectionary in *The Alternative Service Book 1980* (in *The Word for All God's Family* by Francis and Carter, 1996 and Francis and Drayson, 1997) and on the Revised Common Lectionary (in *Learning with the Sunday Gospels* by Francis and Drayson, 1999). A number of other recent catechetical programmes have also placed implicit emphasis on attitude development, although they have tended to make the theoretical underpinning of their approach less explicit.

Can attitudes be assessed?

At the same time as discussing the nature of attitudes, psychologists have been concerned to find ways by which attitudes can be assessed. If, by very definition, attitudes are covert dispositions to respond in certain ways, attitudes cannot be directly observed but can only be inferred from the behaviour to which they give rise. It is verbal behaviour in particular which psychologists have seen as providing the clearest access to underlying and deep-seated attitudes.

Attitude assessment, therefore, tends to be based on sampling people's opinions. While individual opinions may change from day to day, the *pattern* underlying a range of opinions is much more stable. Consequently the techniques of attitude assessment (or attitude scaling) rest on mathematical models of the interrelationship between a range of opinions. While there are several different methods of exploring the mathematical pattern between opinions, one of the best methods in current use was proposed by R. Likert in 1932.

The Likert method of attitude scaling (see Figure 1) invites people to respond to a series of short, sharply focused statements expressing either positive or negative affect. In respect of church, a statement of negative affect might be, 'Church is boring.' People are then able to show the intensity with which they either agree or disagree with the statements by selecting one option on a scale. The most frequently used scale has five points, generally defined as 'agree strongly', 'agree', 'not certain', 'disagree', and 'disagree strongly'.

INSTRUCTIONS Read each of the sentences carefully and think, 'Do I agree with it?'

If you **Agree Strongly**, put a ring round	(AS)	A	NC	D	DS
If you **Agree**, put a ring round	AS	(A)	NC	D	DS
If you are **Not Certain,** put a ring round	AS	A	(NC)	D	DS
If you **Disagree**, put a ring round	AS	A	NC	(D)	DS
If you **Disagree Strongly**, put a ring round	AS	A	NC	D	(DS)

Church is boring	AS	A	NC	D	DS

Figure 1: *Likert attitude scaling*

To construct a new attitude scale psychologists generally begin with a much larger pool of items than they propose to include in the final scale. The items are chosen because they *appear* to reflect the attitudinal domain to be assessed and because they are clearly affective in their tone. These items are then tested in pilot studies in order to discover which ones remain most stable and pattern in a coherent way. To pass the test for further use the smaller set of items selected to form the attitude scale must be both reliable and valid.

Assessing attitude toward Christianity

In the early 1970s, following Likert's method of scaling, Leslie J. Francis set out to develop a scale of attitude toward Christianity capable of assessing attitude change and development during childhood, through adolescence, and into adulthood. Beginning with an initial pool of 110 items, tested through a series of pilot studies, Francis selected 24 items which worked in a consistent way among 8-year-olds and among adults. The story about the development of this instrument and the first 100 or so studies in which it was used is documented by William K. Kay and Leslie J. Francis in their book, *Drift from the Churches: Attitude Toward Christianity during Childhood and Adolescence* (1996).

In order to develop an instrument which would make sense to 8-year-olds *and* to adults, Francis needed to define attitude toward Christianity in a way appropriate for those at the lower end of this age range. Since attitudes are concerned with an affective response rather than with an intellectual response it should be possible to identify items which access the attitudinal dimension equally among 8-year-olds and among adults. Attitude toward Christianity was assessed, therefore, by reference to six components of the Christian tradition accessible even to 8-year-olds, namely reference to God, Jesus, Bible, prayer, church services, and Christian worship and education as experienced in school.

Listening to the evidence

In *Drift from the Churches* William K. Kay and Leslie J. Francis (1996) described a number of studies in which this scale of attitude toward Christianity has been used in order to piece together a picture of the factors which help to shape a positive attitude toward Christianity and a picture of some of the personal and social consequences of a positive attitude toward Christianity. The present chapter draws attention to some of the key findings, namely sex differences, age trends, generational trends, home influences, personality, and school influence.

Sex differences

One of the clearest findings to emerge across the various age groups is that girls and women record a more positive attitude toward Christianity than is the case among boys and men. This is also clearly reflected in the way in which most church congregations contain twice as many females as males.

Other research has tended to suggest that Christianity appeals not only more readily to women than to men, but to women and to men who value the feminine side of their own personality. In other words, churches have become highly feminized environments. The clear strength of being a feminized environment is that churches are able to communicate more readily with those of a feminine predisposition. The clear weakness of being a feminized environment is that churches are much less able to communicate with those of a masculine predisposition.

Local churches should not be surprised, therefore, if they find it easier to recruit and to retain girls as participants within activities arranged for children and young people. As a counterbalance to this tendency toward feminization, churches may need to encourage more men into leadership roles for ministry among children and young people.

Age trends

Another of the clearest findings to emerge from research is that the young person's attitude toward Christianity deteriorates steadily between the ages of 8 and 16. There is no one point at which attitude scores suddenly drop. The decline is basically consistent across the age span, and works in a similar way for boys and for girls, although at each age girls record a higher score than boys.

There are two main theories advanced to account for this decline. One theory attributes growing disaffection from Christianity to be a consequence of maturity into the stage of formal operational thinking. The other theory attributes growing disaffection from Christianity to be a consequence of progressive socialization into a predominantly secular culture. The cognitive development theory would suggest a sudden disruption around the ages of 12–14 years, while the socialization theory would suggest a more gradual and progressive decline. The consistent pattern of decline between 8 and 16 clearly favours the socialization theory over the cognitive development theory.

Local churches may, therefore, want to be particularly aware of the ways in which dominant trends in socialization may hasten the drift of young people away from the churches. Such trends may include attractive alternative pursuits for Sunday morning and environments which are well attuned to shifts in popular culture. To remain relevant to the growing young person's life, church too must appeal as an attractive place at which to be seen.

Generational trends

In 1974 Leslie J. Francis set up a systematic survey throughout two secondary schools in East Anglia in order to be able to assess how young people's attitudes toward Christianity were changing from generation to generation. The survey has been repeated every four years among the next generation of young people sitting at the same school desks.

What this study shows is that throughout the 12-year period 1974–86 there was a consistent decline in the young person's attitude toward Christianity. In 1978 there was a less positive attitude than in 1974. In 1982 there was a less positive attitude than in 1978. In 1986 there was a less positive attitude than in 1982. No further decline, however, took place between 1986 and 1994, the most recent survey reported by Kay and Francis (1996). Clearly, to be in a steady state is preferable to being in an environment of growing alienation.

Home influence

In order to be able to assess the influence of mothers and fathers on attitude toward Christianity among their sons and daughters, two large databases were analysed. The first sample comprised 1,747 11- to 12-year-olds and the second sample comprised 1,635 15- to 16-year-olds.

What this study shows is that the mother's church attendance is the most powerful influence on sons' and daughters' church attendance both in the 11- to 12-year-old age range and in the 15- to 16-year-old age range. While the mother has an almost equally strong influence on both sons and daughters, the influence of the father, at both age levels, is noticeably stronger on sons than on daughters. The influence of the father is particularly crucial with regard to 11- to 12-year-old boys. On the brink of the teenage years the support of the father is particularly influential in promoting the religious socialization of sons.

Given the important influence of parents, churches will want to involve parents as much as possible in their programmes of Christian education for children and young people.

Personality

In order to determine whether individual differences in personality played a part in shaping attitudes toward Christianity, a number of studies have been undertaken using different personality theories (see Chapter 17). One of the most promising theories in this regard has been the three-dimensional model of personality proposed by Hans Eysenck and his associates. Eysenck's model of personality speaks in terms of the three higher order factors defined as extraversion, neuroticism and psychoticism.

Extraversion refers to the outgoing person who is sociable and enjoys meeting people. The opposite of extraversion is introversion. Introversion refers to the person who is less at home in social contexts. Time and time again the data make it clear that there is no correlation between the personality dimension of extraversion and attitude toward Christianity.

Neuroticism refers to the anxious person who tends to worry and to fear the worst. The opposite of neuroticism is emotional stability. The emotionally stable person tends not to experience mood swings or excessive anxiety. Time and time again the data make it clear that there is no correlation between the personality dimension of neuroticism and attitude toward Christianity.

Psychoticism refers to the toughminded person who tends not to care what other people think. The opposite of psychoticism is tendermindedness. The tenderminded person tends to show care and empathy for others and to value harmony. Time and time again the data make it clear that there is a significant negative correlation between psychoticism and attitude toward Christianity. In other words tenderminded individuals hold a more positive attitude toward Christianity.

There are two main theories to account for this consistent relationship between tendermindedness and a more positive attitude toward Christianity. One theory argues that the tenderminded individual is more readily socialized into tenderminded social attitudes and that religion properly belongs to the domain of tenderminded social attitudes. The other theory argues that tendermindedness is properly a feminine personality attitude and that the relationship between tendermindedness and a more positive attitude toward Christianity is part of a wider phenomenon, namely the feminization of the Church.

What is clear is that Churches have more difficulty in attracting toughminded individuals across the age span in comparison with attracting tenderminded individuals.

School influence

One of the real strengths of research which uses attitude scales is that it is possible to employ mathematical techniques to sort out the comparative influence of a number of factors working simultaneously to shape attitudes. Attitude scales are useful, therefore, in studies which try to identify the specific influence of school over all the factors like sex, age, personality, ability and home.

A series of four studies reported in *Religion in the Primary School* by Leslie J. Francis (1987) used such mathematical techniques to address the question as to whether Church primary schools contributed to the development of attitudes toward Christianity among their final year pupils.

The data demonstrated that specific influence could be attributed to both Roman Catholic voluntary primary schools and to Church of England voluntary primary schools. The difference was that, while Roman Catholic voluntary primary schools consistently promoted a more positive attitude toward Christianity, some Church of England voluntary primary schools promoted a more negative attitude toward Christianity among their pupils.

These findings suggest that Churches should be able to work in partnership with Church voluntary primary schools to promote a more positive attitude toward Christianity among their pupils. Such a positive outcome cannot, however, be taken for granted without both strategy and commitment.

References and further reading

Francis, L. J. (1981), *His Spirit is With Us*, London, Collins Liturgical Publications.

Francis, L. J. (1987), *Religion in the Primary School: Partnership between Church and State?* London, Collins Liturgical Publications.

Francis, L. J. and Carter, M. (1996), *The Word for All God's Family: Year 1*, Leominster, Gracewing.

Francis, L. J. and Drayson, D. (1997), *The Word for All God's Family: Year 2*, Leominster, Gracewing.

Francis, L. J. and Drayson, D. (1999), *Learning with the Sunday Gospels: Advent to Pentecost*, London, Mowbray.

Francis, L. J. and Drayson, D. (1999), *Learning with the Sunday Gospels: Trinity Sunday to Christ the King*, London, Mowbray.

Goldman, R. J. (1964), *Religious Thinking from Childhood to Adolescence*, London, Routledge & Kegan Paul.

Goldman, R. J. (1965), *Readiness for Religion*, London, Routledge & Kegan Paul.

Jenkins, P. and Francis, L. J. (1978), *The Lord is Here!* London, Collins Liturgical Publications.

Kay, W. K. and Francis, L. J. (1996), *Drift from the Churches: Attitude toward Christianity during Childhood and Adolescence*, Cardiff, University of Wales Press.

13

Religious and Spiritual Experience

Religious experience and spiritual experience can both be quite elusive concepts. The present chapter proposes to concentrate on two strands of research which have helped to shape understanding of these concepts. The first strand was stimulated by the pioneering work of Sir Alister Hardy and the Religious Experience Research Centre which he established in Oxford. The work here has focused largely on the accounts of religious experience provided by adults, although many of these accounts draw on events that occurred earlier in life. The second strand emerges from a project conducted during the 1990s: the Children's Spirituality Project.

Religious Experience Research Centre

In 1969 Sir Alister Hardy, formerly professor of zoology at Oxford University, set up the Religious Experience Research Centre in Oxford. He was interested in the apparently spontaneous religious experiences which happened in the lives of ordinary people. He set out to gather examples of such experiences.

Alister Hardy's books, *The Divine Flame* (1966) and *The Spiritual Nature of Man* (1979), reveal how his early attempts to gather examples of such experiences were not very successful. He then decided to advertise in religious periodicals inviting people to write to him at Oxford to describe their experiences. Still the response was poor. However, when Sir Alister decided to publicize his programme in the secular press the response was much more enthusiastic.

Quite soon Sir Alister had over 4,000 accounts of experiences in his files. At this stage he saw his role as that of the natural historian, collecting and classifying specimens, somewhat like a Victorian naturalist laying down the factual basis for the theories of twentieth-century biology.

The Alister Hardy Question

Have you ever been aware of or influenced by a presence or power, whether you call it God or not, which is different from your everyday self?

David Hay, 1982, p. 113

Clearly, there are serious limitations with the sampling procedures used to generate the religious experiences recorded in the Religious Experience Research Centre's archives. Nonetheless, it proved to be a very successful method for generating a rich pool of material for classification and analysis.

Later on, in 1976, David Hay tested out Alister Hardy's Question in a national random sample of 2,000 adults. Rather more than 36 per cent of the sample said that they had at some time been aware of or influenced by a presence or a power. Further information about these studies is provided in David Hay's two books, *Exploring Inner Space* (1982) and *Religious Experience Today* (1990).

As Director of the Alister Hardy Centre, Edward Robinson produced three important collections of accounts from the archive, published under the following titles: *The Original Vision* (1977), *This Time-Bound Ladder* (1977), and *Living the Questions* (1978). These books demonstrate how important childhood has been for many people as a time for profound religious or spiritual experiences which have played a formative part in shaping their later lives.

Remembering an experience at the age of six years

The first experience of this kind I had was when I was about six years old. At the time I didn't realise it was unusual. I knew it was a very strong experience and it would be with me all my life, but I had no idea that other people hadn't seen what I had seen.

It was early in the evening. I was alone, and I was walking down the village. I felt perfectly at home; I've always loved the dark; I've always loved silence. And there were these beautiful colours, which gave me a feeling of reverence for the whole of creation. And then I asked other people, 'Wasn't the sky beautiful tonight?' And they said, 'What sky?' It baffled me no end, but even so it was years before I realised that I had really seen something which other people presumably had not, and which in fact had not physically existed.

Quoted in Edward Robinson, 1978, pp. 75–6

Remembering an experience at the age of nine years

Ever since I was quite little I always thought a lot about what life is and where it all comes from, and what's beyond: you know, if there is a periphery to the universe and how to get there; and that sort of train of thought leads you pretty far out ... From the first I always wrote, and that to me was a beginning. In particular I remember one experience: I woke up once when I was nine or ten in the middle of the night and wrote a poem out of the blue; and the fact that I did that has always seemed very odd to me, because the poem sort of came 'whole'. I suppose you could call it a sort of mystical poem because it didn't have anything that I could relate to it; it was a kind of mystical vision of space.

Quoted in Edward Robinson, 1978, p. 48

Two women remembering an experience at the age of sixteen years

M: Yes, that's it. It was a beautiful night, with a full moon. We decided to go out in the middle of the night. This was the first time we'd ever done it; we went out on snow-shoes and skis. It was very quiet; we'd had an enormous snowstorm, the trees were just laden, the snow was waist-deep ... We went through some orchards, through pasture, and to the big rock; and then down to the woods. We kept stopping to lick snow off the branches. It was so beautiful, it was unreal.

L: And then – I don't know who started this – we just started laughing, and hugging the birch branches.

M: I think we didn't talk about it – I don't know for how long. But although we'd both been laughing and hugging the birch trees, we were quite silent on the way home. We didn't really say much after that. I think we were almost afraid that the other hadn't quite the same experience, and that if I said, 'That was fantastic, it never happened like that to me before in my life', I was afraid that she might say, you know, 'Oh pretty', or something like that. But I think we kind of knew, watching each other, a bit after, that we had both felt the same thing.

Quoted in Edward Robinson, 1978, pp. 29–32

The Unattended Moment

Working in a somewhat similar tradition to Edward Robinson, Michael Paffard (1976) set out to search autobiographies and memoirs for accounts of religious experience. He, too, chronicles a number of experiences which had occurred early in life.

Remembering an experience at the age of two years

My first awareness of it came at the age of two, when I was being pushed high in a swing, a small wooden chair slung from the branches of a tree. At the top of my swing I looked up and saw a pattern of green leaves against the blue sky. Boundless delight floated me for one moment up into that sky beside the green leaves, a moment I have never forgotten... This 'floating' experience recurred at odd times, always with an uprush of joyousness; I recognized it when it came upon me but took it for granted; there was no need to put it into words.

Willa Muir in Michael Paffard, 1976, p. 17

Remembering an experience at the age of four or five years

Once as I was looking at a calceolaria, fingering the yellow blossom, marvelling at the mouth that opened and shut and the bulbous under-lip specked with crimson, God was with me in the garden. It was a moment in time and yet out of it. I wanted to prolong it. But I could not. It had passed and I was alone.

Elizabeth Hamilton in Michael Paffard, 1976, p. 17

Remembering an experience at the age of five or six years

I must have been between five and six when this experience happened to me. It was a summer morning, and the child I was had walked down through the orchard alone and come out on the brow of a sloping hill where there was grass and a wind blowing and one tall tree reaching into the infinite immensities of blueness. Quite suddenly, after a moment of quietness there, earth and sky and tree and wind-blown grass and the child in the midst of them came alive together with a pulsing light of consciousness. There was a wild foxglove at the child's feet and a bee dozing about it, and to this day I can recall the swift inclusive awareness of each for the whole – I in them and they in me and all of us enclosed in a warm lucent bubble of livingness. I remember the child looking everywhere for the source of this happy wonder, and at last she questioned – 'God?' – because it was the only awesome word she knew.

Mary Austin in Michael Paffard, 1976, pp. 17–18

Remembering an experience at the age of ten years

I think that in my early boyhood my beliefs were something like this. There existed, above the bright blue sky, a Heavenly City. This was a place pervaded by light and music. I was not unaware of its joys, because one night, when I was about eight or so, I retired to bed on my little iron bed-stead in the small, cold, attic bedroom. I put my head on the pillow and closed my eyes. Suddenly, and for a timeless moment, I had an experience of pure joy. In spite of my closed eyes, I was aware that the room was suffused with a warm light. This effluence was in some indescribable way composed of music. The music was formless, beyond comprehension, and not to be retained in memory.

Vicars Bell in Michael Paffard, 1976, p. 18

Children's Spirituality Project

The Children's Spirituality Project grew out of the concerns of the Religious Experience Research Centre and was shaped by the research perspectives of David Hay. Full details are provided in *The Spirit of the Child* by Hay and Nye (1998). Hay and Nye argue that much of the traditional vocabulary of spirituality is not available to children belonging to a secular culture. This in turn leads to two key problems:
- What conceptual boundaries can be set to the term 'spirituality'?
- How can we identify categories of children's experience which belong to this realm?

In addressing the first question, Hay and Nye quote with approval the following extract from Karl Rahner's *Theological Investigations* (1974, p. 160) which invites us to imagine a world in which all religious institutions have disappeared and the word 'God' no longer exists.

And even if this term were ever to be forgotten, even then in the decisive moments of our lives we should still be constantly encompassed by this nameless mystery of our existence... even supposing that those realities which we call religions... were totally to disappear... the transcendentality inherent in human life is such that [we] would still reach out toward that mystery which lies outside [our] control.

Accordingly Hay and Nye conceive of an innate spiritual capacity in childhood, but recognize that this may focus in particular ways and take different and changing forms as children's other capacities develop.

In addressing the second question, Hay and Nye propose a set of three interrelated themes or categories of spiritual sensitivity, which they define as:
- awareness sensing
- mystery sensing
- value sensing

The first category associated with spirituality, awareness sensing, typically refers to a reflexive or meta-cognitive process, that of being attentive toward one's attention or being aware of a particular sensation or awareness. Four sub-categories of awareness sensing are defined as: here and now, tuning, flow, and focusing.

The second category associated with spirituality, mystery sensing, typically refers to experience that is in principle incomprehensible and indicative of the transcendent. Two sub-categories of mystery sensing are defined as: wonder and awe, and imagination.

The third category, value sensing, emphasizes the role played by emotion in spirituality. Three sub-categories of value sensing are delight and despair, ultimate goodness, and meaning.

In the course of their project a total of 38 children had conversations with Rebecca Nye, 18 of whom were aged between 6 and 7, and 20 between 10 and 11. Of the 38 children, 28 were classified as having no religious affiliation, four were Church of England, four were Muslim and two were Roman Catholic. The children were recruited from one school in Nottingham and one school in Birmingham. Nye had up to three meetings with each of the children, and each tape-recorded conversation lasted about half an hour. The children were interviewed on a one-to-one basis.

The conversation with each child began with a very loosely-structured, light chat about the child's interests and life story. The transition from general issues toward spirituality was typically (but not always) initiated by inviting the children to talk about one of a set of photographs.

Photographs used to stimulate conversation

The following images were included in the project:
- a girl gazing into a fire;
- a boy looking out of his bedroom window at the stars;
- a girl looking tearfully at her dead pet gerbil in its cage;
- a boy standing by himself in a playground, ignored and perhaps unhappy;
- a boy standing on a wet pavement, having dropped some food on the ground, looking up with his hands spread out;
- scenes of waves whipped up in stormy weather.

Hay and Nye, 1998, p. 88

During the major part of the discussion there was no overt mention of religion or religious experience unless the subject was brought up spontaneously by the child. However, toward the end of the sequence of meetings, if religion had not emerged spontaneously as a subject it was introduced, usually by asking about school assembly. Finally, if it seemed appropriate, direct reference to religion or spiritual awareness might be mentioned and the children might be asked whether they recognized this area in their own experience.

The tape-recorded conversations with these 38 children generated over 1,000 typed pages of transcript. Nye decided to approach these data in two ways.

The first approach resembled that of case studies. Nye interrogated the transcripts of individual children in order to identify each child's individual spirituality. Here she spoke in terms of a kind of personal 'signature' for each child. Nye introduced the spiritual signature of a girl named Ruth (Hay and Nye, 1998, p. 85) by drawing attention to the way in which she imagined heaven:

> A mist of perfume, with gold walls, and a rainbow stretched over God's throne... but a transparent mist, like a ... I can't explain it. Like a smell. A real cloud of smell, a lovely smell ... like the smell that you get when you wake up on a dull winter morning, and then when you go to sleep, and you wake up, the birds are chirping, and the last drops of snow are melting away, and the treetops, shimmering in the breeze, and it's a spring morning... (Then she added:) I suppose it's not a season at all, not really, because (it's) just a day in delight, every day.

Interpreting this passage, Nye comments as follows:

> Ruth's imaginative response, drawing on nature, her senses and an appreciation of the mysterious transformations that occur in life, pervaded many of her comments in other 'non-religious' contexts. This could be traced to the opening remarks in her first interview. When offered the choice to draw 'anything at all' while we chatted, she replied: 'I like nature... (Why?)... just because I like it. I don't know. And it's so beautiful to be in the world.'

Reflecting on the 'signature phenomenon', Nye draws the following conclusion (Hay and Nye, 1998, p. 99):

> The practical implication is that one needs to enquire carefully about and attend to each child's personal style if one is to 'hear' their spirituality at all. At a theoretical level this implies that we cannot neatly distinguish the spiritual aspects from the psychological features of a child's life.

The second approach tried to identify patterns or conclusions which were common across the individual children. In this connection Nye identified two different kinds of conversation which were of particular relevance:
- dialogue that employed religious ideas and language;
- non-religious dialogue that implicitly conveyed that the child was engaged in something more than the casual or mundane.

As an example of 'religious dialogue' Nye draws on conversations with 6-year-old John (Hay and Nye, 1998, pp. 101–2). John came from a family which was sympathetic to Christian belief but attended church no more than twice a year. Having listened to John's religious beliefs, Nye asked him how he came to hold his beliefs. In his response John described a religious experience (Hay and Nye, 1998, p. 102):

> I worked about it and I received... one day... I was with my mum and I begged her... um... for me to go to um... some church. And we did it and... I

prayed ... and after that praying ... I knew that good was on my side. And I heard him in my mind say this: 'I am with you. Every step you go. The Lord is with you. May sins be forgiven.'

Later John described his encounter with the Holy Spirit in the following terms:

Well once I went um ... in the night and I saw this bishopy kind of alien. I said, 'Who are you?' And he said, 'I am the Holy Spirit.' I did think he was the Holy Spirit.

As an example of 'implicitly spiritual discourse' Nye draws on a conversation with 10-year-old Harriet. Toward the end of the conversation Harriet generated a flood of unanswerable questions, culminating in wondering about the origin of the universe and human life. Finally, Harriet suggested that, faced with such mystery yet yearning for meaning, 'Perhaps we've got to, like, ask the clouds. The clouds have been there millions and millions of years.'

Nye concluded from this analysis that there is a continuum of children's spirituality. At one end are those who perceive spiritual matters in terms of questions or principles. Then there are those who go on to make unconscious or conscious associations with the traditional language of religion. At the other end of the continuum are those who have experienced their spirituality directly and personally in the form of religious insights.

References and further reading

Hardy, A. (1966), *The Divine Flame*, London, Collins.
Hardy, A. (1979), *The Spiritual Nature of Man*, Oxford, Oxford University Press.
Hay, D. (1982), *Exploring Inner Space*, Harmondsworth, Penguin.
Hay, D. (1990), *Religious Experience Today: Studying the Facts*, London, Mowbray.
Hay, D. and Nye, R. (1998), *The Spirit of the Child*, London, HarperCollins.
Hood, R. W. (ed.) (1995), *Handbook of Religious Experience*, Birmingham, Alabama, Religious Education Press.
Paffard, M. (1976), *The Unattended Moment*, London, SCM Press.
Rahner, K. (1974), *Theological Investigations II*, London, Darton, Longman & Todd.
Robinson, E. (1977), *The Original Vision*, Oxford, Religious Experience Research Unit.
Robinson, E. (1977), *This Time-Bound Ladder*, Oxford, Religious Experience Research Unit.
Robinson, E. (1978), *Living the Questions*, Oxford, Religious Experience Research Unit.

14

Religious Thinking and the Bible

Introduction

The notion of 'religious thinking' came into prominence during the mid-1960s as part of the title of a highly influential book written by Ronald Goldman (1964), *Religious Thinking from Childhood to Adolescence*. Goldman worked as a research psychologist to discover how religious thinking changed or developed during childhood and adolescence. The aims of this chapter are to:

- clarify what is meant by religious thinking
- examine Goldman's research
- assess what can be learnt from this research

What is religious thinking?

The notion of religious thinking can mean different things to different people. Goldman used the words to describe ordinary thinking processes applied to religious subject-matter. He was concerned with how young people thought about religious issues.

Religious thinking

The view I maintain throughout this book is that religious thinking is no different in mode and method from non-religious thinking. Religious thinking is a shortened form of expressing the activity of thinking directed toward religion, not a term meaning separate rationality.

Ronald Goldman, 1964, p. 304

Goldman's definition of *religious thinking* as *thinking about religion* distinguishes this activity from two other rather different activities which may best be described as *thinking religiously* and *thinking in religious language*.

Thinking religiously describes a way of looking at the world and interpreting day-to-day experience through religious categories. The person who sees the hand of God behind good fortune is interpreting that experience religiously or thinking religiously.

Thinking in religious language describes how we use the special forms of language that characterize religious speech. The person who describes God as an 'almighty father' is using everyday language in a special and somewhat odd manner. That person is thinking in religious language.

The strength and the limitation of Ronald Goldman's work is that he was concerned specifically and exclusively with how young people think *about* religious issues.

Research background

Ronald Goldman conducted his research within the theoretical framework of stage development theory established by Jean Piaget. Piaget's view is that children and young people progress and develop through a sequence of hierarchical stages, characterized as pre-operational thinking, concrete operational thinking, and formal operational thinking. According to Piaget these three stages are qualitatively different from one another.

At the pre-operational stage thinking is transductive, that is, inferring one particular fact from another particular fact. Isolated features of a problem only are seen, our understanding is limited by attention to one aspect of a situation. The child mistakes peripheral aspects of a problem for the central aspect. The child finds it difficult to relate one problem to another and cannot see that a partial solution only creates new problems. There is little systematic thinking. Thinking is partial, fragmented and inconsistent. At this stage thought is not reversible.

At the concrete operational stage inductive and deductive logic can be used, but this is limited to concrete solutions, actions, visual and sensory data. Data are correctly classified, systematic thinking is now evident and two or more aspects of a solution can be put together. With concrete data reversibility is evident. The child can concentrate on relating things visibly or tangibly present. The limitations of this stage can be seen in the child's judgement on verbal problems and problem situations which require a more abstract level of thought.

At the formal operational stage the capacity to think hypothetically and deductively is achieved. The data of thinking now changes and solutions are seen in terms of propositions, which may be logically true or false. Logical thinking is now possible in symbolic and abstract terms. Incompatibility of certain facts with an hypothesis is clearly seen. The thinker will often start with an hypothesis and work from that, rather than begin with the facts. Reasoning is reversible in terms of propositions, and reasoning by implication is also evident.

Research method

Those who followed in Piaget's footsteps often spoke in terms of conducting their research by means of clinical interviews. Ronald Goldman followed this tradition. The clinical interview technique meant that Goldman interviewed children in depth one at a time following a structured sequence of questions. The conversation in the interview was driven by two main devices: tape-recorded stories and projective picture tests.

Recorded stories

First, the pupils were asked to listen to three tape-recorded Bible stories: Moses and the burning bush, the Israelites crossing the Red Sea and the temptations of Jesus in the wilderness. For a full appreciation of this part of the research, it is necessary to look at one of the three Bible passages used and to examine the questions employed to probe the passage. Here is the way in which Goldman presented the story of the burning bush, not by using a recognized translation of the account in the Bible, but by creating his own paraphrase:

A man called Moses was one day looking after a flock of sheep in a rather lonely place, close to a mountain.

Suddenly an angel appeared to Moses in a flame of fire, out of the middle of a bush. The curious thing was that the fire was burning away, but the bush itself wasn't burnt.

Moses said to himself, 'I must go and look at it closer, to see why the bush isn't burned.' Now when God saw Moses come nearer to the bush, God called out from the middle of the bush, 'Moses! Moses!' And Moses, not knowing who it was calling, said, 'Here I am.'

And God said, 'Come no closer and take off your shoes. You are standing on holy ground.' Then God spoke again and said, 'I am your father's God, and the God of great men like Abraham and Isaac and Jacob.'

Then Moses hid his face, for he was afraid to look at God.

Here are four of the eight questions which Goldman asked about this passage to probe the children's 'religious thinking' about the story. Only answers to the three questions marked with an asterisk were interpreted to assess Piagetian stages of thinking.

It says at the end of the story that Moses hid his face because he was afraid to look at God.
- Why do you think Moses was afraid to look at God? Any other reason(s)?*
- Should he have been afraid to look at God? Yes/No/d.k. Why?/Why not?
- Would you have been afraid? Yes/No/d.k. Why?/Why not?
Supposing Moses had got over his fear and looked at God.
- What do you think he would have seen?
- What sort of man, face, expression, light, fire, angel?
Why do you think the ground upon which Moses stood was holy?*
- Is God everywhere? Yes/No/d.k./unsure. Then is everywhere holy, or just special places?
- Is this ground holy? Yes/No/d.k./unsure. Why? Why not?
How would you explain the bush burning, and yet not being burnt?
- How do you think such a thing could happen?*

Projective pictures

Second, the pupils were asked to look at three pictures, one at a time, and to answer questions about the pictures. The pictures were used as a 'projective device'. Each picture presented a child of the same sex and age as the child being interviewed. The assumption is that when answering for the child in the picture, the interviewee is answering about himself or herself. The three pictures showed a family going to church, a boy or a girl at prayer, and a boy or a girl looking at a mutilated Bible.

Here are some of the questions Goldman posed about the picture showing a boy or a girl praying:

To whom is the boy/girl praying?
What does the boy/girl pray about?
- For *himself*? What does he pray for himself?
- For *others*? What does he pray for others?
- Are there any favourite prayers he says each time he prays?
Why do you think the boy/girl prays?
Is God/Jesus/Spirit . . . there in the room with the boy/girl?
If He is, how does the boy/girl know He is there?

- Can he hear God's voice?
- Can he see God in any way?
- Can he feel God in any way?

Sample

Employing this amount of material in a clinical interview is time consuming. As a consequence Ronald Goldman based his findings on a sample of 200 pupils, ten boys and ten girls within each year group between the ages of 6 and 17, treating 15-, 16- and 17-year-olds as one age group.

Analysis

Using the statistical technique of scalogram analysis, Goldman interpreted the findings of these interviews as evidence for the view that religious thinking develops through an invariant sequence of stages during childhood and adolescence in line with the Piagetian model. This analysis was based on the pupils' answers to just five of the many questions asked in the interviews. On the basis of this analysis Goldman concluded that before the onset of formal operational thinking, occurring from the age of 13 or 14 upwards, religious thinking was seriously restricted.

The problem Goldman faced in his analysis of the replies to his questions was to distinguish between the *processes* of religious thinking (with which Piagetian psychology is mainly concerned) and the *content* of religious thinking (with which theology is mainly concerned). Rereading Goldman's study, it seems that he valued a liberal theological position more highly than a conservative theological position.

On the basis of the answers to his questions Ronald Goldman illustrated five different stages of religious thinking, which he described as:

- intuitive religious thinking (up to about 7/8 years)
- intermediate intuitive-concrete religious thinking
- concrete religious thinking (about 7/8 to 13/14 years)
- intermediate concrete-abstract religious thinking
- abstract religious thinking (13/14 years onwards)

Each of these stages will be illustrated from Goldman's own writing.

Intuitive religious thinking

The first question was: 'Why was Moses afraid to look at God?' When the child answers, 'God had a funny face' he is introducing an irrelevancy and centring his thinking only upon this. 'Funny', in this context, means horrid or horrible, not 'humorous'. Similarly, the child who says 'Moses was frightened of the rough voice', and another who answers 'It was because he hadn't spoken politely to God' reveal the same problem. This latter is a clear case of transductive thinking, from one particular aspect to another, with no clear evidence to support the inference. To the second question, 'Why do you think the ground on which Moses stood was holy?' one answer was 'Because there was grass on it.' The warning notices in public parks perhaps is the associated off-centre idea...Here is a strong egocentric element. Another child introduces a curious literalism by saying, 'He was standing on a ho.'

Ronald Goldman, 1964, p. 52

Intermediate intuitive-concrete religious thinking

An example of inefficient classifying can be seen in the child's answers to 'Why was Moses afraid to look at God?' which was 'Because God wears a beard and Moses doesn't like beards.' This attempt to relate more than one aspect of the situation, God wearing a beard and Moses' alleged dislike of beards, breaks down simply because the fact that Moses had not yet looked at God is missed. Another boy puts Moses' fear down to the fact that God 'might kill Moses for making the bush on fire', an obvious attempt to relate two features of the story unsuccessfully.

Typical of this period is the circular argument such as the answer to 'Why was the ground, on which Moses stood, holy?' Here the child states, 'It was holy because it said it was. *Why?* Because God blessed it. *Why did God bless it?* Because it was holy!'

Ronald Goldman, 1964, p. 54

Concrete religious thinking

The clear system where several aspects are related, but confined to concrete relations, is seen in answer to, 'Why was Moses afraid to look at God?' Children at this stage see God as a man or a power threatening specific action, sometimes because a specific wrong has been mentioned and punishment is feared for it. For example, 'Moses thought God would chase him out of the holy ground, because Moses hadn't taken off his shoes.' Another, slight variant of this, is 'Moses hadn't been going to Church or anything like that. *Why should that make him afraid to look at God?* God wouldn't like him any more and not make him go up to heaven.' An interesting sidelight on her moral concept of God can be seen when this same girl then states: 'Moses hadn't prayed, and God wouldn't forgive him if he had done anything wrong.' Most other answers at this stage tend to centre upon the light or fire as the source of Moses' fears. 'Because it was a ball of fire. He thought it was coming nearer. It might burn him', says one child.

Ronald Goldman, 1964, p. 56

Intermediate concrete-abstract religious thinking

The attempt to break away from concrete elements can be seen in reasons advanced for Moses' fear of looking at God. At the previous stage children cited a specific wrongdoing as the basis of Moses' fear. Here the concrete wrong gives place to a generalised statement, 'Perhaps he had done evil things. *How would that make him afraid?* He would be ashamed to look at God.' But this proposition is somewhat diluted by the later statement by the same child. 'Moses was afraid because all the names God mentioned were great people. *How would this affect Moses?* Well, Moses had killed a man.' This also illustrates the ability to go outside the story and need to form a hypothesis. The general ideas of Moses' unworthiness is put forward as a propositional statement but often for a concrete reason such as 'he smelled of the sheep.' One girl expressly states 'I'd be scared. *Why?* God is good and if I'd done something wrong I wouldn't like to face him.'

Ronald Goldman, 1964, p. 58

Abstract religious thinking

There is clearly a wide difference in quality between the pupil who had just entered this stage and the older adolescent who had become accustomed to this mode of thought over a period of years. They share, however, the same characteristic of having achieved a liberation from concrete limitations. Consequently in answer to Moses' fear, the general proposition is frequently made that Moses shared with all men a general sense of sin or unworthiness, which made him hesitate to look at God. 'God is holy and the world is sinful.' Sometimes this is stated specifically as 'The awesomeness and almightiness of God would make Moses feel like a worm in comparison.' A girl who had just achieved the abstract stage puts it a little more crudely, 'Moses might be frightened because God was great. He'd never followed him before', but the essence is there. More advanced is the view that Moses like most people of his day, 'would have a primitive feeling of awe'. The critical examination of an hypothesis is well illustrated by one pupil's answers to why the ground was holy, when he said, 'Can God have a greater degree of presence? I'm not sure. Wasn't it supposed to be the Lord's mountain? Wasn't it a volcano and what they couldn't understand they called holy, something dangerous to be left alone?'

Ronald Goldman, 1964, p. 60

Readiness for Religion

A year after publishing his research findings in *Religious Thinking from Childhood to Adolescence* (1964), Ronald Goldman published a second book, *Readiness for Religion* (1965) in which he spelled out the implications of his research findings for religious education in general and teaching the Bible in particular.

The Bible in developmental religious education

I have called attention to both the wasteful effort of teaching the Bible too early and also the difficulties this makes for children of limited development. I would like to correct the widespread misconception that I advocate no Bible teaching before the age of twelve. I do suggest a drastic reduction of Bible material in syllabuses before this age, but the difference does not lie so much in the quantity of Bible material used as in the way in which we use it.

The Bible is the major source book of Christianity *for adults*. It is written by adults for adults and is plainly not a children's book. To help children become familiar with it too early is to invite boredom and confusion.

Ronald Goldman, 1965, pp. 70–1

After Goldman

Goldman's pioneering research encouraged a number of researchers to follow in his footsteps during the late 1960s and the 1970s. They, too, used the clinical interview method and applied this method to other Bible stories and to other projective picture tests. None of these studies, however, made significant advances beyond Goldman's position.

Two other researchers have tried to translate Goldman's theory into pencil and paper tests, namely John Peatling (1974) in the United States and Linnet Smith (1998) in the United Kingdom. Both of these authors have helped to clarify the problems and opportunities in taking seriously research into religious thinking. Critiques of the approaches by Piaget and Goldman are detailed in Chapters 36 and 37. (See also Slee, 1990; Hyde, 1990.)

Conclusion

In essence Goldman's research reminds us that children's minds do not function in the same way as adults' minds. The research does not tell us that we should not teach Bible stories to children, but it does tell us that children will not think about those stories in the same way as we do as adults. Once we discover precisely *how* children think about different Bible stories, then we can make sound judgements about which stories can be taught to best effect at different ages.

References and further reading

Gobbel, R. and Gobbel, G. (1986), *The Bible: A Child's Playground*, London, SCM Press.

Goldman, R. J. (1964), *Religious Thinking from Childhood to Adolescence*, London, Routledge & Kegan Paul.

Goldman, R. J. (1965), *Readiness for Religion*, London, Routledge & Kegan Paul.

Hyde, K. E. (1990), *Religion in Childhood and Adolescence: A Comprehensive Review of the Research*, Birmingham, Alabama, Religious Education Press, Chapters 1, 2 and Appendix F.

Peatling, J. H. (1974), 'Cognitive development in pupils in grades four through twelve: the incidence of concrete and abstract religious thinking', *Character Potential*, 7, 1, pp. 52–61.

Slee, N. M. (1990), 'Getting away from Goldman: changing perspectives on the development of religious thinking', *Modern Churchman*, 32, 1, p. 1–9.

Smith, D. L. (1998), 'That burning bush again: the psychometric assessment of stages in religious thinking', *Journal of Beliefs and Values*, 19, pp. 71–82.

15

Religious Attitudes

Introduction

Some would argue that the most significant dimension of being a religious person is the attitudes shown by that person. To want a child to be religious is to want that child to share these attitudes.

As argued in Chapter 12, our attitudes represent our orientation toward, or away from, something and the way we look on it. They also embody our tendency ('disposition') to behave in a certain way, or to show a particular emotion, toward it. Attitudes are either positive or negative: through our attitudes we show that we are in favour of, or disapprove of, the thing or person or idea in question. This evaluation is usually manifested in our *feelings*, although it also implies certain *beliefs*.

Attitudes are fundamentally *affective*: that is, they are predominantly characterized by feelings, although some attitudes (e.g. neutrality or carefulness) seem to be 'cooler' than others, and may not give rise to emotions. As attitudes are held as dispositions, at any given time they may not be actively producing emotions. So one can dispositionally fear or love someone (i.e. your attitude to them is one of fear or love), even though you are not *feeling* the emotions of love or fear directed to them at this moment.

In his *Introduction to the Psychology of Religion*, Robert Thouless defined religion itself as an attitude: a disposition, orientation or 'mode of adjustment' to reality. Religion, he wrote, is 'a particular kind of attitude toward the world as a whole', an attitude 'which includes reference ... to a spiritual world' whether centred on a belief in God or the gods or not. 'Attitude' is the right word, he argued, because it is 'a generally accepted term for a disposition which includes characteristic ways of behaving, feeling and believing' (Thouless, 1971, pp. 11–12).

This broad 'religious attitude' may be analysed into a wide range of more or less distinctive attitudes to the world (e.g. as created by God), other people (as God's children), and the divine.

The right attitude to religious attitude

The notions of awe, worship and reverence are perhaps *particularly* characteristic of the religious attitude ... It is not the type of *object*, but the type of *attitude*, which defines the activity we want to call 'religion'.

John Wilson, 1971, p. 42

Religious attitudes include:

- assurance and forgiveness
- awe
- commitment
- concern for others
- devotion
- faith
- dread

- gratitude
- hope
- humility
- love
- mercy
- obedience
- openness (to God)

- prayerful attitude
- reverence
- sorrow (for sin)
- trust
- wonder
- worshipful attitude

Many of these underlying attitudes feed emotions and behaviour that carry the same name (love, for example, is also an emotion and 'active love' is an action).

Clearly, most of these attitudes are neither distinctive of – in the sense of unique to – religion, nor do they carry a religious reference, object or orientation 'on their sleeve' (they are only 'implicitly religious'). Other attitudes, such as worship or openness to God, may be regarded as explicitly religious.

Values

To value something is to have a positive feeling toward it. It is to be 'for it', and to believe 'in it'. Such positive evaluations are directed to what are sometimes called our 'values'; our values represent what we value.

When we speak of our 'values' we usually mean those things that we value for themselves, and not just as a means to other ends. These are our 'intrinsic' values – things that we deem to be good in-and-of-themselves. Other things may only be 'instrumentally valuable': we value them as *means* toward the creation of good ends. 'Why do you want to go to church?' is a reasonable question, to which the answer 'to worship God' is a reasonable answer. But how can we answer the question, 'Why do you want to worship God?' (or 'Why do you love' someone?) except by replying, 'Because I just do.' This is an ultimate desire, which we regard as intrinsically valuable. Nothing further is needed to justify it.

Our religious attitudes are to be included in the list of our religious values, because we *value* attitudes such as humility, compassion, trust and forgiveness. Not all of our values may be regarded as religious, however, and some may be rejected by some religions – or at least valued only as means and not as ends in themselves. 'Domination' may be one such value; 'pride' may be another. What do you make of the following list of contentious 'values', and which would you want the children in your church, or your own children, to adopt?

- ambition
- chastity
- excitement
- happiness

- modesty
- pleasure
- popularity
- power

- respect for elders
- success
- wealth
- humility

Meaning

Some have argued that to ascribe value to something is to give it meaning and to love it for its own sake. Ascribing or finding meaning in situations and events is central to our life as human beings. We are 'meaning-making' animals, forever evaluating things – adopting an attitude toward them and prescribing that attitude to others. Religious valuations are central to the 'meaning dimension' of religion. Christian education may be viewed largely as the creation of a Christian world of Christian meaning and of Christian values.

The meaning of meaning

We... know the meaning of something when we know what attitude we ought to have toward it. We know the meaning of a situation when we know what we ought to do in that situation. We know the meaning of life when we know what ideals and objectives we ought to pursue in life.

Vincent Brümmer, 1981, p. 121

Worship

Central to all this is the notion of worship. The English word derives from the Old English *weorthscipe*, which means 'worthiness' or 'acknowledgement of worth'. To engage in religious worship, and to adopt a 'worshipful' attitude, is to ascribe supreme worth and ultimate value and meaning to the object of worship. Only God can be said to be wholly worthy of worship in this way.

John Wilson (1971, 1992) has argued that an essential part of religious education is an 'education of the emotions' in the sense of helping children to become more reasonable in the sphere of religious emotion, educating them about what they ought to feel. The emotions he is particularly concerned with are those that relate to praise, admiration, wonder and worship, especially *awe*. The education of the emotion (and underlying attitude) of awe involves getting children to think rationally about the 'appropriateness' of various objects of awe and worship.

What should we worship?

Religion is peculiarly concerned with *what one worships* which is in turn connected with what one thinks one ought to be in awe of, feel humble toward, reverence, and so forth. It is concerned with certain *emotions* being directed toward certain *objects of emotions:* awe and love for God, guilt for sin, reverence for the Buddha, etc. The crucial questions here are of the form 'What should one worship?', 'Should one worship at all?', or 'Is there anything in the universe of which we should be in awe?' The educator's job is not to answer these questions *for* children, but to give them those qualities and abilities that they need in order to work out possible answers for themselves as reasonably as possible...

We all know that emotions can be in various ways reasonable or unreasonable; they can be excessive or insufficient, directed to proper or improper objects, based on true or false beliefs. To worship Hitler, for instance, is in some ways like wanting to marry the wrong girl, or wanting to be like a gangster hero. Education in religion is education in *one* (very important) sphere in which the emotions enter.

John Wilson, 1992, pp. 11–12

Fundamental attitudes

Donald Evans (1979) characterizes eight 'attitude-virtues' that undergird both religion and morality. Evans' attitude-virtues are intrinsic values (good-in-themselves), but they are also components of human flourishing. This means that we are better and – in a deep sense – happier (more fulfilled) people when we have these. They are all *human* values, but they do have a transcendent role – in fact two roles, because when we adopt them we may be better placed to have an experience of God, and their adoption may only be rationally justified if there is a God who is the proper object of our trust.

Here is Evans' list of attitude-virtues and the opposing 'attitude-vices'. We may think of them as universal 'human' and 'spiritual' values that all children need to develop:

- *Basic trust* [the opposite of which is basic distrust]
  Evans writes that basic trust is an inner stance 'which one brings *to* each situation . . . It is an initial openness to whatever is life-affirming in nature and other people and oneself' (Evans, 1979, p. 2). It is a basic trust-readiness or confidence that reality has meaning, can be accepted and appreciated, and will satisfy our deepest needs. The first years of life is the crucial time for the development of trust, on which all the other virtues build.
- *Humility* [opposites: pride *or* self-humiliation]
  This is the realistic acceptance and exercise of our own powers and freedom.
- *Self-acceptance* [opposite: self-rejection]
  This is the acceptance of oneself and the rejection of pervasive guilt about oneself.
- *Responsibility* [opposite: irresponsibility]
  This is the conscientiousness and competence of a trustworthy person.
- *Self-commitment* [opposite: alienated dissipation of self]
  This is the integration of personality and the attitude of 'being true to oneself'.
- *Friendliness* [opposite: self-isolation]
  This is the willingness of a person to enter an I–Thou relationship of love.
- *Concern* [opposite: self-indulgence]
  This represents a person's willingness to help others pastorally or prophetically.
- *Contemplation* [opposite: self-preoccupation *or* self-consciousness]
  Evans describes this in terms of the stance of a person 'who profoundly appreciates the reality and uniqueness of each particular in the universe', including himself or herself, and is 'liberated from the self-preoccupation and self-consciousness which distort and subjectivise our usual perception of reality' (Evans, 1979, p. 7). It is fostered by various forms of meditation that discipline the attention, cleanse the vision and open the heart. Together with concern and friendliness, it is a species of love.

Other authors have similar lists of 'mature religious attitudes' that we may be concerned to develop in ourselves and our children. Here is another example (Meadow and Kahoe, 1984, pp. 395–8):

- self-objectivity (seeing yourself as others see you)
- acceptance of oneself and others (self- and other-forgiveness)
- concern for ultimate good and courage to live for higher values
- orientation away from idolatry (which is the attitude of ascribing supreme worth to what is partial and limited)

References and further reading

Astley, J. (1994), *The Philosophy of Christian Religious Education*, Birmingham, Alabama, Religious Education Press, Chapters 6 and 9.

Batson, C. D., Schoenrade, P. and Ventis, W. L. (1993), *Religion and the Individual: A Social-Psychological Perspective*, New York, Oxford University Press.

Beit-Hallahmi, B. and Argyle, M. (1997), *The Psychology of Religious Behaviour, Belief and Experience*, London, Routledge.

Brown, L. B. (1987), *The Psychology of Religious Belief*, London, Academic Press, Chapter 6.

Brümmer, V. (1981), *Theology and Philosophical Inquiry: An Introduction*, London, Macmillan, Part 2.

Evans, D. (1979), *Struggle and Fulfillment: The Inner Dynamics of Religion and Morality*, Cleveland, Ohio, Collins.

Francis, L. J. (2001), *The Values Debate: A Voice from the Pupils*, London, Woburn.

Hyde, K. E. (1990), *Religion in Childhood and Adolescence: A Comprehensive Review of the Research*, Birmingham, Alabama, Religious Education Press, Chapter 8.

Jacobs, M. (1993), *Living Illusions: A Psychology of Belief*, London, SPCK.

Lee, J. M. (1984), *The Content of Religious Instruction*, Birmingham, Alabama, Religious Education Press, Chapter 5.

Meadow, M. J. and Kahoe, R. D. (1984), *Psychology of Religion: Religion in Individual Lives*, New York, Harper & Row.

Thouless, R. H. (1971), *An Introduction to the Psychology of Religion*, Cambridge, Cambridge University Press.

Wilson, J. (1971), *Education in Religion and the Emotions*, London, Heinemann.

Wilson, J. (1992), 'First steps in religious education', in B. Watson (ed.), *Priorities in Religious Education: A Model for the 1990s and Beyond*, London, Falmer, pp. 10–25.

16

Children and Prayer

Although prayer is so central to religious faith comparatively few research studies have been undertaken into the place of prayer during childhood and adulthood. Recent reviews of the state of knowledge in the field have been provided by Laurence Brown in his book *The Human Side of Prayer* (1994), and by Leslie J. Francis and Jeff Astley in their reader, *Psychological Perspectives on Prayer* (2001).

The aim of the present chapter is to draw attention to four main strands of research which have investigated different aspects of prayer during childhood and adolescence. Each of these strands will be illustrated by one key study. The first strand, grounded in developmental psychology, has attempted to discover stages in the development of prayer. The second strand has concentrated on mapping changing patterns of belief in the causal efficacy of prayer during childhood and adolescence. The third strand, grounded in social psychology, has attempted to discover the social and contextual influences on individual differences in the practice of praying during childhood and adolescence. The fourth strand, also grounded in social psychology, has attempted to identify the consequences of prayer in the lives of young people.

Stage development

A good example of research concerned with identifying stages in the development of the concept of prayer is provided by the study entitled 'The child's conception of prayer' by Diane Long, David Elkind and Bernard Spilka. This study was first published in 1967 and has been reprinted in *Psychological Perspectives on Prayer* (Francis and Astley, 2001, pp. 37–47).

The aim of Long, Elkind and Spilka's study was to trace empirically the development of the prayer concept as it evolved in the elementary school child. More particularly their concern was with the developmental changes that occurred in the form and content of the prayer concept and in the fantasies and feelings associated with it.

Sample

The subjects for this study were 160 boys and girls between the ages of 5 and 12. Of them, 132 attended one of two private schools in suburban Denver. The remaining 28 were obtained directly from homes in the middle class suburban neighbourhood. The children were selected so that there were 20 at each year of age. They were divided approximately equally between boys and girls.

Each child was individually interviewed. To orient the child and to build rapport, he or she was first shown two pictures in which families were engaged in prayer, and then asked to describe what was going on in the scenes.

In order to explore developmental changes in the *form* of the prayer concept, the following semi-structured questions were employed:
- Do you pray? Does your family pray? Do all boys and girls in the world pray?
- Do dogs and cats pray?
- What is a prayer?
- Can you pray for more than one thing?
- What must you do if your prayer is answered?
- What must you do if your prayer is not answered?

In order to explore developmental changes in the *context* of children's prayer activity and the *fantasies* and *affects* associated with such activities, four incomplete sentences and two open-ended questions were employed. The incomplete sentences were:
- I usually pray when...
- Sometimes I pray for...
- When I pray I feel...
- When I see someone praying I...

The open-ended questions were:
- Where do prayers come from?
- Where do prayers go?

On the basis of the data generated by this study Long, Elkind and Spilka identified three stages in the development of the concept of prayer:

1 In the first stage between the ages of 5 and 7, children had a global conception of prayer in the sense that their comprehension of the term was both vague and fragmentary. Although they had a dim awareness that prayers were somehow linked with the term 'God' and with certain learned formulae such as 'Now I lay me down to sleep', there was little real comprehension of the meaning of prayer. For example, Nancy, aged 5, answered the question, 'What is a prayer?' by saying, 'A prayer is about God, rabbits, dogs and fairies and deer, and Santa Claus and turkeys and pheasants, and Jesus and Mary and Mary's little baby.'
2 In the second stage, between the ages of 7 and 9, children had a concrete differentiated conception of prayer and recognized that it involved verbal activity. At this stage, however, prayer was still an external activity, a routine form, rather than personal and internal. At this stage children never rose above the actual behaviours associated with prayer to its mental and affective aspects which to the older child and adult are its essence. For example, Jimmy, aged 7, answered the question, 'What is prayer?' by saying, 'That we should have water, food, rain and snow. It's something you ask God for, water, food, rain and snow.'
3 In the third stage, between the ages of 9 and 12, children had an abstract conception of prayer in the sense that it was regarded as an internal activity deriving from personal conviction and belief. At this stage prayer emerged as a type of private conversation with God involving things not talked about with other people. Implicit in the replies at this stage was a distinction, that seldom if ever occurred in younger children, between what one *thinks* and what one *says*. For example, Dell, aged 10, answered the question, 'What is prayer?' by saying 'Prayer is a way to communicate with God... Sometimes you just want to talk to somebody, you just can always go to God and talk to him.'

The following age trend was identified with respect to the content of prayer. Among the younger children, the concept of prayer was primarily concerned with the gratification of personal desires. With increasing age, however, there was a shift from asking for particular things for themselves to thanking God for things which they had already received. There was also an increasing concern among the older children with more humanitarian and altruistic requests such as for 'peace' or for the 'poor and the sick'. At the same time there was a decline in the tendency merely to recite standard prayers such as 'God bless mother, father.' Thus, with increasing age the content of prayer became more personal and individualized, but at the same time less egoistic and less self-centred.

Causal efficacy of prayer

A good example of research concerned with mapping changing patterns of belief in the causal efficacy of prayer is provided by the study entitled 'Egocentric thought in petitionary prayer: a cross-cultural study' by Laurence Brown. This study was first published in 1966 and has been reprinted in *Psychological Perspectives on Prayer* (Francis and Astley, 2001, pp. 25–36).

The aim of Brown was to trace empirically the changing pattern of belief in the causal efficacy of prayer between the ages of 12 and 17 in three different samples of young people from different countries.

Sample

The subjects for this study were 398 boys and 703 girls, aged 12 to 17 from selected schools in the United States, New Zealand and South Australia; 489 pupils were from the United States, 263 from New Zealand and 349 from South Australia.

A questionnaire was administered by Brown himself during class time, with a standard introduction which did not specifically maintain that the study was concerned with beliefs about petitionary prayer.

The questionnaire depicted seven situations involving prayer: success in a football match, safety during battle, avoidance of detection of theft, repayment of a debt, fine weather for a church fête, escape from a shark and recovery of a sick grandmother. In relation to each situation Brown addresses two questions: Is it right to pray in this situation? Are the prayers likely to have any effect?

Escape from a shark

James fell into the sea from a yacht. He started to swim toward the boat that was coming to rescue him, but saw the black fin of a shark between him and the boat. He prayed that he might escape the shark.

1 Was James right to pray for his escape?
2 What kind of a prayer might he have offered?
3 Would the fact that James prayed make it more likely that he would escape?
4 If the man in the boat rescuing James prayed too, would James be even more likely to escape?

Brown's main conclusion from his data was that there is a consistent age-related trend away from belief in the causal efficacy of petitionary prayer, and this trend is stable across three Western Christian cultures. Brown also demonstrates that belief in the causal efficacy of prayer is related to the moral circumstances of the prayer. Prayer for the avoidance of detection of theft is thought to be less likely to have a positive effect than prayer for a sick grandmother.

Belief in the causal efficacy of prayer in the situations studied is related to the suitability or appropriateness of a particular situation for prayer. The moral evaluation of situations in which prayer is offered is the most important variable influencing belief about the suitability of prayer and shows one way in which training may overlay the age trend. Situations involving moral disapproval, intervention within natural processes, and trivial actions are thought to be relatively unsuitable for prayer. Such situations are also those in which prayer is believed to be relatively ineffective, particularly when compared with the greater effectiveness of prayer in situations of *personal* danger.

Social and contextual influences

A good example of research concerned with discovering the social and contextual influences on individual differences in the practice of prayer during childhood and adolescence is provided by the study entitled 'The influence of home, church and school on prayer among sixteen-year-old adolescents in England' by Leslie J. Francis and Laurence Brown. This study was first published in 1991 and has been reproduced in *Psychological Perspectives on Prayer* (Francis and Astley, 2001, pp. 98–107).

In an earlier study Francis and Brown had already examined the social and contextual influences on the practice of prayer and on the attitudinal predisposition to pray among a sample of 4,948 11-year-olds. Their data show that, even after controlling for the child's own practice of prayer, which is itself the function of strong social and parental influences, 11-year-old children's attitudinal predisposition to pray is a direct function of their own and their parents' church attendance and denominational identity. While churchgoing 11-year-olds who pray hold a more positive attitude toward prayer than those who pray with equal frequency but do not attend church, churchgoing 11-year-olds who pray and are from churchgoing homes hold more positive attitudes toward prayer than those with similar levels of church attendance and prayer who come from homes where churchgoing is not practised. Furthermore, those identifying with a Christian denomination hold significantly more positive attitudes toward prayer than those with similar levels of prayer, church attendance and parental church attendance who do not identify with a denominational group.

Building on this earlier study, the aim of Francis and Brown's (1991) study was to check whether the same kind of influences held good among 16-year-old adolescents. Moreover, as well as examining the effect of home and church, this study included the influence of Church schools.

Sample

The subjects for this study were 711 pupils attending Year 11 classes in 25 state-maintained secondary schools, including (non-denominational), Roman Catholic voluntary aided and Church of England voluntary aided schools. One whole class was selected from each of the 25 schools.

The questionnaire was administered by the usual class teacher to all the pupils in the

class. The questionnaire included questions about:
- the pupil's pattern of church attendance
- the mother's pattern of church attendance
- the father's pattern of church attendance
- the pupil's practice of private prayer
- a six-item scale of attitude toward prayer
- father's occupation

The data from this study demonstrated that the influence of church is stronger and the influence of home is weaker among 16-year-olds than among 11-year-olds in determining both the attitudinal predisposition to pray and the practice of prayer. While the Roman Catholic schools have no direct influence on their pupils' attitudes toward prayer, after controlling for the influence of home and church, the Church of England schools were shown to exert a small but significant negative influence.

Consequences of prayer

A good example of research concerned with identifying the consequences of prayer is provided by the study entitled, 'The relationship between personal prayer and purpose in life among church-going and non-church-going twelve-to-fifteen-year-olds in the UK' by Leslie J. Francis and Thomas Evans. This study was first published in 1996 and has been reprinted in *Psychological Perspectives on Prayer* (Francis and Astley, 2001, pp. 271–81).

The aim of Francis and Evans' study was to explore the relationship between prayer and perceived purpose in life among a sample of young people between the ages of 12 and 16. Purpose in life is a particularly rich concept explored both by psychology and by theology. Purpose in life is understood to be central to the meaning-making process which counters meaningless. Other research has shown how important purpose in life can be to many aspects of the young person's personal and social development, including areas like good performance at school and resistance to substance abuse. Given the importance of purpose in life, Francis and Evans set out to assess the contribution made by prayer to developing a sense of purpose in life during adolescence.

Sample

The subjects for this study comprised two subsets of respondents from a sample of 4,014 young people between the ages of 12 and 16 who had completed a questionnaire. The first subset comprised 1,640 respondents who reported that they never attended church and that they did not identify themselves as affiliated to a non-Christian religious group. The second subset comprised 669 respondents who reported that they attended a Christian church nearly every week.

Francis and Evans decided to conduct their analyses on these two subsets of their database so that they could explore the correlates of prayer independently of differences in levels of church attendance. In effect their study asked two separate questions:
- Is there a relationship between prayer and purpose in life among young people who never attend church?

- Is there a relationship between prayer and purpose in life among young people who are weekly churchgoers?

The first clear finding from this study is that prayer and church attendance do not necessarily go hand in hand among this age group. A third (33 per cent) of the young people who never attend church nonetheless pray at least occasionally, while 13 per cent of the young people who attend church nearly every week never pray outside their participation in church services.

The second clear finding from this study was that there is a significant positive correlation between frequency of personal prayer and perceived purpose in life both among those who attend church most weeks and among those who never attend church. In other words, here is clear concrete evidence that prayer carries positive psychological benefit for young people who engage in that practice.

Postscript

These four strands of empirical research help to provide an informed context in which we can work when introducing children and young people to prayer:

1 The first strand reminds us that children do not think in the same way as adults and that their thinking about prayer will change and develop radically during the early years of life. The Christian educator needs to listen to the children and to respect the stage of development which has been reached by the individual child.
2 The second strand of research reminds us that adolescents will be thinking critically about the appropriateness and causal efficacy of prayer. Moreover, not all adolescents will be thinking in the same way. When inviting adolescents to engage in prayer we, too, need to be critically aware of the questions being raised by that activity.
3 The third strand of research reminds us that church, parents and school all have a critical influence on the young person's attitude toward prayer and practice of prayer. The Christian educator has a contribution to make alongside these other contributions.
4 The fourth strand of research reminds us that prayer itself can have an important influence on the lives of young people. Young people who learn to pray have been shown to have a greater sense of purpose in life and to enjoy a higher level of psychological well-being. The beneficial effect of prayer seems to hold true both among young people who are regular churchgoers and among young people who never attend church. Teaching young people to pray may, therefore, have significant consequences for their developing lives.

References and further reading

Brown, L. B. (1994), *The Human Side of Prayer*, Birmingham, Alabama, Religious Education Press.

Francis, L. J. and Astley, J. (eds.) (2001), *Psychological Perspectives on Prayer: A Reader*, Leominster, Gracewing.

Hyde, K. E. (1990), *Religion in Childhood and Adolescence: A Comprehensive Review of the Research*, Birmingham, Alabama, Religious Education Press, Chapter 5.

Watts, F. (ed.) (2001), *Perspectives on Prayer*, London, SPCK.

17

Personality and Learning Styles

Introduction

Personality psychology sets out to explore and to understand ways in which people differ at a psychological level. In many fundamental ways it is our basic personality which shapes the ways in which we communicate with others and our preferred teaching styles. In the same way it is individual differences in personality which shape our students' preferred learning styles. The more we can become aware of how our own personality works and the more we can become aware of the individual differences among our students, the more productive will be the interaction in the group.

The aim of this chapter is to provide a brief introduction to the theory of psychological type and the Myers-Briggs Type Indicator, and then to draw out the implications of this personality theory for individual differences in Christian communion and learning styles, both for children and adults.

Psychological type

It is Jung's theory of psychological type which stands at the heart of the Myers-Briggs Type Indicator. This theory identifies two main mental processes:

1 The first process concerns the ways in which we gather information. This is the *perceiving* process. Some people prefer *sensing* (S); others prefer *intuition* (N). According to the theory, these two types look at the world in very different ways.
2 The second process concerns the ways in which we make decisions. This is the *judging* process. Some people prefer *thinking* (T); others prefer *feeling* (F). According to the theory, these two types come to decisions about the world in very different ways.

Jung also suggested that individuals differ in the *orientation* in which they prefer to employ these two processes. Some people prefer the outer or extraverting world (E); others prefer the inner or introverting world (I). According to the theory, these two types are energized in very different ways. Extraverts draw their energy from the outer world of people and things, while introverts draw their energy from their inner world.

Finally, individuals differ in their *attitude* to the outer world. Both introverts and extraverts need to deal with the outer world and both may prefer to do this with a *judging* (J) or a *perceiving* (P) process. According to the theory, these two types display a very different attitude to the outer world.

What the theory understands by these preferences now needs to be explained in greater detail.

Introversion and extraversion

Introversion and extraversion describe the two preferred orientations of the inner world and the outer world. Introverts prefer to focus their attention on the inner world of ideas and draw their energy from that inner world. When introverts are tired and need energizing they look to the inner world. Extraverts prefer to focus their attention on the outer world of people and things and draw their energy from that outer world. When extraverts are tired and need energizing they look to the outer world. Since this chapter is being written by an introvert, the author prefers to present this perspective first, followed by the extravert perspective.

Introverts

Introverts like quiet for concentration. They want to be able to shut off the distractions of the outer world and turn inwards. They often experience trouble in remembering names and faces. They can work at one solitary project for a long time without interruption. When they are engaged in a task in the outer world they may become absorbed in the ideas behind that task.

Introverts work best alone and may resent distractions and interruptions from other people. They dislike being interrupted by the telephone, tend to think things through before acting, and may spend so long in thought that they miss the opportunity to act.

Introverts prefer to learn by reading rather than by talking with others. They may also prefer to communicate with others in writing, rather than face-to-face or over the phone; this is particularly the case if they have something unpleasant to communicate.

Introverts are oriented to the inner world. They focus on ideas, concepts and inner understanding. They are reflective, may consider deeply before acting, and they probe inwardly for stimulation.

Extraverts

Extraverts like variety and action. They want to be able to shut off the distractions of the inner world and turn outward. They are good at remembering faces and names and enjoy meeting people and introducing people. They can become impatient with long, slow jobs. When they are working in the company of other people they may become more interested in how others are doing the job than in the job itself.

Extraverts like to have other people around them in the working environment, and enjoy the stimulus of sudden interruptions and telephone calls. Extraverts like to act quickly and decisively, even when it is not totally appropriate to do so.

Extraverts prefer to learn a task by talking it through with other people. They prefer to communicate with other people face-to-face or over the phone, rather than in writing. They often find that their own ideas become clarified through communicating them with others.

Extraverts are oriented to the outer world. They focus on people and things. They prefer to learn by trial and error and they do so with confidence. They are active people, and they scan the outer environment for stimulation.

<hr>

Introversion and extraversion checklist

Introverts
- prefer being reflective
- prefer working alone
- are drained by too many people
- think before speaking
- are socially detached
- dislike parties
- are reserved
- prefer a few deep friendships
- are private

Extraverts
- prefer being active
- prefer working in groups
- are energized by others
- speak before thinking
- are socially involved
- like parties
- are talkative
- prefer many friends
- are sociable

<hr>

Sensing and intuition

Sensing and intuition describe the two preferences associated with the *perceiving* process. They describe different preferences used to acquire information. Sensing types focus on the realities of a situation as perceived by the senses. Intuitive types focus on the possibilities, meanings and relationships, the 'big picture' that goes beyond sensory information. Since this chapter is being written by an intuitive, the author prefers to present this perspective first, followed by the sensing perspective.

Individuals who prefer *intuition* develop insight into complexity. They have the ability to see abstract, symbolic and theoretical relationships, and the capacity to see future possibilities. They put their reliance on inspiration rather than on past experience. Their interest is in the new and untried. They trust their intuitive grasp of meanings and relationships.

Individuals with a preference for intuition are aware of new challenges and possibilities. They see quickly beyond the information they have been given or the materials they have to hand to the possibilities and challenges which these offer. They are often discontent with the way things are and wish to improve them. They become bored quickly and dislike doing the same thing repeatedly.

Intuitive types enjoy learning new skills. They work in bursts of energy, powered by enthusiasm, and then enjoy slack periods between activity.

Intuitive types follow their inspirations and hunches. They may reach conclusions too quickly and misconstrue the information or get the facts wrong. They dislike taking too much time to secure precision.

Intuitive types perceive with memory and associations. They see patterns and meanings and assess possibilities. They are good at reading between the lines and projecting possibilities for the future. They prefer to go always for the big picture. They prefer to let the mind inform the eyes.

Individuals who prefer *sensing* develop keen awareness of present experience. They have acute powers of observation, good memory for facts and details, the capacity for realism, and the ability to see the world as it is. They rely on experience rather than theory. They put their trust in what is known and in the conventional.

Individuals with a preference for sensing are aware of the uniqueness of each individual event. They develop good techniques of observation and they recognize the practical way in which things work now.

Sensing types like to develop an established way of doing things and gain enjoyment from exercising skills which they have already learnt. Repetitive work does not bore them. They are able to work steadily with a realistic idea of how long a task will take.

Sensing types usually reach their conclusion step by step, observing each piece of information carefully. They are not easily inspired to interpret the information in front of them and they may not trust inspiration when it comes. They are very careful about getting the facts right and are good at engaging in precise work.

Sensing types perceive clearly with the five senses. They attend to practical and factual details, and they are in touch with physical realities. They attend to the present moment and prefer to confine their attention to what is said and done. They observe the small details of everyday life. They prefer to let the eyes tell the mind.

Sensing and intuition checklist

Sensers
- are interested in facts
- are practical
- are sensible
- show concern for detail
- focus on present realities
- are down to earth
- prefer the concrete
- keep things as they are
- prefer to make

Intuitives
- are interested in theories
- are inspirational
- are imaginative
- show concern for meaning
- focus on future possibilities
- are up in the air
- prefer the abstract
- like to improve things
- prefer to design

Thinking and feeling

Thinking and feeling describe the two preferences associated with the *judging* process. They describe different preferences by which decisions are reached. Individuals who prefer thinking make decisions by objective, logical analysis. Individuals who prefer feeling make decisions by subjective values based on how people will be affected. Since this introduction is being written by a thinker, the author prefers to present this perspective first, followed by the feeling perspective.

Individuals who prefer *thinking* develop clear powers of logical analysis. They develop the ability to weigh facts objectively and to predict consequences, both intended and unintended. They develop a stance of impartiality. They are characterized by a sense of fairness and justice.

Individuals with a preference for thinking are good at putting things in logical order. They are also able to put people in their place when they consider it necessary. They are able to take tough decisions and to reprimand others. They are also able to be firm and toughminded about themselves.

Thinking types need to be treated fairly and to see that other people are treated fairly as well. They are inclined to respond more to other people's ideas than to other people's feelings. They may inadvertently hurt other people's feelings without recognizing that they are doing so. Thinking types prefer to look at life from the outside as a spectator.

Thinking types are able to develop good powers of logical analysis. They use objective and impersonal criteria in reaching decisions. They follow logically the relationships between cause and effect. They develop characteristics of being firm-minded and prizing logical order. They may appear sceptical.

Individuals who prefer *feeling* develop a personal emphasis on values and standards. They appreciate what matters most to themselves and what matters most to other people. They develop an understanding of people, a wish to affiliate with people and a desire for harmony. They are characterized by their capacity for warmth, and by qualities of empathy and compassion.

Individuals with a preference for feeling like harmony and will work hard to bring harmony about between other people. They dislike telling other people unpleasant things or reprimanding other people. They take into account other people's feelings.

Feeling types are sympathetic individuals. They take a great interest in the people behind the job and respond to other people's values as much as to their ideas. They enjoy pleasing people.

Feeling types look at life from the inside. They live life as a committed participant and find it less easy to stand back and to form an objective view of what is taking place.

Feeling types develop good skills at applying personal priorities. They are good at weighing human values and motives, both their own and other people's. They are characterized by qualities of empathy and sympathy. They prize harmony and trust.

Thinking and feeling checklist

Thinkers
- are logical
- desire justice
- are concerned for truth
- are truthful
- are sceptical
- are analytic
- are fair-minded
- are firm
- are critical

Feelers
- are humane
- desire harmony
- are concerned for peace
- are tactful
- are trusting
- are sympathetic
- are warm-hearted
- are gentle
- are affirming

Judging and perceiving

Judging and perceiving describe the two preferred attitudes toward the outer world. Individuals who prefer to relate to the outer world with a judging process present a planned and orderly approach to life. They prefer to have a settled system in place and display a preference for closure. Individuals who prefer to relate to the outer world with a perceiving process present a flexible and spontaneous approach to life. They prefer to keep plans and organizations to a minimum and display a preference for openness. Since this chapter is being written by a judger, the author prefers to present this perspective first, followed by the perceiving perspective.

Judging types schedule projects so that each step gets done on time. They like to get things finished and settled, and to know that the finished product is in place. They work best when they can plan their work in advance and follow that plan. Judging types use lists and agendas to structure their day and to plan their actions. They may dislike interruption from the plans they have made and are reluctant to leave the task in hand even when something more urgent arises.

Judging types tend to be satisfied once they reach a judgement or have made a decision, both about people and things. They dislike having to revise their decision and taking fresh information into account. They like to get on with a task as soon as possible once the essential things are at hand. As a consequence, judging types may decide to act too quickly.

When individuals take a judging attitude toward the outer world, they are using the preferred *judging* process, thinking or feeling, outwardly. Their attitude to life is characterized by deciding and planning, organizing and scheduling, controlling and regulating. Their life is goal-oriented. They want to move toward closure, even when the data are incomplete.

Perceiving types adapt well to changing situations. They make allowances for new information and for changes in the situation in which they are living or acting. They may have trouble making decisions, feeling that they have never quite got enough information on which to base their decision.

Perceiving types may start too many projects and consequently have difficulty in finishing them. They may tend to postpone unpleasant tasks and to give their attention to more pleasant options. Perceiving types want to know all about a new task before they begin it, and may prefer to postpone something new while they continue to explore the options.

When perceiving types use lists they do so not as a way of organizing the details of their day, but as a way of seeing the possibilities in front of them. They may choose never to act on these possibilities. Perceiving types do not mind leaving things open for last-minute changes. They work best under pressure and get a lot accomplished at the last minute under the constraints of a deadline.

When individuals take a perceiving attitude toward the outer world, they are using the preferred *perceiving* process, sensing or intuition, outwardly. They are taking in information, adapting and changing, curious and interested. They adopt an open-minded attitude toward life and resist closure to obtain more data.

Judging and perceiving checklist

Judgers
- like to be organized
- like to be structured
- like to be in control
- like detailed planning
- act on decision
- are orderly
- are punctual
- are systematic
- prefer certainty

Perceivers
- like to be spontaneous
- like to be open-ended
- like to be adaptable
- dislike detailed planning
- act on impulse
- are easygoing
- are leisurely
- are casual
- enjoy uncertainty

Teaching and learning styles

Basic differences in personality shape our preferred styles both for teaching and for learning. The more we become conscious of this fact, the easier it is for us to recognize when our own preferred teaching and learning styles may disadvantage some of the children and some of the adults with whom we work. Here are some of the obvious differences:

Extraverts learn best when working with other people, but *introverts* learn best working by themselves. Extraverts benefit from group discussions about what they are thinking, but introverts long for the peace and quiet to discover what is really going on in their own minds. Extraverts often find background sounds stimulating, but introverts find them distracting. When extraverts come into church they often want to talk to people, but when introverts come into church they often want to find their own quiet space.

113

Sensers work best when they are given the basic information and facts that they need, but intuitives become quickly bored with too much information which they do not know how to handle. When studying a passage of Scripture, sensers will enjoy getting to grips with the details in the text, but intuitives tend to find such attention to detail tedious.

Intuitives work best when they are introduced to an overview and to the big theory, but sensers find the big picture difficult to grasp before they have all the details to hand. When studying a passage of Scripture, intuitives like the passage to spark their imagination and to draw links with other areas of life, but sensers find such an approach incomprehensible.

Feelers are more attracted to the Christian faith because to them the gospel is about helping people, about caring for the sick and for the aged, about bringing harmony and peace to those caught up in discord and conflict, and about developing capacity for empathy and sympathy. For thinkers such an approach is seen as too much in the heart and not enough in the head.

Thinkers are more attracted to the Christian faith because to them the gospel is about ultimate reality, about making sense of the world, about theological enquiry, about campaigns for truth and justice, and about seeing that right prevails. For feelers such an approach is seen as too much in the head and not enough in the heart.

Judgers learn best when they are surrounded by structure and discipline, but perceivers learn best when they can be spontaneous and flexible. Judgers expect a routine and pattern to their learning experiences, but perceivers become bored with such apparent predictability.

Perceivers expect to be able to shape their learning experiences as they go along, but judgers become frustrated with such apparent disorganization. When judgers come into church they expect the service to begin and to end on time, but when perceivers come into church they may well arrive late and be prepared to stay all day if they become absorbed in what is going on.

Personality psychology helps us to appreciate that people who learn and behave in ways quite different from our preferences are not *wrong*, but simply *different*.

References and further reading

Baab, L. M. (1998), *Personality Type in Congregations: How to Work with Others More Effectively*, Washington, DC, Alban Institute.

Bayne, R. (1995), *The Myers-Briggs Type Indicator*, London, Chapman & Hall.

Duncan, B. (1993), *Pray Your Way*, London, Darton, Longman & Todd.

Francis, L. J. (1997), *Personality Type and Scripture: Exploring Mark's Gospel*, London, Mowbray.

Francis, L. J. and Atkins, P. (2001), *Exploring Matthew's Gospel: Personality Type and Scripture*, London, Mowbray.

Goldsmith, M. and Wharton, M. (1993), *Knowing Me – Knowing You*, London, SPCK.

Myers, I. B. and McCaulley, M. H. (1985), *Manual: A Guide to the Development and Use of the Myers-Briggs Type Indicator*, Palo Alto, California, Consulting Psychologists Press.

Myers, I. B. and Myers, P. B. (1980), *Gifts Differing*, Palo Alto, California, Consulting Psychologists Press.

PART THREE
CHILDREN AND SCHOOL

18

The Fourth R

Introduction

One of the most thorough studies of religious education (RE) ever made in Britain was commissioned by the Church of England's Board of Education and the National Society, and published in 1970 under the title *The Fourth R: The Report of the Commission on Religious Education in Schools*. The independent commission met under the general chairmanship of Ian Ramsey, Bishop of Durham and formerly Professor of Philosophy of Religion in the University of Oxford. It is often termed the 'Durham Report'. The commission comprised almost thirty theologians, RE specialists, educationalists and Anglican ecclesiastics, and co-opted a further sixteen additional members to its sub-groups. It consulted widely, as well as drawing on evidence from its own questionnaire surveys of educational and Church organizations and from submissions produced by a wide range of organizations and individuals who responded to a public appeal made in 1967.

The resulting seminal report was 380 pages long and considered the following areas:

- the origin and development of RE in England
- theology and education
- religious education and moral education
- RE in county schools (now called community schools)
- RE in independent and direct-grant schools
- RE within other Western societies
- Church schools

Recommendations and responses

The commission sought to place religious education alongside other subjects, justifying it on *educational* grounds and lamenting the fact that it had been singled out as the only 'compulsory' subject in the 1944 Education Act. Nevertheless, the report contended, 'some measure of statutory acknowledgement of the importance of religious education (in which we include school worship) is still required'. The members of the commission argued that this was partly because the educational justification for the subject was not yet sufficiently understood, and partly because the abandonment of legal support would suggest that the nation held religious beliefs 'to be unimportant, false, or vacuous' (p. 275).

The forty-seven recommendations made by the commission included:

- the abandonment of agreed syllabuses and their replacement by handbooks of suggestions and RE advisers employed by the local authorities
- a recognition of the need for 'an extensive research programme' concerning RE
- the strengthening of training for RE teachers
- the appointment of a moderator to assist clergy working in schools and an inquiry into their training and 'diocesan status'

- a more rational distribution of aided schools
- aided schools to give priority to local children 'whatever their denominational allegiance' (p. 283)
- an exploration of more ecumenical co-operation within the dual system of educational provision

Theology and education

It has become routine to complain that Church reports on practical issues are 'too thin on theology'. By contrast, the theological chapter of this report was a substantial one, prepared by a group that included several current, past or future professors of theology in British universities. It first traced the development of theology over the previous one hundred years, citing a large number of works of contemporary theology. There followed a presentation of the report's own 'theology of education', which addressed the following themes. These theological insights informed the more detailed educational discussion of these same topics later in the report.

Religious education

Religious education was to be seen, the report argued, as exploratory, 'fashioned upon the open basis of the Christian's contemporary theological commitments' (p. 58). Indoctrination was comprehensively rejected; by contrast, educational 'self-criticism' and 'reasoned choice', building on substantial knowledge, was commended. It was proposed that religious education should include a wide spectrum of Christian belief.

Open education

The student of religion or morality, the student of science and history, needs to be inducted into the tradition of these disciplines, a process which involves both learning how to think in the appropriate ways and accepting a good deal on authority. An education in any of these fields would be a failure if it produced people who were subservient and uncritical; it would also be a failure if it produced people who supposed that they could themselves rewrite the entire subject from scratch.

Hence 'openness' does not require us to proceed as if we were operating in a cultural vacuum – it cannot mean 'not having any presuppositions, not accepting anything which one cannot here and now justify to any reasonable man, not being prepared to accept anything on authority'. It must mean 'not being doctrinaire, encouraging people to think for themselves, being ready to consider arguments against one's own position'. As such it is compatible with having and with communicating a definite position which one is prepared to defend.

The Fourth R, 1970, p. 80

School worship

Worship in all schools was defended 'on educational grounds' and regarded as an essential part of religious education because it provided an opportunity to experience the rites, ceremonies and other activities of Christian worship (p. 135).

Why school worship?

While the analogies are not wholly exact, religious education without worship is like geography without field studies, the learning of a language without trips abroad, science without its experiments, the theory of music without singing or playing an instrument, learning to swim without entering the water, and studying literature without reading books.

We are maintaining that, just as artistic capacities cannot be developed without being exercised, by painting pictures or making music, so religious understanding cannot be developed without experience of worship.

The Fourth R, 1970, pp. 61, 135–6

The study of other religions

While the report argued that RE should set out from a Christian base, it claimed that this does not preclude learning something of the beliefs, and occasionally sharing the worship, of other faiths, together with some exploration of the reasons for Christianity's claim to distinctiveness.

The moral strand in religious education

Morality was affirmed as autonomous and moral education was recognized as separable in principle from RE, although 'it hardly seems possible to have religious education without moral education' (p. 63). Moral education should be developed self-critically, and remains inadequate and incomplete without reference 'to basic questions of meaning, value and purpose' (p. 77).

The status of religious knowledge

The claims that religious knowledge is poorly founded as an academic discipline, or indeed 'meaningless', were rejected. Such criticisms were seen as ignoring recent developments in both theology and philosophy.

Theology in higher education

The chairman, Ian Ramsey, was himself quoted on the wider task of theology in a university.

Theology in the university

The new prospect for theology arises as and when theology expresses its continuing concern with problems which are of significance to everyone – believer and unbeliever alike; when it arranges for such dialogue between the different disciplines as can provide helpful and informative inroads into a particular problem; and when, as it listens rather than speaks, and learns rather than teaches, it starts to construct theological discourse with a new relevance.

Ian T. Ramsey, cited in *The Fourth R*, 1970, p. 66

Relevance for contemporary educational thought

Religious education, in so far as it is informed by a theological perspective, was recognized as seeking to preserve 'some awareness of a broader area to human nature, of the dimension of "mystery", "depth", "transcendence", of a sense of the unconditioned in human experience' (p. 67).

The report claimed that a neutral position was virtually unachievable over such claims. 'The explicit recognition of the spiritual needs and capacities of children is a far more desirable position ... than either an explicit denial of such needs or a refusal to cater for them' (pp. 70–1). The distinctively Christian doctrine of human nature and its spiritual capacities, and the recognition of the intrinsic, irreducible value of the individual, were seen as challenging more reductive accounts of human beings (e.g. behaviourist and Marxist views). The Christian view is to be characterized primarily by the significance of Christian love.

Love, persons and education

What motivates the Christian in all his various relationships with children, parental, professional, or merely accidental, is a love which reaches out to them in their own condition, and which seeks by force of example to bring home to them a sense of the love of God for them.

Each individual as an object of the love of God has therefore a unique value. Against tendencies to depersonalise and to dehumanise which are prevalent in society the Christian will want constantly to emphasise the importance of personal relationships. The highest analogy he can offer for understanding the being of God is that of the person. The development of the person in all his aspects, religious and moral, as well as physical and mental, is therefore a matter of the deepest importance to him.

The Fourth R, 1970, pp. 71–2

The aims of religious education

The Fourth R adopted a philosophy of religious education that was rather different from that developing at around the same time in the Schools Council's working parties on RE. Their viewpoint – and particularly that of Ninian Smart, their major academic influence – gave rise to a number of publications over the next decade which would radically change the face of RE (see Chapters 20 and 23). Like these later writings, *The Fourth R* attempted to justify RE on educational grounds. Unlike them, however, this report regards the study of a variety of religions as too superficial. Instead it advocates religious education focused on the biblical, historical and theological dimensions of Christianity, with the study of other faiths only being attempted 'where appropriate'. Nevertheless, the educational task is that of helping pupils to 'explore and appreciate', rather than 'to accept', Christianity in the county (community) school. But the more ultimate aim of this exploration is to feed into the child's own quest for meaning.

The aim of RE

The aim of religious education should be to explore the place and significance of religion in human life and so to make a distinctive contribution to each pupil's search for a faith by which to live.

The Fourth R, 1970, p. 103

According to the report, RE should have some 'statutory acknowledgement', but it recommended discontinuing the provision of the 1944 Act and abolishing agreed syllabuses in favour of 'a handbook of suggestions'. According to John Hall, 'these proposals would have removed the Church of England's influence on County schools' (Hall, 1998, p. 36).

As we have seen, the report viewed school worship as a proper part of religious education. Yet it also recognized that the school as an institution is not equivalent to the Church, and the model of school worship proposed is that of a symbolic corporate act that does not presuppose the commitment of all the individuals involved in it. This type of worship is something that is seen outside the school on occasions such as memorial services and remembrance services, which are forms of worship that properly express Christian personal, spiritual and moral values, rather than just secular 'values of a shared humanity' (pp. 138–9).

Church schools

The involvement of the Churches in education in general, and in schooling in particular, is often said to express two concerns:
- a specific, *domestic task* of Christian nurture or instruction – 'seen as the equipping of Christian people for their life in the world' (p. 206)
- a more *general task* of providing an educational service to the whole community

The Fourth R points out that during the period when Church and nation were theoretically one, these two roles were indistinguishable. The Church of England's voluntary schools are now unique in recognizing a general, rather than solely a domestic role, for its Church schools. The report offered a detailed study of theological, educational and economic arguments both for and against Anglican participation in the dual system. Its conclusion was that the Church of England should keep its Church schools. This is not for any denominational advantage, however, but because Church schools represent 'an important opportunity to express in direct service its concern for the general education of the young people of the nation' (p. 252). Ecumenical co-operation between Church schools was explicitly encouraged.

Why Church schools?

Two basic premisses should underline the Church's future thinking and planning:
(a) Church schools are important as providing a means whereby the Church's general presence in education may be realised; (b) individual Church schools are important because they possess certain educational potentialities not

---

necessarily found in schools of other kinds. The Church obviously needs to speak with authority on educational matters, and the only authority which will be heeded today is the authority which is derived from direct experience, such as can be gained from actual involvement at all levels, theoretical, administrative, practical, in the schools themselves. If the Church ceases to be directly involved in the work of education, then few will listen to any comments it may wish to make on education now or in future. Moreover, if the Church withdraws from the challenge of contemporary education, it will cease to be involved with modern society at one of its most creative points, where the Church can both hope to contribute to the development of society and can learn from society.

The Fourth R, 1970, p. 250

The general task of the Church school is here boldly affirmed. Further, the report insists that Church *controlled* schools should give up all attempts to preserve a domestic, rather than a general, educational responsibility. However, Church *aided* schools may retain some measure of distinctiveness; for example, they might be distinguished from county schools in having more frequent religious assemblies, and occasional services in the parish church. But even aided schools should not be seen as having a real domestic, catechetical function, at any rate not as part of the school curriculum. For *The Fourth R*, RE in Church aided schools has the same aim as in other schools, and differs only in the aided schools' 'freedom to achieve this purpose through involvement in one particular religious tradition' (p. 265). The report does not view Church schools as an instrument for delivering denominational instruction.

The distinctiveness of the aided school

For example, through its links with the local congregation and the local clergy its pupils will be able to feel something of what it means to belong to a worldwide Christian society. This will enable them to study the Church from the inside, rather than from the outside. The phrase 'This is what we do, what we believe' will be appropriate in an aided school. This is not to suggest that what others do or believe will never be studied; far from it.

The Fourth R, 1970, p. 265

Nevertheless, voluntary aided schools that were the only 'neighbourhood' schools serving a particular area should consider becoming controlled; and aided schools' admission policies should give priority to local children without reference to denomination.

From today's perspective this philosophy of Church schools seems to many to water down their distinctiveness. The Church of England's recent 'Dearing Report' on Church schools (see Chapter 19) notes that the priority given to 'the service function' (general task) by *The Fourth R* 'has come under increasing challenge', and that governments have recently enacted legislation that has helped the Church 'to foster the Christian character of its schools' (Church Schools Review Group, 2001, p. 13).

References and further reading

Church Schools Review Group (2001), *The Way Ahead: Church of England Schools in the New Millennium*, London, Church House Publishing (the 'Dearing Report').

Commission on Religious Education in Schools (1970), *The Fourth R*, London, National Society and SPCK (the 'Durham Report').

Hall, J. (1998), 'The Church in education: where do we go from here?', in *A Christian Voice in Education: Distinctiveness in Church Schools*, London, National Society and Church House Publishing.

Hull, J. M. (1975), *School Worship: An Obituary*, London, SCM Press, Chapter 4.

19

The Way Ahead

Introduction

The report, *The Way Ahead: Church of England Schools in the New Millennium*, under the chairmanship of Lord Dearing and published in 2001, represents a radical commitment by the Church of England to reshaping its ministry among children through Church schools. The aim of the present chapter is to trace the background of this report, and then describe its main contents.

Background

In November 1998 the Board of Education of the Church of England presented to the General Synod a report under the title, *Church of England Schools in the New Millennium*. The report speaks of 'a moment of opportunity' created by the School Standards and Framework Act 1998. Four opportunities in particular are identified on the opening page of this report:

- Church schools will have the opportunity to develop their identity as a Church school.
- Parishes will have the opportunity to see their Church schools as a significant part of their mission strategy.
- Dioceses will have the opportunity to deepen their service to Church schools and to extend the provision of places in Church schools in response to the needs of the Church and community.
- The Church of England will have the opportunity to recover the energy and commitment to Christian education that founded so many schools in the first half of the nineteenth century.

Overall the report presented to General Synod argued that Church schools stand at 'the centre of the Church's mission to the nation'. Church schools provide a 'vital connection with the community' and with families 'the Church might not otherwise reach'.

Against this background the report made four recommendations:

1. The report urged Diocesan Synods to make more resources available to Diocesan Boards of Education.
2. The report welcomed the opportunities for Church schools to move to the voluntary aided category and encouraged dioceses to support governors in doing so.
3. The report drew attention to the fact that the Church of England owns one in four primary schools compared with only one in twenty secondary schools, and, by implication, encouraged the development of more secondary schools.

4 The report invited the Archbishops' Council to establish a Commission on Church schools and Church colleges.

Archbishop of Canterbury

Speaking in the General Synod debate on the report *Church of England Schools in the New Millennium*, the Archbishop of Canterbury said:

> It was not long ago that the clear trend was to minimise the religious character of Church schools... Now that trend is being reversed. We are more confident today about promoting the distinctiveness of our schools. If people want more of what we can offer, then we must find ways of providing it.

The Most Reverend George Carey, November, 1998

In the Synod debate no one voted against the motion which welcomed more aided schools and urged greater resources for diocesan education teams, but the call for an Archbishops' Commission on Church schools was lost through an amendment. The Church Schools Review Group was set up in place of the lost Archbishops' Commission. Lord Dearing accepted the invitation to chair this group.

The terms of reference given to the review group clearly reflected the conclusions reached by the report presented to General Synod. As originally conceived the review process was scheduled to take three years and to be underpinned by a significant research project. Lord Dearing halved the time required by not requiring the research project. Information was assembled and evaluated by means of wide-ranging consultation.

Terms of reference

In detail, our terms of reference continue:

1. Believing that Church schools stand at the centre of the Church's mission to the nation: to identify what currently contributes to the success and effectiveness of Church schools; and to examine the case for strengthening their distinctiveness and the means by which this might be achieved (effectiveness).
2. To undertake a clear assessment of the need and opportunities to increase the number of all Church schools, but in particular at the secondary phase, and how this might be achieved (strategic development).
3. To develop strategies for increasing vocations to teach; and to review the particular and distinctive role of the Church colleges in the professional formation of Christian teachers and headteachers (both within Church schools and within the education system generally) (vocation).

The Way Ahead, 2001, p. 1

The Way Ahead

The Way Ahead: Church of England Schools in the New Millennium was published on 14 June 2001. Fully in accordance with its terms of reference, the report identified three issues at the heart of its recommendations. To enable the Church of England to discharge its mission through schools, it recommended that the Church has schools that are:
- sufficient in numbers
- sufficiently distinctive in their spiritual life
- staffed by sufficient numbers of Christian teachers

The present analysis of *The Way Ahead* concentrates on the main issues raised in the report: an understanding of what is meant by mission to the nation; the major expansion of secondary provision; the further development of primary provision; the future for controlled status; ecumenical collaboration; a national policy for fundraising; encouraging Christian distinctiveness; shaping admissions policies; teacher recruitment; the role of the headteacher; the role of the clergy; a future for Church-related independent schools; and the role of the Church colleges of higher education.

Mission to the nation

The report recognizes that the Church has a major problem in attracting young people to its services as a means of discharging its mission. By way of contrast, Church schools give their pupils the experience of the meaning of faith and what it is to work and play in a community that seeks to live its beliefs and values. Moreover, the report argues, through the children attending its schools, the Church has an opportunity to reach out to parents.

Reaching parents

The 900,000 children provide access to parents, very many of whom would otherwise have no contact with the Church.

The Way Ahead, 2001, p. 10

The report anticipates two objections to this emphasis on mission within Church schools. The first objection comes from within the Anglican theology of Church schools itself. An earlier report, *The Fourth R* (also known as the Durham Report), published in 1970, had distinguished between the Church of England's two historic roles in education, the role of service (the 'general' function) and the role of nurture (the 'domestic' function) (see Chapter 18). *The Fourth R* identified tension between these two roles and recommended that the Church of England should emphasise the role of service. In changed social circumstances *The Way Ahead* saw 'no dichotomy between the service and nurture purposes of the Church in education' (p. 13).

The second objection comes from the British Humanist Association and the National Secular Society, who argued that faith schools are divisive and exclusive. In response to such criticism *The Way Ahead* asserts that 'the notion of distinctiveness and inclusiveness are not mutually exclusive. A distinct approach to education needs to be matched by openness' (p. 17).

Secondary provision

The major headline recommendation of *The Way Ahead* which caught public attention was the proposal that the Church of England should expand its stake in the state-maintained secondary sector.

In the year 2000 the review group noted that the Church provided around 150,000 secondary places, compared with 774,000 primary places, and calculated that as a consequence only one in five children who attended an Anglican primary school could be accommodated in an Anglican secondary school. The review group argued that the Church was losing contact with most of the Church primary school children 'just at the time in life when they need answers to their questions and support in their faith' (p. 10).

The review group cites support for this strategy from (p. 37):

- increasing demand from parents
- goodwill of the main political parties
- goodwill of many local education authorities

The review group was also encouraged by the Government Green Paper on Schools (CM 5050), which widened the scope for faith communities in education, and proposed a reduction in the governors' capital contribution to the costs of voluntary aided schools from 15 per cent to 10 per cent.

In considering additional provision at the secondary level, *The Way Ahead* invited dioceses to have 'an especial commitment to expanding provision in areas of economic and social hardship' (p. 39).

Secondary schools

The Church should aim to increase Church secondary school places, whether by expansion of existing schools or through additional Church schools (including transfer from the community sector), by the equivalent of 100 schools over the next seven to eight years.

The Way Ahead, 2001, p. 76

Primary provision

The review group noted the uneven distribution of Church primary schools across the dioceses. In particular the review group observed that the densely populated urban dioceses in the south east and the industrial north and midlands were particularly underprovided with Church primary schools. Suburban areas were also generally underprovided.

The Way Ahead seems to assume that the current 'average' provision of Church primary schools should be the target, but recognizes that many dioceses would be unable to reach that target. The report is also careful to note that the Church 'is not in the business of creating surplus places by displacing other schools that are already providing valued service to the community' (p. 35).

Primary schools

At the primary level, dioceses should aim to increase provision where it is most evidently lacking.

The Way Ahead, 2001, p. 77

Controlled status

The 1944 Education Act created two types of Church schools. In the controlled school the Church gave more control to the local education authority, but was absolved from ongoing financial commitment. In the aided school the Church retained more control, but at a cost. Over half of the Church of England primary schools opted for controlled status. The 1944 Education Act made provision for aided schools to revert to controlled status at any time, but only since September 2000 has it been possible for controlled schools to change to aided status without reimbursing the local authority for past expenditure.

The Way Ahead affirms the value of controlled schools, but recommends that, in the case of new schools, preference should be given to aided status.

Controlled schools

Voluntary controlled and voluntary aided schools should rank equally in the care of the Church, and the Church should respond to schools in each category according to their needs.

The Way Ahead, 2001, p. 23

Ecumenical approach

The Way Ahead is sensitive to the advantages of collaboration among the Christian denominations and makes the specific point that the development of new Church schools should be careful not to destabilize other existing denominational provision.

Ecumenical approach

We recommend that in appropriate circumstances the Church should welcome an ecumenical approach to new schools, actively fostering a will for the denominations to work together.

The Way Ahead, 2001, p. 31

Fund-raising

The review group proposes to finance this expansion in Church schools through a nationally co-ordinated initiative. They envisage the appeal seeking support from individual benefactors, charitable foundations, trusts and corporations, but not through an appeal to the parishes.

Cost

To facilitate the proposed expansion, we recommend national fundraising to assist dioceses, and that the objective should be to raise £25 million over seven years.

The Way Ahead, 2001, p. xi

Christian distinctiveness

The Way Ahead maintains that the core principles and values that should unite all Church schools are the gospel values of loving God and one's neighbour. These values will be reflected in how pupils are taught to conduct themselves and to relate to one another and to God's world.

Other signs of Christian distinctiveness are identified as:
- headteacher and staff committed to the Christian character of the school
- meaningful daily worship
- quality religious education
- distinctively Christian ethos
- affirming relationship with a parish church
- observation of the major Christian festivals
- distinctively Christian approach to the curriculum

Christian distinctiveness

No Church school can be considered as part of the Church's mission unless it is distinctively Christian... Today the state is a willing provider, and the purpose of the Church in education is not simply to provide the basic education needed for human dignity. That purpose is to offer a spiritual dimension to the lives of young people, within the traditions of the Church of England, in an increasingly secular world.

The Way Ahead, 2001, p. 3

Admissions policies

The Way Ahead tries hard to balance the two competing claims of Church schools to serve the local community *and* to serve the Christian community. Different problems are faced by the rural voluntary controlled primary school and by the urban voluntary aided secondary school.

The advice given to rural voluntary controlled primary schools is to review their distinctiveness as Christian institutions and to consider whether their local circumstances allow a legitimate case to be made to the local education authority for the inclusion of Christian background within the admissions criteria, providing this does not compromise their tradition and responsibility as a neighbourhood school.

The advice given to urban voluntary aided secondary schools is to offer a proportion of places for local children, especially if they are from disadvantaged sectors of the community. The suggestion is also made that 'some places should be reserved for children of other faiths and of no faith' (p. 29).

Overall, however, the emphasis is on ensuring that Church schools admit at least a substantial minority of pupils with a Christian background.

Admissions policies

In any new primary and secondary schools it should be the policy to establish within measurable time – if it is not possible from the outset – at least a substantial minority of pupils with a Christian background.

In particular, the aim over time in new voluntary aided schools should be to achieve an appropriate balance of 'open' and 'foundation' places, sufficient to ensure that the school is a distinctively Christian institution whilst remaining grounded in the local community in all its diversity.

The Way Ahead, 2001, p. 78

Teacher recruitment

The review group identified the recruitment and training of Christian teachers to be central to the development and expansion of the Church school sector. In particular the review group commends:

- recruitment of teachers from minority ethnic groups
- recruitment of men into the primary sector

Above all, the review group endorses the notion of teaching 'as a vocation of equal status to the priesthood'.

Vocations to teach

Through the dioceses, all parishes should be urged, not just once but repeatedly, to put before people what it means to be a Christian teacher and, in appropriate cases, encourage a vocation to teach.

The Way Ahead, 2001, p. 77

Having stimulated a vocation to teach, the review group recognized the need to raise the morale of the teaching profession in order to enhance teacher retention. The need is to promote respect for teachers in our society and to foster a genuine sense of being valued in the teaching profession.

Leadership in schools

The Way Ahead holds a very high view of headteachers who are described as 'spiritual and academic leaders of the school' (p. 60). They are required to provide 'visionary, inspired leadership and management centred on the school as a worshipping community, where educational and academic excellence for all pupils is pursued in a Christian context' (p. 60).

In order to provide leadership for the expanding sector of Church schools, the review group makes a number of recommendations, including:
- identifying potential leaders
- promoting in-service development
- providing help for headteachers in small primary schools

Developing potential headteachers

Action must be taken now to identify on a national basis, diocese by diocese, Christian teachers of all ages, young and old, who have the potential to provide the necessary leadership. The diocese must see that these teachers have the in-service development needed to move on to senior positions.

The Way Ahead, 2001, p. 77

The clergy

While recognizing that developing the link between the parish church and the local Church school is properly the responsibility of all church members, *The Way Ahead* identifies the special contribution of the clergy. The role of the clergy might include:
- pastor to staff, pupils and families
- ex-officio governor (and, if elected, chair of governors)
- leader of collective worship
- consultant over collective worship and religious education
- chaplain and (voluntary) teacher

Effective contribution to these specialist roles requires appropriate initial training and further in-service professional development. The review group also recommends that the requirements of the local Church school should feature in the clergy appointment procedures.

Clergy appointments

The clergy appointment procedures should ensure that, where there is a Church school in the parish, prospective clergy are given a job description that makes explicit their responsibilities toward that school.

The Way Ahead, 2001, p. 54

Independent schools

The Way Ahead estimates that there are around 500 independent schools which claim explicitly to be Anglican foundations, and over 100 more which are Anglican by association. The report assumes that it is appropriate for the Anglican Church to affirm the independent sector of education, embraces this sector as part of the Church's mission to the nation, and encourages these schools to strengthen their distinctiveness.

Independent schools

Anglican independent schools should always be considered as part of the family of Church schools, and opportunities should be taken to foster the relations between maintained and independent schools.

The Way Ahead, 2001, p. 78

The Church colleges

The remaining Church colleges of higher education play a crucial role in the eyes of the review group for resourcing the expanding network of Church schools. The report encourages these colleges to:

- emphasize their distinctiveness
- appoint a practising Christian as head of teacher training
- promote the Church Colleges Certificate programme in religious studies and Church school studies
- integrate the chaplain into the decision-making process
- become involved in pre- and post-ordination training of the clergy

---

Church colleges

We recommend that the Church should develop a strategic view of its relationship with the colleges and that the Church should affirm the essential role of the colleges through using the colleges as the first source of relevant advice on relevant matters.

The Way Ahead, 2001, p. 81

References and further reading

Burns, J., *et al.* (2001), *Faith in Education: A Response to the Dearing Report on Church Schools in the Third Millennium*, London, Civitas.

Chadwick, P. (1997), *Shifting Alliances: Church and State in English Education*, London, Cassell.

Church of England (1998), *Church of England Schools in the New Millennium*, London, General Synod of the Church of England.

Church Schools Review Group (2001), *The Way Ahead: Church of England Schools in the New Millennium*, London, Church House Publishing (the 'Dearing Report').

Commission on Religious Education in Schools (1970), *The Fourth R*, London, National Society and SPCK (the 'Durham Report').

Dennis, N. (2001), *The Uncertain Trumpet: A History of Church of England School Education to AD2001*, London, Civitas.

Francis, L. J. (2000), 'The domestic and the general function of Anglican schools in England and Wales', *International Journal of Education and Religion*, 1, pp. 100–21.

20

RE in Community Schools

Introduction

'County schools' was until recently the official name for those schools that are owned, maintained and partly controlled by local government (through 'local education authorities') in England and Wales. They are to be distinguished from Church schools (see Chapter 22) and are now officially designated 'community schools'. We may consider them together with 'foundation schools' without a religious character with regard to the teaching of religious education.

The legal framework

Religious education is subject to legislation in all maintained schools in England and Wales. The 1944 Education Act sought to regularize the almost universal teaching of religion in schools. It required that 'religious instruction' should be given in all schools (the only compulsory subject in the curriculum!), subject to conscience clauses for both teachers and the parents of pupils ('the right of withdrawal'). The school day was to begin with an act of 'collective worship', which again was subject to conscience clauses. The term 'religious education' is used in the 1944 Act to cover both teaching ('religious instruction', now normally referred to as 'religious education' and designated as such in the 1988 Education Reform Act) and school worship. In county schools the religious teaching was to be according to an *agreed syllabus* unanimously agreed between four panels comprising representatives of the LEA, teachers' organizations, the Church of England (England only), and other 'religious denominations' in the area. (This meant Christian denominations, but in the 1988 Act it was widened to 'Christian and other religious denominations'.) The 1944 Act took over the Cowper-Temple clause from the Education Act of 1870, which required that no religious doctrine or formulary was to be taught 'that was distinctive of any particular denomination'.

As the framers of the 1944 Act were surely aware of the existence of well-established Jewish schools in England, it would be unfair to say that the idea of 'religion' in the legislation was confined to Christianity, although Government spokesmen at the time referred to 'Christian instruction' and acts 'of Christian worship'. The existence of the conscience clauses, however, together with the provision of worship, make it clear that the fundamental aim in 1944 was that of bringing up children within religion, and that could only mean a specific religion.

Partly in response to pressure from the Churches, the 1988 Education Reform Act intended to strengthen the place of RE and worship in the school, while leaving the basic requirements of the 1944 Act unchanged. The new Act specified 'core' and 'other foundation' subjects in a new National Curriculum, which together with religious education make up 'the basic curriculum', whose task it is to promote the 'spiritual, moral, cultural, mental and physical development of pupils at the school and of society'. New locally agreed syllabuses for RE must reflect the fact that religious traditions in the nation are in the main Christian 'whilst taking account of the teaching and practices of the other principal religions represented in Great Britain'. Community school RE remains non-denominational, although *teaching about* denominational differences is permitted.

Changing aims in religious education

The syllabuses of religious instruction that preceded and followed the 1944 Act were largely composed of biblical passages seasoned by a little Church history (in particular, references to non-controversial saints and heroes of the faith). They were 'Christian', but without much doctrinal content: a consequence of the fact that the history of denominational struggle had shown that doctrine was divisive. Such a curriculum lacked any concrete Church-base and has been described as 'the County Council Creed' and as a new 'Agreed Syllabus Religion'.

Up until the mid-1960s agreed syllabuses and official reports concurred in the view that the aims of publicly funded school education included the children being taught, through instruction in the Christian religion, to 'know and love God' (the 1967 'Plowden Report', p. 207).

In recent decades, the understanding of religious education in schools in Great Britain has undergone two major shifts. The motive power for the first revolution lay mainly with the discipline of educational psychology. The researches of Ronald Goldman into the development of children's 'religious thinking' (see Chapter 14), coupled with empirical reports showing that little of the traditional school RE had had its intended effect on children, led to a new approach and a new generation of agreed syllabuses. These laid more emphasis on so-called 'life themes' and less on biblical knowledge; the Bible stories of the old agreed syllabuses were no longer thought to be appropriate for primary children who (according to Goldman) were not yet capable of abstract religious thinking. The aim of this new RE, however, remained the nurturing of Christianity. Goldman, indeed, referred to it as 'Christian education' and offered a theological justification for teaching it in schools ('Christianity should be taught because it is true').

Such an approach to RE in schools has been described as 'neo-confessional', in that it 'attempts to make "confessional" or dogmatic religious education more acceptable and effective by improving methods and techniques in accordance with the findings of educational research, and especially by constructing syllabuses based on the capacities, needs and interests of the pupils' (Schools Council, 1971, p. 30). The confessional/non-confessional distinction became part of the jargon of discussions about RE in Britain in the 1970s. Essentially, the confessional label was applied to educational activities intended to foster a particular religious commitment.

The second revolution in RE only came with a shift away from such aims to a 'non-confessional religious education' in county/community schools. In the broadest sense this was a revolution in the philosophy, rather than the psychology, of religious education. Things began to change in the late 1960s with a new stress by religious educators and educationalists on 'an unrestricted personal quest for meaning in life in terms of actual experience' (Schools Council, 1971, p. 34). It was felt that RE should encourage children in school to examine the religious interpretation (note the singular noun) of life, and to engage in their own personal quest for meaning, value and purpose. The starting point for such a child-centred course had to be the pupil's own life experience.

Aim of religious education

It should have as its aim the giving to children of a religious view of life and then allowing them freely to make up their minds how that view shall express itself both in belief and practice.

Edwin Cox, 1966, p. 66

Schools Council Working Paper 36 (1971) described this as the 'implicit religion' approach, for it focused on human experiences and attitudes whose 'significance for religion is implied but not directly referred to' (Jean Holm), rather than on phenomena that were recognizably, because explicitly, religious. While some accounts of this approach acknowledged a place for the study of explicit religion, others were in danger of advocating RE programmes that were wholly without any such reference: thus Harold Loukes argued that a lesson on spiders could be as religious as the story of Abraham, provided that it was 'treated personally and set the hearers off into the depth'. A similar criticism is sometimes laid at the door of the more recent 'experiential approach' to RE, exemplified by the work of David Hay and others (Hammond *et al.*, 1990), which seeks to encourage children to explore their own subjective states so as to appreciate the nature of the self and of spiritual experience.

A different criticism of implicit RE is that it was not sufficiently open-ended to constitute an appropriate education in religion for the children of an increasingly secular and pluralistic society. Often this 'personal quest' was a form of 'Christian quest' (Grimmitt, 1973, p. 25). In fact, the revolution in the aims of RE was not completed until the 1970s began to see the promotion in schools of the 'phenomenological' or 'explicit religion' approach. This abandons all responsibility for religious proselytizing or nurture, whether Christian or otherwise, overt or covert.

The primary field of study for the student of RE was now to be seen as the explicit phenomena of religion. Phenomenologists of religion contend that a proper understanding of religion demands empathy with its inside, in addition to a self-disciplined 'bracketing' of the student's own theological and evaluative judgements, so as to let the phenomena speak for themselves.

While the implicit religion element still found a place in this form of RE, there was a tendency to subordinate it to the study of explicit religion, rather than vice-versa. Human attitudes and experiences such as love, trust, hope and fear were sometimes explored in order to understand the experiences of religion. We should note too that this approach also included, even if only for older classes, an attempt to encourage students to evaluate as well as to understand religion: questions of truth and value were not for ever 'bracketed out' of RE.

The distinctive feature of the explicit religion approach to school RE is often taken to be the inclusion of religions other than Christianity in its scope. But the change of aim is more significant than the change in content and it would be possible, although perhaps somewhat perverse, to adopt this approach to RE while restricting the study to Christianity alone. One cannot, however, have a confessional RE that tries to induct pupils into a variety of religions. It is clear that the 'world religions movement' in school RE, which recognizes the importance of studying non-Christian religions at least partly because we all live in a world that is religiously plural and Britain is a multi-faith nation, has considerably strengthened the arm of the non-confessional RE lobby. The first explicit official recognition of the 'outlawing' of confessional RE (contrast

Thompson, 2001) came in the pages of the 1994 Department for Education advisory document, Circular 1/94:

> Syllabuses must not be designed to convert pupils, or to urge a particular religion or religious belief on pupils. (p. 15)

Justifying RE

The phenomenological type of school RE has been generally regarded as much easier to justify on educational grounds than the earlier approaches. Many would regard it as producing uncontroversially worthwhile learning, in an unobjectionable way, with an emphasis on knowledge and understanding. On this view, religions are studied in schools because it is good for children to learn about such significant human phenomena, and to develop tolerance and multi-cultural understanding.

By contrast, a confessional approach to teaching religion (Christianity) would seem to many people only to be justifiable, if at all, on the *theological* grounds that it is true, and that it is right and good for children to be brought up in the true faith. The 'personal quest' RE teacher, on the other hand, teaches religion (or just Christianity) because it is a good thing for children to explore the questions of meaning and to find a (or the) faith by which to live.

The appropriate style for religious education

- *Plural* in the sense that it is not restricted to one tradition but takes seriously the existence of different religions and secular alternatives.
- *Open* in the sense that the scope of the subject and its content are not defined from within one religious tradition.
- *Exploratory* in terms of the attitude it encourages on the part of children and teachers.
- *Aiming at understanding* and so concerned with the development of capacities and attitudes, the exploration of important ideas, and the imparting of factual information.

Schools Council, 1977, pp. 8, 43

The present situation

Current agreed syllabuses for religious education in England and Wales usually add elements from the earlier personal quest approach to an explicit religion syllabus. This reflects a continuing appreciation of the value of reflection on, and indeed development of, the learner's own life-stance and meaning-system (a 'faith to live by'), or a sense of meaning and purpose.

John Hull has described school *religious education* (which includes sensitivity training, moral education, personal relations and so on) as a wider group of subjects 'helping the pupil in his own quest for meaning', with *religious studies* (that is the study of religions) at its core (Hull, 1984, p. 54). Michael Grimmitt writes of RE as a subject that combines phenomenological study (through which the pupil learns about religion) with a version of the experiential/personal quest approach which uses religious insights to stimulate personal insights about the pupil's own identity, values, commitments, etc. (described as learning '*from* religion about himself') and includes the development of self-awareness, interpretative skills and capacities for personal decision-making. He writes:

> The value of studying religions is not merely to be found in the understanding of religious meaning that it promotes, but in what understanding religious meaning contributes to the pupil's understanding of self. Second, the study of religions provides both the occasion and the stimulus for young people to become aware of the centrality of beliefs and believing in human meaning-making activities. (Grimmitt, 1987, p. 165)

Robert Jackson also advocates a middle way in RE in which the study of religions is so conducted that it makes a distinctive contribution to the development of a coherent set of beliefs and values that is personally satisfying to the pupil.

Aims of religious education

Religious education should have two sides to it. It is to help children understand the religious traditions of life and thought that they meet in their environment. It is also to help children to be sensitive to the ultimate questions posed by life and to the dimension of mystery and wonder that underlies all human experience.

Schools Council, 1977, p. 11

Being able to interpret another's world-view is not the only basic aim of religious education, however. The interpretive process starts from the insider's language and experience, moves to that of the student, and then oscillates between the two. Thus the activity of grasping another's way of life is inseparable in practice from that of pondering on the issues and questions raised by it. Such reflective activity is personal to the student. Teachers cannot delay the process of reflection to a later date, just as they cannot guarantee that it will happen. They can, however, enable it by providing structured opportunities for reflection.

Robert Jackson, 1997, p. 130

Although some such expansion of the rather stark explicit religious education aim is now routinely found in British writing about RE in schools, the focus is still on religious *understanding* and the elucidation of religion(s), rather than the promotion of a particular religious *commitment*.

> There is an important sense in which contemporary British RE in county (state) schools should be thought of as a new subject in the curriculum...It is not a natural development of the old RE, which was a domestic activity of the church, but represents a radical break with past traditions, which can be seen as the secularisation, the professionalisation or the liberation of the subject. (John Hull, in Sutcliffe, 1984, p. 285)

Objectives of religious education

Religious education should help pupils to:
- acquire and develop knowledge and understanding of Christianity and the other principal religions represented in Great Britain;
- develop an understanding of the influence of beliefs, values and traditions on individuals, communities, societies and cultures;
- develop the ability to make reasoned and informed judgements about religious and moral issues, with reference to the teachings of the principal religions represented in Great Britain;
- enhance their spiritual, moral, cultural and social development by:
  - developing awareness of the fundamental questions of life raised by human experiences, and of how religious teachings can relate to them
  - responding to such questions with reference to the teachings and practices of religions, and to their own understanding and experience
  - reflecting on their own beliefs, values and experiences in the light of their study;
- develop a positive attitude toward other people, respecting their right to hold different beliefs from their own, and toward living in a society of diverse religions.

School Curriculum and Assessment Authority, 1994, p. 4

References and further reading

Astley, J. and Francis, L. J. (eds.) (1996), *Christian Theology and Religious Education: Connections and Contradictions*, London, SPCK.

Copley, T. (1997), *Teaching Religion: Fifty Years of Religious Education in England and Wales*, Exeter, University of Exeter Press.

Cox, E. (1966), *Changing Aims in Religious Education*, London, Routledge & Kegan Paul.

Grimmitt, M. (1973, 1978), *What Can I Do in RE?*, Great Wakering, McCrimmons.

Grimmitt, M. (1987), *Religious Education and Human Development*, Great Wakering, McCrimmons.

Grimmitt, M. (ed.) (2000), *Pedagogies of Religious Education: Case Studies in the Research and Development of Good Pedagogic Practice in RE*, Great Wakering, McCrimmons.

Hammond, J., Hay, D., Moxon, J., Netto, B., Raban, K., Straugheir, G. and Williams, C. (1990), *New Methods in RE Teaching: An Experimental Approach*, Harlow, Oliver & Boyd.

Hull, J. M. (1984), *Studies in Religion and Education*, Lewes, Falmer.

Hull, J. M. (1998), *Utopian Whispers: Moral, Religious and Spiritual Values in Schools*, Norwich, Religious and Moral Education Press.

Jackson, R. (1997), *Religious Education: An Interpretive Approach*, London, Hodder & Stoughton.

Kay, W. K. and Francis, L. J. (eds.) (1997), *Religion in Education, Volume 1*, Leominster, Gracewing.

Plowden Report (1967) *Children and their Primary Schools*, London, HMSO.

School Curriculum and Assessment Authority (1994), *Model Syllabuses for Religious Education: Model 1*, London, SCAA.

Schools Council (1971), *Religious Education in Secondary Schools*, London, Evans/Methuen.

Schools Council (1977), *Discovering an Approach: Religious Education in Primary Schools*, London, Macmillan.

Sutcliffe, J. M. (ed.) (1984), *A Dictionary of Religious Education*, London, SCM Press.

Thompson, P. (2001), 'The interpretation of religious education legislation: a case study', *Journal of Education and Christian Belief*, 5, pp. 145–58.

Wright, A. and Brandom, A.-M. (eds.) (2000), *Learning to Teach Religious Education in the Secondary School: A Companion to School Experience*, London, RoutledgeFalmer.

21

Assemblies in Community Schools

Introduction

The 1944 Education Act and the 1988 Education Reform Act stipulated that pupils in attendance at a maintained school in England and Wales should take part in daily acts of collective worship. This chapter seeks to explore the historical background of worship in schools and to provide information about some of the current issues of debate in this area.

The early years

Learning how to worship and participating in daily acts of worship were significant features of the lives of these schools from the beginning. The 1870 Education Act, which set up local school boards, contained a clause (the Cowper-Temple Clause) which made it illegal for any board school to provide denominational religious instruction or worship. The new situation raised a question that was to be asked a number of times during the following century, namely, should worship be conducted in state-maintained schools? The vast majority of schools decided that it should, and worship continued to play a significant role in the life of schools in the decades that followed.

The 1944 Education Act

By the 1940s worship was a key feature in the life of most community schools. What the 1944 Education Act did was enshrine its place in law. The Act stipulated that worship was to take place every morning and to be separate from religious instruction. What had taken place previously on a voluntary basis was now required of all state-maintained schools.

In the years that followed the 1944 Act, most British schools conducted an act of worship every morning after registration, and this usually included a hymn, a Bible reading and a prayer (including, of course, the Lord's Prayer). When religious observances had been met it was time to move on to the other aspects of school life. The second part of the twentieth century was a period of great change for British society. Technological and scientific advances heralded major changes in the British way of life. To some extent the faith that people had once expressed in God was substituted by a newly found faith in scientific innovations. Figures showing attendance at places of worship during this period show a steady decline. A further factor was that Britain during this period was becoming a multi-cultural society. Thus, the debate that featured prominently in the 1970s and 1980s was whether worship should be part of life in a modern Western school and if it was, whether it should continue to be exclusively Christian.

The Durham Report (1970)

One of the first influential publications to try to give a balanced account of the debate regarding school worship was *The Fourth R* (1970) (see Chapter 18). It presented a number of arguments in favour of and against maintaining worship in schools and the daily morning assembly. It concluded that it saw no reason to change what was a well-accepted practice in British schools. School worship was deemed valuable because it expressed the corporate life of the school. If it were no longer required by law it would soon wither away; the law protected pupils from the possibility of not experiencing worship at all, and headteachers from local pressure to abandon worship. The legal requirements were also a signal to society of parliament's support for school worship.

School Worship: An Obituary (1975)

A major input into the debate about school worship was made by John Hull in 1975 with the publication of his book *School Worship: An Obituary*. Hull proposed a radical rethink about the role of worship in a modern school, objecting to the existing worship arrangements on several grounds. He claimed that in an era when one of the purposes of education was to encourage children to think for themselves (religious education, for example, encouraged children to explore different belief-systems) it was inappropriate for school worship to demand adherence to a certain set of beliefs. Compulsory worship was not only a contradiction in terms, it also contradicted one of the fundamental aims of modern Western education. While the former assumed belief, the latter scrutinized it. The old style of worship had no place in modern multicultural Britain. It was potentially indoctrinatory and gave a distorted picture of what true worship was like. He proposed a new type of assembly which would provide ceremonies, celebrations and other events which would:
- widen the pupils' repertoire of appropriate emotional response
- encourage a reflective approach to living that transcends the immediacy of experience
- demonstrate the values which are not controversial and upon which democratic society depends (freedom of speech, equality before the law, etc.)
- provide some experience and understanding of what worship is, so that the way of worship (along with other life-styles) will remain an option for anyone who wishes to follow it and so that all will have some insight into what it is like to live a religious life

The trend toward secularization continued. The role of the Church in people's lives diminished and British society became more willing to question its authority. As people were coming increasingly into contact with those from other faith traditions they were also more willing to question whether the Christian path was the only way to God.

The 1988 Education Reform Act

By the late 1980s, it was clear that the legal position of worship in schools needed to reflect the changes that had taken place since the 1944 Act. Sections 6 and 7 of the 1988 Education Reform Act sought to do this. The Act stipulated that school worship was compulsory and that it should take place every day (6.1). Unlike the 1944 Act, which stated that worship should take place at the beginning of the day, the new Act made provision for it to happen at any suitable time. Section 6.2 took into account the fact that in some schools lack of space made it impossible for all pupils to be present. Accordingly, schools could provide for a single act of worship for all pupils or for separate acts for pupils in different age groups.

The Act stated clearly that collective worship should be wholly or mainly of a broadly Christian character (7.1). It fulfilled this requirement if it reflected the broad traditions of Christian belief without being distinctive of any particular Christian denomination (7.2). Most, but not necessarily all, the acts of collective worship in a school should be of a broadly Christian character (7.3). The acts of worship should take into account the family background, ages and aptitudes of pupils (7.5). Withdrawal rights were maintained: teachers continued to have the right to withdraw from collective worship and parents also retained the right to withdraw their children from collective worship (9.2). Finally, the Standing Advisory Council on Religious Education had the responsibility to advise the LEA on matters pertaining to school worship. It could grant a *determination* to vary the requirement that the majority of the acts of collective worship in a particular school should be of a broadly Christian nature.

The new Act did not put an end to the debate regarding whether or not worship was a necessary part of school life. On the contrary, it fuelled an even greater debate. Since 1988, supporters of school worship have claimed that its place in school life should be maintained because it makes a unique and valuable contribution to children's learning. Elaine McCreery, in her book *Worship in the Primary School,* gives the following five reasons for maintaining school worship in the primary school (McCreery, 1993):

- It is a unifier, a time when the whole school community can come together as a single body to share a common identity.
- It is an opportunity to celebrate the values which everyone in the school can be expected to share.
- It provides opportunities to reflect on important issues.
- It can be a preparation for corporate worship, acquainting them with some of the 'ritual, language, and beliefs employed by faith communities in their acts of collective worship' (p. 30).
- It makes a valuable contribution to children's spiritual development.

The main arguments that are put forward against school worship are that it makes worship compulsory when by its very nature it is voluntary; that it is an unnecessary part of the school day and takes up valuable teaching and learning time; that when the whole school gathers together it is impossible for discussion to take place and may, therefore, be indoctrinatory; that when it is badly done it is counter-productive and can put pupils off religion; and that it gives a false picture of what worship is like in a faith community.

What do we mean by worship?

Although the term 'worship' is not defined in the 1944 or the 1988 Acts, schools need to reach a definition that enables them to fulfil the terms of the Act while at the same time not compromising the beliefs and values held by those who take part in it.

Worship in schools has been described in different ways. Here are a few of these descriptions:
- Worship is concerned with reverence or veneration paid to a divine being or power.

- Worship is showing commitment to certain religious beliefs.
- Worship is experiencing periods of stillness, silence and reflection.
- Worship means giving 'worth' (worth-ship) to ideas, concepts, principles and conduct that are worthy of celebration.
- Worship is celebrating shared values.
- School worship is a way of enabling pupils to become familiar with the rituals, language and beliefs employed by faith communities.
- Worship is a time to share in deeper levels of ordinary experience.

Department for Education Circular 1/94, which sought to give advice to schools on the 1988 Education Reform Act's stipulations regarding RE and worship, defined worship as being concerned with 'reverence or veneration paid to a divine being or power'. Such a definition is not without its problems, and some have argued that it goes against the philosophy of British education and of religious education in particular. It raises the question of how we can claim to be open to different belief systems in the classroom and then expect pupils to affirm belief in God in school worship.

Others have emphasized that the definition of worship in schools should be more open and that it should be an experience in which all children should be able to share, regardless of background. The last five descriptions of worship given in the above list might be compatible with this definition.

Collective worship

One significant difference between the 1944 and 1988 Acts was the use of the term 'collective' rather than 'corporate' worship. 'Corporate' implies congregational worship among members of faith communities. By implication, this type of worship is confessional, follows a set pattern, involves fellowship and adoration of the divine. The word 'collective', on the other hand, takes into account the fact that pupils in a school have a variety of backgrounds, beliefs and aptitudes. It recognizes that the nature and level of pupils' response will vary. Collective worship should be part of the broad curriculum offered by every school which promotes the 'spiritual, moral, social and cultural development of children' (Education Reform Act 1988). Consequently its aims, content and organization should differ from that of the worship which takes place within the faith communities.

Assembly and collective worship

A distinction needs also to be drawn between the terms 'assembly' and 'act of collective worship'. As far back as 1970, the Durham Report noted that in many schools the term 'assembly' was used instead of 'worship'. It is a trend that continues to this day. According to *The Concise Oxford Dictionary* the term 'assembly' refers to 'a group of people gathered together'. Within the school context, it refers to the gathering of pupils and staff. Such a gathering is not necessarily an act of worship. It may be limited to notices, team results and admonitions. An act of worship, on the other hand, refers to something more specific. This is the act from which teachers can legally withdraw and from which parents may withdraw their children on grounds of conscience. Nevertheless, in practice, when schools refer to 'assembly' they are usually referring to the gathering together of the school community for the purposes of worship in whichever way it is defined.

'Wholly or mainly of a broadly Christian character'

Perhaps the most controversial part of the 1988 Act was the Section which stated that collective worship 'shall be wholly or mainly of a broadly Christian character' (7.1). Does this mean that school worship should be exclusively Christian, as some heads, teachers and parents fear? Close inspection of the terms of the Act reveals that it is not the intention to make worship restrictively Christian. According to Section 7.2, an act of worship has a broadly Christian character 'if it reflects the broad traditions of Christian belief without being distinctive of any particular denomination' (7.2). The guidelines to the Act indicate that 'broadly Christian' does not mean exclusively Christian, but that 'taken as a whole, the traditions of Christian belief shall be reflected in the act of worship'. Worship is not intended to be narrowly confessional. In the House of Lords debate supporters of the inclusion of the term 'Christian' in this section of the Act were anxious to stress that indoctrination should not be the aim of school worship. Moreover, not every act of worship in a school term needs to be of a broadly Christian character. The terms 'wholly or mainly' are explained in the circular as implying that *most* acts of worship in a term must be broadly Christian. The term 'most' can mean anything from 51 per cent to 99 per cent.

Assembly and spiritual development

One of the areas in which assembly can make a major contribution is children's spiritual development. The 1988 Education Reform Act required that schools should contribute to children's spiritual, moral, social and cultural development (see Chapter 26). Although the last three of these concepts are fairly easy to define, a universally acceptable definition of 'spiritual development' has proved more elusive. The problem is that spirituality means different things to different people. For example, a Christian might argue that to talk about spirituality would be impossible without reference to God; a non-believer on the other hand might stress that spirituality is the quest for truth and meaning and does not necessarily need to involve belief in God at all.

What is spiritual development?

Spiritual development needs to be seen as applying to something fundamental in the human condition which is not necessarily experienced through the physical senses and/or expressed through everyday language. It has to do with relationships with other people and, for believers, with God. It has to do with the universal search for individual identity – with our responses to challenging experiences such as death, suffering, beauty, and encounters with good and evil. It has to do with the search for meaning and purpose in life and for values by which to live.

National Curriculum Council, 1993, p. 2

Those familiar with life in modern schools might make the observation that the promotion of spiritual development as described above has a lot in common with the aims of school assembly as perceived by many educationalists. They might conclude that assembly is a key player in promoting children's spirituality. Assembly is the one time of day when pupils can stand back from the busy-ness of everyday school life to reflect on matters of worth. It can be a time to experience different forms of worship (such as singing and quiet contemplation) and to experience moments of awe and wonder and thankfulness. It might be an ideal opportunity to enable pupils to develop their own beliefs and values, and to develop a respectful appreciation of the beliefs and values of others.

Assemblies today

The debate regarding the nature and desirability of assemblies continues. However, more recent writings in this field have tended to concentrate less on the 'whys' of school worship and more on the 'hows'. The late twentieth century and early twenty-first have spawned a wealth of publications which give schools advice on how best to implement the law's requirements.

In line with the general trend toward increasing accountability within educational institutions, many publications stress the need for schools to produce their own worship policy documents. While the advice given varies from author to author, most agree that an acceptable policy should include details about the following:

- the manner in which worship is defined within the context of the school
- the aims of worship
- how the school interprets and implements the current legislation on worship (for example, what provision is made for pupils who are withdrawn from assembly?)
- how the school's mission statement and shared values can be supported by assembly
- the planning of assemblies (does the school, for example, deliver assemblies through weekly themes; how do individual classes contribute to assemblies?)
- the delivery and presentation of assemblies in school
- how the quality of assemblies is monitored

One of the ways that is commonly suggested for presenting assembly is through the use of themes. The types of theme typically suggested are: themes relating to religious festivals (such as Christmas, Divali, Hannukah); themes relating to the world around us (such as life on earth, pollution and conservation); themes relating to feelings, attitudes and beliefs (such as courage, dreams and jealousy); and themes relating to aspects of the curriculum (such as favourite books). The right theme can be an ideal vehicle for drawing positive attention to the values which the school is trying to promote, and for endorsing the school's mission statement and enabling pupils to reflect appropriately. The advantage of the thematic approach is that it provides structure for assemblies and enables schools to plan ahead as well as to keep records of what has been covered in the past.

Assemblies in the post-1944 period typically comprised hymns, prayers and Bible stories. While this type of assembly is by no means unknown today, most schools recognize the need for more variety in the presentation of assembly for it to maintain the interest of pupils. It is often suggested that assembly activities should include:

- the telling of a story
- the use of prayer
- the singing of hymns or songs
- the use of the children's own written, oral and art work
- role play
- television and radio presentations
- the use of questions and discussion
- using artefacts

- appreciating music or works of art
- listening to a variety of different, carefully chosen and appropriately guided speakers
- experiencing periods of stillness and silence

Even though the law stipulates that worship in schools should be 'wholly or mainly of a broadly Christian character' the content of assemblies today seldom comes exclusively from the Bible. The themes covered and the stories told may come from secular sources or other faiths, in addition to Christian sources.

Hymns and prayers in assembly are more contentious. Some argue that pupils should not be required to sing hymns and say prayers, since doing so may compromise their beliefs. According to this argument, the act of praying and singing certain hymns assumes a belief in God, a belief that not all pupils will necessarily hold. While this may not be an issue in most British schools at the present time, others have substituted silent or shared reflection for prayer and replaced traditional belief-affirming hymns with hymns that are not confessional in nature.

At a time when the school's curriculum has undergone major changes, in response to the changing nature of society, some have argued that worship no longer has a role to play in the life of a school in a modern, secular Western society. Yet school worship has survived. It is no longer seen in most schools as a vehicle to promote the Christian faith but as an educationally valuable time when the whole school can come together to affirm that which is of value and to reflect on that which is of worth to the school community. As numerous school inspection reports produced by the Office for Standards in Education (OFSTED) have testified in recent years, worship, when conducted well, can make a significant contribution to children's spiritual, moral, social and cultural development. As this is one of the key objectives of education as stated in the 1988 Education Reform Act, worship clearly has an important role to play in contributing to the broad, balanced education that is the entitlement of every child in our society.

References and further reading

Commission on Religious Education in Schools (1970), *The Fourth R*, London, National Society and SPCK (the 'Durham Report').

Copley, T. (ed.) (1997), *Collective Worship: Perspectives 57*, Exeter, School of Education, University of Exeter.

Hull, J. (1975), *School Worship: An Obituary*, London, SCM Press.

McCreery, E. (1993), *Worship in the Primary School*, London, David Fulton.

National Curriculum Council (1993), *Spiritual and Moral Education: A Discussion Paper*, London, NCC.

Thatcher, A. (1997), 'Educational arguments for collective worship', in T. Copley (ed.), *Collective Worship: Perspectives 57*, Exeter, School of Education, University of Exeter, pp. 5–23.

Wright, C. (1995), *Delivering Collective Worship: A Guide for Schools*, Westley, Courseware Publications.

22

Church Schools

Introduction and definitions

The state-maintained system of education in England and Wales has its roots in the initiative of many individuals, most of them Christian, in the late eighteenth and early nineteenth centuries. These efforts were given focus with the founding in 1808 of the British and Foreign Schools Society by members of the Free Churches and, three years later, by the founding of the National Society by members of the Church of England. These two societies acted to support local church groups in the creation of schools. For this purpose they received grants from the state. The schools that were founded in this time typically provided 'education for the children of the poor and manufacturing classes in the parish of...'. From these roots grew the system of education that provides education for all but approximately 6.8 per cent of the children between the ages of 5 and 16 in England and Wales today (Department for Education and Science, 2001).

By the 1860s it was apparent that universal elementary education was an urgent need and that the Churches were not going to be able to provide schooling for every child in the country. For this reason, parliament passed the Education Act 1870, which set up the means whereby schools could be created by school boards, locally created, which were empowered to levy rates for the purpose. These school boards were not popular and there was a reluctance to create them in some areas.

In the first half of the twentieth century there were two key reforming acts of parliament. The first in 1902 did away with the school boards and created local education authorities (LEAs), but left the balance between the provision of Church schools and local authority schools – the so-called *dual system* – unchanged. In 1944 an Act was passed which laid the foundation for the education system as it is now experienced. It created two stages of school education, primary and secondary, and also reformed the arrangements for Church schools and for religious education and school worship in all schools.

Within each phase of education it was possible to have schools of four different statuses. These statuses were voluntary aided (VA), voluntary controlled (VC), special agreement (SA) and county. All the Church schools and a few schools founded by secular organizations, such as the City Livery Companies, were in the first three of these categories, while all schools founded by the local education authority were county schools. All four types of school received their basic running costs from the LEA.

This system survived unchanged until 1988, when the Education Reform Act introduced a new type of school – the grant maintained school. In theory, all schools could choose to become grant maintained, which meant that they ceased to receive funding from the LEA but rather received it from the Funding Agency for Schools, a central government quango. In 1998 a change in government led to a further reform.

Grant maintained schools were abolished and all schools within the state system returned to a system of funding and support based on their LEAs. A new category of school was introduced, foundation schools, and the category of special agreement school was also abolished. As a result of the Schools Standards and Framework Act 1998 there were once again four statuses of school: voluntary aided, voluntary controlled, foundation (F) and community (C). As a result of the choices that were possible for individual schools within this framework, the number of schools in VA, VC or F which did not have a religious foundation was significantly increased, and it was therefore necessary to incorporate a new concept into the law to identify those schools to which the arrangements for Church schools should apply. This was schools having a religious character.

To have a 'religious character' the school must meet one of the following tests:

1 At least one of the governors is appointed by a religious faith or denomination to represent that faith or denomination.

2 The premises were provided on a trust that clearly states that it is for religious purposes.

3 The premises were provided on a trust that clearly states that they are for a school to be run in accordance with the principles and practices of a religious faith or denomination.

The full text of the provisions, of which this is a summary, can be found in *The Religious Character of Schools (Designation Procedure) Regulations*, 1998

It is not possible for a community school to have a religious character as defined under the Act. Schools that have a religious character, whether they are voluntary aided, voluntary controlled or foundation, are known as 'Church schools'. These schools are listed in 'The Designation of Schools having a Religious Character (England) Order 1999', its equivalent in Wales or in subsequent supplementary orders. An analysis of that order provides an accurate picture of the numbers of Church schools and their denominational or faith affiliation within the state-maintained part of the education system in England. Table 1 gives details of this analysis. For the purposes of clarity, middle schools are included in either the primary or secondary figures depending on whether they serve 8- to 12-year-olds (primary) or 9- to 13-year-olds (secondary).

For a complete picture of the total number of schools in England that have a religious affiliation, the figures in Table 1 must be increased to include those schools in the independent sector which have a religious foundation or identity. Definitions are difficult to create here. For example, the Anglican report *Youth A Part* (1996) quotes statistics for young people in Anglican schools in the independent sector which were developed by taking only those schools which had claimed an Anglican identity and reflected this by having an Anglican chaplain. By this definition there are just over 200 Anglican schools in the independent sector in England. However, if the requirement to have an identified Anglican chaplain is omitted from the definition the number rises to 598.

These problems make the production of an accurate table of the total number of schools in England with a clear religious character very difficult.

Table 1: Numbers of schools in England with a religious character

Denomination or faith group	Secondary schools	Primary schools	All schools
Christian	19	13	32
Church of England	186	4,531	4,717
Church of England/Christian	1		1
Church of England/Free Church		1	1
Church of England/Methodist	1	28	29
Church of England/Roman Catholic	8	3	11
Church of England/URC		2	2
Congregational		1	1
Jewish	5	25	30
Methodist		27	27
Muslim	2	2	4
Quaker		1	1
Roman Catholic	337	1,771	2,108
Seventh Day Adventist		1	1
Sikh	1	1	2
United Reformed Church		1	1
Total	**560**	**6,408**	**6,968**

The three different statuses within the maintained system

All schools with a religious character must include an ethos statement in their Instrument of Government. This forms the basis on which the governors will develop policies and practices in the school that reflect the school's religious character. Most of the major Christian Churches have developed model ethos statements for their schools.

Model ethos statement recommended by the Church of England and Church in Wales

Recognizing its historic foundation, the school will preserve and develop its religious character in accordance with the principles of the Church of England/Church in Wales and in partnership with the churches at parish and diocesan level.

The school aims to serve its community by providing an education of the highest quality within the context of Christian belief and practice. It encourages an understanding of the meaning and significance of faith, and promotes Christian values through the experience it offers to all its pupils.

In this section each of the three possible statuses of school that can have a religious character will be considered and the differences in certain key areas of the life of the school will be identified. The statements made are generally true, although there may be occasional variations reflecting particular local circumstances. The same wording has been used where the same arrangements apply to schools of different statuses.

Detailed advice on all these matters is available from local dioceses and through the publications of the Catholic Education Service and the National Society.

Voluntary aided schools

These are the schools in which the Churches have the most direct influence. All Roman Catholic schools and just under half of all Anglican schools are voluntary aided.

Admissions: The admissions to the school are under the control of the governing body. The governors determine the admissions policy (although they must consult with other admissions authorities in the area). They administer the policy, although their actions are subject to independent appeal.

Staffing: The governors of the school are the employers of the staff of the school and are responsible for all aspects of their employment. The LEA often provides payroll services and the advice of experts in personnel matters if the governors request this.

Buildings: The schools are owned by trustees (or sometimes religious orders). The governors are responsible for all development work on the buildings and for major repairs with the assistance of grants from the Department for Education and Skills. Routine repairs are undertaken using money delegated from the LEA for this purpose.

Governors: Governors are nominated or elected by the groups most involved with the school, but those governors nominated by the Church are always in an absolute majority over all other governors.

Curriculum: The school must follow the requirements of the National Curriculum but the governors determine the content of the religious education syllabus, which should reflect the religious character of the school.

Worship: School worship should reflect the religious character of the school. Therefore the policy and programme of worship in the school will include material drawn from the usual pattern of worship within the Church, together with material developed by that Church or others to be appropriate to worship for the age group of the school. Within those Christian denominations where the Eucharist is central to the worship of the Church, the school will include a section on the place of the Eucharist in their school policy document.

Voluntary controlled schools

These are schools in which the Church must act in partnership with others in the community to provide the education for the children. Voluntary controlled schools are often seen as a model for a type of co-operation which should exist in areas served by only one school when that is a Church school. Just over half of all Anglican schools and most Methodist schools are voluntary controlled.

Admissions: The LEA controls the admissions. The LEA must consult the governors each year about the admission arrangements for the school.

Staffing: The LEA employs the staff and is responsible for all matters to do with staff appointments. However, under arrangements for delegation of authority to schools most LEAs delegate many of the employer functions to the governing body, who are bound to operate within the LEA policies. Some special provision exists to enable governors to ensure that a headteacher is in sympathy with the ethos of the school and that there are some teachers who can teach religious education that reflects the school's religious character.

Buildings: The schools are owned by trustees (or sometimes religious orders). The LEA funds all building work.

Governors: Governors are nominated or elected by the groups most involved with the school. No single group has overall control.

Curriculum: The school must follow the requirements of the National Curriculum. Religious education is taught in accordance with the agreed syllabus in use in the school's LEA. Parents may request religious education in accordance with the school's religious character.

Worship: School worship should reflect the religious character of the school. Therefore the policy and programme of worship in the school will include material drawn from the usual pattern of worship within the Church, together with material developed by that Church or others to be appropriate to worship for the age group of the school. Within those Christian denominations where the Eucharist is central to the worship of the Church, the school will include a section on the place of the Eucharist in its school policy document.

Foundation Schools

There are a small number of Foundation schools that have a religious character. These are almost all Anglican.

Admissions: The admissions to the school are under the control of the governing body. The governors determine the admissions policy (although they must consult with other admissions authorities in the area). They administer the policy but their actions are subject to independent appeal.

Staffing: The governors of the school are the employers of the staff of the school and are responsible for all aspects of their employment. The LEA provides payroll services and the advice of experts in personnel matters if the governors request this.

Buildings: The school is owned by trustees (or sometimes religious orders). The governors are responsible for all development work on the buildings and for major repairs, with the assistance of grants from the Department for Education and Skills. Routine repairs are undertaken using money delegated from the LEA for this purpose.

Governors: Governors are nominated or elected by the groups most involved with the school. No single group has overall control.

Curriculum: The school must follow the requirements of the National Curriculum.

Religious education is taught in accordance with the agreed syllabus in use in the school's LEA. Parents may request religious education in accordance with the school's religious character.

Worship: School worship should reflect the religious character of the school. Therefore the policy and programme of worship in the school will include material drawn from the usual pattern of worship within the Church together with material developed by that Church or others to be appropriate to worship for the age group of the school. Within those Christian denominations where the Eucharist is central to the worship of the Church the school will include a section on the place of the Eucharist in their school policy document.

Inspection

In all Church schools the inspections conducted by The Office for Standards in Education are complemented by inspections of those aspects of the religious character of the school that are distinctive of its ethos. Provision for these inspections was originally included in Section 13 of the Education (Schools) Act 1992. Subsequently the provisions, as amended in 1993, were incorporated in Section 23 of the Schools Inspections Act 1996. In order to distinguish between the two inspections the convention has developed to refer to the inspections conducted by OFSTED as Section 10 inspections and the inspections of the religious character provisions as Section 23 inspections.

In response to these Acts, the Anglican Church set up a national scheme of inspection, whose framework and training is often used by the Methodist Church for its school inspections. The Roman Catholic Church has a diocesan-based system. It will be already apparent that the way in which Section 23 inspections impact on Church schools will vary with their status. Table 2 is taken from the National Society's *Inspection Handbook* (Brown, Lankshear and Seaman, 2000) and shows the normal situation for inspection.

*Table 2: **The impact of inspection***

	Voluntary aided	Voluntary controlled	Foundation
Religious education	Section 23	Section 10*	Section 10*
School worship†	Section 23	Section 23	Section 23
Spiritual, moral, social and cultural development	Section 23 and Section 10	Section 23 and Section 10	Section 23 and Section 10

*	Section 23 applies where parents have requested religious education in accordance with the religious character of the school.

†	Section 10 inspectors will report on whether the school is complying with the law on school worship in terms of pupil attendance.

Support for Church schools

In both the Roman Catholic and Anglican Churches there are diocesan teams whose work is to support the Church schools in their dioceses. Within the Anglican tradition, these same teams will also be active in the support of religious education, school worship, spiritual, moral, social and cultural development in all schools. The other denominations and faiths involved in the provision of schooling usually provide some support for their schools through a national organization. The national organization responsible for the support of Roman Catholic schools is the Catholic Education Service; and for the Anglican Church it is the National Society, working with the Church of England Board of Education.

The major day-to-day support for Church schools locally is provided by the local priest or minister of the Church, who will usually be an active member of the governing body and will also make a contribution either to the worship in the school or to another area of the school's work where his or her talents are best used.

Conclusions: the future of Church schools

Following the passage of the School Standards and Framework Act 1998, the Churches found that the position of their schools within the national framework of education had been significantly enhanced. The Church of England built on this with a report to the General Synod in the autumn of 1998. The debate on this report passed a resolution, without a single vote against, endorsing the importance of the work of Church schools in the mission of the Church. This has subsequently been followed by similar resolutions in many dioceses, almost all of which have been passed by overwhelming majorities.

Encouraged by this, the Church created a review of its schools whose principal task was to identify the means by which the Church's contribution to the education system of the country could be further developed. The final report of this group, entitled *The Way Ahead*, was published in June 2001 and formally adopted in the autumn of that year (see Chapter 19). There had been widespread consultation over the report, which meant that the government was able to signal its support in principle for some expansion of Anglican school provision in its Green Paper published in February 2001 and in the White Paper published in September. In this latter document the government made clear that it wished schools that had a religious character to be inclusive in their approach. In admission terms this was seen as endorsing the Anglican Church's tradition of ensuring that a proportion of places in the school went to pupils in the school's locality, regardless of the parents' religious affiliation. At the time of writing, the government's proposals are before parliament in what will become the Education Act 2002. It is therefore not clear how this legislation will impact on the development of Church schools, but it may be that the next ten years will see a significant expansion of the role and importance of Church schools. If this is to be achieved, their current high standing among parents and within the tables illustrating the achievements of schools will need to be maintained and developed. This represents a significant challenge to the Churches and in particular to those diocesan and national teams that support Church schools.

References and further reading

Key Anglican texts
Brown, A. S. *et al.* (2000), *Inspection Handbook for Section 23 Inspections in Schools of the Church of England and the Church in Wales*, London, National Society.
Carlisle Commission (1971), *Partners in Education: The Role of the Diocese*, London, National Society and SPCK.
Church of England (1996), *Youth A Part: Young People and the Church*, London, National Society and Church House Publishing.

Church Schools Review Group (2001), *The Way Ahead: Church of England Schools in the New Millennium*, London, Church House Publishing (the 'Dearing Report').

Commission on Religious Education in Schools (1970), *The Fourth R*, London, National Society and SPCK (the 'Durham Report').

Leonard, G. *et al.* (1985), *Positive Partnership*, London, The National Society.

Waddington, R. (1984), *A Future in Partnership*, London, The National Society.

Key Roman Catholic texts

Bishops' Conference of England and Wales (1997), *A Struggle for Excellence*, London, Catholic Education Service.

Catholic Education Service (1994), *Evaluating the Distinctive Nature of a Catholic School* (third edition), London, Catholic Education Service.

Catholic Education Service (1995), *Quality of Education in Catholic Secondary Schools*, London, Catholic Education Service.

Catholic Education Service (1997), *The Common Good in Education*, London, Catholic Education Service.

Key text for Joint Schools

Woollcombe, K. and Henderson, C. (chairs) (1987), *Joint Schools: A Discussion Document on Ecumenical Education*, Norwich and Leominster, Canterbury Press and Fowler Wright.

Other texts

Arthur, J. (1995), *The Ebbing Tide: Policy and Principles of Catholic Education*, Leominster, Gracewing.

Brennan, J. (1995), *The Christian Management of Catholic Schools*, Northampton, The Becket Press.

Chadwick, P. (1994), *Schools of Reconciliation*, London, Cassell.

Department for Education and Employment (1998), *The Religious Character of Schools (Designation Procedure) Regulations*, London, The Stationery Office.

Department for Education and Science (2001), *DfES Statistics of Education: Schools in England 2001*, London, The Stationery Office.

Francis, L. J. and Lankshear, D. W. (eds.) (1993), *Christian Perspectives on Church Schools: A Reader*, Leominster, Gracewing.

Lankshear, D. W. (2000), *Governing and Managing Church Schools*, London, National Society.

McLaughlin, T. H., O'Keefe, J. and O'Keeffe, B. (eds.) (1996), *The Contemporary Catholic School: Context, Identity and Diversity*, London, Falmer.

Sullivan, J. (2000), *Catholic Schools in Contention*, Dublin, Veritas.

Web sites

http://www.natsoc.org.uk/index
http://www.churchschools.co.uk
http://www.cesew.org.uk
http://www.catholic-ew.org.uk/educ/index.htm

23

RE in Church Schools

Introduction

The debate about religious education in 'community', 'county' or 'state' schools (Chapter 20) has had implications for how the subject is taught in Church schools in England and Wales. This chapter explores some of the issues and disagreements that have arisen over this topic.

The legal position

The law treats Church schools differently with regard to the teaching of RE. In Church *voluntary aided schools* the governing body is responsible for the teaching of RE and this must be in accordance with the school's trust deed. The trust deed will specify that RE should reflect the faith and practice of the appropriate denomination; a diocesan or denominational syllabus, published with the authority of the diocesan bishop, will usually be followed. In aided schools, parents may request that their children study RE according to the local agreed syllabus, but only where there is no other convenient school for children to attend. The governors may accede to this request, otherwise the local authority may consider it.

In Church *voluntary controlled schools* (and 'foundation schools' with a religious character) the teaching of RE should normally follow the local education authority's (non-confessional and non-denominational) agreed syllabus for the subject, as in community schools (see Chapter 20). In these schools parents may request that their children should additionally receive denominational RE, and under certain circumstances the school will appoint 'reserved teachers' to provide this teaching. (The clauses in the educational legislation specifying that RE should be non-denominational, and should take account of 'the teaching and practices of the other principal religions represented in Great Britain', do not apply to aided schools nor to any denominational RE that may be provided in controlled schools.)

Parents still retain the right to withdraw their children from RE on grounds of conscience in Church schools (even in aided schools) but governing bodies normally make it clear that they expect parents to be committed to the child's participation in RE (and worship) at the school. Teachers in aided schools and reserved teachers in controlled schools do not have the same right to refuse to teach RE or to participate in school worship as do teachers in community schools.

Should RE in Church schools be different?

On the one hand, Religious Education is an educational activity with the task of helping children to think about faith, to analyse and reflect on it and to bring their critical faculties to bear on it. Religious Education should also make a contribution to pupils' understanding of the world, to their spiritual and moral growth and to preparing them for adult life and responsibilities.

On the other hand, Church schools ought to be 'different'. They ought to be able to demonstrate their faith and values and the centrality of their Christian foundation in the life of the school. Unless they can, there seems little point in their existence. Religious Education is also part of this 'expression of faith', part of the nurturing, or potential nurturing role of the school, providing one of the means by which we hope pupils will see what the Christian faith is about, and how it may be relevant to their own lives.

Diocese of Durham RE Syllabus 2000, 1.13–1.14

In aided . . . schools RE should be able to flower on the stem of the confident Christian ethos of the school.

Alan Brown, 1992, p. 25

To nurture or not to nurture?

The writ against confessional religious education, as described in Chapter 20, does not run universally throughout the maintained sector of education in England and Wales. In addition to recognizing that 'Christianity will be taught from within' (John Hall, 1998, p. 39) throughout voluntary Church aided schools, many parents will also take it for granted that 'confessional Christian education', 'Christian nurture' or 'catechesis' should be an appropriate part of their teaching. Many religious educationalists would agree. James Arthur, for example, argues for a Christian education in Catholic schools that is a 'school-based initiation' promoting 'knowledge and understanding of Catholic beliefs and the free acceptance of these beliefs', as well as 'a sense of belonging to a community of faith' (Arthur, 1995, p. 79).

But a question mark has been raised against this assumption, usually for 'educational reasons' or because of the mixed nature of the student body in these Church schools. According to one survey, over 39 per cent of religious education teachers in a sample of Church of England aided secondary schools denied that the aims of the subject should differ between Church and county (community) schools, a figure that is close to the 36 per cent of teachers in county schools who held the same view (O'Keeffe, 1986, pp. 98, 117).

However, this debate over the place of catechesis within or 'alongside' religious education may be of more significance in theory than in practice, particularly with older children in secondary schools who are often resistant to 'being got at' in RE lessons, even in Church schools.

Should there be nurture in Church schools?

Those for . . .
There should be a style of religious education [in Church schools] which does justice to educational principles but which has value as catechesis: that is, it should not only be concerned with a sympathetic understanding of religion, but also with the development and maturing of faith itself.

Kevin Nichols, 1978, p. 24

Confessionalism of some kind has a place within a Church school, either on legal or historical grounds, or because parents who choose to send their children to Church schools do so in the knowledge that a distinctive and faith-based approach to religious education may be chosen.

Mark Chater, 1997, p. 271

And against...
The classroom is not the right setting for deliberately evangelising pupils nor is it the place where catechesis normally occurs... Religious education leads students to have a sympathetic understanding of religion without attempting to impose or influence their position.

Patrick Purnell, 1985, p. 73

Well, it depends...
While the Religious Education programme provides time for reflection that may enable children to come to understand more fully what they believe, it is not the task of a school in the maintained system of education to seek to bring children to a faith or to nurture them in it. Nor is it the task of a school to undermine a faith in which a child is being nurtured. Religious nurture is the task of the parents and the faith communities. Evangelism is the task of the faith communities. The exception to these general maxims is the Aided school which admits only children from practising Christian homes. These are probably a minority of Church of England Aided schools, but in them some activities identified with Christian nurture may be appropriate.

David Lankshear, 1992, p. 52

Church schools are places where the faith is lived, and which therefore offer opportunities to pupils and their families to explore the truths of Christian faith, to develop spiritually and morally, and to have a basis for *choice* about Christian commitment. They are places where the beliefs and practices of other faiths will be respected. Church schools are not, and should not be, agents of proselytism where pupils are *expected* to make a Christian commitment.

The Way Ahead, 2001, p. 12

'Other faiths' in the Church school

In Chapter 27 we explore the place of learning about 'other faiths' (that is, world faiths other than Christianity) in religious education. However we understand the task of 'teaching Christianity' in the Church school, religious education about the other world faiths remains an educational imperative for all children. Even if the Church school wants to express a particular Christian perspective or 'theology of religions' on these faiths, its pupils can hardly be considered to have become educated about religion if they only know about the Christian faith.

Where the Church school serves a religiously plural group of children and parents, as do many Catholic and Anglican inner-city schools, the teacher of RE will need not only to be sensitive to the various beliefs, values and practices of the different religious traditions, but also to think carefully about the proper Christian attitude to other faiths. In such situations the school functions as a microcosm of society, or at least of some parts of it, and has a Christian responsibility to help pupils to learn attitudes of tolerance and respect, as well as the skills of dialogue, compromise and negotiation of agreement and disagreement.

Church schools and the variety of faiths

To some teachers it would seem inappropriate to teach about religions other than Christianity. Of course, one would expect a Church aided school to spend a considerable time on Christianity and Church teachings. But just as one would expect the school to reach out to other Christian denominations with openness so one would expect it to prepare pupils to meet with people from other faiths.

Alan Brown, 1992, p. 25

It may be helpful to remember that in drawing upon faiths other than Christianity, the concern is to try to help the pupils appreciate and develop insights into religion. Such insights often help and strengthen our understanding of Christianity, for example, the discovery that prayer is not exclusive to Christianity but is found in other religions also, strengthens the teaching of prayer as an essential way of responding to God and of knowing Him. An understanding of prayer in this light is a central idea in Christianity. Many people have found their own commitment to, and understanding of, their own faith deepened through an exploration of religions other than their own...

One of the school's tasks is to help its pupils grow and become part of society. It cannot be denied that this country now reflects a multi-cultural, multi-racial and multi-faith society and however rural or mono-cultural the local school environment is, the world into which our pupils will move out will be one of mixed cultures, races and religions. This will be their world. Schools would therefore be failing in their *educational* duty if they did not prepare children for it. Part of that preparation must be an awareness and understanding of others with different cultural, social and religious backgrounds.

Diocese of Wakefield, *A Handbook of Suggestions for Religious Education in Church Schools*, 1988, pp. 9–10

'Half-way house' RE?

The Church aided school is, of course, still a school. It is not a church. Its buildings are owned by the Church that founded it, and new building work has to be partly funded by the Church, but the recurrent expenditure (including the teachers' salaries) is not provided by the Church. Apart from worship and RE, the school's teaching and other activities must take place according to national guidelines and syllabuses.

We may think of the Church aided school, and even more the controlled school, as operating in a 'mixed economy'. It is a Church institution *and* a state institution. Economically and socially, it may be thought of as a half-way 'house of the gospel' located between the Church and the community's secular streets. The Church's ownership of its buildings (in the case of all Church schools), and even its majority on governing bodies and its contribution to capital expenditure in the case of aided schools, are not sufficient to identify Church schools as 'wholly Church'. Theirs is, rather, a mixed economy of finance, power and educational philosophy that places them on the boundaries between Church and non-Church: threshold places of meeting and mutual influence, comings-and-goings and multiple belongings. Even though the aided school controls its own RE, we may still ask what sort of RE is proper in such a 'half-way house'?

We may argue that for children to understand with empathy the attitudes and emotions of a religious believer, they need to have some experience of the same or similar feelings or affects themselves. You can reasonably well 'learn about' (understand) a belief – and therefore a religious belief – without adopting it, but this is not true of understanding affect. You cannot learn much about any emotion without sharing it to some extent yourself. Since the student of religion has to imagine being 'under the skin' of the religious practitioner, secular religious education must get the student to 'imaginatively rehearse' (Ninian Smart, 1973, p. 75) the feelings of religious people. This may involve evoking in him or her a range of feelings that are at least akin to those that are also components of religious attitudes, emotions, experiences and evaluations, and accompany religious belief and action: feelings of awe, forgiveness, reverence, adoration and 'a sense of creatureliness'. The fuller the understanding of religion that is being aimed at in RE, the wider and deeper these feelings need to be. Therefore empathetic teaching about religion may in principle be said to *overlap* with religious formation, in the sense that it also produces some of the feelings that are so characteristic of and central to religion. Christian nurture and secular religious education remain very different sorts of activities with regard to the broad scope of their outcomes and objectives. But that difference may perhaps best be seen as a difference in (marked) degree, rather than a difference in kind.

How is this discussion relevant to Church schools? We might argue that the Church school, could quite appropriately see itself as encouraging the development of learning outcomes that lie somewhere *between* the educational outcomes of the secular school and those of the seminary or the Church. Such a school might well strive to provide its pupils with a fuller understanding of Christianity than does the community school, by trying to make them in this way somewhat 'more Christian'. In particular, it might seek to produce more by way of Christian feeling: by developing more implicit and characteristic Christian attitudes, emotions and experiences (such as trust, compassion, a sense of awe), and a few of the explicit and distinctive ones (such as reverence for Christ, a positive attitude to the Church, Christian prayer and worship experiences). This should strengthen the pupils' understanding of Christianity, without necessarily developing the *full range* of Christian attributes, especially those beliefs and actions that are more properly the objective of the *Church's* Christian education (such as churchgoing, sacramental practice and belief in the Trinity). In a word, Church school RE should help children to feel more like Christians feel, without *necessarily* getting them to believe like Christians or to engage in Christian practices.

This account allows Church schools to distinguish their own teaching both from that of the secular school and from that of a fully-fledged nurturing Church community. It proposes a sort of 'half-way house RE' which, while focused mainly on understanding, also involves nurturing Christian attitudes, values and emotions.

References and further reading

Arthur, J. (1995), *The Ebbing Tide: Policy and Principles of Catholic Education*, Leominster, Gracewing.

Arthur, J. and Gaine, S. (1996), '"Catechesis" and "religious education" in Catholic theory and practice', in L. J. Francis, *et al.* (eds.), *Research in Religious Education*, Leominster, Gracewing, pp. 335–57.

Astley, J. and Francis, L. J. (eds.) (1994), *Critical Perspectives on Christian Education: A Reader on the Aims, Principles and Philosophy of Christian Education*, Leominster, Gracewing, Part 1.

Brown, A. (1992), *Religious Education*, London, National Society, Chapter 7.

Chadwick, P. (1997), *Shifting Alliances: Church and State in English Education*, London, Cassell, Part 1.

Chater, M. (1997), 'Different approaches to religious education' and 'Critical analysis of different approaches to religious education', in W. K. Kay and L. J. Francis (eds.), *Religion in Education, Volume 1*, Leominster, Gracewing, pp. 257–88, 295–316.

Church Schools Review Group (2001), *The Way Ahead: Church of England Schools in the New Millennium*, London, Church House Publishing (the 'Dearing Report').

Francis, L. J. and Lankshear, D. W. (eds.) (1993), *Christian Perspectives on Church Schools: A Reader*, Leominster, Gracewing, especially Sections 1 and 2.

Hall, J. (1998), 'The Church in education: where do we go from here?', in G. Carey, D. Hope and J. Hall (eds.), *A Christian Voice in Education: Distinctiveness in Church Schools*, London, National Society/Church House Publishing, pp. 29–51.

Lankshear, D. W. (1992), *A Shared Vision: Education in Church Schools*, London, National Society and Church House Publishing, Chapter 4.

Nichols, K. (1978), *Guidelines for Religious Education: 1 Cornerstone*, Slough, St. Paul.

O'Keeffe, B. (1986), *Faith, Culture and the Dual System: A Comparative Study of Church and County Schools*, London, Falmer, Chapter 6.

Purnell, A. P. (1985), *Our Faith Story: Its Telling and Its Sharing*, London, Collins.

Smart, N. (1973), *The Phenomenon of Religion*, London, Macmillan.

Wakefield Diocesan Council of Education (1988), *A Handbook of Suggestions for Religious Education in Church Schools*, Wakefield, Wakefield Diocesan Council of Education.

24

Assemblies in Church Schools

Introduction

One of the difficulties facing anyone who wishes to consider this topic seriously is the use of words. The word 'assembly' has come into common usage in schools to describe what is referred to in the law as school worship. It is important that there is a clear distinction drawn. In practice, schools assemble their pupils for many purposes, not all of which are compatible with worship. This chapter will focus on those occasions on which Church schools assemble pupils together for the purposes of worship. It will not discuss those occasions when the school is assembled for prize-giving, fire-drill or even to be reminded of the rules about behaviour in the playground.

Some aspects of the law of education as it applies to school worship affect Church schools, other aspects do not. It is important to be clear as to what is required and what is not:

- Every pupil must take part in an act of worship every day.
- A particular act of worship may draw together pupils from a single class, a year group, a key stage, a house or any other grouping which is commonly used in the school. In other words, it does not have to be the whole school meeting in one place, but it could be.
- The act of worship can take place at any time of the school day. It may start the day, but it does not have to.

These are all policy, organizational and management issues for the individual school, to be determined ultimately by the governing body and the school's management team. These requirements apply to all schools in the maintained system.

Where a school has a religious character (see Chapter 22) the acts of worship will reflect that character. In all schools in England and Wales that do not have a religious character the worship must reflect the provisions first laid down in the Education Reform Act 1988 and now incorporated in the Education Act 1996. Although they are contained in the text box below, the provisions do *not* apply to Church schools and are included here only because they are frequently referred to and sometimes mistakenly taken to apply to Church school acts of worship.

Education Reform Act 1988

collective worship . . . shall be wholly or mainly of a broadly Christian character.

collective worship is of a broadly Christian character if it reflects the broad traditions of Christian belief without being distinctive of any particular Christian denomination.

By way of contrast, and to make the point that worship in Church schools is different, the following text box contains the opening paragraph of the worship section of the Inspection Handbook produced by the National Society on behalf of the Church of England and the Church in Wales. Every Church school should be reflecting the appropriate traditions from its denomination or faith community in its policy and practice.

In all Anglican schools worship should reflect some of the essential features within the rich traditions of Anglican prayer and worship. Church schools cannot be expected to encapsulate all of that richness, but when planning worship it is useful to have an idea of the important areas to be explored at some time during a pupil's school career. This is appropriate in all phases of compulsory education as the pupil's growing maturity contributes to a broadening and deepening of their spiritual experience and understanding.

Alan Brown *et al.*, 2000, p. 49

General issues within school worship in Church schools

This section will consider some of the important issues that all Church schools will need to consider in planning their programme of worship. These issues are followed by a discussion of some specific issues that will affect some Church schools but not all. They are discussed here for two purposes:

1 To identify the extent to which worship in Church schools is different from worship in churches.
2 To identify the extent to which worship in Church schools is different from worship in schools without a religious character.

School worship must be age-related

It is very important that the worship experience offered to pupils should be related to and appropriate for their age. There are many resources produced from within the faith communities that are designed to enable children and young people to engage with worship. Judicious use of these within the Church school context will help schools enable pupils to engage with the traditions of worship, while still being able to express their own needs and feelings within the context of the activity.

School worship must be educational

Schools are places of education, and everything that happens in school must contribute to the educational aims of the school, therefore school worship must have a place in the education of the pupils. For those pupils who already identify themselves with the faith and denomination of the Church school, school worship will enhance and deepen their experience of worship in their own church and help them to learn more about the tradition with which they are identifying. For pupils of other faiths and denominations, worship in a Church school will help them to understand and possibly value how other people of faith worship, and this should deepen their own experience of worship in their own tradition. For those pupils who have no faith of their own, Church school worship should give them an experience of what it is that people of faith do, what it might be like to participate and what is important to believers. From this very quick summary of three stereotyped positions it will be immediately apparent that most Church schools will have at least this range of pupils at most of their acts of worship, and that there will be subtle shades of difference between different groups within the same school. There will of course be some pupils who, for some of the time, will be positively antagonistic to the whole activity. All Church schools must think through their worship programme and policy in order to provide the best educational experience of worship for the whole range of pupils in their care.

School worship is compulsory

In the preceding paragraph the variety of participants was discussed briefly. What must be remembered by all those planning or leading worship in Church schools is that for the pupils attendance is compulsory. Parents may request that their children be withdrawn from school worship but the pupils may not take that decision for themselves. Many schools will wish to be particularly sensitive to this issue.

School worship has a wide variety of participants

In worship in church or in the faith community, most of those attending are there voluntarily and in part because the pattern of worship adopted within that church has come to be an important part of their expression of their own spirituality. A moment's thought will confirm that the range of individuals present at an act of school worship in a Church school is likely to be much wider. Even in those Church schools that draw pupils mainly from committed members of the faith community these are likely to come from several different places of worship. This variety must be respected and planned for. The National Society Inspection Handbook sums up these issues with the following words:

> For some pupils the experience of worship will be tentative and exploratory. For those who have already developed a growing Christian commitment, worship will be the natural outcome of belief, and a place where their deepest thoughts and emotions can be expressed in communion with God.
>
> Alan Brown *et al.*, 2000, p. 52

School worship in a Church school must relate to worship in church

Most Church primary schools have their roots in a single parish or local church community. In these cases it will be important that there is a direct link between what is experienced as worship in the Church school and what is experienced in worship within the faith community to which it relates. This implies that these schools will draw on the traditions of the faith community in their locality as well as those of the major denomination or communion of which they are a part. This will include, but go further than, joining in or reflecting local celebrations such as the patronal festival of the church or the church's anniversary service. It is probable that the Church school will use some of the prayers and hymns used in the local church and that this overlap of material will be consciously planned.

Use of local church for school worship

Until recently, only voluntary aided schools were able to use their local church for acts of school worship. In other categories of school any act of worship held in a local church did not count as the daily act of worship in the eyes of the law. Since 1998, however, all schools with a religious character have been able to meet their legal requirements by holding a service in a local church. This means that many church schools will need a fresh look at what is appropriate and possible. One of the challenges is to take the school group to the local church safely and with the use of only that amount of time which is justified by the importance of the occasion. This will vary according to local circumstances. In some places the church will be so close that it can be used at any time when a service might be appropriate. In other cases the difficulties of transport, or for secondary schools the size of the accommodation available, will mean that the use of the church for worship will be a rare and carefully planned event. Whatever the difficulties may be, it will be important for all pupils in Church schools to experience worship in church several times during their school career.

Training leaders of school worship in a Church school

It will be apparent that worship in a Church school raises some specific issues that will need to be addressed by the school itself. It may be that a number of local Church schools can come together to discuss how these issues affect them, but each school must eventually make its own policy and develop its own practice. Key to a high-quality provision of worship in the school will be the support that is given to those who take responsibility for leading acts of worship in the school. Many of these people will be teachers, some will be priests or ministers, yet others may be lay visitors to the school. All will have insights to offer and talents to use within the leadership of school worship. Some of them may have worked in other Church schools. All will need support to understand exactly what is required in this particular Church school, not least in understanding the way in which the school has resolved some of the issues discussed above. There are many courses of training offered on school worship. Church schools will need to be satisfied that the ones to which they send representatives accurately reflect Church school issues. Many diocesan teams and Church bodies publish guidance and offer training on these issues. These will be an important resource to the school as it plans and builds up its resources to support those leading school worship.

Every Church school will need to reach an understanding of the way in which these issues should affect its practice and then express that in its policy documents and in the guidance that it gives to those who lead school worship.

Specific issues that affect some Church schools

Although the topics discussed in the following paragraphs will not affect every Church school, they are potentially significant for all because of the light that the issue can throw on the complexity of planning and providing worship in all Church schools.

Church schools and pupils from many faith backgrounds

In some Church schools, most of which will be Anglican, the pupils are drawn from a variety of different faith backgrounds. In a few Anglican schools they are drawn almost exclusively from one or more of the other major world faiths. In schools where there are a number of pupils from a faith background different from that of the school, the school will need to show hospitality and respect to these pupils and their beliefs. This will be reflected in all policies within the school. Schools will then decide within this framework how far they are able to take account of the presence of these pupils in the worship that they provide. The Inspection Handbook produced for Anglican schools has some guidance on this issue.

> Schools may provide opportunities for different faith groups to hold their own acts of worship from time to time. There should always be respect shown for the beliefs of pupils and staff from different religious traditions but one would not expect to see examples of multi-faith worship.
>
> Alan Brown *et al.*, 2000, p. 33

School eucharists

In some of the Christian traditions the Eucharist is so important that it is the central focus of the worship of the Church every week. In Church schools where this is the tradition of the denomination or the parish there will need to be discussion about the role of the Eucharist within the school's pattern of worship. All Roman Catholic and most Anglican secondary schools will have a programme of eucharists in the school. In many Anglican primary schools there will be some debate about whether it is appropriate to hold a eucharistic service when the children are not able to receive. There can be no single policy for Anglican primary schools, and the developing practice in some areas of allowing receipt of communion before confirmation is likely to alter the decisions of some schools and, in the long term, to change the pattern of practice. What is clear, however, is that all pupils in Church schools should become familiar with the meaning of the Eucharist and with some of the elements of the service before they leave the school.

Preparation for sacraments or adult membership

Traditionally, some Church schools have included preparation for participation in the sacraments as part of their programme of religious education or as a special piece of teaching. In recent years this practice has largely died out, sacramental preparation being seen as more appropriate to the parish or home setting. The change of practice within the Church of England already referred to above may change this situation. It seems likely that in some Church schools attached to parishes that admit children to the Eucharist before confirmation, the school will want to arrange for pupils to have the opportunity to receive during school eucharists. This will involve the school in undertaking a programme of preparation with these pupils that parallels that which will be undertaken in a parish setting.

Guidance on school worship in Church schools

For most Church schools this guidance will come from the diocesan organizations or from the national organizations of the faith or denomination. There are a number of publications available which provide practical help as well as Web sites provided by the National Society and the Catholic Education Service, among others. Earlier in this chapter mention was made of the need for schools to be certain that courses on which they send staff and others who lead school worship in Church schools are run by organizations and individuals who are in tune with and understand the issues that are particular to worship in a Church school setting. Where there is any doubt, the school should seek advice from their diocesan or national Church organization before committing resources and time to training based exclusively on a community school model.

Inspection of worship in Church schools

There are two distinct issues here.

Organizational arrangements for inspection

In Church schools the inspection of the quality and content of worship in Church schools is a matter for the Section 23 inspector (see Chapter 22). Such inspectors will have detailed guidance from those responsible for supervising the inspection scheme in their Church. The content of the text boxes in this chapter gives a flavour of the guidance available to those undertaking inspection in Anglican schools. Those inspecting the school under Section 10 of the Act (the team in England from The Office for Standards in Education or in Wales from ESTYN) will report on whether the school is complying with the requirements of the law, but they should not report on issues of quality other than possibly in the context of the contribution that worship makes to the pupils' spiritual and moral development.

In order to inspect a school's provision of worship, the inspector will need to see the school's policy documents and records and to take part in as many acts of worship in the school as time and resources permit.

How can quality of worship be inspected?

This problem is both a practical one, in that worship is being inspected in schools throughout the country on a regular basis, and a spiritual and theological one, in that it is extremely difficult to agree criteria that determine what makes a poor, a satisfactory or a good act of worship. The Anglican Church has, through its Inspection Handbook and the work of its inspectors, developed a detailed schedule that helps inspectors analyse a particular act of worship in order to help the school or the individual leaders improve the way in which they organize and lead worship. This does not in itself go beyond the practical issue. The framework inevitably leaves aside the theoretical question, with which every inspector must wrestle. This problem is best expressed by posing three statements about worship and inspection:

- In order to experience the quality of the worship it is necessary to participate in it wholeheartedly.
- To inspect an activity you must inevitably be, in part at least, an external observer.
- It is very difficult at one and the same time to participate wholeheartedly in worship and to be an external observer of it.

Most inspectors solve this tension by avoiding actions and stances that place themselves outside the worshipping community, such as carrying clipboards or refusing to sing the hymns. They will seek to participate and allow themselves to be drawn into the worship. Immediately it is over, however, they will use an observation framework or other form of organized analysis to recall the details of the act of worship and draw their conclusions from it. Inevitably these conclusions will be coloured by the extent to which the act of worship did enable them to worship with the pupils and the adults in the room.

It will be clear from this brief consideration of the problem of inspecting worship that it is not a totally objective exercise. All that is ever claimed by most Section 23 inspectors is that it is done as carefully as possible, so that the element of subjectivity in the judgements is qualified by a careful consideration of the observed evidence.

References and further reading

Barton, D., *et al.* (1996), *Open the Door*, London, National Society and Oxford Diocesan Board of Education.

Bailey, J. (1999), *Worship!* London, National Society.

Brown, A. S., *et al.* (2000), *Inspection Handbook for Section 23 Inspections in Schools of the Church of England and Church in Wales*, London, National Society.

Catholic Education Service (1994), *The Inspection of Catholic Schools*, London, Catholic Education Service.

Catholic Education Service (1994), *Evaluating the Distinctive Nature of a Catholic School* (third edition), London, Catholic Education Service.

Church Schools Review Group (2001), *The Way Ahead: Church of England Schools in the New Millennium*, London, Church House Publishing (the 'Dearing Report'), pp. 15, 56–7, 83.

The Archbishops' Council (2000), *Common Worship: Services and Prayers for the Church of England*, London, Church House Publishing.

Web sites

http://www.churchschools.co.uk
http://www.natsoc.org.uk/index
http://www.cesew.org.uk
http://www.catholic-ew.org.uk/educ/index.htm

25

Moral Education

Introduction

'Moral education' has always been a major concern of parents, schools and society in general, and therefore of politicians also. It is a term that covers all those processes that promote the learning of moral attitudes and virtues, moral beliefs and understanding, moral dispositions and motivation, and the skills of moral reflection and decision-making.

Always educating?

We, as adults, parents, teachers or whatever our relationship with young people may be, are involved in moral education, in passing on values, in helping or not helping our children to find and apply solutions to their interpersonal problems whether we like it or not, whether we accept the role or not. By what we are, or are not, by what we do or fail to do, by what we profess or do not profess, we educate boys and girls in behaviour through our everyday unselfconscious contacts with them.

Peter McPhail *et al.*, 1972, pp. 11–12

The make-up of a *morally educated person* has been analysed in a number of ways. One list (adapted from Wilson, 1973, pp. 136–7) includes the following attributes:
- feelings and attitudes of respect and concern for others, based on an ability to identify with them and a belief that they 'count'
- an awareness of one's own and others' emotions
- knowledge of the relevant facts about a situation and the 'know-how' or social skills for dealing with it
- an ability to recognize moral situations, to make moral decisions to act in the interests of others, and to carry out such decisions in practice

Education and values

Four approaches to education and values are often distinguished (Halstead and Taylor, 1996, Chapter 1):
- The *character education* approach is a form of moral education which results in the transmission of moral values and forming the child in them.
- The *values education* approach concentrates on exploring and developing the children's own values (also called 'values clarification').

- The *moral reasoning* approach assists children to move to higher levels of moral reasoning through the discussion of moral dilemmas.
- The *just community* approach seeks to develop responsible behaviour through sharing group norms in community. (The school is sometimes seen as a 'moral community' for this purpose.)

'Values education'

This is the most controversial of these approaches. Advocates often argue that it is not the same thing as moral education, but is rather a technique for enabling children to make up their own minds and to engage in properly respectful discussion about the values each person holds. In values education no code of values is promoted, the children are not told how to think or behave, and the teacher's views carry no more authority than those of the pupils. This is thought to be a better way of developing responsible behaviour, by encouraging unforced consensus among the learners as they make their own values explicit and assess for themselves the 'effectiveness' of these values for the well-being of themselves and other people (cf. Robb, 1994).

The approach recommends what has been called 'procedural neutrality' or *neutral chairmanship* on the part of the teacher in discussions of moral issues. This stance has been criticized on the grounds that 'teaching is an essentially moral transaction', at least in so far as it demands the transmission of the 'classroom virtues' and of the common 'civil or societal values... upon which society is founded' (Mary Warnock, in Halstead and Taylor, 1996, pp. 49, 52, 53). Such sweeping criticisms may be unfair, since teacher neutrality is usually proposed only for significantly controversial matters: for example, for debates about the ethics of developing GM crops, but not in discussion on the sexual abuse of children. But the difficulty here is knowing exactly what and who allows us to say that a moral issue is so 'significantly controversial' that teacher neutrality is demanded in discussing it. Abortion will be in this category for some but not others; and the same may be said about under-age sex.

Liberal moral education

The deep truth expressed by liberalism is that morality is a sphere in which freedom of thought and conduct is of undeniable significance; any moral education worthy of the name must therefore be one in which young people are equipped with capacities for wise and principled decisions about how they will live their lives, as well as with some sense of personal responsibility for their own decisions. But in the course of affirming the moral primacy of freedom and resisting that which might threaten to inhibit it, liberal views often seem to have gone overboard in endorsing a certain agnosticism about moral truth... so that any one personal choice is as morally valid – and deserves the same respect – as any other. And when this idea is combined with the equally suspect view that if the choices of young people are to be really free, then we should refrain from their instruction in any moral attitudes and conduct on pain of jeopardising that freedom, we have a very potent cocktail of nonsense indeed.

David Carr, 1996, p. 10

Yet the method has its uses, if only because creating a deliberately 'cool' situation, however artificial, encourages children to talk about and reflect on what they really believe, to be less defensive about their own values and less naively dismissive of different viewpoints. But the clarification of the pupils' own values cannot be all that the school, home or church provides for children at the crossroads where values and education meet. This is partly because to make a moral judgement is to claim that it applies to everyone else faced by the same moral situation: such a judgement is, as moral philosophers say, *universalizable*. It is not like a fashion statement or an opinion about whether you like peanut butter.

David Carr has identified two broad approaches to moral education: the 'traditional-paternalist' and the 'liberal-progressive'. The first approach covers the character education listed above; the second would include values education. Carr sees them both as expressing genuine truths about the nature of moral life and education, but in his view liberalism contains the most risks.

Formation and criticism in moral education

Values education is one way of reflecting on our own and others' values. We may think of it as a form of *critical moral education* in which the learner is encouraged to reflect critically on morality (that is, to evaluate or assess it from her own standpoint). In *formative moral education* (or *moral formation*), by contrast, a moral tradition or culture is 'passed on' and received by the learner. As moral criticism must itself be based on moral principles and insights, critical moral education can only really take place within some framework of moral formation or nurture. This framework is normal and natural to social beings, and should not be rejected as moral 'indoctrination' or 'interference'. Moral formation builds the moral platform from which we launch moral criticism.

We sometimes hear assertions such as, 'Surely it's always wrong to make moral judgements?' and 'We must wait until the children are older and can decide for themselves what is right and wrong.' The first claim acknowledges tolerance as a virtue (which it is) but refuses to set any bounds to it – yet surely we should not be encouraging tolerance of the intolerant and the vicious? The second claim also self-destructs, for on what grounds will our children 'choose' their values unless they have some values in the first place to serve as the basis of that selection?

But the liberal may wonder if there is any room for the *autonomy of the learner* if we encourage parents and schools to form children in values. In fact, children today are far more likely to adopt uncritically the values of their peer group or the advertising industry, who may not have the child's best interests at heart, than to be too influenced by parents and teachers. In any case, the learner is only formed in and converted to values when they become *her* values, and even then the changed learner will continue to reflect on, judge and assess the values she has received. The learner is always in the centre of the frame of moral education.

Our *respect for others* demands that we take our children – and therefore their moral valuing – seriously. But our *respect for morality* demands that we take our own values seriously to the extent that we will share them with our children. (Tolerating someone's actions or beliefs is quite compatible with trying to change their minds.) In moral discussion with children, the best place to start is often with their own values and their own morality. But education cannot just end at the start. We begin where the learners are; but if we want them to learn we must want them to change.

Moral education should not just do one thing. It isn't just about teaching rules or encouraging social action. A good formative moral education will pass on a host of different moral elements to children (cf. Astley, 2000, Chapter 9). These include:

- fundamental moral concepts, rules and principles that define morality (e.g. 'Keep your promises', 'Don't harm other people')
- ways of moral thinking (e.g. 'If I were in her situation, would I agree to this?')
- some sort of 'moral vision' (which some will think of as an objective perception of moral value, but others just as a way of looking on things – seeing other people *as* children of God, for example)
- moral attitudes, character dispositions and feelings (e.g. kindness, compassion or outrage), and their proper exercise
- patterns of moral action, which are important because we act ourselves into different ways of feeling and valuing (thus Baron von Hügel's claim that he kissed his child not only because he loved her, but also in order to love her, and Aristotle's argument that we learn the virtues by *practising* them)
- the social skills required for sensible moral action
- some acquaintance with individuals and communities that exemplify the virtues, and with stories of individual moral exemplars or 'moral heroes', so that 'we learn to be as they are'
- perceived membership of a 'moral community' of shared judgements, attitudes, feelings, reasoning, etc.
- the knowledge and understanding relevant to moral decisions (e.g. about the likely consequences of actions)
- for religious believers, the accounts given in revelation and religious tradition of the will, character and purposes of God.

Educating the virtues

Nothing is more legitimate, indeed urgent, than for teachers and other educationalists to appreciate that the moral education of children, the job of acquainting them with those homely and familiar human excellences called the moral virtues – honesty, tolerance, fairmindedness, courage, persistence, consideration, patience and so forth – is the highest and more important task of education. The schools which best provide this firm foundation for living well . . . are those in which children are taught by teachers who are themselves clearly committed to integrity, truth and justice and who have sought to transform the school and the classroom into the kinds of communities where a love of what is right, decent and good is exhibited as often as possible in the conduct of those into whose care they have been given.

David Carr, 1991, p. 269

For a *complete* moral education, however, the child should also learn how to make her own moral judgements. At least sometimes this will involve her in negative criticisms of the morality that has been passed on to her. This is not at all the same thing, however, as learning cynically to dismiss all her moral upbringing, all moral authorities and the whole 'moral tradition' of her society. But each of us needs to recognize when certain aspects of the morality that we have learned must themselves be judged by other ideals and principles.

The hidden moral curriculum

The 'hidden curriculum' is a set of experiences through which children learn, but which do not come wearing their educational role 'on their sleeves'. The explicit curriculum (classroom talk-and-chalk, individual and group work, projects, experiments, reading textbooks and so on) is rather more up-front with regard to their educational intentions. But even these activities are no more than the visible part of the iceberg, below which lurks the bulk of a more hidden learning that can shipwreck good education – or support and enrich it.

The school teaches values, moral attitudes and the skills of moral behaviour very largely through its hidden curriculum. The school both expresses and forms itself in moral and spiritual values through human interactions between teacher and pupil, and between pupil and pupil, in its corridors, cloakrooms and playgrounds, as well as through its structures, rules and policies, its rewards and punishments, and its displays and notices.

The moral life of schools

The unintentional outcomes of schooling, the ones teachers and administrators seldom plan in advance, are of greater moral significance – that is, more likely to have enduring effects – than those that are intended and consciously sought ... Many of the unintended influences are in operation *all or most of the time*, whereas the intended ones are more episodic and self-contained. The rules that structure the classroom, assumptions that undergird the curriculum, and the teacher's style or character are almost always present. They may seldom be the focus of attention but they remain in operation all the same.

Philip Jackson *et al.*, 1993, p. 44

References and further reading

Astley, J. (2000), *Choosing Life? Christianity and Moral Problems*, London, Darton, Longman and Todd, Chapters 8 and 9.

Bottery, M. (1990), *The Morality of the School: The Theory and Practice of Values in Education*, London, Macmillan.

Carr, D. (1991), *Educating the Virtues: An Essay on the Philosophical Psychology of Moral Development and Education*, London, Routledge.

Carr, D. (1996), *The Moral Role of the Teacher*, Edinburgh, Scottish Consultative Council on the Curriculum.

Halstead, M. and Taylor, M. J. (eds.) (1996), *Values in Education and Education in Values*, London, Falmer.

Jackson, P. W., *et al.* (1993), *The Moral Life of Schools*, San Francisco, California, Jossey-Bass.

McPhail, P., *et al.* (1972), *Moral Education in the Secondary School*, London, Longman.

Midgley, M. (1991), *Can't We Make Moral Judgements?* Bristol, Bristol Press.

Robb, W. (1994), *Values in Education: Can It Alleviate Social Problems?* Aberdeen, CAVE.

Straughan, R. (1988), *Can We Teach Children to be Good? Basic Issues in Moral, Personal and Social Education*, Milton Keynes, Open University Press.

Van der Ven, J. A. (1998), *Formation of the Moral Self*, Grand Rapids, Michigan, Eerdmans.

Wilson, J. (1973), *A Teacher's Guide to Moral Education*, London, Chapman.

Wilson, J. (1990), *A New Introduction to Moral Education*, London, Cassell.

26

Spiritual, Personal and Social Education

Introduction

The subject of this chapter is closely related to moral education. Indeed, 'moral' is often added to the list of adjectives we are considering here to specify a broad category of educational activity. Despite this overlap, however, both 'spiritual education' and 'PSE' (personal and social education) take us beyond the domain of moral education.

The preamble to the 1944 Education Act referred to the responsibilities incumbent upon every local authority to 'contribute toward the spiritual, moral, mental and physical development of the community'. (Interestingly, Archbishop William Temple approved the introduction of the word 'spiritual' into this legislation in preference to the word 'religious', seeing it as a broader and more inclusive term.) Over forty years later, the 1988 Education Reform Act (Section 1.2) required schools to provide a 'balanced and broadly based curriculum' that:

(a) promotes the spiritual, moral, cultural, mental and physical development of pupils at the school and of society; and
(b) prepares such pupils for the opportunities, responsibilities and experiences of adult life.

In 1993 the *Framework for Inspection* for OFSTED had defined these different elements along the following lines:
- *Spiritual* development relates to 'that aspect of inner life through which pupils acquire insights into their personal existence which are of enduring worth. It is characterized by reflection, the attribution of meaning to experience, valuing a non-material dimension to life and intimations of an enduring reality.'
- *Moral* development is concerned with 'knowledge, understanding, intention, attitudes and behaviour in relation to what is right or wrong'.
- *Social* development includes 'the competences and qualities needed to play a full part in society'.
- *Cultural* development refers to the 'understanding and command of those beliefs, values, customs, knowledge and skills which, taken together, form the basis of identity and cohesion in society and groups'.

Although the adjective 'personal' seems to have been sidelined in these documents, it remains key to educational debate and practice. 'Personal and social education' is a phrase that has often been used in the discussions about the school curriculum to focus a particular set of educational outcomes:

Personal and social education is concerned with qualities and attitudes, knowledge and understanding, and abilities and skills in relation to oneself and others, social responsibilities and morality. It helps pupils be considerate and enterprising in the present, while it prepares them for an informed and active involvement in family, social, economic and civic life. (Department for Education and Science, 1989, p. 1)

Contributions to the personal and social development of pupils in school are made by many subjects (especially literature and drama, history, RE and PE) and many cross-curricular themes (e.g. health education and environmental education). The hidden curriculum of relationships and school structures also makes a major contribution in this area. Although 'PSE' is usually not specifically timetabled in primary schools, explicit PSE courses exist in many secondary schools. Topics dealt with in such courses include:

- health
- careers
- politics
- economic and legal issues
- sexual and family relationships
- parenthood
- personal relationships and responsibilities
- study skills
- community and social studies
- communication skills

The contexts in which learning about such topics takes place include individual and group work (especially discussion-based work), reflective and imaginative learning experiences (especially role-play exploration), and undertaking visits to and welcoming visitors from the world outside the walls of the school. This last element shades into extra-curricular activities such as clubs and societies, charitable fund-raising projects, outdoor education experiences and service in the community.

All of these aspects have a moral dimension, and PSE is usually seen as an important area for developing personal and social knowledge, abilities and skills of a moral nature, including moral understanding, making moral judgements and acting upon them (see Chapter 25). Fundamental to PSE is the development of a range of attitudes and broad outcomes, as shown in the box that follows.

Schools should support the development of certain personal qualities and attitudes among all pupils:

- independence of mind;
- self-reliance, self-discipline and self-respect;
- an enterprising and persistent approach to tasks and challenges;
- consideration for others;
- a sense of fairness, together with respect for the processes of law and for the legal rights of others;
- respect for ways of life, opinions and ideas different from one's own, provided they are based on consideration for others;
- readiness to act on behalf of the legitimate interests of others who cannot effectively so act themselves;
- a commitment to promoting the well-being of the community through democratic means;
- concern for conservation of the natural world, and for the physical, including the built, environment.

Department for Education and Science, 1989, pp. 13–14

All of these may be recognized as value-laden. While PSE courses spend considerable time on the knowledge and understanding, abilities and skills that are essential components of this aspect of education, the development of the *attitudes* and *values* implied by them represents the core of the subject.

Coming to terms with educational jargon

PSE   = 'personal and social education'
PSHE = 'personal, social and health education'
PSME = 'personal, social and moral education'
SPACE = 'social, personal and careers education'
SMSC = 'spiritual, moral, social and cultural' development/education

Affective education includes all educational work that is concerned with the student's feelings and emotions, particularly directed to her personal and social development, and the positive encouragement and support that schools provide in these areas.

Education in citizenship

The 'rights and responsibilities of citizenship' have always been seen as central to the social responsibilities addressed by PSE, and in recent years politicians of every hue have underscored the subject's importance in the statutory education of our children. Citizenship education forms part of the National Curriculum in England at key stages 3 and 4, with an emphasis on pupils learning to play an 'active role as future citizens and members of society' through social and moral responsibility (an essential prerequisite), community involvement and political literacy.

Citizenship means different things to different people. For some it is restricted to a knowledge of duties and responsibilities, and a commitment to these as a moral and active member of society. For others, however, the notion extends to developing children's critical faculties, so that society might be reformed 'by individual understanding, knowledge and prejudice reduction' (Chris Wilkins, in Bailey, 2000, p. 26). However, those who argue in favour of this broader, 'empowerment model' of citizenship education, as central to the development of personal responsibility and society's concern for justice and equality, are more likely to see citizenship as a moral stance that leads not just to understanding but to the transformation of individuals and their liberation from oppressive social conditions.

We aim at no less than a change in the political culture of this country both nationally and locally: for people to think of themselves as active citizens, willing, able and equipped to have an influence in public life and with the critical capacities to weigh evidence before speaking and acting; to build on and to extend radically to young people the best in existing traditions of community involvement and public service, and to make them individually confident in finding new forms of involvement and action among themselves. There are worrying levels of apathy, ignorance and cynicism about public life. These, unless tackled at every level, could well diminish the hoped for benefits both of constitutional reform and of the changing nature of the welfare state.

Qualifications and Curriculum Authority, 1998, pp. 7–8

The 'spiritual' in education

As we have seen, the spiritual development of pupils is required as an outcome of school education, and is subject to inspection by OFSTED. It is an aspect of education that is not limited to any one subject or part of school life, although RE and school worship certainly contribute toward it.

In 1993 the National Curriculum Council (NCC) issued a discussion paper entitled *Spiritual and Moral Development*. Spiritual development was described there as 'applying to something fundamental in the human condition' and as an element that was by no means restricted to the overtly religious (p. 2). According to the OFSTED Framework for Inspection: '"Spiritual" is not synonymous with "religious"; all areas of the curriculum may contribute to pupils' spiritual development' (cf. Office for Standards in Education, 1994, p. 8).

The 'aspects of spiritual development' outlined by NCC included some very broad categories indeed, among them:

- the development of personal beliefs
- a sense of awe, wonder and mystery
- feelings of transcendence
- search for meaning and purpose
- self-knowledge and self-respect
- an ability to develop relationships and a sense of community
- exercising the imagination
- being moved by beauty or kindness; and hurt by injustice or aggression

Some have criticized this breadth. Thus John Beck argues that important differences are glossed over, and clarity sacrificed 'for the sake of an at least partially misplaced togetherness' (in Thatcher, 1999, p. 166). From a different perspective, Adrian Thatcher writes that 'there is no essence of spirituality that philosophers can help to provide or define into existence, no ideological middle-ground (despite Government attempts to inspire one), and no minimalising solution to the problem of diversity'. It would be better, he argues, for us to begin with an account of *Christian* spirituality. Thatcher understands this in terms of 'the practice of the love of God and neighbour': that is, spirituality is about being in the right relationship to God

---

Theology and spiritual development

A spiritual person is, in Christian faith, someone who is, at least to some extent, holy. Holiness is not measured by overt religious piety but by the extent to which one has oriented one's life towards the love of God and neighbour. Spirituality is about growth in, or into, the Christian life, and the Christian life is the love of God and neighbour. The OFSTED version of 'spiritual' just cited is hard to reconcile with the gospel version of it. OFSTED thinks spiritual development is about cultivating the individual's 'inner life'. A Christian account of spiritual development is relational, about our relationships with God, with our neighbours and ourselves, which are suffused with glimpses of divine love. OFSTED characterizes it by reflection and the 'attribution of meaning to experience'.

Adrian Thatcher, 1997, pp. 88–9

---

and other people, a self-giving relationship (Thatcher, 1996, pp. 119–20). This is a particular, and rich, conception of spirituality that Thatcher contrasts with the generalized ('Enlightenment') values of a universal search for identity and for meaning and purpose in life. It is also one that balances the individualism and self-love, which is implicit in much secular rhetoric about spiritualities, with a neighbour-love that Jesus expressed in terms of loving your neighbour as yourself (Thatcher, 1999, pp. 51–2). Here is a debate between, on the one hand, a historical religious tradition with its appeal to the teaching of Jesus (the Great Commandment, the Parable of the Good Samaritan) and, on the other, broad, nebulous categories like 'experience', 'value' and 'meaning'. Similar voices of criticism have been heard from elsewhere. Thus in 1993 the Roman Catholic Bishop Vincent Nichols described the spiritual quest in theological terms that contrast with educational rhetoric, as 'that of recognizing the God who comes to meet us, and of having a free heart with which to respond'.

Certainly, the Church school is a place where this *explicitly Christian* dimension of spirituality can find a proper place. On the other hand, the 'common' (community/county) school may regard itself as being in no position to teach Christian spirituality, or Christianity more generally, 'from within' as 'our faith'. It is inevitable, therefore, that an inclusive definition of the spiritual area should be adopted. Thatcher and others are critical both of the NCC document and of the subsequent process devised by the School Curriculum and Assessment Authority (SCAA), later replaced by the Qualifications and Curriculum Authority (QCA), of a 'National Forum for Values in Education and the Community'. This sought a wide-ranging consultation 'to discover whether there are any values upon which there is common agreement within society', through discussions involving delegates from a variety of world religions. Inevitably, it produced a list of 'consensus' moral and spiritual values (under the headings of *the self, relationships, society* and *the environment*) which made little reference to God or distinctively religious traditions, and only passing reference to school worship and RE as promoting spiritual development (SCAA, 1996). This reconstructed, inclusive concept of spiritual development has been embraced not only by humanists but also by many religious leaders, as well as by teachers.

Is this, implicitly secular, consensus approach to spiritual values to be welcomed, or should we instead derive our 'understanding of spirituality and spiritual development from within a religious tradition' (Thatcher, 1999, p. 51; cf. Wright, 2000, pp. 119–23)? The generalized understanding of spirituality in education may well eventually overtake and subjugate any remaining educational endeavours focused on the particularity of religion within the school. It is noteworthy that a politically seemly 'spiritual education' is allowed to be quite 'confessional' in its commitment to the development of pupils' beliefs and values, at a time when education in religion is often instructed to confine itself to *teaching about* specific and explicit religious claims and traditions.

Andrew Wright attempts to square the circle of liberal education and the spirituality of tradition by advocating a conversational dialogue between pupils and the plurality of these traditions. This should not attempt 'to mould children into a preconceived framework', but should rather encourage 'an ongoing journey of exploration, one that is not dependent on any prior agreement about the nature of spirituality' (Wright, 2000, pp. 80, 101). Schools may nurture children in spiritual values, provided that they *also* encourage them in 'autonomous critical thinking' about those values (p. 127).

The Christian teacher's contribution?

- The first contribution Christians should make – and make boldly – is to ensure that, alongside other opinions and views, Christianity has a fair hearing. It seems popular in some publications to scour the world for insights into human problems while missing key Christian understandings that have deeply influenced our own culture.
- The second significant contribution that Christians should be making to this area of education is to live the life they profess, to *put into practice what they say they believe.* Faith, in the Christian sense, is not just an intellectual assent to a set of beliefs, but personal commitment to the Christian Way. Humility in making truth claims, a spirit of repentance for our weaknesses and a genuine love for people, will help validate our claims to understand truth. If Christians are seen to live the life they profess... then they can have a powerful impact on children. It is essential to practise what we preach.

Brian Wakeman, 1984, p. 38

References and further reading

Bailey, R. (ed.) (2000), *Teaching Values and Citizenship across the Curriculum: Educating Children for the World*, London, Kogan Page.

Best, R. (ed.) (1996), *Education, Spirituality and the Whole Child*, London, Cassell.

Best, R. (ed.) (2000), *Education for Spiritual, Moral, Social and Cultural Development*, London, Continuum.

Department for Education and Science (1989), *Personal and Social Education from 5 to 16*, London, HMSO.

Erricker, C. and Erricker, J. (2000), *Reconstructing Spiritual and Moral Education*, London, RoutledgeFalmer.

Francis, L. J. and Thatcher, A. (eds.) (1990), *Christian Perspectives on Education: A Reader in the Theology for Education*, Leominster, Gracewing, especially Sections 13 and 14.

Office for Standards in Education (1994), *Spiritual, Moral, Social and Cultural Development: An OFSTED Discussion Paper*, London, HMSO.

Pring, R. (1984), *Personal and Social Education and the Curriculum: Concepts and Content*, London, Hodder & Stoughton.

Qualifications and Curriculum Authority (1998), *Education for Citizenship and the Teaching of Democracy in Schools*, London, QCA.

School Curriculum and Assessment Authority (1996), *The National Forum for Values in Education and the Community: Final Report and Recommendations*, London, SCAA.

Thatcher, A. (1996), '"Policing the sublime": a wholly (holy?) ironic approach to the spiritual development of children', in J. Astley and L. J. Francis (eds.), *Christian Theology and Religious Education*, London, SPCK, pp. 117–39.

Thatcher, A. (1997), 'Theology of education and Church schools', in W. K. Kay and L. J. Francis (eds.), *Religion in Education, Volume 1*, Leominster, Gracewing, pp. 61–99.

Thatcher, A. (ed.) (1999), *Spirituality and the Curriculum*, London, Cassell.

Wakeman, B. (1984), *Personal, Social and Moral Education: A Source Book*, Tring, Lion.

Wright, A. (2000), *Spirituality and Education*, London, RoutledgeFalmer.

27

Learning about Other Faiths

Introduction

There are strong educational and moral arguments for teaching children about religious faiths other than their own or that of their parents. A child's particular school, village, town, city or even county may not be very 'multi-faith', but the world as a whole certainly is. An understanding of the different religions is essential to an understanding of the history, culture, society, geography, politics and future of many parts of the world – and other parts of the child's own country. Ignorance breeds prejudice (i.e. judgements that are not based on evidence or experience) and hatred of difference. Living together in harmony demands a tolerance of difference and diversity, including religious diversity.

There are strong Christian arguments in favour of tolerance of religious diversity, although historically these have often been eclipsed by arguments for eliminating difference. Biblical themes and texts that encourage a more inclusive theology of religions include:

- the importance of welcoming the 'stranger' or 'sojourner' (Deuteronomy 10.18–19; Matthew 25.35)
- Jesus' ministry to pagans and religious outcasts (e.g. Matthew 8.5–13; Luke 10.29–37; Mark 7.24–30)
- the universalist emphases in parts of the Old Testament (e.g. Isaiah 45.1)

Many Christians (though by no means all) would affirm that other religious traditions contain profound insights into the human condition and the nature of the divine, often expressed in literature and art of great beauty and intrinsic worth. In studying other religions, Christians may be helped to have a clearer view of the particular logic and practice that marks out religious commitment, belief and expression from other ideologies and ways of thinking and living. The study of particular religions can also give special insights into Christianity, both where it is similar and where it markedly differs.

People often accuse the teaching of world religions of encouraging the beliefs that 'all religions are the same' and that 'it doesn't matter what you believe'. But these views more usually come from people who *haven't* studied the range of very different beliefs and cultures associated with these different faiths, and who ignore the passion and commitment with which they are expressed. Good religious education does not lead to such a naive form of relativism, which downgrades the significance of the believer's concern for religious truth and meaning.

Studying religion as a phenomenon

The 'phenomenological study of religion' draws on the work of philosophers who claimed that experience must be judged by our standing back from it and distancing ourselves from it, particularly by attending to phenomena solely as they are presented to the mind, without considering judgements about their truth or value. This is the 'suspension of pre-conceived judgement before the phenomenon in order to let it speak for itself' (Dhavamony, 1973, p. 17). This method of *epoché* has come to be spoken of in terms of students 'bracketing out' their own assumptions and conclusions, to avoid distorting their understanding of the phenomenon being studied. The suspension of judgement leads to a certain academic 'coolness' and 'distance' from one's own viewpoint.

Other people's shoes?

The North American Indians used to say, 'Never judge a man until you have walked a mile in his moccasins.' The phenomenological approach to religion embraces this principle in advocating *empathy*, the capacity to enter into another's experiences and vicariously experience their thoughts, attitudes and emotions. This 'feeling in' another is paradoxically conjoined with the distancing approach of phenomenology to produce 'a mixture of standing back and warmth' (Ninian Smart, 1984, p. 258), as we strive to 'get the feel of' what it is like to be a Muslim on pilgrimage to Mecca, a Buddhist engaged in meditation or a Jew facing persecution. We are meant to identify with their feelings even though we do not directly share them, rather like a method actor or novel reader does, in seeking to understand a character by imaginatively participating in that character's world.

Beyond the descriptive

Ninian Smart, an academic whose influence on the phenomenological approach to RE has been immense, argued that, while RE should 'emphasise the descriptive, historical side of religion', it needs also to 'transcend the informative' by initiating students 'into understanding the meaning of, and into questions about the truth and worth of, religion' (Smart, 1968, p. 105). The first part of this movement beyond the descriptive is achieved by focusing on the inner life as well as the externals of religion through the exercise of empathy, but the second part takes us beyond a full-blown, purely phenomenological approach to religion by including an evaluation of its truth claims, self-understanding and values with the help of philosophical, historical and ethical criteria, as from the point of view of an 'outsider'.

The dimensions of religion

Ninian Smart has also been very influential in his account of the different dimensions that make up a religion. In studying the different world faiths (including Christianity, of course) it is important for teachers and syllabuses to include something of each of these seven dimensions:
- the doctrinal or philosophical dimension
- stories, sacred histories and myths (story-metaphors or 'moving pictures of the sacred')
- ethical codes, laws and rules
- ritual actions and practices, such as prayer, worship, pilgrimage and meditation
- the experiential or emotional dimension: religious experience itself and the emotions that accompany religious practice and belief
- the organizational or social dimension: the social institutions of the religion and other expressions of religious belonging

- the material or artistic dimension: material objects and sundry artefacts of religious significance (e.g. the Ka'aba in Mecca and the River Ganges; temples, churches, statues and icons)

Smart later added the dimension of the political and economic effects of religion.

Empathy and evaluation in religious education

Empathy
This includes:
- the ability to consider the thoughts, feelings, experiences, attitudes, beliefs and values of others;
- developing the power of imagination to identify feelings such as love, wonder, forgiveness and sorrow;
- the ability to see the world through the eyes of others, and to see issues from their point of view.

Evaluation
This includes:
- the ability to debate issues of religious significance with reference to evidence and argument;
- weighing the respective claims of self-interest, consideration for others, religious teaching and individual conscience.

Adapted from School Curriculum and Assessment Authority, 1994, p. 6

Difficulties

The phenomenological approach to RE is often unfairly criticized for being 'superficial' and 'concerned only with externals'. It is very much more than that. More serious objections include the following claims:
- It is simply too difficult for children to set aside their own assumptions and beliefs in the way advocated by this approach, and in any case RE needs to attend to the children's own views as well as teaching objectively about the faith of other people. These views include their evaluation of other faiths and their 'personal relevance'.
- 'More' (faiths studied) often means 'less' (depth of study). Few teachers *really* know about many religions, and over-simplification and misrepresentation is likely on this sort of approach. Further, it is sometimes argued that 'more faiths' means 'more confusion' between the different faiths in the minds of children, and there is some empirical evidence for this claim.
- 'The attempt to be fair to all traditions, by being equally tolerant of all and non-judgemental, can lead like a slippery slope from well-intentioned neutrality to profound scepticism about religion', or at least to a subjectivist or relativistic analysis of it (Watson, 1993, p. 45).
- Unless the phenomenological approach is transcended and supplemented (as Smart advocated) by an exploration and evaluation of the truth-claims of each religion, and an assessment of its moral, historical, personal and social value, the method is not truly *educational* (in the sense of *critical* education).

- Even photographs can only be taken from a particular viewpoint or perspective; a different view is to be had by standing here rather than over there. There is no neutral standpoint or 'view from nowhere' to be had on anything; no 'Archimedean point' outside the world from which to gain a leverage of understanding.

The problem of selection

No teacher can teach everything: teachers must be *selective* about what they teach. Clearly the teaching of any subject matter must depend on the prior level of knowledge and understanding, and intellectual and other capacities of the learners. These 'pedagogical' factors will affect which aspects of a religion are chosen for teaching to particular pupils at their particular age and stage of development and schooling. But there are other, sometimes hidden, factors that influence the selection of the 'salient' features of religions in syllabuses and classrooms, and many of these raise general theological issues and questions.

- Should teachers concentrate on what they think are the 'loftier' or 'purer' aspects of a religion, and pass over those of which they – and their pupils – might be more critical? 'There is a danger of a certain "domestication", of filtering out controversial issues and conflicts within the traditions' (Jackson, 1997, p. 125).
- Should we lay most of the emphasis on features of a religion that are unique to it, or *distinctive* of it, rather than those features that, while being *characteristic* of this religion, are shared by other faiths? (Should we, for example, concentrate on what makes Sikhs obviously different from Muslims or Christians, rather than on what they have in common?)

Approaches to teaching about other faiths

A variety of teaching methods may be adopted for the teaching of other faiths. These are often employed in a complementary fashion:

- the study of faith themes across the religions, where several religions are used to illustrate a common concern: e.g. 'sacred writings', 'creation stories', 'good versus evil'
- the systematic study of the different religions, 'one at a time': this involves an integrated study of the 'whole faith' and its scriptures, history, beliefs, worship, etc.
- the use of visits and visitors so that pupils experience the worship of a religion in a temple, church or mosque, and hear the religious adherents' own accounts of their faith
- the study of general curriculum topics that include a 'world religions dimension': e.g. 'families', 'myself', 'friends and enemies' or 'symbols'

Are we taking them seriously enough?

Metaphors such as 'quest', 'search', 'exploration', all self-consciously tentative and non-committal, seem primed to conceal the ultimate character which religious commitment must have, to distance the student from what he or she studies and perhaps avoid the main reason for studying it – viz. because religious adherents believe their faith is true and through it they find salvation. Ninian Smart's famous book *The Phenomenon of Religion* opens with the words 'In the whole firmament of intellectual values there is scarcely a more delightful, baffling and profound pursuit than the exploration of religion.' So be it; but this apparently leisured approach to the subject might easily obscure the fact that religious issues are matters of life and death.

Adrian Thatcher, 1990, p. 279

References and further reading

Chater, M. (1997), 'Different approaches to religious education' and 'Critical analysis of different approaches to religious education', in W. K. Kay and L. J. Francis (eds.), *Religion in Education, Volume 1*, Leominster, Gracewing, pp. 257–88, 295–316.

Dhavamony, M. (1973), *Phenomenology of Religion*, Rome, Gregorian University Press.

Erricker, C. (ed.) (1993), *Teaching World Religions: A Handbook Produced by SHAP*, Oxford, Heinemann.

Hull, J. M. (1985), *World Religions for Christian Children*, Redhill, National Christian Education Council.

Hull, J. M. (1991), *Mishmash: Religious Education in a Multi-cultural Britain*, Derby, CEM.

Jackson, R. (1997), *Religious Education: An Interpretive Approach*, London, Hodder & Stoughton.

Kay, W. K. and Francis, L. J. (eds.) (2000), *Religion in Education, Volume 3*, Leominster, Gracewing.

School Curriculum and Assessment Authority (1994), *Model Syllabuses for Religious Education: Model 2*, London, SCAA.

Smart, N. (1968), *Secular Education and the Logic of Religion*, London, Faber.

Smart, N. (1973), *The Phenomenon of Religion*, London, Macmillan.

Smart, N. (1984), 'Phenomenology of religion', in J. M. Sutcliffe (ed.), *A Dictionary of Religious Education*, London, SCM Press, pp. 257–8.

Smart, N. (1996), *Dimensions of the Sacred: An Anatomy of the World's Beliefs*, London, HarperCollins.

Thatcher, A. (1990), 'The recovery of Christian education', in L. J. Francis and A. Thatcher (eds.), *Christian Perspectives for Education*, Leominster, Gracewing, pp. 273–81.

Watson, B. (1993), *The Effective Teaching of Religious Education*, Harlow, Longman, Chapters 4 and 7.

Appendix to Part Three
Key Stages

National curriculum key stages for schools in England and Wales

Key stage	Age range	Year groups	
R	5		Infant/Primary School
KS1	5–7	1–2	Infant/Primary School
KS2	7–11	3–6	Junior/Primary/Middle School
KS3	11–14	7–9	Secondary/Middle School
KS4	14–16	10–11	Secondary/Upper School (GCSE)
KS5	17	12	Lower Sixth (GCE 'AS' level)
KS5	18	13	Upper Sixth (GCE 'A2' level)

PART FOUR
MINISTRY AND
CHILDREN

28

All-age Learning and Worship

Introduction

All-age learning and worship has become a key concept in the Churches' understanding of ministry among children and young people. The concept is grounded in the approach to children advocated by the British Council of Churches' report, *The Child in the Church*, published in 1976 (see Chapter 7). The concept was given further examination by the Church of England's report, *Children in the Way*, published in 1988.

Theological models

In *Children in the Way*, the concept of all-age learning and worship is underpinned by a theological examination of the nature of the Church and of the different models which can be developed to illuminate our understanding of it. Three models are scrutinized in turn: the 'school' model, the 'family' model, and the 'pilgrim' model.

The 'school' model

The school model of the Church has been found to be unhelpful for a number of reasons. There are so many fundamental differences between day schools and the nature of the Church:

1   Schooling is highly organized, compulsory and staffed by professional teachers. Church groups are voluntary, loosely structured and generally staffed by volunteers.
2   Children are clearly expected to grow out of the day school. Compulsory schooling keeps them within the system to a specified age, and after that they are liberated into the world of adulthood. It would be unfortunate if the same model were transferred to the Church.

The school model of Church

The school model also tends to put the teacher or leader into the role of the one who knows and the children into the position of those who need to know: teacher and taught, instructor and instructed. For many reasons this is not always helpful.

Children in the Way, 1988, p. 29

---

3 The day school carries some very clear signals regarding the relationship between children and adults. In this context the adult world constructs the curriculum, initiates the child into the curriculum and routinely assesses the child's performance against notional pre-established criteria. The Church may wish to model a somewhat different understanding of the relationship between children and adults.

The 'family' model

At its best, the family model of the Church offers a range of positive and constructive insights. An 'ideal family' can be conceptualized as a group of people who are naturally dependent on one another, and whose various skills and knowledge are used for the good of the whole group. In the ideal family some activities are undertaken by the whole family acting together, while other activities are pursued by individual members alone or with friends outside the family.

An ideal family can be the place where we are able to be ourselves and where we can be accepted for who we really are.

The family model of Church

In the image of the Church as a family, there are some attractive ideals for considering Christian nurture. For example, a church can arrange some activities for all its members to share, some joint for particular groups within the fellowship. The model suggests a need to work out appropriate ways of sharing skills and leadership, to recognise the possible power of the weakest members, and to sort out ways of passing on stories and appropriate rituals.

Children in the Way, 1988, p. 31

On the other hand, there are some very significant disadvantages with the family model of the Church. It has to be recognized that for many people the 'ideal family' has never existed. The family can be the source of conflict and violence. The family can restrict human growth as well as release individual potential.

For some, the family can become inward looking and exclusive. The family can be used to keep other people away and to shut other people out.

The emphasis on family services, the family Eucharist and family days can marginalize individuals who do not themselves live as part of a traditional family structure. Single people in particular may begin to wonder whether there is a proper place for them within a Church which continually expresses its self-understanding in terms of the family model.

The 'pilgrim' model

In place of the school model and the family model, *Children in the Way* advocated the pilgrim model of the Church. According to this model, both children and adults are travelling the same faith journey, and both may learn from each other.

The pilgrim model of Church

The image of the Church as a pilgrim community adds new dimensions which may be helpful. While the school model can all too easily be interpreted as teacher and taught, and the family model may feel too restricted, the pilgrim community comprises a band of people all sharing in and learning from common experience.

Children in the Way, 1988, p. 33

The pilgrim model of the Church offers the following kinds of images. As children and adults set out on the common journey together, both contribute to the shared experience at their own level. Children raise questions and generate insights which enrich the experience of the adults. Adults draw on their own fund of wisdom to provide depth and wider interpretation for the children. In this sense teaching comes from all members of the community and the learning arises just as much from informal as from formal situations.

All those involved on the common journey are bound up one with the other. All have some sense of responsibility for the others. All are learning and sharing in the common life.

The pilgrim Church is moving on from the past to the future the whole time. As a growing, living, moving body, the pilgrim Church must give permission for some individuals to go off on their own and to shape their own pilgrimage. At the same time the pilgrim Church must be alert to new members joining the pilgrimage and travelling with us.

Educational practice

All-age learning and worship provides an opportunity for the theological insights of the pilgrim model of the Church to be put into practice. Key to successful working in this area is a team of leaders who are committed to making all-age learning and worship really happen. In particular two dangers need to be avoided:

1 The first danger is that it is often so much easier to revert to a more traditional model of adult leaders recreating a school-based experience for the children. In all-age learning and worship the leaders must remain willing and able to learn from the children as well as for the children to learn from the leaders.

Educational practice

Leaders must genuinely believe that *all* are learners and fellow worshippers and have the ability to convince others – adults and children – that this is and can be so. For many leaders the pattern of hived-off age or interest groups may be so ingrained that the possibility of alternatives is difficult, if not impossible, to contemplate, and they will need help to understand and, if possible, experience what is being envisaged.

Children in the Way, 1988, p. 56

---

2   The second danger is that all-age worship can degenerate into worship for children in which the adult worshippers feel marginalized. While adults need to be respectful of the preferred modes of worship favoured by the children, the children in their turn need to show respect for the traditions valued by the adults.

A number of recent books provide examples of how local churches have put all-age learning and worship into practice. For example, in their book *All God's People*, Leslie J. Francis and Anne Faulkner (1997) set out to encourage clergy and lay people to tell the stories of what was happening in their own parishes, or in their own areas. Their book presents the following examples.

Candlemas

Michael Sturdy, a member of the education committee at All Saints', Wokingham, describes a half-day Saturday workshop which prepared for the Sunday Eucharist on the theme of Candlemas.

Programme

12.00 p.m.	Time together – bring your own lunch
12.45 p.m.	Introduction
1.00 p.m.	First activity session
2.15 p.m.	Tea and squash
2.45 p.m.	Second activity session
4.15 p.m.	Run through in church
5.00 p.m.	Service of Light
5.15 p.m.	Finish

Between 40 and 50 people came to the workshop. There were ten different activities available during the two sessions:
• church choral music
• church decoration
• baking
• candle making
• banner making
• preparing the readings
• poetry and psalm writing
• liturgical dance
• Bible study
• preparing the intercessions

The Saturday concluded with an informal Service of Light. At the beginning the dancers performed their dance. Candles were provided by the candle-making group. It was a moving service enhanced by the presence of parents who were not at the workshop but who had arrived early to collect their children.

On the Sunday morning candles were handed to the congregation on arrival. The relevant activity groups led the Old Testament and gospel readings, the intercessions and the gradual hymn. Instead of a sermon the activity groups not otherwise involved in leading parts of the service gave short accounts of what they had done. The banner was displayed, church decorations were pointed out, rolls from the baking group were shown and two poems were read. After the communion came the Candlemas procession, in which the congregation sang a hymn while candles were lit throughout the church by members of the candle-making group, using the candles they had made.

All Saints

Margaret Dean, Diocesan Children's Education Officer for the Diocese of Guildford, describes a service held in Guildford cathedral on the evening before All Saints' Day:

An invitation was given to everyone from all parishes of the diocese. As a result of this invitation, the service was attended by families, youth groups, old folk, disabled groups, and uniformed organizations. Some travelled together as parties, some arrived alone or with just one or two others.

The celebration began at 7.30 p.m. in the cathedral. About 2,000 had crowded into the cathedral, with 500 more waiting outside. The service took the theme of the light of Christ coming into the world and being passed first to the apostles and then down the centuries to the present day. The service featured four saints, male and female, active and contemplative. Those selected were St Mary Magdalene, St Paul, St Benedict and St Teresa of Avila.

After the first reading, a simple candle was lit at the top centre of the chancel steps. This was later used to light a further four large candles on the chancel steps. Each of these four candles was lit after someone told the story of one of the four saints, and how, having received the light of Christ, they passed it on to others.

Before the closing prayers, scouts and guides distributed candles to the whole congregation. The four candles on the chancel steps were used to light tapers from which the whole congregation took their light. Then everyone left the cathedral, taking their light outside into the darkness.

Once outside the theme of light was continued with a professional firework display which lit up the night sky. Good fortune brought a clear night. The display was a great success, full of colour, life, unpredictability, noise, delicacy and beauty. As the cathedral is set on a hill, it meant that the display could be seen, heard and enjoyed by the entire city and surrounding area.

Volunteers were on hand to clear up the firework remains the next morning.

Pentecost

Anne Faulkner, Parish Development Adviser for the Buckingham Archdeaconry, describes an activity day organized by the education committee of the Deanery Synod.

Programme

10.00 a.m.	Arrival and welcome
10.15 a.m.	Bonfire and parachute games
10.45 a.m.	Story of first Pentecost (Acts 2)
11.00 a.m.	First activity session
12.30 p.m.	Lunch
1.00 p.m.	Second activity session
2.30 p.m.	Tea and squash
3.00 p.m.	Eucharist
3.45 p.m.	Pentecost cake for the Church's birthday
4.00 p.m.	Finish

On arrival, the first thing the 90 people who attended the day saw was a large graffiti board headed with the questions, 'What is Pentecost? What does Pentecost mean to me?' Quite quickly a collection of words, images and pictures appeared on the graffiti board.

Next came experiences of fire and wind, two of the traditional symbols of the Holy Spirit. A bonfire had been prepared, complete with a safety barrier. The fire was lit with a cheer and the spontaneous, unplanned singing of 'Camp fires burning'. Children and adults alike were happy to watch the fire grow and burn for ten or fifteen minutes. When attention began to waver, a parachute was produced well away from the fire and simple games were played. The parachute made a wonderful wind for all to feel.

At 10.45 a.m. the graffiti board was taken into church with everyone following. People were asked to reflect on their experiences of the fire of the bonfire and the wind of the parachute, calling out further words and images to add to those already on the board. The story of the first Pentecost was related to these images.

Activity sessions designed to explore the Pentecost theme included:
- art and craft
- modelling
- cooking
- music
- dance
- prayer
- science
- puzzles and word games
- two 400-piece jigsaws

At the end of the afternoon children and adults brought to the church and displayed all that had been produced during the day. The service concluded with a procession into the church hall, where candles were lit on the birthday cake and 'Happy Birthday' was sung to the church.

References and further reading

British Council of Churches (1976), *The Child in the Church*, London, BCC.

Church of England (1988), *Children in the Way: New Directions for the Church's Children*, London, National Society and Church House Publishing.

Francis, L. J. and Faulkner, A. (eds.) (1997), *All God's People: Working with All Ages*, Leominster, Gracewing.

Jamal, D. (1990), *Leaves on the Tree: All-Age Learning and Worship*, London, National Society and Church House Publishing.

Sadler, J. (2000), 'Learning together: all-age learning in the Church', in J. Astley (ed.), *Learning in the Way*, Leominster, Gracewing, pp. 113–23.

White, J. W. (1988), *Intergenerational Religious Education*, Birmingham, Alabama, Religious Education Press.

29

Using the Lectionary

Introduction

The *Revised Common Lectionary* has been designed to provide a continuous series of readings for the Sunday services over a three-year period. These readings have been chosen according to two main principles. First, shape is given to the lectionary by the shape of the Church's year. Each of the three years of the lectionary follows the same basic shape. Second, a major way in which the three years differ one from another concerns the gospel readings. The first year concentrates on Matthew's Gospel, the second year on Mark's Gospel, and the third year on Luke's Gospel. While each of these three years concentrates on one of these three Synoptic Gospels, parts of John's Gospel are introduced into all of the three years.

Three-year cycle

Some of the advantages of the three-year cycle of readings are that it:
- ensures a range and variety of readings from the Bible
- reflects the seasons within the Church's year
- helps to ensure that over time there is the opportunity for preaching and learning across issues drawn from every aspect of the Christian life

Because the *Revised Common Lectionary* now plays such a key part in the worship provided by many churches across the denominations, a series of books have been prepared to help make the lectionary accessible for ministry among children and for all-age learning and worship. This chapter provides an introduction to the Church's year and illustrates how the scheme of work devised by Francis and Drayson in *Learning with the Sunday Gospels* (1999) provides a concrete theme for each of the Sundays in the lectionary year which follows Matthew's Gospel. Their book offers similar ideals for the year of Luke and for the year of Mark.

The Church's year

For the Church the new year begins on the first Sunday in Advent. The Church's season of Advent then includes four Sundays in the run up to Christmas. The season of Advent is followed by Christmas and then by the season of Epiphany.

The season of Epiphany is followed by the season of Lent. Lent is the penitential period leading up to the events of Holy Week and the crucifixion on Good Friday. Then Lent gives way to the joy of Easter Day.

The season of Easter continues to celebrate the good news of the resurrection and culminates in the Day of Pentecost when the Church celebrates the outpouring of the Holy Spirit among the early disciples.

A week after the Day of Pentecost the Church celebrates Trinity Sunday to commemorate the Christian revelation of God as Father, Son and Holy Spirit.

The long period after Trinity Sunday ends on the Sunday before Advent, sometimes called the celebration of Christ the King.

Season of Advent

The word 'Advent' is derived from the Latin verb meaning 'to come'. Advent is a season of preparation for the coming of Christ in two senses. The people of God prepare themselves both for the annual celebration of Jesus' nativity and for the second coming of the Lord. The second coming strikes the two notes of hope and of judgement.

Traditionally, the season of Advent is a period of sombre preparation for the Church. It is a penitential season. Often churches mark Advent by using purple vestments, by omitting the joyful Gloria from the communion service and by removing flowers and decorations from the church. When the church is then decorated for Christmas the contrast is that much greater.

The *Revised Common Lectionary* gospel readings for the first Sunday of Advent emphasize both the unpredictability of the hour and the sharpness of the judgement. The gospel readings for the second Sunday of Advent concentrate on the theme of the repentance proclaimed by John the Baptist as the proper act of preparation. The gospel readings for the third Sunday of Advent adopt a gentler tone. These readings continue to focus on John the Baptist, but now emphasize his role as forerunner. The gospel readings for the fourth Sunday of Advent move attention to the person of Mary who, in her unique way, prepared for the incarnation.

While the Church's calendar prepares for Christmas through a season of penitence and repentance, the young people within the Churches' congregations are living their lives in a busy secular world where the mass media, the shops and the schools are preparing for Christmas in a very different kind of way. The Church cannot ignore these powerful and pervasive influences on children. Work with children, therefore, needs to try to bridge the gulf between the themes of the lectionary and the pervasive influence of the excitement and anticipation which surround the children's view of getting ready for Christmas. This can be done through the use of appropriate linking themes.

Season of Advent: themes

Day	Theme
First Sunday of Advent	Advent candles
Second Sunday of Advent	Christmas cards
Third Sunday of Advent	Wrapping presents
Fourth Sunday of Advent	The manger

Christmas and Epiphany

At the first service of Christmas (often at midnight) the Church comes out of the penitential season of Advent into a period of celebration and joy. Churches are richly decorated. Purple vestments are exchanged for vestments of white or gold.

Both the Church and the secular world remain conscious of the twelve days of Christmas between Christmas day and the feast of the Epiphany (6 January). This twelve-day period within the Church's calendar provides opportunities to explore the nativity and Epiphany narratives within the Gospels.

Often, however, these important narratives are not used to best effect on the Sundays within this twelve-day period, when the children of the church may have the best opportunities to explore those stories and to share them with the adult members of the congregation. For this reason, some churches choose to develop the gospel lections appointed for Christmas Day and for the feast of Epiphany as alternatives to the gospel readings appointed for the first and for the second Sundays after Christmas.

The lectionary suggests three gospel passages for Christmas Day. The two passages suggested from Luke's Gospel focus on the shepherds and on the angelic chorus. The passage suggested from John's Gospel is the Prologue, which begins with those famous words, 'In the beginning was the Word.'

The gospel passages suggested by the lectionary for the first Sunday after Christmas (which some churches choose not to use) explore the first twelve years of Jesus' life by focusing on the flight into Egypt and return to Nazareth, on the encounter with Simeon and Anna in the temple, and on the boy Jesus being found in the temple talking with the teachers. Young children may be surprised to encounter these narratives so quickly after Christmas Day and before the feast of the Epiphany.

While only one gospel passage is suggested for the feast of the Epiphany, this is a rich narrative which can be explored from several different angles. The Epiphany story tells of the magi visiting the infant Jesus.

Christmas and Epiphany: themes

Day	Theme
Christmas Day	The shepherds
Epiphany	Christmas star

Season of Epiphany

The period following Christmas and Epiphany is known as the season of Epiphany. The Greek root of the word 'Epiphany' means 'to bring to light' or 'to reveal'. The season of Epiphany begins when the infant Christ is revealed to the wise men from the East. In a sense, the Sundays after Epiphany and before Lent continue this theme.

Because the date of Easter is fixed by the phases of the moon and therefore varies from year to year, the number of Sundays between the feast of Epiphany and the beginning of Lent also varies. The lectionary deals with this by following the first, second, third and fourth Sundays of Epiphany with Sundays counted before Lent. When Easter is early, fewer of the Sundays before Lent are used than when Easter is late.

In all three years, the first Sunday of Epiphany celebrates the baptism of Jesus, when the divine revelation addressed Jesus with the words 'You are my Son, the Beloved; with you I am well pleased' (Mark 1.11). In all three years, the last Sunday before Lent celebrates the transfiguration, when the divine revelation once again addressed Jesus in similar words (Mark 9.7), 'This is my Son, the Beloved; listen to him!'

In all three years, the second Sunday of Epiphany draws on themes of revelation from John's Gospel: Andrew's testimony that 'We have found the Messiah'; Nathanael's affirmation, 'You are the Son of God'; and the wedding at Cana where Jesus performed the first of his signs and revealed his glory.

In the first year of the lectionary the Sundays between the third Sunday of Epiphany and the Sunday before Lent draw on the opening chapters of Matthew. The call of the first disciples is followed by five extracts from the Sermon on the Mount.

In the second year of the lectionary the Sundays between the third Sunday of Epiphany and the Sunday before Lent draw on the opening chapters of Mark. The call of the first four disciples is followed by four accounts of healing and then by the call of Levi.

In the third year of the lectionary the Sundays between the third Sunday of Epiphany and the Sunday before Lent draw on the opening chapters of Luke. These readings begin with Jesus teaching in the synagogue of Nazareth, followed by Jesus' rejection at Nazareth, by the great catch of fish and by three extracts from the Sermon on the Plain.

Season of Epiphany: themes

Day	Theme
Baptism of Christ	Water
Second Sunday of Epiphany	Names
Third Sunday of Epiphany	Fishermen
Fourth Sunday of Epiphany	Favourite drinks
Fifth Sunday before Lent	Salt
Fourth Sunday before Lent	Anger
Third Sunday before Lent	Teddy bears
Second Sunday before Lent	Birds
Sunday Next before Lent	Mountain

Season of Lent

Traditionally for the Church the season of Lent is a sombre period of fasting and preparation. As during the season of Advent, many churches return to the purple vestments. Once again flowers are often removed from the church. Some churches refrain from using the Gloria in the communion service.

Traditionally Lent is also a time for fasting. Through fasting the people of God prepare themselves to commemorate the events of Holy Week, the betrayal, crucifixion and death of Jesus. The traditional themes of Lent include temptation, repentance and renewed dedication.

The gospel readings for the first Sunday of Lent focus on the temptations of Jesus in the wilderness. The significance of this theme at the beginning of Lent is concerned with exploring the models of Messiahship which Jesus rejected. In the temptations Jesus refused to turn stones into bread, to throw himself from the pinnacle of the temple, and to seek lordship over the kingdoms of the world.

In contrast with the first Sunday of Lent, the gospel readings for the second Sunday of Lent focus on the model of Messiahship which Jesus embraced, the model which led inevitably to the cross. Here are three readings which predict Jesus' death on the cross: the prediction of the passion to Nicodemus, the prediction of the passion to the disciples, and the prediction of the passion in Jerusalem.

The gospel readings for the third Sunday of Lent select three images of the new beginning which is offered to the people of God through the death and resurrection of Jesus. In these readings living water brings eternal life, the old temple is replaced by the new temple, and the fig tree is given a new chance.

The fourth Sunday of Lent is sometimes kept as Mothering Sunday and seen as a day of refreshment during the middle of Lent. The gospel readings illustrate the relationship between Jesus and Mary his mother. In these readings Mary is portrayed at key points in Jesus' life, as the young mother who brings her infant to the temple, and as the ageing mother who stands by the cross at the hour of her son's death.

The gospel readings for the fifth Sunday of Lent anticipate the death of Jesus and foreshadow the resurrection. Here we hear about the raising of Lazarus, about the grain of wheat which dies before leading to new growth, and about Mary who anointed Jesus' feet.

The last Sunday of Lent introduces the events of Holy Week by celebrating Jesus' triumphal entry into Jerusalem on the back of the donkey. The crowds spread their cloaks on the road and tore branches from the trees to spread in his way. They shouted, 'Blessed is the one who comes in the name of the Lord!'

Season of Lent: themes

Day	Theme
First Sunday of Lent	The magician
Second Sunday of Lent	Christus Rex
Third Sunday of Lent	Running water
Mothering Sunday	Mary caring for Jesus
Fifth Sunday of Lent	Tombs
Palm Sunday	Processional crosses

Season of Easter

Just as the season of Advent leads into Christmas, so the season of Lent leads into Easter. Once again the purple vestments of the penitential season give way to the white or gold vestments of celebration and joy.

The season of Easter begins with Easter Sunday and concludes with the Day of Pentecost. There are six Sundays between these two major festivals.

The gospel readings for Easter Sunday tell the story of the empty tomb from the perspectives of the three Synoptic Gospels. Matthew, Mark and Luke each have their own distinctive emphases on this key celebration within the Christian year.

The gospel readings for the second Sunday of Easter (sometimes called the first Sunday after Easter) present John's account of Jesus' appearing to the disciples on the evening of Easter Day and then again a week later on Easter octave. While on Easter Sunday the emphasis is on the empty tomb, on the second Sunday of Easter the emphasis is on the evidence for the resurrection.

The gospel readings for the third Sunday of Easter portray the disciples meeting with the risen Jesus in the ordinary affairs of life. Jesus travels with two of the disciples on the road to Emmaus. Jesus eats fish with the disciples in Jerusalem. Jesus takes breakfast with the disciples by the lakeside.

The gospel readings between the fourth Sunday of Easter and the seventh Sunday of Easter all focus on images of Jesus from John's Gospel. This cycle begins on the fourth Sunday of Easter with images of Jesus the good shepherd. The fifth Sunday of Easter follows the theme of the good shepherd with the three images of the way, the vine and the new commandment. The sixth Sunday of Easter draws to a close the period of the resurrection appearances and anticipates the Ascension and the Day of Pentecost. The gospel readings are from the farewell discourses of John and point to the ongoing life of the Christian community after Jesus is taken from them and the Holy Spirit has been sent to them. The seventh Sunday of Easter is also the Sunday following the ascension. The season of Easter comes to a close with the Day of Pentecost when the early Church received the gift of the Holy Spirit.

Season of Easter: themes

Day	Theme
Easter Day	Easter eggs
Second Sunday of Easter	Sense of sight
Third Sunday of Easter	Sharing bread
Fourth Sunday of Easter	Sheep
Fifth Sunday of Easter	Maps
Sixth Sunday of Easter	The guide
Seventh Sunday of Easter	Royal crowns
Date of Pentecost	Wind

Trinity Sunday to Christ the King (the Sunday before Advent)

The Day of Pentecost is followed in the Church's year by Trinity Sunday. On Trinity Sunday the Church contemplates and celebrates the mystery of the revelation of God as Father, Son and Holy Spirit.

The period following Trinity Sunday through until the next Advent gives space for the main gospel themes to be explored. Each of the three years works through its chosen Gospel, Matthew, Mark or Luke. Mark's Gospel is shorter than the other two and the lectionary takes the opportunity to insert seven passages from John's Gospel in the year which is based on Mark's narrative.

The Church's year ends with the celebration of Christ's kingship. Here is the triumphal acknowledgement that Christ reigns. In year one the image offered from Matthew's Gospel is that of the Son of Man coming in his glory and with all the angels with him. 'There he will sit on the throne of his glory.' In year two the image offered from John's Gospel is from the conversation between Jesus and Pilate. Pilate asks Jesus the direct question, 'Are you the King of the Jews?' Jesus takes this as an opportunity to define his kingdom as 'not from this world'. In year three the image offered from Luke's Gospel is the moment of crucifixion. The contrast is between the mocking voice of the soldiers saying, 'If you are the King of the Jews, save yourself', and the pleas of the penitent criminal, 'Jesus, remember me when you come into your kingdom.'

Trinity Sunday to Christ the King: themes

Day	Theme
Trinity Sunday	Waterfall
Proper 4	Foundations
Proper 5	Repair shop
Proper 6	Friends
Proper 7	Pets
Proper 8	Welcome
Proper 9	Children's games
Proper 10	Farmer
Proper 11	Summer walk
Proper 12	Hidden treasure
Proper 13	Picnic
Proper 14	Gales

Day	Theme
Proper 15	Removing barriers
Proper 16	Rock
Proper 17	Suffering
Proper 18	Hide and seek
Proper 19	Mending what is broken
Proper 20	Prizes for all
Proper 21	setting traps
Proper 22	Vineyard
Proper 23	Birthday invitation
Proper 24	Coins
Proper 25	Feeling loved
All Saints' Day	Signposts
Fourth Sunday before Advent	Signs
Third Sunday before Advent	Batteries
Second Sunday before Advent	In business
Christ the King	Fairground

References and further reading

Buetow, H. A. (1995), *God Still Speaks; Listen: Cycle A,* New York, Alba House.

Buetow, H. A. (1996), *All Things Made New: Cycle B,* New York, Alba House.

Buetow, H. A. (1997), *Ode to Joy: Cycle C,* New York, Alba House.

Francis, L. J. and Drayson, D. (1999), *Learning with the Sunday Gospels: Advent to Pentecost,* London, Mowbray.

Francis, L. J. and Drayson, D. (1999), *Learning with the Sunday Gospels: Trinity Sunday to Christ the King,* London, Mowbray.

Harrington, W. J. (1996), *The Gracious Word: Year B,* Dublin, Dominican Publications.

Irvine, C. (1996), *Celebrating the Easter Mystery: Worship Resources for Easter to Pentecost,* London, Mowbray.

Kitchen, M., Heskins, G. and Motyer, S. (1997), *Word of Life: Year C,* Norwich, Canterbury Press.

Sayers, S. (1989), *Focus the Word: The Complete Three Year Cycle,* Rattlesden, Kevin Mayhew.

Soards, M., Dozeman, T. and McCabe, K. (1993), *Preaching the Revised Common Lectionary,* Nashville, Tennessee, Abingdon Press (12 volumes).

Thomas, S. (1997), *Come to the Feast: All Age Services for the Church Year based on the Revised Common Lectionary,* Rattlesden, Kevin Mayhew.

┌─────┐
│ 30 │
└─────┘

Evangelism and Outreach

Introduction

Evangelism is defined by the *Shorter Oxford English Dictionary* as 'the preaching or promulgation of the Gospel'. It is derived from the Greek word *euaggelion*, which is translated as 'gospel'. In discussions of the Church's ministry and mission generally, a distinction is made between 'nurture' which is concerned with developing the faith of church members, and 'evangelism', which is concerned with bringing to faith those on the outside of the Church. This present chapter is concerned with evangelism and outreach.

Children's evangelism

Children's evangelism is a kingdom activity rather than a narrow concern for Church recruitment. In working with children whose links with the church are tenuous, Christians are making a long-term investment in society at large. The Sunday schools and other children's ministry of past decades have given much toward a moral consensus in this country while at the same time accustomising people to the stories and concepts that come alive for many in a later adult commitment.

All God's Children? 1991, p. 2

The most sustained analysis of evangelism among children in recent years was provided by the report *All God's Children?*, published in 1991. The working party which produced this report was set up jointly by the Board of Mission and the Board of Education of the Church of England. The report took a wider view than that of one denomination. The working party included a Methodist, a Roman Catholic and a Baptist. The report favours the definition of evangelism as 'activities designed to help people discover the good news' (p. 39).

All God's Children? focused on a number of main issues which continue to be the key areas for consideration. The present chapter follows the same pattern. The first five sections focus on the context in which evangelism among children takes place today, namely the demise of Sunday schools, the emphasis on family church, the need to appreciate the constraints shaped by the wider culture, the role of the school and the factors which shape the child's world-view. The following sections focus on the theological questions which need to be asked, a discussion of the aims of evangelism among children, and the place of evangelism within schools. The practical issues, like organizing and running evangelistic events, are covered in the later section of this book as practical ministry.

The demise of Sunday schools

Originally the Sunday schools seem to have been established more for the benefit of those children of parents who did not attend church or chapel than for the benefit of those children who were brought up in practising families. In this sense Sunday schools functioned as a powerful form of evangelism and outreach among children, and such evangelism and outreach was regarded as a proper and legitimate aim for Sunday schools.

The Sunday school model had clear strengths and clear weaknesses. The main strength was the capability of reaching a high proportion of young people in an age when attendance was taken for granted as a 'national custom'. The main weakness was that Sunday school was seen to be linked more closely with the idea of school than with the idea of church. Growing up meant leaving behind both school and Sunday school.

This form of Sunday school was unable to survive the secularization of Sunday and unable to compete with the growing body of alternative attractions available to young people. The demise of the Sunday school has now been well documented (see Chapter 6; Nixon, 1985; Cliff, 1986).

Church of England Sunday school attendance

A survey conducted during the late 1980s estimated the total number (N) of children in specified age groups attending Church of England Sunday schools, and calculated these figures as a percentage of the total population of children living in England.

Age group	Male		Female	
	N	%	N	%
under 2	2,500	0.4	2,500	0.4
2–5	32,050	2.6	39,550	3.4
6–9	54,600	4.7	74,800	6.8
10–13	23,250	1.9	36,850	3.2

Leslie J. Francis and David W. Lankshear, 1991, p. 9

Family church

In the 1960s, Sunday schools were being replaced by strategies based on the notion of 'family church'. A good account of this strategy is provided in Michael Botting's book, *Reaching the Families: The Planning and Conduct of Family Services* (1969). There were two sound theological principles behind this movement: the evangelization of children and of their parents properly takes place in the same context; the church properly functions as a family embracing all ages.

The problem, however, is that the family church strategy reached little beyond the children whose parents were prepared to come. The boundaries within which evangelism could take place were seriously curtailed.

The family service

A family service, then, is a service designed to speak to all the family at the same time. While it is deliberately made simple and probably shorter than other services, it is not only for the children. Such names as 'children's church' or 'young people's service' do not describe it, because the service is just as much, if not more, for adults as for children.

Michael Botting, 1969, p. 20

Cultural context

The demise of the Sunday school movement has been associated with a significant shift in the religious cultural climate of the wider society. A key contribution made by Sunday schools concerned their reinforcement of the basic Christian 'story' among a large proportion of society. This shared story helped to create a 'Christian' society. One perspective on the points of contact between the 'implicit' religion of contemporary society and the Christian gospel is provided by Professor Edward Bailey (1997, 1998).

Today children are growing up in a post-Christian society in which the Christian story cannot be assumed to be part of their shared and common heritage. This defines the context in which evangelism has to work.

There is less consensus, however, regarding what has taken the place of the Christian story in today's cultural context. The notion that Christianity has been replaced by a secular world-view among young people is becoming increasingly less convincing. Rather, young people seem to be creating their own 'religious' world-view, drawing on an amalgam of ideas, embracing horoscopes, magic and supernatural powers. Here, at least, is a context with which evangelism can engage.

School context

While the 1944 Education Act assumed a close alliance between Church and state in the provision of religious (Christian) education, a clear distinction has now been made between the *educational* role of the school and the *evangelistic* or *catechetical* role of the church. The job of community schools, at least, does not seem to include initiating young people into Christian faith (see Chapter 20).

The distinction between the roles of school and church has stimulated a particular debate regarding the potential distinctiveness of Church schools. While the Roman Catholic Church has tended to see Church schools as primarily serving the children of Church members, the Church of England has tended to see Church schools as serving the wider local community. As a consequence, many children in Church of England schools come from non-Church backgrounds. Some argue that Church of England schools have a clear mandate to engage in evangelism. Others argue that Church of England schools should be places through which the Church can serve the nation. The most influential Church of England statement on this issue was *The Fourth R,* published in 1970, which steered the Church away from seeing Church schools as agents of evangelism (see Chapter 18). The recent report *The Way Ahead* (see Chapter 19), while recognizing that church schools are at the centre of the Church's mission, denies them a role as agents of proselytion or conversion.

The child's world

Evangelism needs to take seriously all that can be known about the child's own world. This is a world which is being shaped by many influences beyond the immediate environment of home and school. The child's world-view is being shaped by:

- television
- videos
- computer games
- Internet
- advertising

The child's world-view

Elements in our society are combining to create for today's children a prematurely adult and somewhat lonely world that accustoms them to materialism, hedonism, sexual amorality, the unseriousness and even normality of violence, the possibility of spiritual power through an openness to the occult – and all this against an ever-weakening acknowledgement of the truth and relevance of Christianity.

All God's Children? 1991, pp. 32–3

Facing the issues

The report *All God's Children?* raises four key issues which need to be debated by those concerned with evangelism among children:

1 The first issue asks the question, 'Does God have a focused concern for children in themselves outside the family?' The question has to be asked because some would argue that it is 'unbiblical' to attempt to minister to children outside the family unit. The report concludes from its reflection on Scripture that a specific ministry toward children is entirely appropriate.

Children and the family

Those who call for a return to biblical patterns of family must recognize the very different world in which we live.

Francis Bridger, 1988, p. 140

---

2 The second issue asks the question, 'Is evangelism an appropriate thing to do with children?' The question has to be asked because some would argue that evangelism may take advantage of the young person's immaturity and may be seen as a form of manipulation or indoctrination. The report concludes from its reflection on the very nature of evangelism that evangelism properly construed is appropriate among children. The report argues that evangelism is about the creation of formats and contexts within which people can discover the gospel for themselves. This definition has much in common with contemporary understandings of the educational process. Evangelism of children needs to be seen in terms of education rather than persuasion.

3 The third issue asks the question, 'How should the churches relate to the parents of those children who take part in their activities?' The question has to be asked because some would argue that there is a danger of conspiring with the children against their parents. The report argues that parental support and approval should always be sought and that parents should be informed about the activities in which their children participate.

4 The fourth issue asks the question, 'How do churches handle a situation where children from other faith communities attend their gospel-sharing activities?' The question has to be asked because of the growing multi-faith nature of society and the growing emphasis on respect for other faiths. Here is the crucial question which the report fails to answer.

Defining the outcome

Those who engage in evangelism among children need to be clear about what they are setting out to achieve. The child's response to evangelism cannot be measured in the same way as the response of an adult. We should not look for a public conversion, promises of lifelong commitment, or even regular church attendance. We should not look for responses which are characteristically adult, but for those which are realistically appropriate within the child's own stage of development.

According to *All God's Children?* there is, however, one particular response that children's evangelists should desire, and that is 'children should want to pray' (p. 57). The report argues that children can be taught to know a loving God to whom they can talk naturally. Simple trusting prayers learnt during childhood remain to shape and to educate an adult spirituality in later years.

Children finding faith

What, then, are we doing when we preach the Gospel to children? I think...
we are doing several things that might best be described as pre-conversional.

First, we are *sowing seed for the future*. Children who hear the Gospel may not yet be ready for the act of surrender and the stage of owned faith but they can store away the truth for the time when it will become relevant...

Second, we may be *persuading a child simply to switch his affiliation* ... It is unlikely given what we know about the structure of child development, that a junior child who comes along to a mission or Sunday school will be converted in the adult sense of making an independent decision to reorientate his life. What is much more likely is that the child...has decided to start a new affiliation...The desire to give his loyalty to a new group (the mission, church or whatever) can represent a genuinely heart-felt act...

But the meaning of such a commitment may lie in affiliation to the complex of persons and beliefs which make up the group, rather than to a personal acceptance of a set of truths...

Francis Bridger, 1988, pp. 120–21

Evangelism in schools

The 1988 Education Reform Act protects the provision made by the 1944 Education Act both for statutory religious education and for a daily act of collective worship.

Many schools invite clergy and lay members of Churches (as well as of other faith communities) to contribute to the act of collective worship and to religious education classes.

In accepting such invitations we need to respect the primary educational purpose of schools. This is not a context in which it is appropriate either to assume that pupils have faith or to try to win converts to faith. It is, however, totally appropriate to help pupils to experience and to understand the perspective and practices of those of us who belong to faith communities.

Outside the statutory provision for religious education and the act of collective worship, many schools permit and encourage voluntary activities in lunch-time and after-school hours. Within this context there is an opportunity for voluntary Christian activities and sometimes these are affiliated to national networks.

Voluntary Christian activities of this nature not only nurture the witness of committed Christian children who attend, but may have a positive outreach among children who would otherwise have no contact with the Church. The management of such groups requires sensitivity so as not to abuse the privilege of being allowed to meet on school premises and so as not to antagonize other 'interest' groups which may be discouraged from forming active cells within the schools.

Conclusion

All God's Children? identifies what it styles an 'evangelistic imperative' for evangelism among children. This imperative, the report argues, has three bases:

1   The first basis is a *moral* imperative. It is not wise to leave evangelism until later in life. Already during early childhood hearts and minds are being moulded for later life.
2   The second basis is a *spiritual* imperative. The kingdom of God belongs to children. They need to be helped to see that there is a God to whose kingdom they belong.
3   The third is an *ecclesiastical* imperative. If children remain outside the Church, those who are inside are themselves impoverished. The Church needs children as much as children need the Church.

References and further reading

Bailey, E. I. (1997), *Implicit Religion in Contemporary Society*, Kampen, Netherlands, Kok Pharos.
Bailey, E. I. (1998), *Implicit Religion: An Introduction*, London, Middlesex University Press.
Botting, M. (1969), *Reaching the Families: The Planning and Conduct of Family Services*, London, Falcon.
Bridger, F. (1988), *Children Finding Faith*, London, Scripture Union.
Butler, P. (1992), *Reaching Children*, London, Scripture Union.
Church of England (1991), *All God's Children? Children's Evangelism in Crisis*, London, National Society and Church House Publishing.
Cliff, P. B. (1986), *The Rise and Development of the Sunday School Movement in England, 1780–1980*, Redhill, National Christian Education Council.
Francis, L. J. and Lankshear, D. W. (1991), *Continuing in the Way: Children, Young People and the Church*, London, National Society.
Frank, P. (1992), *Children and Evangelism*, London, Marshall Pickering.
Nixon, R. (1985), *Who's the Greatest? A Study of the Sunday School in Contemporary Society*, London, National Society.

31

Home and Family

Introduction

For the great majority of children in our society, the first and foremost community of nurture is the family, rather than the school or church. This central arena of education has been described as 'the first and vital cell of society', the 'school of deeper humanity' and as a 'community of love' (Vatican II). For Christian families the educational experience it provides is, or should be, some form of Christian nurture.

Social scientists often describe the process in terms of 'socialization', meaning here the learning (and sometimes teaching) of a 'social role' – that is, the way in which people behave in a social context. This involves transmitting a whole cluster of beliefs, attitudes, values, ways of perceiving and understanding the world (a 'world-view'), and of speaking and acting within it.

Home

Home is the place where, when you have to go there,
They have to take you in.

Robert Frost, 'The Death of the Hired Man', 1914

A family may be broadly defined as a group of people who are bound to each other in a way that they intend to last, and who regard themselves as responsible for each other's well-being. On this definition, families may or may not include children. The 'nuclear family' of mother, father and children differs from the larger group of relatives (the 'extended family') of other cultures and earlier generations, as well as from the increasingly familiar units of one-parent family and same-sex couples. In all cases, the family comprises a set of interdependent relationships and a commitment to mutual growth and support, particularly emotional support.

Family variety

No single form of the family is a kind of God-given ideal, in relation to which every other form has to be compared and evaluated. For this reason, Christian citizens of the modern Western world need to acknowledge quite explicitly that Christianity is not just for those who belong to nuclear families and who believe that nuclear families are 'the ideal'. What needs to be affirmed and celebrated instead is that the new life that God has shown to us in Christ is universal. It is God's gift to all people to enable them to grow into the image of God both as individuals and in their life together.

206

> Certainly, the Christian Gospel impels us to accept the transformation, not only of our inner life, but of the forms and patterns of our corporate life as well. However, this cannot be taken to imply that there is only one form of the family which is right for everyone. The diversity of God's creation and the wide range of human experience do not support such a view.
>
> Board for Social Responsiblity, 1995, p. 87

Meeting needs

According to James Fowler, the family 'uniquely and indispensably' meets our essential needs in a number of areas (in Astley and Francis, 1992, pp. 320–6). These include:

- our need for communion with, and a valued 'place' among, others – in short our need for a 'home'
- our need to develop the ability to be separate, to stand alone and to be responsible for our actions – but always with the assurance of a welcome when we return
- our need to find meaning in our world, sharing with others a set of values and an orientation to life – particularly conveyed by participating in 'ritual' acts and words within the family
- our human needs for food, shelter and sexual identification, which are basic needs that undergird the satisfaction of all our other needs

It is often argued that the health and vitality of the family is finally determined by a proper balance between the needs and demands of its individual members and those of the whole family. Herbert Anderson writes that the secret of family life is 'how its members learn to be separate together' (Anderson, 1984, p. 15).

> ### *'Being separate together'*
>
> The phrase ... is intended to convey the equal importance of both community and individual. It is not possible to be an individual except in relation to community... Being together is as natural as being separate ...
>
> At the same time, the possibility of community presupposes being separate. There is no intimacy without identity. Separateness and togetherness are organically interrelated. The family provides the communal setting for growth in particularity, which in turn fosters interdependence.
>
> Herbert Anderson, 1984, pp. 60, 62

Learning the trick of being separate together is like learning to keep one's balance on a bicycle or a tightrope. This is a delicate and often unstable midway position, always subject to the temptation and tendency to fall off into one extreme ditch or the other: either by becoming too separate and selfish, or by not learning to be an *individual* personality at all. The home is the school where we first learn to live together. It is here that we learn the limits of selfishness; it is here that we learn first the importance of sharing, of responsibility and of altruism. And it is in the home that children gain their initial insights into what it means to be a parent. If we are lucky with our parents, we will learn in the home the virtues and joys of self-giving love, and the pain and pride of eventually 'letting go'. As the proper exercise and limiting of power and possessiveness is the distinctive mark of the character of the Christ-like God (see Philippians 2.5–8), it is not surprising that the love of God is often modelled on that of a parent, or that people sometimes speak of their home as the place where they *felt*, as well as heard about, the divine love and forgiveness (cf. Hosea 11.1–9). Yet homes are also the places where human relationships can go so disastrously wrong that what the child learns and experiences there is more satanic than divine. Parenting is a Christian vocation, and perhaps one of the most difficult.

Church versus home?

The family, then, appears to be our first and society's primary expression of community. But some Christians will agree with Stanley Hauerwas that the family should *not* be given the primary role in character formation, but rather that 'the first family of every Christian' is the *church*.

The family in theology

In its consistent monotheism, its abhorrence of idolatry, and its advocacy of the headship of Christ, the Bible offers a powerful *corrective* to any tendency to give 'the family' an inflated importance. The gospel stories of Jesus calling disciples to leave their kinship and household ties to follow him are a dramatic expression of this (cf. Mark 1.16–20; Matthew 10.34–37; Luke 9.57–62 etc.). The fact that the Church so readily adopts a 'familist' ethos and ethic is surely surprising in view of the evidence that Jesus himself did not marry, that he expected disciples to subordinate family ties for his sake, and that he spoke in quite pessimistic terms about what his followers ought to expect from their natural kin (cf. Mark 3.31–35; 10.28–30; 13.12–13)...

There is no sense in simplistic distinctions between the Church as a structure of grace and 'the family' as one of nature. This is to claim too much for the Church and too little for 'the family'. It also fails to do justice to the widely held view that the Church itself is *a kind of family*, and conversely, that 'the family' has a *sacramental* quality.

Stephen Barton, 1993, pp. 9–11

It is certainly true that the Christian family needs the help of a supporting, serious, nurturing congregation to offer three things: a wider perspective, a less fraught and forced set of relationships (sometimes), and a Christian context that is more explicitly related to the Jesus story. Where the church complements and completes the Christian nurture started in the home, taking the child on to new explorations of discipleship, this is greatly to be applauded. But it cannot be *guaranteed* in the church any more than it can in the family.

We need to look and see what sort of a 'family' the church is, judging it by the same standards as we apply to the family. Is the church one of those selfish and self-seeking families; or does it provide a caring, forgiving and concerned home? Good churches can save us from bad families; they naturally support and work with the ministry of good parents. But bad churches are worse than an embarrassment: they can work against the family's proper fulfilment of its role as religious mentor and sustainer. The ideal situation is one of complementarity between home and church. Nevertheless, parents must recognize the possibility that the church may *oppose* the values of the home, and that when it does so it is sometimes the church that is in the wrong.

Family stages

Just like individuals, families have 'life cycles', developing through a sequence of stages which present different emotional and social demands of family members. For a family with children, the realignment of relationships caused by the new demands of parenthood extend beyond the couple themselves to relationships with other relatives, friends, neighbours and work colleagues. As the children get older, the family has to take account of a new group of their own friends, teachers and other significant relationships. After the often traumatic period of the child's adolescence, parents have to face a mini-bereavement as children move on to higher education, the world of work or to set up homes of their own. Their departure leaves the original couple (older, and maybe wiser) facing one another across the 'empty nest' in a realigned relationship that mirrors, but is never going to recapture, the intimacy of their first childless home.

Throughout all these stages of the family life cycle, both the children and the parents have aged and developed, and their interrelationships have been continually reformed. In particular, the parents have had to learn to relate to the same child in very different ways, as that child moves from a totally dependent baby, through the different stages of maturation and the growing separation and independence of childhood and adolescence, through to the fully grown 'adult child' with whom an adult-to-adult relationship is now possible – and necessary.

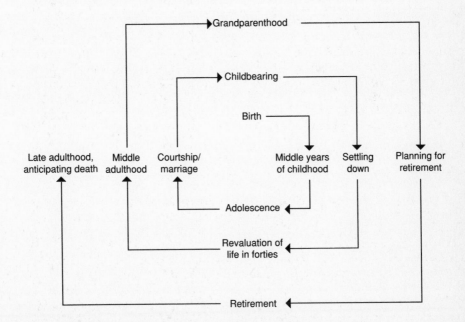

Figure 2: *Family life spiral*

Source: after Lee Combrinck-Graham, in James C. Hanson (ed.) (1983), *Clinical Implications of the Family Life Cycle*, Tunbridge Wells, Aspen, p. 38.

The interrelated, complementary development of the three generations of child, parent and grandparent, with the associated life-cycle crises and physical, emotional and psychosocial changes, may be represented in the picture of a 'family life spiral' (see Figure 2). Each generation has to cope with its own changes and realignment of relationships, for example as the parents relate on the one hand to their child's adolescent demands and on the other to their own mid-life readjustment of priorities and their concerns about the ageing of their own parents.

References and further reading

Anderson, H. (1984), *The Family and Pastoral Care*, London, SPCK.

Barton, S. C. (1993), 'Towards a theology of the family', *Crucible*, Jan–Mar, pp. 4–13.

Barton, S. C. (ed.) (1996), *The Family in Theological Perspective*, Edinburgh, T. & T. Clark.

Board for Social Responsibility (1995), *Something to Celebrate: Valuing Families in Church and Society*, London, Church House Publishing.

Borrowdale, A. (1994), *Reconstructing Family Values*, London, SPCK.

Clapp, R. (1993), *Families at the Crossroads: Beyond Traditional and Modern Options*, Downers Grove, Illinois, InterVarsity Press.

Durka, G. and Smith, J. (eds.) (1980), *Family Ministry*, Minneapolis, Minnesota, Winston.

Fowler, J. W. (1992), 'Perspectives on the family from the standpoint of faith development theory', in J. Astley and L. J. Francis (eds.), *Christian Perspectives on Faith Development: A Reader*, Leominster, Gracewing, pp. 320–44.

Grimer, M. (1994), *Making Families Work: A New Search for Christian Family Values*, London, Chapman.

Hyde, K. (1990), *Religion in Childhood and Adolescence: A Comprehensive Review of the Research*, Birmingham, Alabama, Religious Education Press, pp. 224–37, 254, 262–3, 315, 328–30.

Neff, B. J. and Ratcliff, D. (eds.) (1984), *Handbook of Family Religious Education*, Birmingham, Alabama, Religious Education Press.

Pyper, H. S. (1996), *The Christian Family – A Concept in Crisis*, Norwich, Canterbury Press.

32

Pastoral Care, Parents and Education

Introduction

It should go without saying that a Christian approach to children must be essentially *pastoral*. This word derives originally from the Latin *pastor* or 'shepherd', and is related to the verb for 'feeding' or 'grazing'. The image of the person in charge of a congregation as its 'shepherd' is an old one which views the ministerial role as one of guiding or leading, caring and protecting. 'Pastoral' has come to mean a healing concern particularly for those in trouble or distress; but it also refers more generally to a 'carefulness' for the soul – hence to 'the giving of spiritual guidance'. This last definition rubs shoulders in the dictionaries with another core sense of 'a teacher's responsibility for the general well-being of pupils or students' (*Concise Oxford Dictionary*, 1999).

Pastoral parenting?

Parenting is the first and fundamental pastoral ministry, for its basic orientation is to care for, protect, nurture and guide children (see Chapter 31). Although these roles may properly be expected of a child's parents for many years, the ways in which parents show care for their offspring naturally change dramatically as the child grows, matures and establishes her independence.

It is in the first years of life, however, that we most need pastoral parents. According to the psychologist Erik Erikson, the first task of the ego in the child's developing sense of identity is a sort of psychological battle between trust and mistrust. A caring, accepting, stable, *secure* relationship is necessary for the development of basic trust: a trust in the mother, or other primary carer, in others and in the child herself. If children are denied the conditions for the development of basic trust at an early stage (Fowler's faith stage 0, see Chapter 10), their later development may be badly affected. The consequences of mistrust are shame, guilt and a sense of inferiority. And if we do not trust Mummy when we are little, how will we be able to trust anyone – including God – later?

> ### Erikson writes
>
> Mothers create a sense of trust in their children ... [which] forms the basis in the child for a sense of identity which will later combine a sense of being 'all right', of being oneself, and of becoming what other people trust one will become ... Parents must not only have certain ways of guiding by prohibition

and permission; they must also be able to represent to the child a deep, an almost somatic conviction that there is a meaning to what they are doing...

The parental faith which supports the trust emerging in the newborn has throughout history sought its institutional safeguard (and, on occasion, found its greatest enemy) in organized religion. Trust born of care is, in fact, the touchstone of the *actuality* of a given religion...

The clinician can only observe that many are proud to be without religion whose children cannot afford their being without it. On the other hand, there are many who seem to derive a vital faith from social action or scientific pursuit. And again, there are many who profess faith, yet in practice breathe mistrust both of life and man.

Erik Erikson, 1977, pp. 224–5

Pastoral teaching?

All education may be seen as an expression of care, in terms of its provision of and devotion to the welfare and protection of others. Similarly, all teaching may be seen as in some sense 'ministry' or service. There is, indeed, something intrinsically pastoral about education. Teaching itself is a helping relationship, and for many people learning is a healing, indeed a 'salvific' (saving) experience. Education, writes William Willimon, is 'one aspect of pastoral care'.

Christian education as pastoral care

People can be healed, supported and cared for by helping them clarify their values and concepts, by putting forward a conceptual framework upon which they are able to make meaning of their often disordered world, by telling them the Story in terms that can be heard and affirmed as *their* story, by proclaiming the faith in such a way that it becomes *their* faith.

William Willimon, 1979, p. 125

Most adults, however negative their attitude may be to their own schooling, have a memory of a teacher who 'meant something' to them, particularly because she or he was truly a carer.

The pastoral teacher

One looks back with appreciation to the brilliant teachers, but with gratitude to those who touched our human feelings. The curriculum is so much necessary raw material, but warmth is the vital element for the growing plant and for the soul of the child.

Carl Gustav Jung, quoted in Graham, 1998, p. 26

Some teachers may be 'pastoral' in this way simply by being good teachers, and particularly by being enthusiastic for, indeed 'in love with', their subject. The effect of the teacher played by Robin Williams in the film *Dead Poets' Society* was partly the contagion of his enthusiasm for his subject, but it was also the effect of his commitment to its seriousness and value. Parker Palmer has written of the teacher's relationship with the subject in terms of a friendship that he wants to share with his pupils. Initially the subject is a stranger to the children, but their fear of this stranger is overcome when they see the 'friendship that binds subject and teacher' – a friendship that is not possessive or protective, but open to others. The teacher wants to *share* this love.

Friendship teaching

The metaphor of friendship helps identify some demands of this sort of teaching. The teacher, who knows the subject well, must introduce it to students in the way one would introduce a friend. The students must know why the teacher values the subject, how the subject has transformed the teacher's life. By the same token, the teacher must value the students as potential friends, be vulnerable to the ways students may transform the teacher's relationship with the subject as well as be transformed. If I am invited into a valued friendship between two people, I will not enter in unless I feel that I am valued as well.

Parker Palmer, 1993, p. 104

Pastoral education?

Many claim that if we examine the fundamental principles that underpin the work of schools, education will be recognized as fundamentally pastoral. Here is one list of such principles (Best *et al.*, 1995, pp. 288–97):

- Education must begin from a commitment to meeting the developmental needs of the individual.
- Education must be oriented toward the development of the whole person.
- The identification of the educational needs of the individual requires the willing participation of the learner.
- Education involves respect for persons, valuing children for themselves.
- Education involves equality (similar treatment being given to all in similar conditions, without groundless discrimination).
- Children are entitled to learning experiences that promote their personal, social and moral development.
- Teachers have a right to exercise their professional judgement – and a right to pastoral care as well.
- Schools should be organized and resourced to the ends of pastoral care and personal and social education.

Pastoral care in education

Although some have objected to the term as implying too much dependence and not enough autonomy, 'pastoral care' has become an accepted term in British education. According to Her Majesty's Inspectorate, it is concerned with:

promoting pupils' personal and social development and fostering positive attitudes: through the quality of teaching and learning; through the nature of relationships amongst pupils, teachers and adults other than teachers; through arrangements for monitoring pupils' overall progress, academic, personal and social; through specific pastoral structures and support systems; and through extra-curricular activities and the school ethos ... It offers support for the learning, behaviour and welfare of all pupils, and addresses the particular difficulties some individual pupils may be experiencing. It seeks to help ensure that all pupils, and particularly girls and members of ethnic minorities, are enabled to benefit from the full range of educational opportunities which a school has available. (Department for Education and Science, 1989, p. 3)

This is a very wide-ranging concept. Pastoral care of pupils is promoted, or as educationalists now like to say 'delivered', by a number of specific structures and activities, as well as through the ethos and climate of the school as a whole. They include:
• the school's 'house' or 'year' system
• the child's tutor and tutor group
• counselling services
• careers education
• chaplaincy (in some Church schools)

It should be added that the management and leadership in a school provides an indirect facilitation of the pastoral well-being of the child, and an additional, rather more direct, impact on the pastoral needs of the teachers.

Pastoral lessons?

The most important method of giving pastoral care to pupils and of enhancing their personal growth cannot occur in a parallel pastoral system. It occurs continually in and through the everyday lessons of the school.

John McGuinness, 1989, p. 41

Guidance and counselling

This phrase is often used in educational circles to cover:
• advice-giving, helping relationships where information is given and diagnoses of the pupils' needs offered ('guidance')
• more non-directive activities in which the child is helped to work through his or her own problem and make his or her own decisions ('counselling')

There is sometimes a tension between the two activities, and this parallels the tension the priest or minister often feels between offering spiritual or moral guidance to a parishioner, and adopting a much more neutral role that facilitates the 'client's' own self-understanding and decision-making processes.

Love in teaching and learning

Talk of warm relationships and friendship in education, and developing a caring atmosphere and good personal relationships, carries some risks. Richard Pring stresses the importance of teachers 'respecting' their pupils, but adds the following.

Respect

At no time... should respecting persons be confused with liking, let alone loving, them. Good *personal* relationships do not require having an affection for the person I am relating to. Indeed, affectionate personal relationships could get in the way of personal respect in so far as sometimes these might be of a selfish nature, blinding one to the real interests and welfare of the other, or being pursued irrespective of those interests.

Richard Pring, 1984, p. 29

But what is love? The Jewish scholar Martin Buber once wrote of the educator as showing a 'lofty asceticism'. He should not be in thrall to *eros*, the Greek word for a love that is evoked by the loveableness of its object, what some have called 'need-love'. Need-love is natural, in education as elsewhere (including parenting, of course), for it is natural to all human relationships. Teachers *need* to teach, and in that sense they need their students. The best teachers love to teach and to experience the joy of seeing other people flourish, increasing in knowledge and understanding, coming to an insight or mastering a skill. But need-love is not enough on its own in education, or in life. It must be transformed by what Buber called 'inclusive eros', but the New Testament labels *agapē* or 'gift-love': the unlimited, other-regarding, unconditional love that is not dependent on our feelings or the loveableness of the other. This species of love is love in action; it is a function of the will and is only found perfectly in the love of God. It is a kind of loving that is also a kind of giving.

Influence not interference

Eros is choice, choice made from an inclination. This is precisely what education is not. The man who is loving in Eros chooses the beloved, the modern educator finds his pupil there before him. From this unerotic situation the greatness of the... educator is to be seen... [The teacher] enters the school-room for the first time, he sees them crouching at the desks, indiscriminately flung together, the misshapen and the well-proportioned, animal faces, empty faces, and noble faces in indiscriminate confusion, like the presence of the created universe; the glance of the educator accepts and receives them all. He is assuredly no descendant of the Greek gods, who kidnapped those they loved. But he seems to me to be a representative of the true God. For if God 'forms the light and creates darkness', man is able to love both – to love light in itself, and darkness toward the light...

In education, then, there is a lofty asceticism: an asceticism which rejoices in the world, for the sake of the responsibility for a realm of life which is entrusted to us for our influence but not our interference – either by the will to power or by Eros.

Martin Buber, 1947, pp. 94–5

Teaching is not for the teachers, therefore. It is not for their self-aggrandizement or the satisfaction of their needs. It is *for the learners*. However passionate it may be, ultimately it must be *disinterested* – that is, unbiased and uninfluenced by the teacher's personal benefit, profit or advantage. True teaching is not self-serving, but self-giving.

In the world of higher education, research and publication is usually ranked higher than teaching. Of one academic theologian it was said after his early death, 'He really should have devoted himself more to his own work, rather than to encouraging the work of his students.' Perhaps. But his students probably thought differently. The love for a subject – even the subject of religion – that does not flow over into a helping relationship with others, that they may come to love it too, is a rather narrow species of love. And it is not teaching. The teacher *facilitates* others: their learning, their insight, their research. Good teachers, whether in schools or universities, often take on a sort of John the Baptist role: 'decreasing' that the others (the learners) may increase (see John 3.30). Parents, of course, must also fulfil this role if they are to allow their children truly to flourish and to become themselves.

Taking each other seriously

In his book, *Taking Each Other Seriously*, Bob Graham made some telling points about the effects of the teacher and the nature and purpose of schools.

The point of schools

Schools can be very dangerous ... and very crazy places too, if they are not at least good enough ...

We have to recognize that schools and teachers are there, if they are to have any truly reputable purpose, to take people seriously, and essentially for that alone.

Bob Graham, 1998, pp. 82, 89

Graham recognized the real power and influence of schools on the lives of their pupils. Schools, as well as homes, are places that can make or break children, by either helping them find a home, a place and a purpose, or by confirming them in an emotional lostness that is very difficult to change.

He proposed the discipline of 'taking people seriously' as a way of reconciling the extremes of realism and idealism in education. This is not, however, a matter of doing everything for them. It is 'primarily about acknowledging people, which is a very long way from being the same thing as sorting out their problems for them' (pp. 96–7). He argued that taking others seriously does not mean doing anything very much. But anyone who has suffered at the hands of those teachers who felt themselves to be above such little things, or has been redeemed through the educational ministry of those who have felt that 'acknowledging people' is part of the job (part of the job of *living*, perhaps?), will know what a difference can be made by doing, or avoiding doing, 'nothing very much'.

References and further reading

Best, R. *et al.* (eds.) (1995), *Pastoral Care and Personal-Social Education: Entitlement and Provision*, London, Cassell.

Buber, M. (1947), *Between Man and Man*, London, Kegan Paul.

Department for Education and Science (1989), *Report of Her Majesty's Inspectors on Pastoral Care in Secondary Schools*, Stanmore, DES.

Erikson, E. (1977), *Childhood and Society*, London, Granada.

Graham, R. (1998), *Taking Each Other Seriously*, Durham, Fieldhouse Press/University of Durham School of Education.

Jacobs, M. (1988), *Towards the Fullness of Christ: Pastoral Care and Christian Ministry*, London, Darton, Longman & Todd.

Lyall, D. (1995), *Counselling in the Pastoral and Spiritual Context*, Oxford, Oxford University Press.

McGuinness, J. (1989), *A Whole School Approach to Pastoral Care*, London, Kogan Page.

McGuinness, J. (1998), *Counselling in Schools: New Perspectives*, London, Cassell.

Palmer, P. J. (1993), *To Know as We are Known: Education as a Spiritual Journey*, San Francisco, California, HarperSanFrancisco.

Pring, R. (1984), *Personal and Social Education in the Curriculum: Concepts and Control*, London, Hodder & Stoughton.

Willimon, W. H. (1979), *Worship as Pastoral Care*, Nashville, Tennessee, Abingdon.

33

The Law and the Child

Introduction

This chapter will introduce key aspects of the law as it affects children in the United Kingdom. One problem in this area is how the word 'childhood' is defined in British law. In the Children Act 1989, childhood is seen, for some purposes at least, as extending to 16 years or above.

The material is arranged under the following headings:
- the United Nations Convention on the Rights of the Child
- education
- protection and neglect
- special needs
- independence and the growth of responsibility

The United Nations Convention on the Rights of the Child

This convention was ratified by resolution 44/25 of the General Assembly of the United Nations on 20 November 1989, with the intention of coming into force on 2 September 1990 in those countries that were signatories by that date. This convention replaced the Declaration of the Rights of the Child adopted by the United Nations General Assembly in 1959. This convention is very important to any consideration of the law as it impacts on children, as it provides the international standard against which national legislation can be assessed. Article 1 of the convention makes it clear that for the purposes of the convention the upper limit of childhood is a child's eighteenth birthday unless the law of the country states that the child attains majority earlier.

United Nations Convention on the Rights of the Child – Article 14

1 States... shall respect the right of the child to freedom of thought, conscience and religion.
2 States... shall respect the rights and duties of the parents and, when applicable, legal guardians, to provide direction to the child in the exercise of his or her right in a manner consistent with the evolving capacities of the child.
3 Freedom to manifest one's religion or beliefs may be subject only to such limitations as are prescribed by law and are necessary to protect public safety, order, health or morals, or the fundamental rights and freedoms of others.

The inclusion of text from Article 14 at this point has two purposes. The first is to illustrate the way in which the articles are generally worded and the duties that they put on states to implement the articles. The second is to draw attention to the fact that religious matters are covered within the convention.

Education

Articles 28 and 29 of the United Nations Convention on the Rights of the Child particularly address the issue of education and the importance for all children to have access to schooling. In the system of education provided in England and Wales these issues have been covered by a number of Education Acts since the Churches initiated provision of primary education for all during the nineteenth century. Perhaps the most famous of these Acts of Parliament is the Education Act 1944, which set up much of the system of schooling that is still in use. Following an increase in the amount of legislation for education during the 1980s, the law as it applies to schools (with the exception of school inspection) was consolidated into a single Education Act in 1996. This has since been subject to further amendment, most notably by the School Standards and Framework Act 1998 and the Learning and Skills Act (2000). At the time of writing, the government is preparing a further Education Bill, which is expected to become law during 2002. Current documentation, therefore, needs only to refer to the Education Act 1996 or to subsequent legislation.

Education Act 1996, Sections 7 and 8

(7) The parent of every child of compulsory school age shall cause him to receive efficient full-time education suitable –

    (a) To his age, ability and aptitude, and

    (b) To any special educational needs he may have, either by regular attendance at school or otherwise.

(8) (1) Subsections (2) and (3) apply to determine for the purposes of any enactment whether a person is of compulsory school age.

    (2) A person begins to be of compulsory school age when he attains the age of five.

    (3) A person ceases to be of compulsory school age at the end of the day which is the school leaving date for any calendar year –

        (a) If he attains the age of 16 after that day but before the beginning of the school year next following,

        (b) If he attains that age on that day, or

        (c) (unless paragraph (a) applies) if that day is the school leaving date next following his attaining that age.

    (4) The Secretary of State may by order determine the day in any calendar year which is to be the school leaving date for that year.

The law (Education Act 1996) places the responsibility for making arrangements for the education of children firmly on the parents. For all but a small minority of parents, all children between the ages of 5 and 16 normally attend school unless their parents make formal arrangements for them to be educated at home. The effect of this provision is to make attendance at school compulsory for all children, unless their parents are able to provide education at home consistent with definitions of 'suitable education' developed in case law.

Law heavily circumscribes the content of education at school, in that the Education Act 1996 requires schools to provide all the subjects which together are defined as the 'basic curriculum'. The basic curriculum is defined as religious education and those subjects that make up the National Curriculum. The content of the National Curriculum is defined by a series of orders. The law also provides for the creation of local syllabuses for religious education which all schools must follow unless they have a 'religious character'. If a school has a 'religious character' the governors determine the syllabus for religious education in accordance with the school's Ethos Statement. As well as being involved in the provision of church schools, the Church is deeply involved in the systems created by the Education Act 1944 for the development and support of local syllabuses for religious education.

Education before or after compulsory school age is voluntary and is provided by a range of different types of institution or group. Provision has been made in education law for this mixed economy of provision and for defining the standards that have to be met for receiving funding from the state.

Protection and neglect

The United Nations Convention on the Rights of the Child gives a great deal of space to the need for children to be protected from abuse, exploitation and violence. This important issue seems rarely out of the news and the legislative framework has developed considerably in the last 15 years, partly at least in response to the scandals of previous generations. The development of this body of legislation has also led the Churches to review their practice in this important area. The legal framework for child protection is contained in the Children Act 1989, particularly Part V. The implications for church practice of the developing law on child protection are dealt with in Chapter 34.

Special needs

The Education Act 1996 contains the current definition of special educational needs. This definition applies to all children under the age of 19 and lays duties on both local education authorities and school governors to make provision for the education of these children. The definition contained below is not as comprehensive as many people might wish, and in particular does not make it clear how a child with a temporary learning difficulty should be regarded. Nevertheless, it does provide an important basis for channelling help to many children who might otherwise not receive it.

The Act makes provision for an assessment of a child's particular needs, and after consultation with the parents in certain circumstances the authority may make a formal statement of these needs (Education Act 1996, section 324). The law also goes on to make provision for parents to appeal against the contents of that statement if they are not satisfied with it.

One of the persistent difficulties with the law on this issue is the question of the resources that are needed to make proper provision for these children. At certain levels of statement the responsibility lies with the governing body. When a child is assessed as having particularly pressing needs, the responsibility shifts from the governors to the authority. Unfortunately, the argument about the provision of resources can sometimes slow down the delivery of these resources to the children who need them. It is to be hoped that further reviews of this aspect of the law will improve this situation.

Education Act 1996, part IV, chapter 1, section 312

(1) A child has 'special educational needs' for the purposes of this Act if he has a learning difficulty which calls for special educational provision to be made for him.

(2) Subject to subsection (3) (and except for the purposes of section 15(5)) a child has a 'learning difficulty' for the purposes of this Act if

    (a) He has a significantly greater difficulty in learning than the majority of children of his age,

    (b) He has a disability which either prevents or hinders him from making use of educational facilities of a kind generally provided for children of his age in schools within the area of the local education authority, or

    (c) He is under the age of five and is, or would be if special educational provision were not made for him, likely to fall within the paragraph (a) or (b) when or over that age.

(3) A child is not to be taken as having a learning difficulty solely because the language (or form of language) in which he is, or will be, taught is different from a language (or form of a language) which has at any time been spoken in his home.

Independence and the growth of responsibility

The United Nations Convention on the Rights of the Child defines childhood as ending at 18 unless individual countries define it as ending earlier. In the United Kingdom the law has developed a gradualist approach to the end of childhood. A variety of acts have defined different ages as the point at which children and young people are allowed to participate in the activities that are associated with adulthood. The following issues represent only a small selection of these.

Leaving children on their own

There is no law that determines the age at which a child may be left alone without adult supervision. There is, however, provision that if a parent or other adult supervising them leaves them alone when doing so puts them at risk, then this is an offence. The National Society for the Prevention of Cruelty to Children has put guidance on this issue on their Web site, an extract from which appears below.

Extract from NSPCC guidance on leaving children at home alone

- Never leave a baby or very young child alone at home, whether asleep or awake, even for a few minutes. It does not take long for unsupervised young children or babies to injure themselves.
- Most children under thirteen should not be left for more than a short period.
- No child under sixteen should be left overnight.

Buying cigarettes

The Children and Young Persons (Protection from Tobacco) Act 1991 has 16 as the minimum legal age for buying cigarettes. This Act strengthened provisions in the Children and Young Persons Act 1933.

Drinking alcohol

Children are allowed to enter a public house if they are over the age of 14, but they cannot consume alcoholic drinks there nor can they purchase drinks. For both these purposes they must be 18.

The Criminal Justice and Police Act 2001 makes it an offence to buy or attempt to buy alcohol for young people to consume in a bar. The law takes a different view of young people being bought alcohol if it is consumed to accompany a meal. Under these circumstances, children as young as five could consume alcohol. Young people aged over 16 may purchase beer, porter, cider or perry if they consume it with a meal. The Children Act of 1908 prevents the giving of alcohol to children under the age of five except under medical supervision. An act came into force in 1995 which allowed magistrates to issue a 'children's certificate' so that children under 14 can be admitted to bars or pubs holding such a certificate.

Criminal justice system

This section draws heavily on the work of Bell and Jones on the chronology of policy and legislative provisions. The Children and Young Persons Act 1933 created a range of age-related limits concerning how the law deals with children and young people.

The Children and Young Persons Act 1933 section 50, as amended by the Children and Young Persons Act 1963 section 16 (1), states that children cannot be held responsible for their criminal actions if they are below the age of ten. By contrast, the Crime and Disorder Act 1998 abolished the common law assumption that a child under the age of 14 did not know the difference between right and wrong.

The Criminal Justice Act 1991 raised the age of young people who should normally be dealt with in Youth Courts from 16 to 17, thus ensuring that all those accused of offences who are under 18 are dealt with in such courts unless they appear as joint defendants with adults.

The Criminal Justice Act 1991 gave protection to witnesses under the age of 14, who can give their evidence unsworn.

Consensual sex

This is a controversial area and there has been a series of changes in the law in recent years changing the legal view of the age of consent for homosexual sex. Until 1967 such acts were illegal. The Sexual Offences Act 1967 made it legal for adults defined as over 21 to have homosexual sex in private. Subsequent acts have changed the minimum age, which is now the same as it is for heterosexual activities.

The Sexual Offences (Amendment) Act 2000 states clearly that 16 is the age at which it is deemed that a child can give consent to having sexual intercourse. If an adult has sex with a child below this age this is child abuse. Adults (that is people over the age of 18) in a position of responsibility for children under 18 who have sexual intercourse with them are committing an offence, even if the child is over the age of consent.

Sexual Offences (Amendment) Act 2000 section 3 (1)

Subject to subsections (2) and (3) below, it shall be an offence for a person aged 18 or over:

a) To have sexual intercourse (whether vaginal or anal) with a person under that age [18]; or

b) To engage in any other sexual activity with or directed toward such a person,

if (in either case) he is in a position of trust to that person.

The exceptions referred to in the quotation above ensure that the provision is not retrospective and that ignorance of the circumstances can be a defence. People who have responsibility for persons between the ages of 16 and 18 need to understand the change that this law has made to their position.

Right to vote

The Representation of the People Act 1969 set the age at which people could vote in elections in the United Kingdom at 18. Before this the age had been 21 since 1928 (for women) and 1918 (for men).

Driving a motor vehicle

Currently this age is set at 17 for a car and the provision determining this is the Motor Vehicles (Driving Licences) Regulations 1996. There are various categories of vehicle and the age at which an individual may drive them also varies. At 16 it is permissible under these regulations to drive an invalid carriage or a moped. At 17 people can drive agricultural and forestry tractors and small vehicles (including cars, and motorcycles with engines smaller than 125cc or with low power-to-weight ratios). In order to be able to drive medium or large vehicles, minibuses and high-powered motorcycles, an individual must be 21 or over.

Fireworks

The Fireworks (Safety) Regulations 1997 raised the age at which young people could legally buy fireworks from 16 to 18. Some low-powered items such as caps, cracker snaps and party poppers may still be purchased by young people aged over 16.

Conclusion

It will be apparent from this brief survey of some of the ways in which the law affects children and those who work with them that the legal understanding of childhood extends far beyond that currently in daily use. In common usage we tend to refer to those of primary school age or younger as being 'children' and then those older than this as 'teenagers' or 'young people'. For some legal purposes, however, young people are still children at 17. It is, of course, natural that children should enter adulthood slowly in legal terms, taking on more of the privileges and responsibilities of adulthood as they grow older.

Perhaps three things should be clear to those who work with children and young people:

1 Both the United Nations Convention on the Rights of the Child and many parts of the law of the United Kingdom take a high view of the rights of the child and seek to ensure that these rights are respected.
2 Those who work with children and young people must behave with great responsibility and personal discipline and must work toward ensuring the greatest possible protection for children.
3 Children are recognized as individuals who have specific needs which, when we seek to serve them, we must take into account.

None of these ideas should be difficult for those working with children and young people in a church context to understand or implement, as they have parallels within the Church's theology of service to and work with children.

References and further reading

Jones, G. and Bell, R. (2000), *Balancing Acts: Youth, Parenting, and Public Policy*, York, York Publishing Services/Joseph Rowntree Foundation.

Government Legislation
United Kingdom Parliament (1908), *Children Act 1908*, London, HMSO.
United Kingdom Parliament (1933), *Children and Young Persons Act 1933*, London, HMSO.
United Kingdom Parliament (1944), *Education Act 1944*, London, HMSO.
United Kingdom Parliament (1967), *Sexual Offences Act 1967*, London, HMSO.
United Kingdom Parliament (1969), *Representation of the People Act 1969*, London, HMSO.
United Kingdom Parliament (1989), *Children Act 1989*, London, HMSO.
United Kingdom Parliament (1991), *Children and Young Persons (Protection from Tobacco) Act 1991*, London, HMSO.
United Kingdom Parliament (1991), *Criminal Justice Act 1991*, London, HMSO.
United Kingdom Parliament (1996), *Education Act 1996*, London, The Stationery Office.
United Kingdom Parliament (1998), *School Standards and Framework Act 1998*, London, The Stationery Office.
United Kingdom Parliament (2000), *Sexual Offences (Amendment) Act 2000*, London, The Stationery Office.
United Kingdom Parliament (2000), *Learning and Skills Act 2000*, London, The Stationery Office.
United Kingdom Parliament (2001), *Criminal Justice and Police Act 2001*, London, The Stationery Office.

Web sites
http://www.legislation.hmso.gov.uk
http://www.unicef.org/crc/
http://www.unhchr.ch
http://www.nspcc.org.uk
http://www.dvla.gov.uk

Child Protection

Introduction

The Education Reform Act 1988, the Children Act 1989, the Education Act 1996, the Police Act 1997, the Protection of Children Act 1999 and the Criminal Justice and Court Services Act 2000, provide an integrated system of legislation for the protection of children in the United Kingdom.

The Children Act

Anyone who has access to and is responsible for children, in whatever role, must comply with the requirements of the Children Act 1989. This Act has been described as the most significant reform of legislation relating to children in our times. It has been designed to support and encourage good practice and safety in all aspects of work and involvement with children.

The requirements of the Act, which took effect from October 1991, apply to local authority services and to privately run and voluntary organizations, with respect to children's homes, community homes, adoption, fostering, child-minding and day-care for young children, and for connected purposes.

The Children Act contains the following main principles:
- The welfare of the child must be the paramount consideration.
- Children should be brought up in their families wherever possible. Moving them must be a last resort. If moved away then the aim is to return a child as soon as possible.
- Local authorities have a duty to provide for children in need.
- Partnership and integration with parents are key aims in this Act.
- Services provided must be appropriate to the child's race, culture and linguistic background.
- Children should be safe and protected, when necessary by intervention. Intervention by local authorities must be open to challenge.
- Substitute care, in place of parental care, should be of a high quality.
- Children must be consulted and involved in decisions which affect them.
- Situations where children are cared for away from home must be open to scrutiny.
- The concept of a parental responsibility replaces that of parental right. A child can no longer be seen as a parent's possession.
- Court procedures and decisions must be responsive to the needs of children. A principle of 'no delay' is introduced and court orders are to be avoided unless it is better for the child that an order be made.

Practical implications

Those involved in ministry to children, whether salaried or on a voluntary basis, must be aware of and uphold the principles set out in the Children Act.

The first principle underpins the ethos of the whole Act in its statement on the necessity for the welfare of the child to be always paramount. The further statements focus on the major issues which arise in the nurture and care for children when their welfare is considered.

The following principles take into account all aspects of the child's welfare, the concerns and actions which can be seen to cover the whole provision for the child, including protection from any form of abuse or harm. Protecting the child from physical, emotional and sexual abuse or neglect is critical if the child's experience is to be a happy and fulfilling one which encourages healthy emotional, social, physical, academic and spiritual growth.

Safe from Harm

Following the Children Act 1989, the Home Office issued a code of practice for safeguarding the welfare of children in voluntary organizations in England and Wales, under the title *Safe from Harm*.

Safe from Harm

This code of practice sets out principles and guidelines which will help voluntary organizations to safeguard the welfare of the children and young people under 16 years of age with whom they work.

Safe from Harm, 1993, p. 3

In order to safeguard the welfare of the children and young people in their charge, *Safe from Harm* recommends that voluntary organizations should consider the issues raised by each of the following statements of principle and then, if they wish to do so, take any action which they deem to be appropriate in the light of their circumstances and structures, and the nature of their activities:

- Adopt a policy statement on safeguarding the welfare of children.
- Plan the work so as to minimize situations where the abuse of children may occur.
- Introduce a system whereby children may talk with an independent person.
- Apply agreed procedures for protecting children to all paid staff and volunteers.
- Give all paid staff and volunteers clear roles.
- Treat all would-be paid staff and volunteers as job applicants for any position involving contact with children.
- Gain at least one reference from a person who has experience of the applicant's paid work or volunteering with children.
- Explore all applicants' experience of working or contact with children in an interview before appointment.
- Find out whether an applicant has any conviction for criminal offences against children.
- Make paid and voluntary appointments conditional on the successful completion of a probationary period.
- Issue guidelines on how to deal with the disclosure or discovery of abuse.

- Train paid staff and volunteers, their line managers or supervisors, and policy-makers in the prevention of child abuse.

Practical implications

All organizations should have a clear written policy on the protection of children in their care. Drawing on the guidelines of the Home Office document *Safe from Harm*, churches should prepare a clear policy statement for ensuring the safety of children. Such a statement might include the following points:
- This church is committed to the welfare, nurturing and safekeeping of children.
- This church is committed to supporting and resourcing those who work with children.
- No one will be expected to work in this church with children unsupported.
- This church will ensure that those who work with children, and those in whom children place their trust, know how to handle a situation where a child or young person is considered to be at risk through abuse or neglect.
- Children are part of this church today, have much to give as well as receive, and will be listened to. In worship, learning, teaching, and evangelism we will respect the wishes and feelings of children.
- This church is committed to providing a safe, warm and friendly environment for all.

Child abuse

The abuse of children and young people can occur among families of any background and within any institutions, even those statutory bodies and structures set up to protect children.

An allegation of abuse against a child, even an anonymous phone call, will be acted on by Social Services or the NSPCC. Along with the police these agencies have powers to intervene. Other key agencies are health and education authorities, which will monitor and make referrals. It is important that people know the procedure and know their own limits. If there are reasonable grounds to suspect that a child is being abused in any way, this should be reported immediately to Social Services. If there is some doubt, it is possible to discuss such things in confidence without necessarily disclosing the name of the child involved. It must be stressed that it is not for the clergy or lay leaders to launch into further investigations in what may be a criminal action. Guidelines for procedures should be found in the Child Protection Policy adopted by your church.

The document *Working Together: A Guide to Arrangements for Inter-Agency Collaboration for the Protection of Children from Abuse* (published by the DHSS in July 1988) outlined the following categories of registration for abuse:
- *Neglect*: the persistent or severe neglect of a child (for example by exposure to any kind of danger, including cold and starvation) which results in serious impairment of the child's health or development.
- *Physical Abuse*: physical injury to a child, including deliberate poisoning, where there is definite knowledge, or reasonable suspicion, that the injury was inflicted or knowingly not prevented.
- *Sexual Abuse*: the involvement of dependent, developmentally immature children and adolescents in sexual activities they do not truly comprehend, to which they are unable to give informed consent, or that violate the proper limits enshrined in family roles.

- *Emotional Abuse*: the severe adverse effects on the behaviour and emotional development of a child caused by persistent or severe emotional ill-treatment or rejection. All abuse involves some emotional ill-treatment; this category should be used where it is the main or sole form of abuse.
- *Grave Concern*: children whose situations do not currently fit the above categories, but where social and medical assessments indicate that they are at significant risk of abuse. This could include situations where another child in the household has been harmed or the household contains a known abuser.

Development of legislation and the protection of children

The Police Act 1997

Part 5 of The Police Act 1997 provides for new arrangements for the safety of children in allowing employers, voluntary organizations, and other recruiters, greater access to criminal records information.

The Protection of Children Act 1999

The Protection of Children Act 1999 makes provision for the newly set up Criminal Records Bureau to provide information from the lists of those who have come to notice as being unsuitable to work with children and have been placed on the lists maintained by the Secretary of State. The Criminal Records Bureau was set up to facilitate safer recruitment to protect children and vulnerable adults.

In this way, the Government has established the strong framework of a coherent cross-sector scheme for identifying people considered to be unsuitable to work with children. The system prevents identified people from gaining access to children through their work. It also makes provision for the Criminal Records Bureau to provide information on those persons who have been placed on the list as unsuitable to work with children.

The Criminal Justice and Court Service Act 2000

The Criminal Justice and Court Service Act builds on these various systems and processes to help create a comprehensive and integrated system of child protection. The new procedures require that applicants for posts which involve working with children apply to the Criminal Records Bureau for clearance. Details of the individual and the proposed employment are taken by the local Criminal Records Bureau office and a form is returned to the applicant. The applicant checks the details of the form, signs it and sends it to an appointed counter-signatory who, in turn, signs the form and returns it to the Criminal Records Bureau. The Criminal Records Bureau enters any information from the Criminal Records Bureau on the form and a copy is sent to the applicant and the counter-signatory. If there are problems to be dealt with, the officer will contact the church's Child Protection Officer (see p. 229) who will in turn contact the applicant and follow through the necessary procedures.

Selection of personnel

The appropriate supervision and care of children is central to any policy and procedures which may be drawn up for their protection. One of the major issues that arises in child protection is the state of trust to which all adults in a child's life must commit themselves. Those who have children in their care must ensure that trust is not betrayed.

Selection

The responsibility for those who lead the ministry to children is to ensure that all who work with the children are appropriate persons to do so. These persons are supervised in their work and the state of trust is upheld. It is essential that care must be taken at all times in the recruitment of paid persons and volunteers intending to work with children. Once appointed to a specific task, it is recommended that a contract is signed by adults working with children and by the supervising minister.

Most regional or national Church structures now provide a recommended proforma and procedure to help local churches in the proper recruitment, vetting and selection of personnel to work with children and young people. Although clear variations exist between the different Churches, a good example can be provided by examining the policy adopted by the Church in Wales. If you are working in another Church you should check the arrangements which apply in your circumstances. They are likely to contain most of these features.

Example guidelines for child protection

The Provincial guidelines for child protection, *The Care and Protection of Children: Statement of Policy and Guidance Implementation,* was produced by the Church in Wales in 1997. Diocesan Child Protection Officers were appointed and parishes were given support to draw up child protection policies and implement the required good practice for the safety of children. All these procedures aimed to provide safe, appropriate supervision and care for children. Procedures include recommendations that all who work with children complete a police check form and referees are required for every appointment made. Lists must be compiled of those who have completed the check forms and job descriptions drawn up to include the procedures for the care and safety of children. Parishes are required to appoint a named person as a contact for child protection issues, and the clergy and parochial church councils are responsible for the appropriate procedures being actioned in the parish. All information is kept in The Archbishop's Registry for the Church in Wales.

Intervention procedures

Any system of child protection must ensure that children have the facility to appeal to an independent person if concerned about another adult's behaviour. The person chosen for this role should not be directly concerned with the child in a teaching or learning situation. This will enable intervention on behalf of the child to take place appropriately if necessary.

Procedures

If a case of child abuse is reported, then it is critical that all those directly or indirectly involved with the child must be aware of the reporting procedures. This is a difficult and sensitive area with which to deal.

The welfare of the child comes first, so the procedure which reports child abuse should be put into action immediately if an incident is brought to light. It is essential that the policy for child protection clearly outlines the reporting procedures to follow. Any confusion in procedures could have a disastrous effect on all concerned.

Practical provisions

Supervision

In the early stages of the implementation of child protection in organizations working with children, there appeared to be some confusion over the statements regarding the adult/children safety ratios and the guidelines on child protection supervision procedures. The following figures were given as a guideline on a sensible ratio of adult/child supervision when working with groups of children. For children under two years of age there should be one adult for every three children; for 2- to 3-year-olds there should be one adult for every four children; for 3–7-year-olds there should be one adult for every eight children; for those over the age of eight there should be one adult for every 13 children. Under 18s may not be included in the staff ratio and may not be put in charge of a group. These figures relate to what is sensible in the number of adults required to safely supervise children of varying ages.

However, child protection procedures demand the use of more than one adult in every situation in which the supervision of children is required. This is related to the need to protect the child from abuse and harm which could arise in one-to-one situations and to protect the adult from any false accusations in such circumstances. It is generally recommended that, as far as possible, a mixed group of boys and girls should be supervised by both male and female adults.

Accommodation

The venues for meetings must be of a high recommended standard and safe for the children. Strangers or unauthorized visitors should not be able to enter premises. Once on premises the children must not be allowed to leave unless they are supervised. If a child needs to leave, only an authorized leader should be allowed to accompany that child. At least three adults should be present at any group meeting. Collection of children at the end of a session must be supervised with care to ensure that no unauthorized person leaves with a child.

Situations where children are cared for away from home must be open to scrutiny. The Children Act requires that all organizations caring for children under eight years old for two hours or more must register. In a home this will only apply if offered for reward, but elsewhere it applies whether for reward or not.

Facilities which are provided for less than six days each year are exempt, but the local authority Social Services department must be informed in advance of the intention to provide any facilities which involve the care of under eights for more than two hours, even though a registration is not required.

The registration will check the following factors: the person offering care; the suitability and safety of the premises; whether other people who are employed on the premises where the care is offered are fit to be in the 'proximity' of children.

There are additional safety requirements which need to be observed for events which include overnight stays, even when church halls or schools are used for this purpose. For example, exits need to be properly signed and illuminated, fire drills need to be conducted, and appropriate information needs to be available for medical support.

Safe from harm check list

The following check list may help to ensure that the proper provisions are in place:
- Are first aiders and an up-to-date first aid kit available both on the premises and for activities away from the premises?
- Do leaders know who the first aiders are and where they can be contacted?
- Are all accidents recorded?
- Do regular fire drills take place?
- Are fire notices displayed informing people what to do in case of fire?
- Are fire appliances suitable and serviced regularly?
- Has the local Fire Prevention Officer visited the premises?
- Is there suitable access and provision made for disabled people?
- Is a register kept of all those in attendance?
- Has a parental consent form and health form been completed for each child?
- Is appropriate and adequate insurance in place?
- Have adequate checks been conducted on all leaders?
- Have leaders been properly introduced to the work, adequately supported and offered training?
- Do leaders know what to do if a child tells them of abuse?
- Are adult/child ratios appropriate for the group and for the activity?
- Are the meeting places safe and secure from unwelcome people?
- Is it possible for children to 'slip' outside without leaders noticing?
- Is this check list reviewed annually?

Acknowledgement
Some material has been adapted from *Better Safe Than Sorry* with the permission of the Training and Parish Resources Department of the Diocese of Oxford.

References and further reading

Bradford, J. (1995), *Caring for the Whole Child: A Holistic Approach to Spirituality,* London, The Children's Society.

Churches Child Protection Advisory Service (1998), *Guidance to Churches: Dealing with Child Abuse and Appointing Children's Workers,* Swanley, CCPAS.

Church Pastoral Aid Society (1998), *Who Cares? Effective Pastoral Care of Under 11s in Church Based Groups,* Warwick, Church Pastoral Aid Society.

Hancock, M. and Mains, K. B. (1987), *Child Sexual Abuse: A Hope for Healing,* Guildford, Highland Books.

Hershman D. and McFarlane, A. (2001), *Hershman and McFarlane Children Act Handbook 2001,* Bristol, Family Law.

Hyson, J. and Gear, A. (2000), *Better Safe than Sorry,* Oxford, Diocese of Oxford.

Parkinson, P. (1997), *Child Sexual Abuse and the Churches,* London, Hodder & Stoughton.

Smith, D. R. (1993), *Safe from Harm: A Code of Practice for Safeguarding the Welfare of Children in Voluntary Organizations in England and Wales,* London, The Stationery Office.

PART FIVE
CHILDREN AND CHANGE

35

Babies and Infants (0–3 years)

Adult knowledge of the mental world of the pre-school child owes a great deal to the work of the Swiss psychologist Jean Piaget (1896–1980). Adult knowledge of the emotional world of pre-school children draws upon a different tradition running through Bowlby and Freud.

Becoming aware of the external world

Piaget observed the behaviour of his own three children and, from a large number of observations, was able to put together a theory about *The Origin of Intelligence in the Child,* the English title of the book he published in French in 1936. He argued that the simple instinctive reflexes of the baby, which are mainly grasping and sucking reflexes, are gradually adapted to the external world. After a few days the child notices the difference between sucking a nipple rather than a finger but, even so, continues to suck blankets, toys and other inedible objects. This suggests that sucking reflexes are adapted to a range of things and are later carried out for their own sake rather than simply to obtain milk. The same pattern is likely to occur with other reflexes.

Within the early months recognizing faces, smiling in recognition, recognizing voices and making repetitive sounds all occur. Piaget uses the term 'schema' to describe a pattern of activities. There may be a 'looking' schema or a 'grasping' schema which become co-ordinated so that the child sees something and then attempts to grasp it and suck it. This coordination of schema is the basis for later mental organization through which intelligence is developed.

Piaget writes:

here we reach the organisation of the grasping schemata. These schemata become organized among themselves from the fact that they adapt themselves to the external world ... hence such schemata constitute 'structures' of a whole ... but above all these schemata are organized in coordination with schemata of another kind, the chief of which are those of sucking and vision ... everything that is looked at tends to be grasped and everything that is grasped tends to be sucked and then looked at ... an object which can be simultaneously grasped and sucked, or grasped, looked at and sucked becomes externalised in relation to the subject quite differently from one which can only be grasped. (1977, pp. 142, 143)

The early learning of the baby is to do with the baby's own body and immediate physical surroundings and has been labelled by Piaget as belonging to a 'sensori-motor' stage because it concerns the senses and motor activity (the mastery of bodily movements).

The permanence of objects

Piaget noticed a seemingly surprising reaction in his children when they reached about six months of age. The baby would be shown a toy and would reach out to grasp it, but if the toy was then hidden behind a cushion or under a handkerchief the child would immediately lose interest, as if the toy had simply vanished out of existence. Even when the child saw the cloth being placed over the toy, the child would show no interest in removing the cloth. Piaget deduced that children of this age had no sense of the permanence of objects. Images floated before them without their having an ability to connect these images with physical permanence.

A few months later when the activity was repeated the children would appreciate that the toy might be hidden under the cloth and reach forward to remove the cloth and grab the toy. If the toy were hidden under a second nearby cloth, the child would still grab the first cloth where the toy used to be. Piaget interpreted this as showing that the child presumed the action of grabbing the cloth produced the toy. In other words, before the child understands the toy as having a permanent existence, it links the appearance of the toy with an action that it performs. This, again, supported his notion that mental activity is really built up from physical activity in the early years of life.

Language

The first year of life is basically prelinguistic. The child begins to coo from about six weeks and produces sounds associated with pleasure. After about six months, repetitive monosyllables are produced like 'mama', 'baba', 'dada' or even 'dadadada', and by twelve months these may be associated with particular people, though without precision. 'Mama', for example, may be applied to grandparents or sisters or simply be a general cry for comfort. For this reason it is difficult to say exactly when children begin to talk.

If, however, the child can say three words at 12 months, by 24 months the vocabulary may have increased to about 250 words, though a very sharp distinction needs to be made between words that children understand and words that children actually use. The use category may be only about 50 words by 20 months of age. However it is measured, there is clearly a language explosion in the second year of life. Words begin to be put together in a grammatical form. One-word sentences ('milk' meaning various things like 'I want some more milk' or 'I don't like my milk') give way to two-word sentences like 'Teddy sleep' meaning 'Teddy is asleep' or 'Teddy wants to get to sleep' etc. At the same time, the overextension of meaning (one word applied to a lot of similar things: for example, 'moon' referring to nail clippings or the reflection on the surface of a cup of tea) continues.

In the first stage of grammatical speech, children will produce utterances unlike any they have heard an adult say. For example 'all gone sticky' means 'the sweet is finished'. In the second stage, the child begins to use grammatical inflections by putting the plural and possessive 's' on words and marking past tenses with 'ed'. This results in sentences like 'I doed it' for 'I did it' and words like 'wented' for 'went'. The point to notice is that children's language is experimental and creative and not simply imitative.

This raises an important issue about human linguistic ability. The early creative nature of language use has persuaded many linguists that the human brain is predisposed to language. For this reason language learning is unlike other forms of learning. It is unique and special. And it is partly so because language is nearly always associated with a social context. Words are said in social situations. 'Bye bye' is said when someone leaves. 'Thank you Jesus' may be said before meals. The social situation serves as a clue to the meaning of the words and the words take their meaning from the social situation.

Language and thought

The onset of language has enormous implications for the processes of thought. Language immediately permits the labelling, and therefore the classification, of all kinds of objects in the external world. At the same time, the achievements of the sensori-motor stage remain to be built on, and eventually transformed, through the symbols and images which language facilitates.

By about four years of age children show signs of being able to appreciate superordinate and subordinate categories. They might understand that dogs are animals, that 'dog' is the subordinate category and 'animal' is the superordinate category, and begin to see how everything can be put into various hierarchical groups.

Emotional development

John Bowlby (1907–90) dealt with delinquent children whose lives had been disrupted by the 1939–45 war. Bowlby developed and refined the concept of attachment over a number of years, drawing on the psychodynamic theory of Freud and ethology (the study of animal behaviour). Bowlby suggested that infants have a desire to explore the world around them and that this need takes the child away from the primary caregiver. There is a tension between the need for care and the desire to explore.

The following scene is typical. The mother and the child are together when a visitor arrives. The 1-year-old child at first stays close to her mother. Later she sits apart and plays as mother and the visitor talk. She looks at her mother quite frequently and sometimes smiles. Every so often she calls her mother or points to something in the room. On one occasion when her mother leaves the room for a few moments she follows too, ignoring the visitor's invitation to play. On another occasion when her mother leaves she cries, resists the friendly advances of the visitor, and then, when the mother returns, greets her with a hug.

In *Childcare and the Growth of Love* (1965), Bowlby wrote:

> What is believed to be essential for mental health is that an infant and young child should experience a warm, intimate, and continuous relationship with his mother (or mother-substitute – one person who steadily mothers him) in which both find satisfaction and enjoyment. (p. 13)

If the child does not form a warm emotional bond with his or her mother or mother-substitute the child suffers from maternal deprivation that Bowlby thought was likely to have serious consequences in later life. Bowlby's conclusions were based on:
- observation of infant behaviour with mothers
- the view that attachment to mother automatically makes it difficult to form bonds with other caregivers
- observation of children who have been separated from mothers, for example while in hospital (these children protested, despaired and finally became detached, and so emotionally flattened).

Research by Mary Ainsworth (originally a student of Bowlby's) suggested that patterns of attachment between mother and child could predict the types of relationship people would develop later on in life. Moreover, observation can determine how sensitively or responsively the mother interacts and that this, in turn, forms the basis within the child for feelings of *self-worth* and *self-confidence*.

In an experiment where the mother leaves the room (so that the child is in the presence of a stranger) and then returns, four basic patterns were observed:

1 The child cries during separation from the mother but is easily comforted upon the reunion; the child preferred the mother to the stranger. This is the *secure* type (type B).
2 The child initially shunned contact with the mother on reunion; the mother and stranger were treated in similar ways throughout the experimental situations. This is the *anxious/avoidant* type (type A).
3 The child was upset when the mother left the room and was not easily comforted on the return; the child showed anger to the mother on reunion. This is an *anxious/ambivalent* pattern (type C).
4 The child appears dazed, confused or apprehensive and shows no coherent system for dealing with separation or reunion. This is the *disorganized* pattern (type D) and was seen frequently in families where there was abuse or high social risk.

In 1988 when cross-cultural comparisons were made, 57 per cent of West German, 75 per cent of British, 67 per cent of Dutch, 75 per cent of Swedish, 64 per cent of Israeli, 68 per cent of Japanese, 50 per cent of Chinese and 65 per cent of United States parents showed the type B pattern.

One of Bowlby's original concerns related to the welfare of young children in long-term residential care. Further research has suggested that 59 per cent of children under the age of three years who spend more than 20 hours a week in non-maternal care are likely to be secure, as compared with 74 per cent of those who spend less than 20 hours a week in non-maternal care.

With regard to the origins of religious feelings, some scholars (Bittner, 1991) have made connections between the 'oceanic feelings' that stem from the young child's oneness with the mother, and the overwhelming sense of unity that can occur during foundational religious experiences. As the child feeds from the mother and feels safe within the warmth of her arms, so the adult, it is argued, rediscovers this sense of nurture and emotional warmth in the love of God. This connection, which is almost impossible to test empirically, has an intuitive attractiveness, especially to scholars influenced by psychoanalytic explanations of human development. It may be, then, that another important result of good relationships in babyhood is that these may later inform mystical religious experience.

Size and shape

In concentrating on the mental and emotional life of the intelligent baby it is easy to forget how weak and helpless babies are. Babies are literally incapable of surviving without adult attention. They need to be fed, cleaned, clothed and protected. The baby is, as adults are often surprised to find, very small. For example, the width of the baby's palm may just cover an adult thumb joint. At the same time the baby is disproportionate in adult terms. The baby's arms cannot reach above the head properly because, in relation to the size of the body, the head is enormous. Since the head is heavy the baby is unable to rise to a sitting position: the baby's muscles simply cannot support the weight of it and, of course, the baby's legs cannot support the weight of the body.

The first year or two of life is taken up with learning to control the outer regions of the body and then, in the third year, beginning to develop some form of dexterity. At first, for example, holding a pencil is extremely difficult. Manipulating it is almost impossible. Similarly, the problem with tying a shoelace is the practical one of grasping the laces and forcing them into the right shapes.

Because babies are small and clumsy, they often hurt themselves. Falling over or bumping into hard objects is commonplace and painful. Objects like doors are not designed for babies or small children, while even small dogs are frightening. In addition, babies are prone to illness and may suffer colds, earache, eczema and discomfort in teething.

All these factors, together with the inability to understand language, lead to distress, tears and confusion. Only the comfort of adults, and particularly the mother, can offset the perplexing start to life.

Food and toilet training

Food and excrement occupy the child's attention and are usually of concern to the busy, and perhaps harassed, parents. Should the mother feed the child at the breast or at the bottle? Should the parents feed the child according to a prearranged schedule or 'on demand'? Anthropological studies as well as the influence of modern child rearing practice have tended to argue that 'nature knows best'. For example, the child fed on demand from the breast may eventually be more adaptable and cheerful – presumably because the early years of life have been less stressful. The other side of this coin suggests that the over-indulged child is lazy and unable later in life to exercise self-discipline.

Miriam Stoppard argues that 'breast feeding is good for both you and your baby', and that it may be recommended for other reasons:
- Breast-fed babies are less prone to illness than bottle-fed babies.
- Breast milk is more easily digested than cow's milk.
- Breast-fed babies rarely become overweight.
- Breast-feeding is the most convenient method.
- Breast-feeding is good for a mother's figure.
- Breast cancer is rarer in parts of the world where breast-feeding is traditional.

Learning to be clean and control the bowels can become the focus of a battle of wills between baby and parents. Again, there is a choice between attempting to enforce discipline upon the child by producing the potty according to a schedule, or allowing the child to learn to ask for it when it feels the need.

Miriam Stoppard advises:

> Let your child decide whether or not to sit on the potty. You can suggest that she does but you should never force the issue.
>
> I am whole-heartedly against toilet training. For me there are no arguments in favour of it, only arguments against it. I believe that toilet training... should be eradicated from child care and child development... it is impossible to train a child to do anything unless the body has developed to a point where it is anatomically and physiologically able to perform the tasks demanded of it... if you insist on a toilet programme when your child is not ready for it, the end can only be sadness. The relationship with the child will deteriorate. (Stoppard, 1990, p. 159)

It is generally agreed, however, that during the first 18 months of life the child has no proper bowel or bladder control, just the toilet timing reflex. By about 30 months two-thirds of children can be dry most of the time. Training, therefore, by sitting a child on a potty after meals, can often begin from about 24 months (Green, 1984).

Both food and toilet training, then, can be conducted with more or less rigour, but modern child-care experts are clearly against coercion and in favour of what might be called a natural approach, one that does not put pressure on the child to conform to predetermined patterns, but encourages the sort of behaviour that enables the child to participate in social life beyond that of the immediate family circle.

References and further reading

Bittner, G. (1991), 'Against religious headbirths: a psychoanalytic critique', in J. W. Fowler, K. E. Nipkow and F. Schweitzer (eds.), *Stages of Faith and Religious Development,* London, SCM Press, pp. 180–91.

Bowlby, J. (1965), *Childcare and the Growth of Love,* Harmondsworth, Penguin.

Green, C. (1984), *Toddler Taming: A Parents' Guide to the First Four Years,* London, Century Hutchinson.

Piaget, J. (1977), *The Origin of Intelligence in the Child,* Harmondsworth, Penguin. (First published in French as *La Naissance de l'Intelligence Chez L'enfant* in 1936.)

Stoppard, M. (1990), *New Baby Care Book* (second edn), London, Dorling Kindersley.

36

Pre-school Children (3–5 years)

The intelligent baby becomes the intuitive child. According to Piaget the sensori-motor intelligence that is in use up to the age of 24 months gradually gives way to a new kind of thinking. The baby's intelligence is expressed through action and the schemata associated with it. At the next stage the baby must move into the world of concepts:

> At the outset, two innovations place conceptual thought in opposition to sensori-motor intelligence and explain the difficulty of transition from one of these two forms of intellectual activity to the other. In the first place, sensori-motor intelligence seeks only practical application, that is, it aims only at success or utilisation, whereas conceptual thought leads to knowledge as such and therefore yields to norms of truth. (Piaget, 1954, p. 359)

The baby is concerned to manipulate the environment and his or her own body. The baby wants to grab the spoon, lift the toy or be comforted, but is not concerned with matters of fact or truth. The baby does not argue whether an event happened last week or a week before, or whether there are two or three fish in the pond. The young child, by contrast, begins to be interested in what Piaget calls 'norms of truth'. This interest leads to the second difference in the way the young child thinks:

> Sensori-motor intelligence is an adaptation of the individual to things or to the body of another person without socialization of the intellect as such; whereas conceptual thought is collective thought obeying common laws. (Piaget, 1954, p. 360)

Of course, the great new tool of thought is language. By the age of three years the child is able to understand and communicate. Stories, rhymes, prayers, riddles and even jokes are part of the child's experience of language. Yet the transition from one kind of thinking to another kind of thinking is difficult for the child who does not 'at first succeed in reflecting in words and concepts the procedure that he or she already knows how to carry out in acts' (p. 361). There is, then, a mismatch between what the child understands through activity and what the child can use language to explain. But there is a further complication. Almost by definition sensori-motor intelligence is egocentric: it only operates from the point of view of the child. This is the reason, Piaget believes, that the speech of children is, in their infant years, so centred on themselves. Only as they act socially do children come to realize that other points of view are possible. Thus only as they act *socially* is their *intellectual* egocentrism gradually exchanged for a group view. This egocentrism is most clearly shown in children's conversation and in the mountain experiment.

Conversation

Records of the conversation of children of nursery age show how common monologue is. Speech accompanies action:

1, 2, ... 3, 4, 5, 6, 7 ... 8, 8, 8, 8, and 8 ... 9. Number 9, number 9 (singing) I want number 9 [this is the number he is going to represent by the drawing]. Now I'm going to do 9, 9, I'm doing 9, doing 9, look teacher, 9, 9, 9 ... number 9. (Piaget's record of one of his own children.)

This sort of speaking then develops into collective monologues where children talk to themselves in groups. The children are not really interested in the replies of anyone else – they are simply talking aloud in front of others.

What can we say of the questions that children ask at this stage? Although there are a lot of 'Why?'s in the interchanges between children and adults, most of these are not the 'Why?'s of causality. They are not questions about the reasons for events. Indeed, one observer does not expect to find the word 'because' used correctly before about the age of six years. In Piaget's view, most of the questions asked by children between three and five years of age are to do with actions and intentions: 'And my scissors, can you see them?'; 'Are you going to play at Indians?'; 'I'm working, are you?'; 'I didn't hurt you, did I?'; 'How shall I paint the house?'; 'Are you coming this afternoon?' are real examples of children's speech. The remaining questions appear to be related to facts and events, to time and place, and to word meanings or evaluations: 'What does "behind" mean?'; 'Is it pretty?'.

The mountain experiment

The child is presented with a model about a square metre in size representing three mountains in relief. The child has to reconstruct the different perspectives through which a toy doll or teddy views the various mountains. So the doll or teddy is placed at right angles to the child and the child is asked what the toy can see. The child consistently replies that the toy can see exactly what he or she can see. Because of the layout of the mountains, it is obvious to an adult that the position of an observer makes views quite different from different angles. But children treat their own position as an absolute one. What is odd about this is that children in the sensori-motor stage are perfectly capable of understanding that objects look different from different perspectives. But since the sensori-motor stage depends on actively handling an object, there is no need to break from the egocentric perspective. Only gradually, then, do social relations lead children away from their original egocentrism.

Social development

Children's social development takes place in line with their intellectual development. One of the ways that social development of pre-school children is observable is in their play. Play usually involves other children or an adult. The sensori-motor stage of intellectual development is expressed through solitary play that involves repetition, practice and the mastery of behaviours acquired through imitation. In other words, the sensori-motor stage precludes anything but the most basic social development, even though this phase of development, as we have seen in the previous chapter, is critically important.

Between the ages of three and six years, children begin to use objects and actions symbolically, but in their play together they are still largely egocentric. They engage in 'parallel play' where they all play at the same time with particular toys, but they do not actually play with each other.

Another indication of social development is to be found in the quality of the child's family life. Studies (Baumrind, 1971) of white suburban families show styles of parenting that have been classified into three types:

- permissive-indulgent (rules not enforced)
- authoritarian (rigid enforcement of rules)
- authoritative (firm enforcement of rules)

These three types of parenting are linked with the child's usual behaviour. Permissive-indulgence is associated with noncompliance with adults, low self-reliance, general cheerfulness, aggression and impulsiveness. Authoritarianism is associated with fearfulness, apprehension, moodiness and vulnerability to stress. Authoritativeness is associated with self-reliance, high energy levels, cheerfulness and friendly relations with peers.

Where there is more than one child, the social development of the children takes place as they relate to each other. Where the mother talks to the first-born child about the new baby before its birth, there is evidence that the first-born is more likely to be more friendly to the new child a year later. This friendliness is accentuated if the children are of the same sex, at least in the 8–14 month period. Typically the mother's relationship with the first-born child changes when the new baby arrives; the mother becomes attentive to the younger child and may provoke jealousy in the older one. The older child may copy the baby's behaviour to gain attention or, alternatively, may show signs of independence to show that he or she is 'grown up'. In either case the older child may relate more to the father if the mother is focused upon the baby.

As part of their social development children learn to dress, tie up shoe laces, brush their teeth, bath, feed the hamster, expect presents for birthdays and turn on the television. They may begin to count, take biscuits from a tin and notice the habits of adults. Although all these activities represent an increase in a range of skills, they also have social implications. Children are not totally dependent on adults any more but can begin to look after themselves a little, to contribute in conversation and action to what goes on in the home and to express preferences that alter adult behaviour ('Don't make green soup. I don't like it.').

Emotional development

From their facial expressions it is reasonable to conclude that newborn babies feel simple and intense emotions. They are content, frustrated or upset. As the child grows up these emotions become more varied.

Even from an early stage children reflect the emotions of those around them. A baby may show signs of distress if mother pretends to cry. The sensitivity of infants to the emotions of others is thought to lead them through copying the emotions of others (laughing when adults laugh with them) to egocentric empathy (where the child tries to comfort others). The empathy is egocentric in that the child offers what he or she would like. So when the dog is hurt, the child offers it a sweet.

The emotional range of the child is extended through its sensitivity to adults. The child learns from the adult that particular emotions to people, objects and situations are appropriate. If inappropriate emotions are shown – for instance if the child is frightened of a sheep in a field – adults will help the child not to be afraid. On the other hand, if the child shows no fear of the fire, the adult will try to help the child appreciate that there is a danger of pain in going too close to flames. Other emotions are similarly modelled so that the child learns to laugh at humorous situations and to distinguish these, especially in slapstick comedy, from genuinely painful ones.

Clearly the emotional development of the child is tied up with the child's social development. Some emotions are suppressed or considered unacceptable ('Big boys don't cry') while others are encouraged. Without close adult relationships the child will not learn how emotions should be handled and what particular feelings mean. Thus without someone to say, 'Don't get so excited', the child does not know what excitement is. Emotional development therefore takes place along a path marked out by adults. Social development – playing with others and becoming emotionally involved with them – is partly driven by the emotions. If children do not feel excited by going to a party, they will not want to go. In general, then, we may say that young children's emotionality is shaped by adults in a socially desirable direction. For example, the egocentric nature of play leads children to arguments and squabbles over such matters as whose turn it is to use a special toy. The adult then introduces the concept of sharing or of taking the toy in turns and, by this means, social development takes place through the erasing of anti-social emotions.

States not operations

Piaget considers the child under seven years of age to be at a pre-operational stage. By this he means that children cannot reverse the effects of actions in their minds. They believe that there is more plasticine in a large flat patch than a ball, even though they have seen the ball rolled out into the patch, because they cannot imagine the converse operation of the patch being rolled back into a ball. The child attends to *states* rather than to changes between states. Transformations of all kinds are too complex to appreciate because they require the child to appreciate many factors at once. As a result the child is satisfied with a 'happy ever after' end to a story where the hero and heroine have reached a changeless state. Similarly, children of this age are content to think that it is raining or it is sunny without wondering about the water cycle.

As we shall see in the next chapter, at the next stage the child's mind begins to cope with the complications of change and the viewpoints of other people.

Criticisms of Piaget

Bryant (1974) carried out many of Piaget's experiments with minor but significant variations. He was able to show that children are able to grasp concepts associated with concrete operational thinking at a younger age than was previously thought and that some of their apparent failures result from lapses of memory rather than lapses of understanding. Donaldson (1978), also using a set of variant experiments as her basis, argued that children are able to 'decentre', that is, to see things from more than one point of view, much more early than Piaget had thought and that the failure in Piaget's design stemmed partly from the kinds of questions he asked. His questions did not 'make human sense' to the children and so they responded inappropriately.

Brown and Desforges (1977) were more comprehensive in their onslaught. They argued that the Piagetian concept of 'stage' was unworkable because, by definition, a stage required a 'coherent integration of operations'. Since this definition presumes that high correlations will exist between tasks designed to measure the same sort of intellectual functioning, and since this is not observed, the notion of stage falls to pieces. Moreover, if a problem with the same form but different content is carried out by students with significantly different results, it is clear that the presumed dissociation between form and content is questionable.

Moore and Harris (1978) address the issue of language. They are able to show that children who fail at conservation tasks succeed in understanding and producing passive sentences from active ones. Since the transformation from active to passive may be thought of as parallel to the reversibility necessary for conservation, it is arguable that Piaget's notion of conservation does not apply to language.

Such criticisms have not prevented the continued flourishing of Piagetian studies and the organization of large annual conferences by the Jean Piaget Society. However cogent the critics of Piaget believe themselves to have been, those who see in his work a valid account of mental development find the criticisms fail to demolish the central contentions of stage developmental theory and its impressive empirical base.

References and further reading

Baumrind, D. (1971), 'Current patterns of parental authority', *Developmental Psychology Monographs* 1, pp. 1–103.

Brown, G. and Desforges, C. (1977), 'Piagetian psychology and education: time for revision', *British Journal of Educational Psychology* 47, pp. 7–17.

Bryant, P. (1974), *Perception and Understanding in Young Children*, London, Methuen.

Donaldson, M. (1978), *Children's Minds*, Glasgow, Collins.

Moore, T. E. and Harris, A. E. (1978), 'Language and thought in Piagetian theory', in L. S. Siegel and C. J. Brainherd (eds.), *Alternatives to Piaget: Critical Essays on the Theory*, London, Academic Press, pp. 131–52.

Piaget, J. (1954), *The Child's Construction of Reality*, London, Routledge & Kegan Paul. (Originally published in French in 1937.)

Sugarman, S. (1987), *Piaget's Construction of the Child's Reality*, Cambridge, Cambridge University Press.

Sutherland, P. (1992), *Cognitive Development Today: Piaget and his Critics*, London, Paul Chapman.

37

Primary School Children
(5–11 years)

Introduction

This chapter covers a longer period of time than the previous two chapters. During the junior years children pass through what can be the happiest points of childhood. Most begin to read fluently, to enjoy playing with friends, to acquire new skills and to satisfy their enormous curiosity about the world in which they live. Physically they have passed the growth spurt at the very beginning of childhood and now grow at a steady rate, becoming slightly taller and stronger with each passing year and able to master a range of physical activities from playing table tennis, riding bicycles, swimming, kicking balls to needlework and drawing accurately. Emotionally, these years are often calm and untroubled, free from the potentially disruptive feelings that can accompany adolescence. Where children are afraid, it is usually of such things as ghosts, graveyards, being alone in the dark and some animals like big dogs and snakes which are unlikely to trouble them in the ordinary course of events.

Intellectual development

Piaget considers that most children pass through a watershed at about the age of seven when they pass from the pre-operational stage of thinking to the concrete operational stage. This transition considerably increases children's power to use their minds to predict the behaviour of the external world. During the pre-operational stage the child is unable to cope with transformations but, once operational capabilities are reached, the child can mentally reverse physical actions, and this has enormous repercussions. The classic Piagetian experiment involves showing a child two glass tumblers. One is tall and thin and the other is short and fat. First, the tall thin tumbler is full of water, and then water is poured out of it into the short fat tumbler. Naturally the water level in the fat tumbler is lower (because its diameter is greater). When the child is asked whether there is more water in the tall or short tumbler, the child at the pre-operational stage invariably replies that the tall tumbler has more water. The child simply concentrates on the level of water and, because it is higher in the tall tumbler, thinks it contains a greater volume of water. Once the child reaches the stage of concrete operational thinking, it becomes mentally possible to reverse the activity of pouring water out of the first tumbler into the second and therefore to realize that the amount of water concerned has remained the same.

This ability allows children to perceive the invariance of physical objects with changeable properties. It also enables children to perceive relationships between parts and wholes more precisely. For example, four quarters of a pie can be taken apart or put together again, showing that the combined parts comprise the whole.

As we shall see when considering the young adolescent, the concrete operational stage is marked by an ability to deal with the logic of classes and relations. The class of human beings is made up of the class of adults and the class of children. The logic of classes allows us to say that the class of human beings minus the class of children equals the class of adults. This sort of logic can be extended indefinitely with all the classifications children use, and is obviously used in part–whole understandings. The logic of relations concerns statements such as, 'Paul is my brother.' It presupposes that, just as I stand in a brotherly relation to Paul, he stands in a brotherly relation to me. Up to the age of about ten years, many children tend to confuse these relations and so are unable to say how many brothers there are in the family. They know that they have only one brother and they may see that Paul has only one brother but they may still find difficulty in seeing that there are altogether two brothers in the family.

More complicated relationships between parts and wholes occur where children are asked to perform tasks involving seriation, that is, placing objects in ascending or descending order according to a particular physical characteristic. If children are given a series of wooden blocks of varying size and asked to arrange them into a staircase, the child working at the concrete operational stage can form a 'schema' (the Piagetian term for a mental construct) of the finished staircase and arrange the blocks without trial and error. If given a new block the child can place it at the correct point in the sequence. The child at the pre-operational level, however, finds this a much more difficult task and is unable both to insert a new block without starting again from the beginning, or of appreciating that it is just as easy to start from the small end and work to the larger end as it is the other way round.

The onset of concrete operational thinking leads to a better ability to understand numbers and, in understanding numbers, to understand age and time. Younger children at the pre-operational stage do not appreciate that age is dependent on birth order, thinking instead that age differences become modified over time. 'Is your granny older than your mother?' '*No.*' 'Are they the same age?' '*I think so.*' This leads to other odd results. Because of their failure to grasp the ideas of succession and duration operationally, some children think that they were born before their parents. Only at about the age of seven or more can children be expected to give correct replies to questions involving birth succession.

This set of difficulties means that children have very little conception of historical time. It is more or less impossible for them to appreciate periods of several years and a block of time like a century or a millennium is quite beyond their horizons. 'Was this motorway built at the time of Jesus, Dad?' Here the problem is not only to do with the order of events but also to do with the relatively large numbers involved. Big numbers are inclined to be undifferentiated. Only toward the end of the junior school years will some children begin to appreciate time in a more adult way but, even here, huge time periods like those relating to cosmology are quite unreal.

In addition to the changes brought about by concrete operational development, gradual changes take place with regard to the understanding of the external world as a whole. For example, younger junior children tend to identify the name of an object with the object itself. The name is the essence of the thing. This form of realism extends into dreams which are thought to be 'really there'.

Causes are at first not fully understood. Ask a young child to draw a bicycle and a very inaccurate picture will be produced. The child of four might simply say that the pedals work the engine. Only after about the age of eight years are children generally able to provide a mechanical explanation and drawing of a bicycle and to appreciate the functions of the different parts. At the same stage as this occurs, however, similar mechanical explanations tend to be applied to such things as clouds, which must be pushed by little motors inside them.

A more subject-based account of intellectual development, stemming from a different branch of psychology than Piaget's, takes note of the appearance of specialist abilities in children during the junior school years. From about the age of six, verbal abilities begin to be discernible and from about the age of eight, if not before, musical abilities begin to be obvious. A similar pattern may be observed with drawing. These specialist abilities are linked with general intelligence but are distinct from it, so that a child might be very advanced in its ability to produce a likeness but not particularly able in other areas. As the child passes up the junior school these abilities begin to become more apparent.

Social development

Children between the ages of five and 11 years gradually become more independent of their parents in the routines of daily life. The experience of school introduces a repertoire of new behaviours. It becomes necessary to keep to some kind of school timetable and to begin to conform to the norms and expectations of the peer group. Fashion and competition can become important. At the upper end of the junior school, some of the girls will be sexually mature and show an interest in boys that may lead to undercurrents of rivalry in the classroom. Jewellery and lingerie can become badges of sophistication.

Play changes from being a solitary activity where mastery of physical skills is practised for pleasure and becomes a team concern. The junior years find children beginning to appreciate collective rule-based activity that, as we shall see, parallels their moral development. Team games are an expression of social development because, in them, the child learns to submerge its own egocentric interests in the aspirations of the group.

Moral development

The Piagetian account of moral development concerns the understanding by children of rules. Although morality is a matter of values as well as rules, it is rules that form the easiest component of morality to identify. In a series of studies carried out on children's understanding of moral rules, Piaget identified three separate stages which correspond with the child's general intellectual development:

1 In the *first* stage adult authority is the final arbiter. Cheating is wrong because teacher says so; lying is wrong because parents say so. Rules are absolute and apply in all circumstances regardless of any other factors. The child functions in a pre-operational way and this lasts up to about the age of seven or eight.
2 The *second* stage occurs between about eight and 11 when there is a progressive sense of social equality, though obedience to authority still takes precedence over justice. There is, at this point, the beginning of an understanding of motive.
3 The *third* stage occurs from the age of 11 or 12 onwards and occurs on a basis of social equality between peers. Moral rules are seen as being integral to co-operative relationships and seen to derive their force from mutual agreement as to their value. Thus moral development moves from the external imposition of apparently arbitrary moral rules to the free acceptance of rules on the basis of equal relationships. Moreover, once children are able to move out of the egocentrism of early childhood, they are able to take motive into account in any moral judgement they make.

Consider this story:

> Tony and Timmy attend a birthday party where the children sit down for a meal that ends with jelly and cakes. Tony becomes annoyed with one of the other children and throws a jelly across the table at him. Timmy, meanwhile, trying to be helpful, carries a tray of jellies into the dining area from the kitchen. Unfortunately he trips and drops six jellies all over the floor. Which child has been naughtiest?

The pre-operational child will assume that Timmy is naughtiest because he has ruined more jellies. The older child will note that Tony's motives were bad and that therefore his behaviour is really morally worse than Timmy's even though Timmy has done more damage.

Reading

The ability of the child to read builds up steadily in the junior years and by the age of seven the most able children in a class will be comfortable with simple books. By the age of ten brighter children will read full-length adventure stories for pleasure. The competition between reading and watching a story on video or TV usually favours the visual medium. If children are asked whether they have read a particular book they may answer 'yes' even though what they mean is that they have seen the book adapted for the screen. Such is the power of the visual medium that, when comparisons are made between text and screen, children will often assume that the screen version is the 'real' one even though it may be inferior and simplified.

Children's ability to understand stories moves from a stage where they can recall the events of a narrative in the correct order and comprehend the behaviour of its characters, to a stage where they can appreciate the moral or spiritual purpose the story is intended to convey.

Within the current National Curriculum for England and Wales, Key Stage 2 pupils (aged 7–11) should read texts with 'more complex narrative structures and sustained ideas' that include 'figurative language both in poetry and prose' and which have 'a variety of structural and organizational features' (Department for Education, 1995). And as one of their keys skills pupils should be:

> taught to consider in detail the quality and depth of what they read. They should be encouraged to respond imaginatively to plot, character, ideas, vocabulary and organization of language ... in literature. They should be taught to use inference and deduction ... Pupils should be taught to evaluate the texts they read.

Studies of children's understanding of the Bible have been carried out since the 1960s. An important investigation into children's understanding of parables (Murphy, 1979) studied the ability of children to appreciate the non-literal meaning of a parable. Murphy was able to show that, in comparing the Good Samaritan, The Rich Fool, The Pharisees and the Tax Collector, The Sower, The Two Houses and The Lost Sheep, children's performance varied between the parables. Nearly all children understood The Good Samaritan better than The Rich Fool. For instance, 90 per cent of 10-year-olds understood the non-literal meaning of The Good Samaritan whereas only 35 per cent of 10-year-olds reached the same level with The Rich Fool. In some cases, children's understanding could be improved by a modernized version of the Bible though, in the case of The Good Samaritan, modernization made no difference – presumably because the outline and details of story were sufficiently clear in most versions.

Religious development

Studies of the religious development of children in Britain have sometimes taken place from a Freudian perspective (Lee, 1965) and, at other times, from a Piagetian one, and most studies have looked at religious development in relation to Christianity rather than at other world faiths. The best known and most influential study of religious development among young people was conducted by Ronald Goldman and published in 1964 (see also Chapter 14). He asked children questions about their understanding of three Bible passages and, on the basis of the children's answers, concluded that junior school children, who were at the age of concrete operational thinking, were largely unable to understand the correct meaning of biblical texts. This was because biblical texts have an abstract meaning or because their meaning must be inferred from narrative details. In either case young children are incapable, so Goldman argued, of proper comprehension.

Goldman's work has been severely criticized and its conclusions, when stated in an extreme form, do not hold water (e.g. Slee, 1992). While it is true that young children understand biblical texts in a way different from older children and adults, there are numerous biblical narratives and parables which are well within the grasp of children and which have significance for them and for their religious development. It would be foolish, and indeed irresponsible, to deprive young children of Bible stories on the basis of Goldman's research.

An alternative approach to religious development has been developed by James Fowler, working largely within a Piagetian paradigm (see Chapter 10, and Astley and Francis, 1992). Fowler's research suggests that children of junior school age operate at the stage of *mythic-literal faith*, in which children attach their faith to story-telling and the sense of meaning and belonging which can come from telling the story of the particular community (like the church) or group.

References and further reading

Astley, J. and Francis, L. J. (eds.) (1992), *Christian Perspectives on Faith Development: A Reader*, Leominster, Gracewing.

Department for Education (1995), *English in the National Curriculum*, London, The Stationery Office.

Goldman, R. J. (1964), *Religious Thinking from Childhood to Adolescence*, London, Routledge.

Hyde, K. E. (1990), *Religion in Childhood and Adolescence: A Comprehensive Review of the Research*, Birmingham, Alabama, Religious Education Press.

Lee, R. S. (1965), *Your Growing Child and Religion*, Harmondsworth, Pelican.

Murphy, R. J. L. (1979), 'An Investigation into Some Aspects of the Development of Religious Thinking in Children Aged Between Six and Eleven Years', unpublished PhD dissertation, University of St Andrews.

Slee, N. (1992), 'Cognitive developmental studies of religious thinking', in J. W. Fowler, *et al.* (eds.), *Stages of Faith and Religious Development*, London, SCM Press, pp. 130–46.

38

Early Adolescents (11–15 years)

Intellectual development

According to the Piagetian model of intellectual development, early adolescence marks an important change from concrete operational thinking to formal operational thinking. This is a profound and complex change which results in the arrival by the adolescent at an adult mental capability. This is not to say that the adolescent thinks like an adult, merely that for the first time the adolescent has at his or her disposal the capacity to meet adults on their own intellectual terms. This potential equality, as we shall see, has other consequences.

Formal operational thinking is the ability to use propositional logic and to superimpose this on the logic of classes and relations. Propositional logic is the logic which can be expressed in sentences such as 'If the rod is made of brass, it will be sufficiently flexible.' In other words, propositional logic deals with possibilities and conditions. By contrast, the logic of classes and relations, which is characteristic of concrete operations, deals much more readily with the here and now. It arranges groups of objects into hierarchies by placing smaller and subordinate classes inside larger ones. The class of human beings is made up of the class of adults and the class of children. The logic of classes allows us to say that the class of human beings minus the class of children equals the class of adults. This sort of logic can be extended indefinitely with all the classifications children use. The logic of relations deals with the relations between two or more things or people: it requires the ability to see the relationship from both points of view. Mr Smith taught me French, and I learnt French from Mr Smith; Peter lent me money, and I owe Peter money; and so on.

Piaget was able to demonstrate that all that had previously been understood by children using concrete operations, that is, mental representations of actions relating to physical objects, can be re-understood using a logical system made up of propositions. This is why formal operational thinking must come after concrete operational thinking. It is a transformation of concrete operational thinking into a more abstract and symbolic form. The advantage of formal operational thinking, however, is that it allows young people to think systematically through *all* the various possibilities that might determine the solution to a particular problem. Using a complicated set of demonstrations, Piaget was able to show that adolescents working in the formal operational mode are able to appreciate every possible combination of propositional pairs. If there are four factors, brass rods and non-brass rods, and rods which are flexible and rods which are not sufficiently flexible, there are 16 possible combinations that can be enumerated, and only 16. As we shall see, since this way of thinking is akin to scientific problem-solving, adolescence is strongly associated with an awakening interest in scientific knowledge.

All this may seem a long way away from the average adolescent, but it is important to notice in general terms that the young adolescent can now begin to use abstract ideas with some confidence and to reason using abstract terms. For example, the young adolescent can begin to say, 'If democracy is important, then everyone should have a vote.' Democracy is an abstract idea but the young adolescent can grasp this and reason from its implications. Similarly, the young adolescent can begin to reason about the abstract attributes of God: 'If God is wise, then the ordinances and sacraments of the Church ought to express God's wisdom.'

The combination of an ability to appreciate abstractions (often expressed by symbols, but not necessarily) and the capacity to use propositions to work with possibilities leads to the idealism characteristic of mid-teen adolescents. Intoxicated by the variety of possibilities confronting them, adolescents may become enthralled by ideological systems or the glittering achievements of science. Why not build a better world? Why not abolish poverty, eradicate hunger, explore space, evangelize the earth and get rid of all weapons? Every problem appears tractable. Even at a less exalted level, young people may think that the problems of unemployment must be easy to solve and that they can, in any case, do better than the unimaginative older generation.

Critics of Piaget suggested that the proportion of the population who operate naturally at the level of formal operations is more restricted than he believed and that, in any case, most people only operate in this way within domains with which they are particularly familiar. The aboriginal hunter will consider hypotheses and possibilities when tracking down an animal but, confronted by a new numerical problem, will be reduced, like the rest of us, to counting with his fingers. The lawyer will understand new parliamentary statutes, but be slower than the child in exploration of unfamiliar software. But even critics of Piaget recognize the value of his description of the quality of thinking available to adolescents and recognize the coherence of his explanation.

Emotional development

Sex education in schools is intended to prepare girls for the onset of menstruation and to prepare both sexes for responsible intercourse in the context of a loving relationship, though not necessarily within marriage.

Sexual maturity produces a new set of powerful emotions. Whereas during the junior school boys tended to play with boys and girls with girls, there is now a breaking down of single-sex groups and a realization that the attractiveness of the opposite sex demands the cultivation of new friendships. For most young people, going to school in co-educational environments, the formation of friendships that have sexual overtones is relatively easy. But there is a re-orientation of social relationships, and self-confidence can be won or lost in the first groping embraces with the girl- or boy-friend.

Alongside this discovery of sexual emotions there is an inevitable negotiation with parents or authority figures about limits and boundaries. Typically, adolescents want to stay out later than their parents wish and typically parents are more concerned about the safety and well-being of daughters than they are of sons. Thus emotional changes take place on two fronts: in respect of the peer group (Does this girl like me? Is that boy interested in me?) and in respect to the home (All the other 13-year-olds in my class are allowed to go to this pop concert, why can't I?).

One way of viewing these emotional developments is in relation to the growing reasoning abilities of young people. It is arguable that unless young people have learnt to cope with the simpler non-sexual emotions of childhood they will be in for a rough ride during adolescence. The 8-year-old who can cope with disappointment or can learn to be patient in waiting for a game or party is more likely to handle the minor rejections of adolescence with dignity and self-esteem intact. Growing reasoning abilities allow young people to understand how their own emotions operate and what sort of tactics they need to pursue in order to restrain themselves. Of course, growing reasoning abilities also allow young people to argue volubly and cogently with adults and, at the same time, to pursue their emotional desires with imagination and intrigue. In either case, the powerful emotions generated by sexual maturity have an impact upon the interests, social relations, family relationships and academic progress of young adolescents.

Social development

The interests of teenagers diversify intellectually while, at the same time, coming under the influence of the youth culture that is endemic to the Western world. This culture can be traced back to the period after 1945 when, for the first time, young people began to be in the position of having disposable income. By spending money on products that interested them, they supported a burgeoning music and fashion industry. This industry, now broadened to include a variety of magazines, videos, CDs, Web sites and clubs, feeds the interests of young people in style (expressed most obviously in music and clothes), relationships, sex and travel.

The general tendency of young people to move from childhood dependence on adults to a position of complete independence passes through the teenage years when these two extremes are held in tension. On the one hand, teenagers wish to be independent, grown-up, treated as adults and, on the other, they wish to call upon the emotional and financial resources of parents or responsible adults in times of difficulty or uncertainty. During this time teenagers find their peer group an increasingly important source of values. Whereas in childhood they accepted and respected the opinions of their parents, now they turn to the opinions of the peer group and set these against parental opinion. Arguments in the home occur as teenagers articulate the views of their peer group against the 'restrictive', 'old-fashioned', 'out of date' and 'irrelevant' views of their parents. And given the additional intellectual capacities now available to young people, these arguments can be difficult for adults who, quite suddenly, find themselves unable to out-think their children. To some extent the network of peer group relations replaces the network of family relations and provides the guidance and support the family used to provide.

Not surprisingly, there is evidence that the transition from childhood to adulthood is painful for many young people. About a third of young people 'often long for someone to turn to for advice' (Francis and Kay, 1995, p. 27) and the person they turn to in the home, for both males and females, is the mother. She stands in quite a different relationship to most teenagers from the father. Nearly half of young people do not find it helpful to talk with their fathers, and the implied friction is far greater among girls than boys. The mother, by contrast, is much more likely to be perceived as being sympathetic. As many as 58 per cent of girls and 43 per cent of boys find their mothers helpful. The only other adult who appears remotely to approach the mother as a confidant is the doctor, in whom about two-thirds of young people feel some emotional trust.

When the figures are analysed more closely by gender, it becomes clear that, whereas girls are much more likely to find help in talking to their circle of friends, boys are reluctant to take this course of action. The stereotype of the tongue-tied male who is unable to express himself to anyone about his emotional difficulties is an unfortunate reality. As many as 24 per cent of young males have sometimes considered taking their own lives, and an even higher figure of 30 per cent applies in the case of females. Thus although more females experience negative emotions, it is also true that females are more likely to have a support system in their family and social relationships. Churchgoing, however, is an important source of help and support, and churchgoers, as a group, whatever the denomination, are less likely than their non-churchgoing peers to experience either depression or suicidal thoughts.

Whenever a picture of teenagers is drawn from survey findings, it is important to stress that such characterizations are general. While there is a general impact of the peer group on the teenager, there are many young people who manage to balance the pull of their contemporaries and the influence of their parents without undue stress. Similarly, while many teenagers find it almost impossible to resist the dictates of fashion, others learn to see behind the facade to the commercial exploitation perpetrated by the youth culture industries. And again, while some teenagers are depressed and unable to speak with parents, at least a third have good relationships at home and move through their adolescent years relatively free of trouble.

Young people's interests and concerns continue to be centred on school:

Young people in overwhelming numbers enjoyed the social side of school life. They like the people with whom they go to school and they describe themselves as happy at school. Their criticisms, however, fall heavily on teachers. (Francis and Kay, 1995, p. 40)

A small minority, about 10 per cent, is alienated from school and most of the norms and values of society as a whole. These young people frequently have low academic aspirations, dislike the area where they live, can see nothing wrong in minor acts of vandalism or theft and approve of the taking of narcotics and stimulants.

A rather larger minority, about 25 per cent, is concerned with the wider world, with pollution of the environment, poverty in the third world, pornography and nuclear war, and most of these young people take the view that there is something *they* can do to help solve the world's problems. In other words, they manifest the idealism identified by Piaget. This active and engaged minority is well represented among churchgoing young people; indeed, churchgoing among young people may even cause the sense of empowerment and self-esteem that leads to activism, as well as foster and sustain moral and spiritual values (cf. Gill, 1999, pp. 55, 66, 200–2).

Educational development

Junior schools are relatively safe havens for children. Each year they spend most of their time with a single class teacher who knows them well and is able to monitor not only their academic progress but also their general well-being. The secondary school is different in two main ways. First, children must learn to move between lesson and lesson and teacher and teacher, with the result that pastoral problems are much less easily detected. Second, children are placed in bigger institutions containing older pupils who are young adults. The dangers of bullying and of failing to make academic progress are real; about a quarter of pupils worry about being bullied and nearly two-thirds worry about their school work (Francis and Kay, 1995, p. 32).

Assuming young people navigate their way through these difficulties, they must then choose from the academic menu on offer in their school. Exam courses usually start in year 10, which means that decisions about which subjects to study must be made in year 9 or at the age of 13 plus. Particular talents, like those in music, gymnastics or mathematics, will be evident and, for the fortunate few, choices about what to study will be easy. For others, the onset of formal operational thinking opens up doors into the world of science. Whatever the academic aptitude of pupils, important decisions will often have to be made on the basis of a relatively small amount of information. It is here that the advice of parents and the liaison between the school and the home is crucial.

Unhappily, for a lot of young people parental guidance is absent. As many as two-thirds of young people admit to often hanging around with friends 'doing nothing in particular' (Francis and Kay, 1995, p. 125). For those parents who *do* try to influence their children's academic development, there is a delicate pathway to be trod between being over-anxious and therefore putting too much pressure on children, and being too distant and unconcerned and therefore signalling that school work does not matter.

Churchgoing children are consistently more likely to be favourable to school than non-churchgoers and therefore more likely to succeed within the teaching and learning environment (Francis and Kay, 1995, p. 36). One problem that may affect religious young people occurs at the apparently warring frontier between science and religion. There is considerable research evidence showing that it is possible to adopt an attitude of scientism which is formed round the belief that ultimately all problems can be addressed scientifically and that only scientific knowledge is true knowledge (Kay and Francis, 1996). This hard-line position is antagonistic to religious faith and, where religious young people meet it, they are often unprepared for the intellectual conflict that arises.

A more moderate and mediated intellectual position occurs as young people begin to appreciate the levels and layers of meaning that different descriptions of the same events can give. Thus there is a chemical description of the composition of the human body: it contains certain quantities of protein, trace elements and the like, but this chemical description can in no way equate with a literary description of a person who is 'my best friend' or 'my sister'. The two kinds of description of the same person belong to two realms. As young people progress to their mid-teens they become aware that it is possible to hold apparently contradictory descriptions of similar events in their minds. A scientific description of creation can co-exist with a theological description of creation without either impugning the validity of the other. Without this ability to discriminate between different domains, and especially where young people have been taught that particular interpretations of biblical texts are the *only* possible ones, churchgoing young people may find that their religious faith is overthrown. It is important, then, that church workers who deal with young people equip them with the tools necessary to interpret Scripture. For example, it would be helpful to show young people that the basic account in the first two chapters of Genesis emphasizes the overall creative power of God. In doing so, it provides an order of events that locates the start of life in the sea and then charts its progress to the land. All this culminates in the arrival of human beings. Such an approach is more helpful than to insist that each of the days within the biblical account must have consisted of exactly 24 hours.

Religious development

Again, the work of Fowler (see Chapter 10, and Astley and Francis, 1992) provides a perspective on religious development which may be added to what has been said about the educational development of the young teenager. According to Fowler, between the ages of about 11 and 12 until around 17 or 18, many young people operate with a conforming faith. Although they develop the ability to think abstractly and to appreciate multiple interpersonal perspectives, they tend to hold their faith in an uncritical and unreflective way. Faith tends to be concerned with the formation of identity rather than with the intellectual arguments and overall coherence of the implications of belonging to a particular religious tradition. The meaning-making aspect of faith, therefore, is usually at second hand and derived from bits and pieces of the world-views of others, especially parents, teachers and the peer group.

References and further reading

Astley, J. and Francis, L. J. (eds.) (1992), *Christian Perspectives on Faith Development: A Reader*, Leominster, Gracewing.

Francis, L. J. (2001), *The Values Debate: A Voice from the Pupils*, London, Woburn.

Francis, L. J. and Kay, W. K. (1995), *Teenage Religion and Values*, Leominster, Gracewing.

Gill, R. (1999), *Churchgoing and Christian Ethics*, Cambridge, Cambridge University Press.

Hyde, K. E. (1990), *Religion in Childhood and Adolescence: A Comprehensive Review of the Research*, Birmingham, Alabama, Religious Education Press.

Kay, W. K. and Francis, L. J. (1996), *Drift from the Churches*, Cardiff, University of Wales Press.

39

Late Adolescents (15–19 years)

Intellectual development

According to Piaget, with the arrival at formal operational thinking intellectual development has been completed; there are no further stages through which to pass. It may appear to be misleading to suggest that intellectual development is completed, because we all change our ideas and views during the course of life, but what Piaget means is that the capacity for abstraction and systematic thought which can be reached in the early teenage years is not later superseded by a new and more inclusive stage.

This said, it is important to remember again that formal operational thinking may be less prevalent than Piaget realized and that it may only be commonplace in specialist domains. It is also true that there have been suggestions that a further stage *might* be possible in the sense that thinking about thinking opens the way for further levels of abstraction and generalization, but most writers would argue that the cognitive structures attainable through formal operations are *not* qualitatively changed by further development. What happens instead is that formal operational thinking begins to be applied to the full range of intellectual issues and curriculum areas. The tools of formal operational thinking can be turned upon all the problems of life, and in this sense intellectual development continues.

Alongside this sort of change, particular intellectual talents blossom more obviously in the higher sections of the secondary school. Music, mathematics, art and literature begin to open their doors to more gifted pupils who find pleasure in intellectual appreciation and achievement. The gap between the most able and the least able musician at the age of 15 is far greater than it was at the age of five, and the same goes for the other special abilities.

For the majority of pupils, it has to be said that learning is not so much a delight as something that has to be done in order to get a qualification and ultimately a job. One very practical question is the one about which options to take in year 9. Would it be better to take biology and German or should I choose French and history? In this respect intellectual development is not the crucial issue. What matters to the child is whether he or she likes a teacher and whether close friends are taking one option or another. The usual advice given to young people is that they should try to keep as many possibilities open to themselves as they can, and this is best done by keeping one foot within the arts or humanities and the other within the sciences. In British schools, the public has access to league tables so that it is possible to spot which school departments are likely to deliver the best exam results, and judicious and concerned parents may well try to guide their child into an option where an experienced and consistent teacher holds sway.

The problems of choice that occurred at year 9 occur again at year 11 as pupils move on into the next stage of their education. And they occur again at year 13 for those pupils who wish to go on to further or higher education. In one respect intellectual development through these years is marked by a series of educational hurdles and social filters that are designed to usher pupils into their eventual place within the job market. In another respect, intellectual development takes place independently of the grades and examinations by which success is measured. Pupils can widen their range of interests, become confident in their own powers of reasoning and understanding, plan their own leisure time, form their own relationships and projects and defend a personal point of view in discussion and debate. This sort of intellectual development is part of 'growing up' and becoming autonomous human beings.

Careers guidance at this point usually works on the general principle that the interests and aptitudes of pupils should be matched with particular families of jobs. Those who go to careers guidance interviews are asked questions such as: Would you like to work out of doors? Would you like to work in an office? Would you like to work on your own or with people? Are you good with figures? And on the basis of the answers given, the Careers Guidance Service can recommend a job in one environment or another and take account of the pupil's aptitudes and abilities. Such guidance is only general, and the problem for pupils is that they may want to do a particular job but not obtain the necessary qualifications or, alternatively, they have the qualifications but do not know which of several job possibilities they should choose. At some point pupils need to look at the entry qualifications for specific jobs and then take an appropriate course. Such a match is most obvious with vocational courses like those associated with dentistry, nursing or teaching which, in the light of the costs of further and higher education, are becoming increasingly popular. Starting salaries for these jobs are known and so the repayment of student loans can be anticipated.

Emotional development and its consequences

Most teenagers will be familiar with birth control methods and, by the time pupils reach the mid-teens, a significant proportion of them will have had heterosexual experience of one kind or another. Full intercourse is rarer, but in 1994 figures showed that 18.7 per cent of females aged 16 to 19 had experienced sexual intercourse before the age of 16. There is clear statistical evidence that the age of first intercourse is dropping and that the percentage of males and females who have their first intercourse before the age of 16 is rising (Wellings *et al.*, 1994).

Moreover, whereas in the 1950s and before males were more likely to seek early intercourse and females were more likely to abstain, there is now a trend for growing convergence between the sexes. Of those who have experienced intercourse before the age of 16, the ratio of males to females is now 3 to 2, whereas 40 years ago this ratio was 7 to 1.

Sexual behaviour by teenagers is certainly influenced by educational, social-class, ethnic and religious factors. Higher social classes tend to delay first intercourse by as much as an average of three years. Age at first intercourse also increases with educational level and this differentiation is apparent for both sexes.

Compared with their graduate peers, non-graduate men are more than three times as likely to have sex before their 16th birthday, and non-graduate women nearly twice as likely. (Wellings *et al.*, 1994, p. 53)

Social differences between graduates and non-graduates are likely to be less noticeable in Britain with the arrival of the era of mass higher education. In this new millennium there will be more British graduates than ever before and many of them will display the social traits previously associated with non-graduates.

Ethnicity is also significant. Pupils of Pakistani, Bangladeshi and Indian origin are much less likely to report sexual intercourse before the age of 16 than are those from other ethnic groups, this tendency being even more marked for women. By contrast, Wellings *et al.* (1994, p. 54) suggest that black men and women are *more* likely to report intercourse before the age of 16. Whites fall in an intermediate position between these two extremes. Religious affiliation to Christian denominations is also likely to delay intercourse, though Roman Catholics appear an exception to this tendency (p. 55), probably because of the working-class composition of the Catholic sample. Religious affiliation to non-Christian religions is even more marked in its association with a delay in first intercourse. Finally, there is no evidence that there are systematic regional differences of age at first intercourse across the United Kingdom, either from north to south or between rural and urban areas.

The use of contraception at first intercourse varies according to the age when this took place but, where intercourse occurs before the age of 16, 'nearly half of young women and more than half of young men report no method used either by themselves or by a partner' (p. 58). The most common method of contraception at first intercourse is the condom.

Social development

Social development is usually seen as following a trajectory from infantile dependence on parents through growing independence in the teen years to a mature relationship of equality. The late teen years are marked by stages of legally recognized independence (see Chapter 33).

Erikson (1995) has traced the psychosocial development of modern Western individuals through eight stages, two of which take place during the teen years. The first, which occurs at puberty, concerns the struggle for identity against role confusion. In Erikson's view identity is achieved by identifying with clear social roles, but this is linked with the beginnings of active sexuality. Confusion can arise if there are no appropriate social roles on which to fasten one's hopes. It can also arise if sexual emotions lead to the idealization of an unattainable person or to some forms of hero worship. The resolution of the problem is achieved by 'falling in love' and so 'projecting one's diffused ego image on another and by seeing it thus reflected and gradually clarified. This is why so much young love is conversation' (Erikson, 1995, p. 236).

The second stage occurs later when identity has been achieved and a balance must be struck between intimacy and isolation. 'The danger of this state is that intimate, competitive, and combative relations are experienced with and against the selfsame people' (p. 237). On one side, there is a danger of ego-loss or the dissolution of identity by absorption in close friendships and sexual unions, and on the other there is the danger that other people will be rejected because they pose a threat to the young person's hard-won individuality. Somehow a balance must be achieved between retaining identity and developing intimacy. In Erikson's view this intimacy is that which leads to the eventual bond with a life partner.

Erikson's work strikes a note with most people because he has taken account of the entire life cycle in his description of human development. He sees the teenage years, quite logically, as a preparation for the life work of the individual and, by blending social and psychological factors together, provides a convincing interpretation of what typically happens.

Faith development

According to Fowler, the fourth stage of faith development is that of a self-reflective, critical faith into which many people come in late adolescence, though others do not arrive until mid-life. Many others, perhaps a quarter of the total population, do not make this transition at all. The stage of *individuative-reflective* faith involves a 'critical distancing from one's previous... value system' (Fowler, 1981, p. 179) and the deliberate choice of a style of believing. 'My world-view is held explicitly, and in a self-aware fashion relying on my own authority for my own beliefs and values. That is why I need to be clear about things to have a coherent and consistent – and tidy – faith' (Astley and Kay, 1998, p. 157).

This stage of faith (see Chapter 10) is characterized by a break with external forms of authority that are supported by a particular matrix of social relations. The new stage is much more personal, a matter of my own decision, feelings, values and intellectual choice. It originates in the achievements of formal operational thought and in the enlargement of social horizons. It is part of the process of finding oneself or realizing one's identity. In this respect Fowler draws upon Erikson's insights (Moseley *et al.*, 1992, p. 52). The identity so formed and the faith now articulated is clear, unambiguous and in some respects rigid. It is rational, and defended rationally, and may be regularized into theological systems.

From the point of view of the churchgoing young person, this stage of faith follows on quite naturally from the commitments made at confirmation. By discussions and arguments in the youth group, young people begin to hold up their faith for examination and to learn and appreciate the arguments for the particular religious position which they decide to take up. 'I am an evangelical therefore I believe in the authority of Scripture'; 'I am a Methodist and therefore I believe in the importance of Wesley's hymns.'

Transition to young adulthood

There is evidence that the political opinions of young people tend to develop later than their religious opinions. Certainly, according to the findings of a huge data set collected by Leslie Francis, confidence in the main British political parties does not reach higher than 20 per cent and most young people feel that their lives will not be altered whatever political party happens to be in power. Typically about 40 per cent of young people feel too uncertain to make a judgement about political parties (Francis and Kay, 1995; Francis, 2001).

The transition to work is, in the upper reaches of secondary education, looked forward to positively. Over three-quarters of young people (77 per cent) believe that a job gives you sense of purpose and only a small minority (9 per cent) would rather be unemployed than join a government scheme intended to ease the way into work. Such findings are compatible with the discovery that over two-thirds of young people (68 per cent) 'often hang about with their friends doing nothing in particular' – they are aimless and waiting for something other than school on which to expend their energies.

In general, survey findings suggest that, while the great majority of young people are ready to seize the opportunities of further or higher education or employment, there is a small minority (about 10 per cent) that is alienated from the mainstream and feels in some way let down by school, parents, society, the Church or life in general. It is these alienated young people who are most vulnerable to the siren voices of political radicalism and to hard rather than recreational drugs.

References and further reading

Astley, J. and Kay, W. K. (1998), 'Piaget and Fowler', in W. K. Kay and L. J. Francis (eds.), *Religion in Education, Volume 2*, Leominster, Gracewing, pp.137–68.

Erikson, E. H. (1995), *Childhood and Society*, London, Vintage.

Francis, L. J. (2001), *The Values Debate: A Voice from the Pupils*, London, Woburn.

Francis, L. J. and Kay, W. K. (1995), *Teenage Religion and Values*, Leominster, Gracewing.

Fowler, J. W. (1981), *Stages of Faith: The Psychology of Human Development and the Quest for Meaning*, San Francisco, California, Harper & Row.

Moseley, R. M. *et al.* (1992), 'Stages of faith', in J. Astley and L. J. Francis (eds.), *Christian Perspectives on Faith Development: A Reader*, Leominster, Gracewing, pp. 29–57.

Wellings, K. *et al.* (1994), *Sexual Behaviour in Britain*, Harmondsworth, Penguin.

PART SIX
MEANS AND METHODS

40

Art and Craft

Introduction

There are almost limitless ideas for work with art and craft with children: ideas from school journals, books, magazines, children's comics and so on. Here are a few which have been tried and tested. These activities can be fitted as appropriate within workshops, fun days, all-age events and even, as illustrated in one example, in worship. All art and craft activities have to be carefully organized and must always address issues of children's safety under the Children Act 1989. If children are working indoors, safety issues have to be taken into account (for example, that equipment like easels and boards are stable and will not fall over, paint and glue are washable and non-toxic, scissors are safe with rounded ends). If children are working outdoors, there are different safety issues (for example, that the working space has clear boundaries and is enclosed, so that children cannot wander away and so that unwelcome visitors cannot enter; that sharp fences, prickly bushes and poisonous plants are not within reach). Whether children are working inside or outside, all these art and craft activities need a considerable amount of adult supervision. It is not necessary for there to be a large presence of adults who are artistically inclined, but adults are needed who can supervise and encourage the children in what they do, and in some cases, join in with them.

Large Holy Week puppets

These puppets were made in the Sundays of Lent prior to Holy Week in the usual Sunday morning children's work slot of about 40 minutes. The puppets were made to represent the characters surrounding Jesus in the Holy Week story. Any characters could be chosen, but the characters chosen for this particular project were St Peter, St John, Judas Iscariot, Herod, Pontius Pilate, Mary the mother of Jesus, Mary Magdalene, Caiaphas, Simon of Cyrene, a soldier and Joseph of Arimathaea. Two different characters were taken each week in the children's session. Their role and their involvement in the story, how they may have felt, what they did, why they did it and all these kinds of things were traced according to the point of view of that particular character. Great care needs to be taken not to simplify complex human characters into bland categories of 'goody' or 'baddy'. It is not helpful for characters in this story to be classified in this way, and it leads to all sorts of extraordinary ideas, and even to anti-Semitic thinking if we are not very careful. The stories need to be told fairly straight and factually, exercising some empathy with each of the characters involved in the story.

Required for each puppet

- one garden cane, 4 feet long
- one garden cane, 3 feet long

- garden tape to bind them together
- two large sheets of A1 coloured sugar paper in the same colour
- bits and pieces to decorate and make symbols
- two large paper plates

A puppet was made for each character. These puppets were gathered together and displayed in church as they were completed week by week. They were used in the Holy Week worship for adults and for children.

Making the puppets

Each week the children made the puppets in the following way, doing most of the assembling of the puppets themselves, but with supervision:

1   Bind the two canes at right angles, the shorter cane going horizontally (to form a cross shape) in position for arms.
2   Cut the A1 paper into a very stubby T shape for clothes. The arms of the T need to be very long; the body needs to be as wide as possible.
3   Decorate the sheets of A1 paper to look like (one sheet) the front and (one sheet) the back of each figure. The children can dress the characters with belts, buttons, coloured stripes on the clothes, and any other trimmings they can think of. It is quite important to make sure that the back and the front look vaguely similar so that when finished the puppet looks like the back and front of the same character. How the character is decorated will depend on who they are. The figure of a soldier should be very different from the figure of Mary the mother of Jesus.
4   Take two large paper plates and on one of them make the face for the character. On the back of the other, make the back of the head of the character concerned. The face of the character may have a beard, dark or light skin and red cheeks. The back of the head may be covered with a head-dress.
5   Staple the two parts of the head together, leaving the bottom of the plates, the neck edge, open.
6   Create an appropriate paper head-dress from different coloured sugar paper: a veil, a turban or a crown. Make sure it fits onto the head of the character concerned. If it covers the back of the head, there does not need to be any hair on the character, but if it does not, then make sure that the back of the head is presentable, and the figure does not look bald.
7   To assemble the character, staple the two T-shaped front and back body parts together down the sides, leaving the shoulders open. Take the cross shape and fit it inside the body piece. Staple two rows above and below the horizontal cane to fix the body. Put the head over the top of the vertical cane and staple it as close to the neck as possible so that it does not wobble.
8   Make the symbols or other additions to the characters and fit these to the puppets. For example, in the characters that we have chosen for this project, the following symbols were used. Peter carried a net which was a net used to contain oranges bought in the supermarket. John had a cup (to signify the cup at the Last Supper), which was made out of a plastic beaker covered with silver foil and strung from one arm of the puppet. Judas had a drawstring money bag because he was supposedly the keeper of the money. Herod had a crown to show that he was a king. Pilate was dressed in a Roman toga and so he was fairly distinctive. Mary was dressed in blue, the traditional colour in which the mother of Jesus is often portrayed. Mary Magdalene had a perfume pot which was the shape of an

alabaster jar. Caiaphas was dressed as a high priest with a high priest's breast plate. Simon of Cyrene had a cross in his hand to signify him carrying the cross for Jesus. The soldier was dressed in Roman armour and had a sword. Joseph of Arimathaea was dressed as sumptuously as possible to make him look like a rich man. All sorts of other symbols could be used for people in the story of Holy Week.

The puppets were used in a number of the Holy Week events in the church and they were on display around the church. They were used creatively by the adults who wrote Stations of the Cross to fit the characters in a different Holy Week workshop. Then the puppets and the words that the adults had created were put together at a service of the Stations of the Cross on Good Friday morning. The puppets remained on display in the church and were also used in an Easter Sunday afternoon family service.

Mosaic banners

This was a Lent project for a modern church with tall, bare white painted brick walls. The Lent theme for the whole parish was darkness to light and the teaching on Sundays was centred around that, progressing through Lent to the light of Easter.

The adult Lent course happened on Wednesday evenings. Each two hour evening session was structured in the following way. A short input by one of the clergy was followed by group work. The input and the group work continued the theme of darkness to light, took a Bible passage and explored it, or some other idea associated with the theme.

After a coffee break, the second half of the evening was spent working on the mosaic banners. This project of making mosaic banners was essentially one for adults and teenagers and was not suitable for younger children. Even with adult supervision the careful painting necessary was very monotonous for children even if they had the required skills. It is not recommended for children under about eight or nine, and only then for short periods of time. There was an alternative activity for those adults who did not want to join in the banner making project.

Preparing the banners

Very careful preparation in advance led to the success of this particular project. There were six banners and they were each made from vertical strips of wallpaper. Each banner was 8 feet long and 3 feet wide and was divided into 3-inch squares which were measured out carefully and ruled out in pencil on the banner. A number was pencilled in each square to represent the colour to be used. The darkest colours were on the edge, black, dark blue, deep purple, getting lighter and brighter, red, orange and yellow into the middle, where there was a cross in white. All the numbers were put on the banners. Each banner was slightly different but the overall effect was the same.

The relevant colours of paint were all mixed carefully in advance and PVA glue was added to the paint to stop it from running and to give it a thickness of texture. Brushes were available in various sizes, but none of them very wide.

Making the banners

The banners were made one at a time, one person being responsible for overseeing the whole project. Although there were many other people involved, everyone was answerable to the person in charge. The banners were laid out on the floor of the church hall and they were put on the stage when the hall was in use in between sessions, with the curtains drawn and all sorts of dire warnings should anybody go on the stage.

The squares were carefully painted with the pre-arranged colours. This was quite straightforward because the numbers were clearly written on each of the squares. It was a good inclusive exercise as once the adults were convinced that no artistic skill was actually needed, they entered into it with a great deal of enthusiasm and care. The main difficulty was the sore knees which ensued from kneeling on the floor of the hall to paint. It was a surprisingly quiet exercise in which people became very absorbed.

People said that they found themselves reflecting on the colour they were painting at the time and what it represented to them in terms of the Passion story. For example, one man said that when he was painting the purple, he had not really thought about purple representing the Roman Empire before. Therefore he pursued the whole idea of what it must have been like to have been subject to the Roman rule and the Roman authorities and he tried to imagine what it might have been like for him. One woman said that, as she painted blue, which to her seemed to represent the sky, she thought about there being one sky over one world and actually how close we are to the parts of the world where these events actually happened and how close we are today to the people of the world. This set her thinking about what it meant to proclaim the Gospel all over the world and her part in that proclamation.

The adults' thoughts were very diverse. An unplanned part of the project was that as the adults were clearing up or as they took a break to stretch their knees, they talked to each other about their thoughts during the painting session.

As Lent progressed it became obvious that the banners were not going to be completed in just the hour available on a Wednesday evening. As a consequence more and more people became involved in the project. The church hall was opened most evenings, under supervision, when it was not being used for other things. People came in and did half an hour or an hour's painting and then went away again. In this unexpected way, during the last two weeks of Lent, the Lent course seemed to happen every night of the week and was extended to people who were not present on Wednesday evenings.

The end result

The banners were hung on the walls of the church for Easter Day. They were very dramatic and people were stunned at the impact that they made. The darkness to light theme was explored in the Easter Day services and the threads from the whole of Lent pulled together. The biggest impact was really upon those people who had not been part of the painting project. People who were not normally in church throughout Lent but who were there on Easter Sunday, stood in amazed silence in front of these enormous banners with the white crosses in the middle and the dark edges. They certainly had an amazing impact on Easter in that church in that particular year.

Hands and feet banners

Introduction

This work was part of a Holy Week event called 'Walking with Jesus', which was organized in a rural church for children when Holy Week happened during the school holidays. It was a traditional church building with a nave and with chairs, some of which were reasonably easy to move. This activity is one that needs quite a lot of adult helpers. On this occasion the adults were joined by teenagers who were very willing to help with this particular activity because it was such fun.

Equipment needed

- a roll of wallpaper, 8 feet long (x 2, one for each banner)
- plastic sheeting and newspaper in abundance
- paint mixed into trays: the most useful trays are the paint trays which take rollers for painting domestic walls as they are flat and fairly stable

Plastic sheets were spread between the choir stalls in the chancel to cover the whole of the floor so that were was no opportunity for paint to get onto the floor of the church. The two banners, which were just sheets of wallpaper, were put down on top of the plastic on the floor. At one end of the choir stalls, nearest to the nave, several chairs were laid out so the children could sit down and take off their socks and shoes. At that end of the chancel, also on the plastic sheeting, were the trays of coloured paint. At the other end of the choir stalls (the altar end) were two baby baths of warm water, soap, plenty of towels and some more chairs.

The activity went like this. The children were called from other activities that they were involved in, probably about eight at a time, to take off their socks and shoes at the nave end of the choir. They then stepped into the paint, which was thickened so that it was not too messy and runny, and then they walked the length of the banner, making careful footprints on the banner. When they got to the other end, they washed their feet, went through the actual choir seats barefooted, and put on their socks and shoes at the other end of the chancel. It is quite important to keep the queue moving because all the children will be anxious to have a turn. Once they have all had the opportunity to do this, then of course they can have a turn again. The second time is often even more fun, as they have a much clearer idea about what they are doing.

The end result was an amazing banner of footprints in all colours, and of course in all sizes, but predominantly all going in the same direction. One of the other activities that the children did in that particular workshop was to cut out black letters which spelled out the words 'walking with Jesus' twice. Once the banners were dry, these letters were stuck down on each of them. The banners were then nailed to wooden batons and hung from two of the pillars in the nave of the church ready for Easter day. The impact was very dramatic. Most people who saw them loved them or were deeply impressed by them and felt they said something, but a few people objected very strongly to the children having walked in paint, and one lady objected to the letters being in black. The banners provided a good teaching focus for the Easter season.

Resources and further reading

Adams, L. (1998), *Make and Learn Bible Toys,* San Diego, California, Rainbow Publishers.

Bruce, E. and Jarvis, J. (2000), *The Paintbox Project,* Birmingham, National Christian Education Council.

Cooling, M. (1996), *Art and Music Toolkit,* Swindon, British & Foreign Bible Society.

French, R. and French, J. (1991), *Puppet Drama,* London, Scripture Union.

Godfrey, J. (1995), *Praise, Play and Paint,* London, National Society and Church House Publishing.

National Christian Education Council (1988), *What a Good Idea,* Birmingham, National Christian Education Council.

Slee, N. M., Francis, L. J. and Pedley, B. (1999), *Ready, Teddy, God!* Birmingham, National Christian Education Council.

Thompson, K. (2001), *Bumper Instant Art, Make and Do,* Buxhall, Kevin Mayhew.

41

Festival Workshops

Introduction

School holidays are a very good opportunity to gather children together and to give them substantial time to learn about festivals. Festivals in church are generally not very well kept with children. Leaders of children's groups work very hard to prepare children particularly for Christmas and Easter, but when the festival actually comes along, there is very little *provision* made for the children to keep these festivals on the day. Children are either absent or they are in an adult act of worship with their parents, or with other adults. One way around this difficulty is to use the school holiday time to give the children a day or a half day workshop leading up to an act of worship on or as near to the festival as possible. These can be held quite separately from the fun days (see Chapter 42) or they can be amalgamated so that some of the fun activities and some of the more festival-linked teaching can be mixed together in a way that provides a very good experience for the children.

The Children Act permits events of two hours or less to be held without involving clearing leaders with Social Services. Many churches find that this is easier, but of course it is always on the understanding that all the teachers and the leaders and all those who are involved have been cleared and have signed declaration forms according to their denominations.

Keeping harvest

Introduction

This was an attempt to prepare children for a harvest festival which a church kept fairly early in September and very soon after the children had gone back to school. This meant that there was very little opportunity for the children's work in the Church to prepare the children. The children were gathered together for a Saturday afternoon workshop for two hours on the day before the harvest festival was kept with that particular congregation.

Programme

2.00 p.m.	Arrival and welcome
2.05 p.m.	Children taken out into the churchyard, local gardens, or the grass verges, to notice anything that grew and could be classified under the heading of *harvest* in the widest sense of the word
2.20 p.m.	Back together for chatting and discussion

2.40 p.m.	Into four groups to make large banners
3.20 p.m.	Sharing some of the produce
3.40 p.m.	Discussion and thanking God with closing worship

As the Programme shows, the children were encouraged to go out to look and to think about things that grew and what God provides to make them grow: the right soil conditions, sun, rain, and so on. The children went out in small groups with a leader who could talk with them about what they were seeing. At 2.20 p.m. the discussion session started by talking about what they had seen, what they had brought back with them, and what they had found. It moved on to talking about what they had seen in shops, or grew in their gardens. There were some vegetables and flowers there for them to see. The older children were able to make a particular contribution when discussion moved on to what would be classified as the harvest of the sea, of fish and shell fish and seaweed, and the ways in which that can be used. They also had ideas about what happens to what comes from under the ground: coal and oil, and precious stones and gems. The wide-ranging discussion was relevant to children of various ages. At 2.40 p.m. they moved into four groups, with the purpose of making four large banners. The banners were each different. They represented the harvest of the sea, the harvest of the earth, the harvest of the farm, and the harvest of the garden. Each banner was about eight feet by two feet, made from wallpaper lining paper, and they were designed to be hung from four of the pillars in the main part of the church.

The banner which dealt with the harvest of the garden was divided into plots and looked rather like an allotment from a bird's-eye view. The children were able to cut things out of garden catalogues and stick them very carefully all over this banner so that there were flowers, cabbages, carrots and so on all in separate plots. It looked very effective. It had to be carefully planned so that the right sized pictures were available to the children. The farm banner was made to look like a large field with tractors and machinery, with crops in various stages of growing and harvesting being shown. This was made with cut-out pictures and pictures that the children coloured or drew and stuck on a basic field. The third banner, which was the harvest of the sea, was made of tissue paper to represent the sea. Most of it was depicted underneath the sea with a trawler on the surface of the water and a huge net hanging down with all sorts of fish in it. The under-the-earth banner was divided in half, so that half the banner showed a mine above the ground and the other half showed a shaft with coal and with jewels and a drill going down to find oil. This banner was sketched out by leaders, coloured by children and augmented by children, who stuck on jewels and bits of coal.

By 3.20 p.m. the banners were almost finished. The children were gathered together and they were invited to eat some of the harvest produce, including celery, carrots and apples. There were various fruits and vegetables which the children could eat raw and which they nibbled, together with a drink. It was interesting to note which children ate which vegetables, and which children did not like any vegetables, and how they might be encouraged to try some of them. The children were each given a paper plate and again plenty of food catalogues, and food pictures cut out of advertisements in women's magazines, home magazines and cookery magazines. They were asked to put on that plate what would constitute one of their favourite meals, and to glue the pictures on. That led into a discussion about these, and a discussion about thanking God and the need for us to remember to thank God for our food. A similar discussion then took place about parts of the world where there is little or no food and where people cannot just walk and get food. A sense of the children realizing how fortunate they were was carried into a closing act of worship, the children going home at 4.00 p.m.

An Advent workshop

The purpose of a two-hour afternoon Advent workshop at the end of November was to cut across all the hype and excitement there is in children's lives at this time of the year, including Christmas preparations they do at school, the Christmas parties, Father Christmas, and shops and decorations. In all that, the children often lose Advent completely. Advent becomes just a time of enjoying Christmas, practising plays, and so on. The purpose of this workshop was to give the children some sense that Advent is a time of waiting for Christ to come. This afternoon was spent dwelling upon Advent as a season, as opposed to losing it completely.

Programme

2.00 p.m.	Signing in, and making Advent calendars by everybody individually
2.45 p.m.	Gathering together to talk about Advent and to sing the Advent song, followed by drinks and biscuits
3.00 p.m.	Into four groups to represent the four parts of the Advent song
3.30 p.m.	Making Advent rings
3.45 p.m.	Worship and lighting Advent candles
4.00 p.m.	Afternoon finished

The first activity in which the children were involved was making Advent calendars. The advance preparation for this needed to be quite careful. Twenty-five pictures were chosen, depicting things that were associated with getting ready for Christmas and Advent, including candles and trumpets, evergreens and angels, presents and bells. These pictures included, of course, a picture of the nativity. The pictures were reduced so that they were more or less the same size. They were glued onto a sheet of A4 paper and photocopied enough times so there would be one sheet for each child. Blank sheets of card were divided into 25 spaces and these were photocopied so that again there were enough copies for every child. Small removable self-stick notes were provided which just covered the pictures to make a window effect. They had numbers on the outside and they opened by being folded back. Glitter glue pens were also provided together with stars and other shapes for the decorations. The card used was coloured card, but the pictures were all photocopied onto white paper.

As the children arrived for the afternoon, they were given a small envelope with 25 pictures in it, plus an empty card; there was glue available together with anything else that might be needed. The children glued the pictures on the card in any order they liked, but they were encouraged to put the nativity picture in the middle. They glued on all 25 pictures. They then put on their removable self-stick notes, and if they were able, they wrote numbers 1 to 25 on each of the removable self-stick notes, before decorating the calendars. If you are familiar with working with glitter glue pens, you will know that they do make a mess, so there is a considerable amount of supervision needed. They also take quite a while to dry, so you need to be able to put the Advent calendars in a safe place while the rest of the activities happen so that they can dry before the children go home. This was a very successful activity. Many of the children had never done anything quite like it before, and it took much longer than was anticipated. About three-quarters of an hour should make sure that most children finish.

When the children gathered together, the entry into the discussion was provided by the 25 pictures that they had incorporated and their own Advent calendars and what they knew about Advent and about the symbols they had stuck on their cards. They were quite forthcoming about that. They then learnt the Advent song, a modern version of 'The Holly and the Ivy'.

The song provides excellent teaching material for the four sections ('one is for God's people', 'two for the prophets', 'three for John the Baptist' and 'four for Mother Mary'), far more material than you actually have time to use in a fairly short slot.

The four groups

The four groups each made a picture of the four verses of the song. It involved quite a lot of careful planning and preparation because some of the concepts, particularly the prophets, are not easy for children. These pictures were made to be displayed on a wall in church, with the words of the headings from the chorus under each picture so that it was very clear to members of the congregation what the pictures were about.

The first group concentrated on the theme of all God's people. The children each drew themselves in a fairly basic triangle with a head sort of shape and they went round encouraging other people to draw themselves too, so that everybody there had the opportunity of being represented. These figures were then coloured and stuck on to a very large sheet of paper, together with pictures of a church, a school, a home, a factory and a shop. There was a sense of all God's people going to church, but also living in the world.

The second group concentrated on the theme of the prophets. The children used smallish paper plates for the basis of the heads. They made the heads with beards and used fabric to provide head-dresses and long robes. The figures were stuck on two pieces of A1 card because they were too heavy for A1 paper. The background was of desert with sky and shrubs. This was painted directly onto the sheets of card and some children chose to paint rather than to make the figures.

The third group concentrated on John the Baptist who was portrayed as standing up to his knees in the River Jordan. The leader of this group actually did a pre-prepared John the Baptist, taking an outline of a large figure from a book. The children did everything else, including a river of paint and the crowds. They placed figures in various places in the picture: some were on the bank of the river, some were in the river, some were a long way away. The whole thing looked like a very busy scene with John very much the dominant character.

The fourth group concentrated on Mary. The children were consulted as to how they would like to portray Mary. They decided on a Botticelli type of Mary surrounded by cherubs and angels which were made out of doilies and paper plates. These figures were grouped around Mary, who was herself made from tissue paper. The result was a very big figure of Mary surrounded with the heavenly host. All the pictures were double A1 size so they were fairly dramatic.

As children finished from all these four groups, they were given letters to colour (which the leaders had cut out in advance) which gave the titles of the large pictures. These were then stuck on long strips of paper. It is fairly useful to have something for children to do when they finish, because clearly with big pictures like these you cannot keep a group of ten or 12 occupied all the time, and the letters provided something to fall back on.

At 3.30 p.m. most of the children were ready for a break, having concentrated hard. They went out with leaders armed with secateurs and the leaders clipped greenery with the help of some of the older children. All the children came back with handfuls of small stones. They made three Advent rings on large round trays. Because the trays take the weight of the greenery, there was no need to do anything very fancy or elaborate in winding the greenery together. The stones which the children had collected were arranged in the middle of each tray and the greenery was placed all around it, so that the whole tray was completely covered. Tubes looking like paper candles were made to stand on the tray among the stones. Paper candles were used rather than real candles for safety and because it is much easier to get paper candles to stand up than wax ones. However, there was one Advent ring already made which was more substantial and which had four real candles, so that at the time of the worship, these candles could be lit. There were three Advent rings with pretend candles and one Advent ring with real candles. The Advent song was sung and the children were reminded that it was still the beginning of Advent. They had three weeks to look forward before Christmas, three weeks in which candles on the Advent ring would be lit Sunday by Sunday in church and in all the meetings of the children's groups between then and Christmas.

Resources and further reading

Church Pastoral Aid Society (1994), *Making the Most of Harvest*, Warwick, Church Pastoral Aid Society.

Currie, N. and Currie, S. (1998), *Seasons and Saints for the Christian Year*, London, National Society and Church House Publishing.

Currie, N. and Thomson, J. (1992), *Seasons, Saints and Sticky Tape: Ideas and Activities for Celebrating Christmas Festivals*, London, National Society and Church House Publishing.

Faulkner, A. (1999), *My Book of Special Times of Year*, Oxford, Bible Reading Fellowship.

Francis, L. J. and Drayson, D. (1999), *Learning with the Sunday Gospels: Trinity Sunday to Christ the King*, London, Mowbray.

Francis, L. J. and Faulkner, A. (eds.) (1997), *All God's People: Working with All Ages*, Leominster, Gracewing.

Irvine, C. (ed.) (1996), *Celebrating the Easter Mystery: Worship Resources for Easter and Pentecost*, London, Mowbray.

Lamont, G. and Lamont, R. (1997), *Children Aloud! Adults and Children Worshipping Together*, London, National Society and Church House Publishing.

Ludlow, L. (1992), *Festival Fun*, Oxford, Lion.

MacNaughton, P. and Bruce, H. (1997), *Together for Festivals: Resources for All-Age Worship*, London, National Society and Church House Publishing.

Parkes, K. and Parkes, S. (2000), *Feast of Faith – Celebrating the Christian Year at Home*, London, Church House Publishing.

Sayers, S. (1989), *Focus the Word: The Complete Three Year Cycle*, Rattlesden, Kevin Mayhew.

Thomas, S. (1997), *Come to the Feast: All Age Services for the Church Based on the Revised Common Lectionary*, Rattlesden, Kevin Mayhew.

Thompson, K. (2000), *The Jesse Tree*, Buxhall, Kevin Mayhew.

42

Fun Days

Experiencing a fun day

'I never expected it to be like this. I thought it would be . . . well, churchly and a bit boring.'

Abigail (aged 8)

Introduction

There's never enough time on a Sunday morning to get much done with children. Leaders work very hard to use a wide range of materials and activities to interest and involve children of mixed ages. They are very aware of the limitations of the time available and mostly they use it effectively and creatively. But, at the most, the majority of those who lead junior church (or whatever it is called in your church) have about 40–50 minutes for work with the children. This often has to include time for the children to gather and to share their news, a time for singing and worship, some teaching and an activity or two to reinforce the teaching. These parts come in any order and in all kinds of guises, but most leaders feel under pressure to fit in as much as possible. In addition, leaders have to have the children ready (and quiet), so that at the moment the message is received, they can all return to church to join the congregation.

Even when the children's work is mainly focused on a midweek club or an after school session, there is still pressure on the leaders to deliver a fairly formal lesson or to read a Bible story. When so many young, and not so young, people know little of the Bible, it is understandable that leaders feel they want to fit as much direct teaching into a session as they can.

Although most leaders do an excellent job in these circumstances, sessions are often very rushed, with no opportunity for important aspects of learning and development, fun and play. So why not arrange a fun event when there will be more time for the children, when the programme will give space for everyone to have fun without pressure of time?

Saturdays or a midweek day in school holidays are usually best. Choose a time when the majority of people do not go away: after Christmas, during the February half-term, or after Easter are times when parents and carers are pleased that there is something for their children to do.

A fun event is just that – a time when children gather together to have fun. The *main* purpose is not for them to learn or even to worship, although both will probably happen, but to have fun. We do not have enough fun in our churches and we tend to burden children with our anxiety that they learn all that we want them to know. We know in theory that children learn through play but in our churches there is little evidence that we put this theory into practice.

A fun day in church and churchyard

For such a day you need not go far away. Your church building can serve you well, especially if you have some outdoor space too (like the churchyard). Here is an account of one event.

Sample programme

10.00 a.m.	Signing in and labels
	Treasure hunt in church
10.15 a.m.	Games
10.45 a.m.	Drinks
11.00 a.m.	First hobbies group
11.40 a.m.	Second hobbies group
12.20 p.m.	Singing together
12.30 p.m.	Packed lunch
1.00 p.m.	Parachute games
1.30 p.m.	Third hobbies group
2.00 p.m.	Making music
	Movement/Drama
2.45 p.m.	Drinks
3.00 p.m.	Sharing what we have done (perhaps in worship)
3.30 p.m.	End

The day was held in a traditional church building with a high roof. It was possible to move some of the furniture but, as there were some fixed pews, the whole nave could not be cleared. It is a good idea to look creatively at your church building and to inspect all the spaces that are not usually used or which are used in a certain way. Many of our buildings are far more versatile than we think – we just need a 'new' eye to explore and to re-imagine the ways they can all be used. Ask yourself questions like: Can corners be cleared of chairs (or boxes)? Can a vestry or flower room provide more space? If we put down a piece of carpet would it make a space more useable?

We are all required to meet the demands of the law when we arrange such an event. This particular church has a kitchen and a toilet. If yours does not, make arrangements to use the facilities of a nearby house. Before the event happened, considerable care was taken to make sure that the premises were safe. Hazardous things like trailing flexes, ropes, microphones and steps, were removed, hidden, or made safe.

The programme

Registration

The law requires that all those taking part or leading such a day be registered on arrival. This means that if you have to evacuate the building quickly, you know how many people there are and if they are all out or not. At this event everyone wrote their name in coloured pen on the flip chart by the door, and made themselves a coloured label to wear.

Treasure hunt

The treasure hunt was started as each child arrived, so that everyone had something to do immediately. There was no sitting and waiting for things to begin. The clues were simple so that the children enjoyed taking part. The treasure hunt was not planned to test their knowledge, but to make sure that they had fun exploring and going into the parts of the church that they did not normally see closely. There were plenty of adults available to help, especially with reading and explaining the clues.

An example of a clue

Take a wax crayon and some paper. Make rubbings of as many different surfaces inside the church as you can reach from the floor. Try to find at least six.

The games

As the day was fine, the games were held out of doors in the churchyard. If this would cause offence, or if your churchyard is not safe for children, it would be best to hold the games in the church or in a nearby hall, garden or open space.

Simple games, like 'cat and mouse', 'hide and seek' and 'stick in the mud' were very successful. It is as well to remember that although adults often think that children need new and complicated games to play, it is often the familiar, well-tried games which are the greatest success.

Hobbies groups

While the children were outside playing, a few adults prepared the drinks and biscuits, and took them outside to the children. Another larger group of helpers prepared the hobbies groups in spaces round the church. When the children came in from their games, they could go straight into hobbies groups without waiting for them to be set up.

On this occasion, the hobbies groups were painting, woodwork (outside in the church porch), tapestry, pegdolls, making musical instruments, clay modelling (outside on the path) and making a video.

Painting

Large paper, plenty of ready-mixed paints, assorted brushes and pots for paint and for water are needed. If you are using the church, a large plastic sheet (available from DIY stores or garden centres) helps to save the floor from being painted.

Children often ask, 'What shall I paint?', so have some ideas ready, or have a theme for your day. The theme for this fun day was 'spring' as it was held in late February. Have cloths for mopping up and hand washing facilities readily available.

Woodwork

This workshop was in great demand every time it was offered. Off-cuts of wood of all kinds, a work bench or two, some nails, screws and glue, some simple but good tools and interested adult help are all that is needed. Good tools are less frustrating than 'children's tools' which usually do not work well. Children are much more careful than we give them credit for but even so, this is not a hobby group for the under fives.

Tapestry

It has to be said that this group tended to attract the girls, but once a man volunteered to help, some of the boys were brave enough to join the activity.

Everyone had a piece of tapestry that represented some aspect of spring (a lamb, a flower, a tree, etc.) and they were encouraged to fill it in using a simple (not very small) cross stitch. At the end these pieces of tapestry were mounted to form a picture of spring. It went so well that a week or so later, the finished article appeared as an altar frontal in one of the side chapels in the church.

Pegdolls

This rather old fashioned activity proved to be very popular. Most of the children had never seen the doll-shaped pegs and they caused much interest. As well as the pegs, this hobby group needed bits and pieces of fabric, scraps of lace and other trimmings, scissors, small buttons, wool of all colours. Needles and cotton were provided but most of the children (boys and girls) preferred to use fabric glue to stick the clothes and trimmings on the pegdolls, rather than to sew them.

A useful hint for the pegdoll group

It is a good idea to have some dark fabric and some 'combat' coloured bits, as the boys mostly wanted to make 'action man' type figures.

Making musical instruments

This was kept as simple as possible with a wide range of 'instruments' on offer. Drums were made from tins, filled with dried beans and decorated with coloured paper or, for some of the older children, with spirit-based markers. Shakers were made from plastic tubs and bottles of all kinds, with the tops fixed or with greaseproof paper over the opening fixed with elastic bands. Kazoos are simple to make with combs and paper. The children are bound to want to use the instruments, so allow enough time for this; they will also want to take them home.

Clay modelling

This is very messy and should only be done outside, where it is possible to wash down the area used, preferably with a hosepipe. Everyone needs to wear an overall or large plastic apron. However, it is worth the mess to share in the delight of the children, many of whom may never have used real clay before. Clay can be bought at good toy shops or craft shops, and care should be taken to store it in an airtight container when not in use so that it does not dry out. At this workshop the children worked at a large plastic topped table set up on the church path, with buckets of water handy to keep the clay moist and cloths for mopping up readily available. The children were not urged to make anything specific but to enjoy the feel of the clay, to have fun with it and to see where their exploration led them. Most ended up making something, and being very proud of their creations.

Making a video

This is an activity for a small group, unless you have access to several video cameras. So that they actually have the chance to use the camera themselves, rather than watch the process, there should only be a group of about four children per camera. On this fun day, those who took part in this hobby group were not asked to produce anything, but just to have fun. However, each group contained some budding young film producers who drove everyone into making a short but memorable piece of video.

Comment from the video group

My dad never lets me touch the camcorder at home. On the fun day I did a bit by myself.

9-year-old boy

Parachute games

Parachute games are a success with children and adults of all ages and sizes, and all energy levels. It is a very inclusive activity. With care and sensitivity people can take part sitting down, and people in wheelchairs enjoy it greatly. These games can be played with ten people round the parachute, or fifty, even a hundred if the parachute is big enough. But a big space is needed with plenty of height, as the parachute will billow up into the air. On this fun day parachute games were held inside the church, as it was too windy outside.

Play-parachutes and details on how to play with them are available from:

Gasworks
Children's Play Equipment Company
Bridge Mills
Mills Street West
Dewsbury
West Yorkshire
WF12 9AE

Making music/movement and drama

This half-hour session was for everyone together. It was great fun but rather chaotic. The adult leaders chose some songs and hymns that were fun and had a clear rhythm and the children chose how they responded. The music was played at a loud level and different groups worked in different parts of the church, each group with an adult and each group working on their own, but to the same music. Some used the musical instruments that they had made in the hobby groups, some danced in an organized way, some just danced, one group chose to do aerobics. Another group decided to act out a drama of spring coming into life, using the music to guide them but speaking over it. This was not really planned but it arose out of one of the movement groups.

Worship

The day ended with worship, which seemed the best way to share all that had happened and to offer the fun and the joy of the day to God. There was singing, praising, dancing to the glory of God. Most of what was done was the result of the day together, but every attempt was made not to see it as a series of performances. Everyone was free to join in everything in a fairly spontaneous way. This made worship fun.

A song for the worship

The song 'Thank you Lord for this fine day' is very easy to adapt so that the words express whatever we want to say.

Thank you Lord for...
  This fun day
  Music and dance
  Paint and clay, etc.

It also has an easy rhythm for clapping and percussion, and for the home-made instruments.

Going away for a fun day

If you prefer to go off-site, or you do not have a hall or the kind of church building which is suitable for a fun day, or the church council is not keen for the church building to be used, there are endless possibilities for such an event somewhere else.

The days of the Sunday school trip to the seaside are long since gone (in most places), but we must not forget that many of our children lead very busy lives. With homework, and activities like music lessons, extra coaching and organized sports training, some have little time for fun. Days in the local park, or in the country exploring, playing games, sharing a picnic can be much more fun than we expect. We do not need to go very far away and we should always try to keep the costs as low as possible so that all children can join in.

We adults are often so keen for children to 'get something out of life' that we organize trips and treats that are always about learning (visits to museums, exhibitions, historical sites, etc.). Children usually end up writing up what they discovered in the form of a project or a diary. Of course, this is often appropriate and useful, but so is a day just for the sheer joy of having fun and not having to remember what was done or learnt.

An important reminder

If you are planning to take children out for anytime at all, you MUST do all that is required under the Children Act. Forms must be signed by parents, leaders must be checked, and legal requirements for different age groups properly observed. If in any doubt check with your denomination's officers.

Our children must be well protected.

A day out in the local park looked like this

Games like football and rounders are very simple to organize, but they do need good equipment. Children should not be expected to play with bats and balls that are not appropriate or too small for them to handle properly.

Races and games of skill (throwing, tossing, jumping, etc.) are easy to invent and there are plenty of games books which can help you with ideas.

A programme for a day in the park

10.00 a.m.	Time to explore and run about
10.30 a.m.	Hide and seek

11.15 a.m.	Drinks and biscuits
11.30 a.m.	Football/rounders or ball games for the younger ones
12.30 p.m.	Packed lunch
1.00 p.m.	Parachute games
2.00 p.m.	Races and skill games
2.45 p.m.	Scavenger hunt
3.30 p.m.	Go home

A scavenger hunt for children of all ages is the best sort. Select a word or phrase which contains different letters (for example, FIELDWAY PARK). Ask the children to find something to bring back to their leader beginning with each letter. Give each child a polythene bag and make some basic rules: things must not be alive, they must not be picked from flowerbeds, how far they can explore (children must be very carefully supervised by adults *all over* the area in which they can play). As the children return with their bags of treasures, they lay them out on a sheet of newspaper to make the word. If there is a high number of small children, suggest they work in pairs with a bigger one helping a younger one.

Points to remember when planning a fun event

- The times are meant to be fun and relaxing, not focused on direct learning.
- Adult leadership is key to all such events. The more adults there are, within reason, the easier such an event is to organize.
- Remember safety and child protection regulations.
- Always get permission in writing from parents or guardians.
- Always have a first aid kit on the premises and make sure there is a qualified first aider with the group.
- If the adults join in and enjoy themselves, that will mean that the children will have even more fun.
- Have all equipment to hand so that the children do not have to wait between activities. It is not fun for children to be bored.
- Have spare activities for those children who finish quickly, or who want something else.

Resources and further reading

Bond, T. (1988), *Games for Social and Life Skills,* Cheltenham, Stanley Thornes.

Bruce, E. and Jarvis, J. (2000), *The Paintbox Project,* Birmingham, National Christian Education Council.

Cooling, M. (1996), *Story and Drama Toolkit,* Swindon, British & Foreign Bible Society.

Egan, P. (1982), *Together for Holidays,* London, CIO Publishing.

Farley, J., Goddard, E. and Jarvis, J. (1997), *Under Fives Alive,* London, National Society and Church House Publishing.

Fountain, R. (1999), *Go for Gold,* London, Scripture Union.

Francis, L. J. and Faulkner, A. (eds.) (1997), *All God's People: Working with All Ages,* Leominster, Gracewing.

Fuller, J. and Slee, N. (2001), *Songs of Life (Workbook* and *Study Guide),* Birmingham, Christian Education.

Goodland, P. (1998), *Over 300 Games for All Occasions,* London, Scripture Union.

Marguerat, D. and Bourquin, Y. (1999), *How to Read Bible Stories,* London, SCM Press.

National Society (1996), *Jump Up if You're Wearing Red,* London, National Society and Church House Publishing.

Schreiber, G. (1996), *Saints Alive: Stories and Activities for Young Children,* Mystic, Connecticut, Twenty-Third Publications.

43

Keeping Holy Week

Introduction

This was a five-day workshop of two hours each morning, held during a Holy Week after the school term had ended. The workshop was held in a traditional church building with all the limitations and opportunities provided by that environment. Each daily session lasted only two hours, so that special clearance and permission was not needed from Social Services. There was a considerable number of parents and other helpers, as well as junior church leaders and clergy, involved in this workshop, which was attended by some 40 to 50 children between the ages of 4 and 12. Because it was known that there would be older children, special provision was made for them, and this provision will be described later.

Programme for the first four days

10.00 a.m.	Arrive and register; arrival game linked to the symbol for the day
10.15 a.m.	Welcome, story and singing
10.30 a.m.	Activities in age groups
10.55 a.m.	Refreshments
11.05 a.m.	Change the activity, move around
11.30 a.m.	Game, outside if possible
11.40 a.m.	Return to the story and share the children's work; discussion and questions
11.50 a.m.	Closing worship including singing
12.00 p.m.	Go home

The older children participated within this programme right through, except for the activity periods where their activities were different. When the programme did not meet their needs, in particular with the games aimed at younger children, this was addressed and they were asked to help so that the very young children had somebody older with them in slightly more boisterous games.

The first four days of the workshop followed the same basic pattern. On the fifth day of the workshop, which was Good Friday, the plan for the morning was slightly different, and that will be explained later.

The plan

The planning group met well in advance. It consisted of five or six people who had knowledge of the different age groups and of the skills needed in various activities. It was decided that there would be a theme for each day and that the story of the events of Holy Week would be told in little bits during the course of the week, drawing attention to how these events affected the disciples and Jesus.

The theme for Monday was the donkey; Tuesday's theme was money; Wednesday's theme was bread; and Thursday's theme was the cross. On arrival the children were asked to register by writing their names on a sheet of paper and by providing themselves with a label. When they had done this they were then given a picture of the item which was the theme for the day. They took that picture and they stuck it on a card which was their own personal attendance card for the week. This was an A5 sheet with Holy Week Workshop and the year on the front, and sections inside with the headings Monday, Tuesday, Wednesday, Thursday, and Friday. The children glued the symbol for the day as a way of showing that they had attended on that day. These cards belonged to the children. The cards were kept during the week, but the children were allowed to take them home at the end of the week as a reminder of the holiday club.

Each day the arrival game was linked to the theme so that on Monday the arrival game was the blindfold game of putting the tail on the donkey. On Tuesday the arrival game was finding as many different coins as they could. These were cardboard coins and play coins which had been collected from leaders, parents and children in advance, and some of them had actually been bought from toy shops. These were spread around the church and the children found as many different ones as they could. On Wednesday the theme was bread, and the arrival game was for the children to be blindfolded and to taste as many different kinds of bread and see what they could say about them. This meant that some of the older children did not join in the game, but helped the younger children because most of this needed one-to-one supervision, certainly with the smaller ones. A variety of different breads were bought from supermarkets, or made at home. The different breads were cut into small pieces and the children talked about which were crunchy, which were soft, which they liked, which they did not like, which was onion, which was herb and which was apricot, and so on. They chatted together about the breads. On the fourth day, Thursday, the symbol was the cross. A wide range of different sorts of small crosses, and pictures of small crosses, were photocopied and turned face downwards all over the church. As the children arrived they were given a card with twenty slots on it as we had twenty different sorts of crosses. They had to go around the church, turning over the small pictures of crosses and collecting all twenty different ones; if they picked up the same cross that they had already got, they turned it back face downwards and went on to find another one. It was necessary to have glue and tables available so that as they found the crosses they could glue them on their cards.

Welcome, story and singing session

Having the welcome, story and singing session at 10.15 a.m. allowed time for children to arrive late and for various conversations to happen with parents at the door. The children gathered together and names were shared. Children were asked to stand up if they had been in a church before or if they had not. All sorts of welcoming activities and words were used so that the children mixed together. There was a mixture of children who had not been to the church's normal children's Sunday activities or had not been to a workshop like this before, and there were others who were very familiar with their surroundings. It was important that all the children were made welcome and made to feel comfortable, and that the children who came on their own were identified so that they did not remain on their own.

Each day a different part of the Holy Week story was told. On Monday, when the symbol was the donkey, the story concerned the arrival of Jesus into Jerusalem riding on the donkey. On Tuesday, when the symbol was money, the story concerned Jesus driving the money-changers out of the temple in Jerusalem. On Wednesday, when the symbol was bread, the story concerned the events of the Last Supper. On Thursday, when the symbol was the cross, the story concerned the events surrounding and building up to the crucifixion of Jesus.

It was important to recognize that many of the children would know at least the outline of these stories, but some of them might not. Quite considerable sensitivity had to be used in making sure that all the detail of the story was included, but the children's knowledge was valued and those who knew the story were involved in being able to display that knowledge in an appropriate way.

Simple songs are best used; children like to join in songs that they know. It was worth finding out from the leaders of the junior churches, Sunday school, and indeed the day school, which songs the children knew so that at least some of those could be included. It is not always necessary to have a pianist, as children sing quite well unaccompanied – particularly if they have got one or two adults who are confident enough to sing with them. Some of the songs that the children knew were adapted slightly to make sure that there was an appropriate song to fit with the theme for each of the days.

Activity slot

Two constant activities were provided each day in addition to a variety of activities which changed from day to day. The first activity which happened every day was a quiet corner where children who did not want to work with others, or children who were unsettled in one way or another, were encouraged to go. In the quiet corner there were pictures to colour, word searches to do, quizzes, sheets to complete, and paper for the children to do their own drawing or their own writing. They could then work alone or with others as they chose.

The second activity that happened each day was a workshop responsible for making a frieze for display in the church. In this workshop children did the appropriate part of the story on two sheets of A1 paper joined together to create a frieze which built up during the week. The frieze was then put on the wall of the church ready for adults to see at the worship at the end of the week.

On Monday, there was a group which made palms which could be waved in the worship and these were made out of folded paper. There was another group which made donkey masks out of large brown paper bags to go over their heads. On Tuesday, when the story concerned Jesus driving the money-changers from the temple, a very energetic group took part in a drama activity, acting out the story with a great deal of energy and shouting. Another group made angry faces on paper plates and put them on sticks so that they could hold them up to their faces to look very angry and very frightening. On Wednesday, everybody had the opportunity to make bread. This was an extremely popular activity and the morning had to be carefully organized so that it was possible for the children in groups to go to the kitchens in two local houses to make bread mix, knead it into shapes, and leave it to prove, so that adults could then cook it and bring it back at the end of the morning for the children to take home. It was made quite clear to the children right from the beginning that they would not necessarily take home the piece that they had shaped, but every effort was made to try and match them. Bread was also provided for the Wednesday evening Eucharist in the church and for the Maundy Thursday Eucharist which was held the following day.

The activity for Thursday was linked to the cross and there was an opportunity for some children to make simple wooden crosses and for another group to make bookmarks in the form of a cross. Some of these were so attractive that the adults actually asked to buy them and to give the money for the children's work in the church. Not all children were keen to part with them, but some very definitely were.

The refreshments then followed. The children were moved to a different part of the building in the main nave, a place where the activities had not happened, where they could sit quietly and have drinks and biscuits. On Friday they were given hot cross buns.

The activity session that followed the refreshments consisted of the same activities, but with the children choosing a different group to work in.

Games

The idea of having a game at 11.30 a.m. was to make it as noisy, as exuberant, and as energetic as possible. For most of the time, the children were very happy just to have running games or some balls outside. If it was not possible for the children to be outside, the main nave of the church would have provided a good space for controlled races and quite a lot of simple games could be played there. These could involve the children in jumping or hopping on the spot, or reaching up high, or curling up small. These sorts of activities allow the children to use physical energy and to exercise their bodies in order to unwind from the fairly focused activity groups which they had been involved in.

Final twenty minutes

At the end the children were gathered together and they were reminded of the theme and the story. They shared what they had done and their work was all collected together. If the children were able to take it home, they were given the opportunity to do that. If it was for display in the church, then that was explained very carefully and they had some idea where it was going to be and how it was going to be displayed. All this was brought together into a very short closing act of worship which included songs and prayers about the theme they had been exploring during the course of the morning. It is important to end an event like this on time because parents often have other engagements or activities to go to, and small children are very often used to having their lunch quite early.

Good Friday

As it was the custom of the church where this holiday workshop was being held to have a Good Friday morning children's service, the workshop was amalgamated with the service. The workshop started at 10.00 a.m. and the children's service was scheduled for 11.30 a.m. Parents, members of the congregation, and children who had not been at the workshop were encouraged to come for this service at 11.30 a.m. On Good Friday, the arrival game involved pulling together all the symbols that they had explored during the week: the donkey, the money, the bread and the cross. The children were given a sheet of paper, divided into four sections, and they were asked to draw their own version of these symbols and write a little bit underneath explaining what they were about (the younger ones needed help with this). At 10.15 a.m. they gathered together, as they had on the other four mornings, for the welcome and the singing. The story was a reminder of the events of Holy Week, and also a pointer to the fact that although this day, Good Friday, was a sad day in many ways, it also pointed forward to a very happy day, Easter Sunday. There was some conversation about what happened on Easter Sunday and about how the children could be involved in an Easter Sunday afternoon service where there would be Easter eggs. The resurrection would be celebrated and their work would all be displayed in the hope that their parents, their families and friends would come.

The 10.30 a.m. slot on Good Friday took a very different form. Children were given the opportunity to prepare for that morning's act of worship. Some children were invited to read, some wanted to act, particularly the bits of the story about the money-changers which they had done as drama the previous Tuesday. Others wanted to show some of the work they had done throughout the week, so this was displayed or carried and shown by the children. They also needed to practise singing and waving palm branches; they were taught to shout the great shouts of Holy Week, 'Hosanna' and 'crucify him', and eventually of course the great shout of 'Alleluia'. They joined in these with gusto. At 10.55 a.m. the refreshments were served and at 11.05 a.m. the children started to prepare to welcome their visitors, by waiting by the church door or on the path. They handed out service papers and they sat with their parents if they wanted to. They showed their parents what they had done where this was available.

The 11.30 a.m. Good Friday service took everybody through the events as they had been looked at during the week of the workshop, and each section was separated with prayer and with a song. The whole worship was finished by about 11.55 a.m., so there was no sense of the service being too long for some very small children who had been brought to it.

Older children

As has been explained, the older children joined in most of what was on offer all through the week, but there were separate activities available for them every day between 10.30 a.m. and 11.30 a.m. They did not change activity groups, but stayed in one group. Two or three leaders undertook to work with this age group, who were encouraged to write a play about the events of Holy Week, one which could be performed in the form of a radio play. The original idea was that the children would stand at a microphone behind a sheet and they would read this play as part of the service on Good Friday. What actually transpired was that despite the protestations of being shy, they did not want to be unseen and invisible; they wanted to partly act this out. So in the end it turned out to be a scripted play of the events of Holy Week with a few props and with the younger children coming in to add to the crowd noise. It was surprisingly successful and the children had a very good sense of what they wanted to say. It was not very biblical in places, but it was certainly full of feeling and definitely in their own words. Many parents and adults who attended the service found it really quite moving that the children were able to express their own feelings in this way around these very emotional events of Good Friday.

Resources and further reading

Atkins, K. (2001), *Bumper Instant Art for Lent and Easter*, Buxhall, Kevin Mayhew.

Blarry, M. (1988), *Know How to Use Dance in Worship*, London, Scripture Union.

Church Pastoral Aid Society (1994), *Making the Most of Easter*, Warwick, Church Pastoral Aid Society.

Edwards, P. (1993), *Times and Seasons: Clip Art for the Liturgical Year*, Great Wakering, McCrimmons.

Egan, P. (1981), *Together for Holy Week: A Resource Anthology,* London, CIO Publishing.

Faulkner, A. (1999), *Easter Alphabet,* Oxford, Bible Reading Fellowship.

Francis, L. J. and Drayson, D. (1999), *Learning with the Sunday Gospels: Advent to Pentecost,* London, Mowbray.

Francis, L. J. and Faulkner, A. (eds.) (1997), *All God's People: Working with All Ages,* Leominster, Gracewing.

Gardner, J. and Leonard, C. (2000), *The Road to Easter,* Oxford, Bible Reading Fellowship.

Herbert, C. (1993), *Prayers for Children,* London, National Society and Church House Publishing.

44

Out of Hours

Introduction

When we work with older children in our churches we need to be imaginative. It is very easy for this age group to be bored. They are quite sophisticated in their normal lives and many of them are well travelled, but they are often unfamiliar with simple pleasures. It is quite easy with a little imagination to give them an enjoyable experience costing very little. The two events described in this chapter were for young people aged between 10 and 14 and happened in half-term school holidays when it did not matter if their usual routine was disrupted.

The usual safeguards apply. There must be a generous ratio of adults to young people. There must be a qualified first aider present at all times and all adults involved must have gone through the procedures required by the Children Act. If there is to be any walking along roads at night, consult the local police about safety requirements and necessary lights. It is a good idea to hold a meeting of parents before such events happen so they can be reassured about the safety precautions and supervision. Be cautious about involving parents in the whole of the programme because one of the attractions of such events for young people is that their parents are not there. If parents are involved, do so on a rota basis so that all the young people have the freedom to enjoy the event at the same level.

An all-night event

Programme

7.30 p.m.	Welcome, programme outline and games (games out of doors, if possible)
9.00 p.m.	Cook supper
9.30 p.m.	Eating supper and clearing up
10.30 p.m.	Craft activities in groups
11.30 p.m.	Drink
11.45 p.m.	Midnight walk
1.00 a.m.	Prayers by candlelight
1.30 a.m.	Hot drink
1.45 a.m.	Activities: girls activity and boys activity
4.00 a.m.	Sharing the activities, preparation and rehearsal for worship
5.00 a.m.	Breakfast
6.00 a.m.	Short brisk walk
6.30 a.m.	Eucharist
7.15 a.m.	Tidy up
7.30 a.m.	Depart

Introduction

This took place in the May half-term in a modern urban church on a large estate. It was not easy to get more than three or four adults to be present all night, but members of the congregation were invited to volunteer for specific responsibilities, which they did with enthusiasm.

There was also a general invitation to the congregation to pop in whenever they wanted to, and particularly to be there for any worship events, especially the 6.30 a.m. Eucharist. It was decided to stage the event in the church building, not using the adjoining hall unless essential. One side aisle of the church was cordoned off with chairs so that sleeping bags and cushions could be made available for those who really could not stay awake all night. The point of an all-night event is to keep going, and for participants to go through their thresholds of tiredness and to sustain each other. If they really do need to have a sleep, provision should be made for this in comparative comfort. One adult took responsibility for any young people who needed a rest, but this resting happened within the setting of the whole event.

Welcome, programme outline and games

The young people all knew each other so this part of the programme consisted of reminding them about the programme they had helped to plan, and setting some ground rules (such things as not going outside unless everyone went together, not going off in pairs, joining in all parts of the programme unless resting). These rules were kept to the absolute minimum, but it was important that they were understood.

The games were held on a piece of grass outside the church, but they were also planned so that they could have been held in the church hall had it been wet. They were planned to be noisy, energetic and exuberant.

Supper

Pizza bases had been bought and a variety of possible toppings provided. The young people chopped peppers, tomatoes and onions, grated cheese, opened cans of tuna, and did everything to prepare the toppings. They then loaded up their own pizza base and put it in the oven. As there were quite a lot of pizzas; they had to be cooked in relays and so there were quizzes, word searches and pencil and paper games available for the young people to use while they were waiting for their pizzas to cook.

Craft activities

The craft activities were designed for the sheer joy of doing them. The group really enjoyed craft and handiwork and chose three particular activities: spittal painting, work with clay and wood carving.

Spittal painting
You will need the following equipment:
- toothbrushes of all shapes and sizes, enough for everyone to have one each at least
- small sticks which can be dragged across the toothbrushes or, failing that, pencils which can be washed afterwards
- an assortment of small and large nail brushes or floor scrubbing brushes and any other sort of brushes with hard bristles which might be available
- overalls if you can get people to wear them, or they might choose to bring their own

- trays for the paint
- any other protective covering like plastic or newspaper that is appropriate to the setting

The spittal painting took place in the dark. This is an indescribably messy process as the paint goes in all directions. A piece of paper was spread on a car park outside with newspaper around it for people to kneel on. Brushes were dipped into the paint and held level over the trays so that the worst of it dripped off, and then held just over the end of the paper. The side of the stick or the pencil is run across the brush fairly briskly away from the body so the paint flew all over the sheet. All the colours can be superimposed and people took it in turns to work on the same sheet. The outcome was a large sheet of paper which looked like nothing, but which they had enormous fun doing. They then decided that they would use a second piece of paper and, after much discussion, they created an abstract picture of the theme darkness and light. They graded the paint so that the dark was all at one end, the light was all at the other and the middle was a mixture, and they talked about moving from the darkness of not knowing Jesus into the light of knowing Jesus.

Work with clay
The work with clay also took place outside. We were fortunate enough in having external lighting round this church. Tables were set up, bowls of water were on hand, and real clay was used. Unlike the first workshop, nothing corporate came out of this. One or two young people produced what they considered to be masterpieces and they were allowed to take them home. The hour was spent quite happily enjoying the clay.

Wood carving
The idea of wood carving had come from a man in the congregation who seemed to have an unending supply of wood, some of which was soft balsa wood which he was prepared to give to the young people. He offered to come and supervise this and, as in the clay activity, this group was allowed to experiment with the wood and to carve it in whatever way they wanted. Presumably because it was an event that was happening in church, quite a lot of them came up with variations on crosses. These were used and offered at the final Eucharist and the young people were allowed to take them home.

Refreshments

After the clearing up from the activities had happened, hot or cold drinks and light snacks were available. It is always well to remember that young people have substantial appetites and they need to be fed and watered fairly regularly if they are to stay happy.

Midnight walk

The young people had all been told to wear suitable clothing and to bring a coat, although the evening had not been either wet or cold when they had arrived. Two adults had planned the walk and they came specially to lead it. This meant that the adults who had been leading the earlier activity workshops were not involved in anything else and those adults who were to be there all night had a break. It is important that the adults leading the walk have tried the route, know where the pitfalls are, are well equipped with torches and lights and quite clear about how long it will take. The delights of this particular midnight walk for town children were the joys of all being together, and of listening and experiencing the night in a new way.

Prayers by candlelight

Everyone returned from the walk excited and quite cold. They came into a warm church to find that it had been prepared by the adults who remained behind. The Lady chapel was illuminated only by candles, with large cushions or hassocks on the floor. Everyone was encouraged to take off coats and shoes, and to sit on the floor in the candlelight. This was a complete contrast from what they had experienced earlier in the night. The prayers by candlelight were gentle and quiet, with some singing and some silence. As a focus for them to look at, there were articles such as pictures and some of their craft work in clay and wood. They settled down and enjoyed it enormously. Altogether it only lasted about twenty minutes, and so the young people managed that very well. This was followed by more drinks and more light refreshments.

Group activities

By 1.45 a.m. the young people had been divided into two separate groups, each of which had a clear purpose. The girls were in a group in a local house where there were sewing machines and fabric. The plan was for them to make circle skirts and then practise a dance wearing these skirts. The boys remained in church, where they were given the task of presenting the gospel in a series of overhead projector transparencies, to be created in whatever way they felt appropriate.

Girls
Some of the circle skirts had been cut out in advance so that some of the girls could get on with supervised sewing of them, while others cut out their own and pinned the parts together. Most of the girls had done no sewing of any sort, so there was considerable excitement at the idea of doing this. The plan was not only that they would dance at the final Eucharist of the night, but that they would form a dance group which would eventually dance in the worship in church.

Boys
The boys considered the gospel and decided they were going to produce a series of drawings which overlaid each other in the form of cartoons on overhead projector transparencies. They divided into pairs and took parts of the story each. Each part of the story had six or seven different overhead projector transparencies used to build up a picture.

Integration
The girls each managed to make a skirt, which fitted well enough. The skirts were finished except for the hems which were left until later. There was an enormous sense of satisfaction that they had done this. The boys too finished their task and their sophisticated use of different colours of the overhead projector pens was really quite impressive.

The young people then all met in church with more food and more drinks and talked to each other about what they had done. That was followed by a rehearsal of these activities for use in worship. A very simple dance was worked out by the girls, with the boys helping them. The boys presented their gospel story, with the girls making some suggestions. This session was the only one that overran, as it did not finish until about 5.30 a.m. This did not matter as breakfast was prepared by new helpers who came especially for that. By the time the food was ready to eat, the young people were quite tired and were delighted to be presented with a cooked breakfast.

Short brisk walk

At about 6.00 a.m. the young people were taken for a quick walk to keep them awake. They came back and found the Eucharist ready and their spittal painting being used as an altar frontal, along with clay and wood models round the altar. About eight or ten additional adults turned up in church at 6.30 a.m. to share the Eucharist. It was a simple informal celebration and thanksgiving, the focus being the offering of the work and the lives of the young people, the night's activities and all they had done. The two parts which were predominantly led by the young people, the dancing to one of the hymns and the gospel story with the overhead projector transparencies, were much appreciated by all those who attended.

Evaluation

At the next meeting of the youth group the event was evaluated as a resounding success. Some said that they had felt very tired when they got back from the midnight walk. Almost none of them had slept at all. One or two had a sit down or a lie down, but that was all. They felt incredibly pleased with themselves and wanted to know when the next such event was going to happen.

An early morning walk with breakfast

Programme

5.00 a.m.	Meet and walk
6.30 a.m.	Hot drinks and morning prayers
7.00 a.m.	Cook and eat breakfast
8.00 a.m.	Walk
9.00 a.m.	Arrive back and go home

Introduction

This was a much simpler event, much shorter and easier to organize, but equally interesting and exciting because it started at a time when the young people were normally in bed.

The setting for this event was a rural community during October half-term, before the clocks changed so the mornings were really quite dark. This was a gathering of young people from several churches, not all of which were Anglican.

We were keen that there would be a cooked breakfast for the young people, but equally keen that they did not have to walk carrying a considerable amount of equipment. So adults volunteered to go by car to a pre-arranged place, taking all that was needed for breakfast. This made walking much more pleasant, and it meant that the breakfast was set up and ready by the time the young people arrived at the agreed venue.

The walk

The young people gathered at the church at 5.00 a.m. and were given the pilgrims' blessing by the vicar, who was with them throughout the whole event.

Two adults had undertaken to plan the route. They knew exactly where they were going, but they had maps available so that those young people who were interested in map reading could follow their progress. The walking was mostly across well-defined footpaths in the countryside. It was of course still dark so the usual safeguard of lights had to be observed. The walk allowed the young people to get a balance between experiencing the dark and yet feeling safe. Because the young people were not used to walking very far, the route was only between three and four miles.

Despite the fact that most of the food and drink for breakfast had gone with the adults in the cars, the walking adults carried flasks of drinks because it was quite cold. The hot drink break took place at about 6.00 a.m. rather than 6.30 a.m., and it was agreed that morning prayers would take place at the same time. Some adults had brought candles, and morning prayers with singing happened just as the sun was beginning to rise. It was almost dark, but for the young people it was a very special and unique experience to be in a field singing and praying at that time in the morning.

After the drinks and the prayers, the walk continued until the 7.00 a.m. breakfast rendezvous was reached. When the young people arrived, they found that the adults who had taken everything in their cars had set up the breakfast, and all the young people had to do was to divide into groups and to gather around the calor gas cookers and, under adult supervision, to cook their breakfast. They were all able to choose what they ate from quite a wide range of items. There was much laughter and bantering, and it was greatly enjoyed. The adults who had come in the car had been thoughtful enough to bring ground sheets and blankets for the young people to sit on, and a few folding chairs for any weary adult who had walked with the young people.

The clearing up took place and everyone was back walking by soon after 8.00 a.m. It was deliberately planned that the walk after breakfast would not be very long so that the young people did not get very tired. They arrived back at church at 8.59 a.m., went into church and received a blessing and dismissal from the vicar.

Evaluation

It was generally regarded by the young people that it had been a very successful event. They had got to know some people that they had not known previously, and they had had a new experience of walking in the countryside in the dark, and being on their feet walking and watching as the sun rose.

Resources and further reading

Baptist Missionary Society (1992), *Fool's Gold: Drama with a Mission*, Didcot, Baptist Missionary Society.

Challingsworth, N. (1982), *Liturgical Dance Movement*, London, Mowbray.

Charter, A. and Hardwick, J. (1995), *The Ultimate Holiday Club Guide*, Oxford, Bible Reading Fellowship.

Farley, A. and Westcott, N. (1991), *Act it Out*, Birmingham, National Christian Education Council.

Francis, L. J. and Faulkner, A. (eds.) (1997), *All God's People: Working with All Ages*, Leominster, Gracewing.

Harding, N. (2000), *Festivals, Milestones, Young People and God: DIY Resources*, Warwick, Church Pastoral Aid Society.

Hopwood, D. (1995), *Acting Up,* London, National Society and Church House Publishing.
Powell, P. (1994), *Scenes and Wonders,* London, National Society and Church House Publishing.
Privett, P. (ed.) (1993), *Signposts,* London, National Society and Church House Publishing.
Rich, R. (1995), *More Surprise Sketches,* Birmingham, National Christian Education Council.
Thompson, K. (1990), *Sketch and Tell,* London, Scripture Union.

Indexes

Index of Names

Index of Subjects